THE SABBATH IN JEWISH AND CHRISTIAN TRADITIONS

Stanley M. Wagner, General Editor

EDITORIAL COMMITTEE

Ralph R. Covell
Gregory A. Robbins
Nicholas E. Persich, C.M.
Jane Smith

The publication of this volume has been generously supported
by the Rabbi C.E.H. Kauvar Publications Fund.

THE SABBATH
IN JEWISH
AND CHRISTIAN
TRADITIONS

Edited by

Tamara C. Eskenazi
Daniel J. Harrington, S.J.
William H. Shea

Crossroad   New York

1991
The Crossroad Publishing Company
370 Lexington Avenue, New York, NY 10017

Library of Congress Cataloging-in-Publication Data

The Sabbath in Jewish and Christian traditions / edited by Tamara C.
  Eskenazi, Daniel J. Harrington, William H. Shea.
    p.   cm.
  Papers originally presented at a symposium at the University of
Denver, May 24–26, 1989.
  ISBN: 0-8245-1093-3
  1. Sabbath—Congresses. 2. Sunday—Congresses. 3. Rest—
Religious aspects—Congresses. I. Eskenazi, Tamara Cohn.
II. Harrington, Daniel J. III. Shea, William H.
BV111.S32 1991
296.4'1—dc20   91-7626
                                                          CIP

Printed in the United States of America

CONTENTS

FOREWORD

O ne of the most meaningful programs of the Institute for Interfaith
Studies at the Center for Judaic Studies, University of Denver, is our
academic outreach to three of Denver's great theological seminaries – The
Iliff School of Theology, Denver Seminary (Conservative Baptist), and St.
Thomas Seminary (Roman Catholic). We have been enriching the cur-
riculum of these seminaries for the past fifteen years by providing nine
courses in Judaic Studies over a three-year period in Bible, Jewish history,
rabbinic literature, and Jewish theology. We, too, have been enriched by the
exciting classroom dynamic involving bright, enthusiastic, and spiritually
wholesome Christian seminarians.

After one of the sessions I instructed as part of this program, Wayne
Austin, a Seventh-day Adventist, approached me with a request. He
handed me a tape recording of a lecture delivered in Denver by Dr.
Samuele Bacchiocchi, one of the Adventists' leading historians and theologians, and he asked me to listen to it. Being generally responsive to
students' requests, I was happy to do so; however, never did I expect to be
so moved and impressed by a lecture.

As an Orthodox Jew and, hence, a strict observer of the Sabbath, I have
personally experienced the loveliness and joy of this holy day throughout
my life. In my own religious circles, the meaning and significance of the
Sabbath are well known, and our devotion to the Sabbath is an integral
part of our spiritual life. Yet, despite my very broad and intimate association with Christian leaders and laity, I had never known a Christian who
shared, in any way, this commitment to the Sabbath.

I was absolutely overwhelmed, therefore, by Dr. Bacchiocchi's address,
in which he spoke about the Sabbath in the warmest, most loving terms I
had ever heard from the mouth of a Christian. It was then that I felt the
time had come for Jewish and Christian scholars to meet to explore our
respective traditions relative to the Sabbath and I flew to New York to meet

with Dr. Burt Beach and his colleagues to discuss the possibility of jointly sponsoring a conference on this subject. The rest is history, and the by-product of that history is this splendid volume.

I wish to express my gratitude personally to Dr. Tamara C. Eskenazi, whose tireless efforts were greatly responsible for the success of the conference. To her coworkers, Dr. Alice Knotts, who has been especially helpful in bringing the manuscript to its final form, Anne Clark, Kimberley Shinabery, and Diana Steinbicker, to all of the participants in the conference, and especially to Dr. Burt B. Beach and The General Conference of the Seventh-day Adventists movement, we extend our gratitude for their cooperation and involvement. Thanks, too, to Dr. Paula Bernstein and the Phillips Foundation for their substantial funding of the Institute for Interfaith Studies.

It is written in the *Zohar* (Genesis 48a) that "the Sabbath is a mirror of the world to come." May the image in that mirror become clearer as a result of the knowledge we obtain from this important work.

Dr. Stanley M. Wagner, Director
Center for Judaic Studies
University of Denver
September 20, 1990

INTRODUCTION

Remember the Sabbath day, to keep it holy.
(Exodus 20:8)

Observe the Sabbath day, to keep it holy, as the Lord
your God commanded you.
(Deuteronomy 5:12)

The biblical commandment to remember or observe the Sabbath
Exodus 20:8; Deuteronomy 5:12) seems straightforward enough at
first sight. Upon reflection, however, it quickly generates questions that
continue to puzzle, provoke, and preoccupy Jews and Christians: Where
does the Sabbath commandment come from? How significant was it in
biblical times? Why has it been so important to Jews throughout the
centuries? When and why did certain Christians take Sunday instead of
Saturday as their Lord's Day? Why do some Christians such as Seventh-
day Adventists observe Saturday rather than Sunday? Is the Sabbath
mainly a day of rest or worship? Is Sunday mainly a day of rest or worship?
Should Christians transfer everything said about the Sabbath in the Bible
to Sunday? What role does the Sabbath play in contemporary lives of Jews
and Christians? How can Jews and Christians best hand on the religious
and human values associated with the Sabbath and Sunday?

These and other related questions were examined at the symposium
entitled "The Sabbath in Jewish and Christian Traditions," held May
24–26, 1989, at the University of Denver. This event was cosponsored by
the Center for Judaic Studies at the University of Denver and the General
Conference of Seventh-day Adventists. For the first time in the long history
of debates, Jewish, Protestant, Roman Catholic, and Seventh-day Adventist scholars came together to explore the ancient and modern significance
of the Sabbath. They brought diverse perspectives to the discussion,

including the historical, philosophical, liturgical, and legal. The papers and responses from that meeting appear in this volume.

The symposium on the Sabbath brought about a rare meeting of representatives from varied religious traditions to address a topic that both divides and unites them. The combination of theoretical and practical aspects renders the Sabbath uniquely appropriate for such an undertaking, because the Sabbath is observed in one form or another by all of these religious groups. The symposium was intended not as a "summit meeting" to produce a consensus statement but rather as an opportunity to set forth and explore various theologies and practices associated with the Sabbath and Sunday in order to enhance interfaith understanding.

The authors are scholars in various disciplines and write from their own academic specializations, but they are also people committed to the religious traditions of Judaism and Christianity, who do not hesitate to step outside their academic objectivity to say what they think in a frank and forthright manner. Their papers have been arranged in six categories. Respondents analyze and evaluate some specific papers, raise new questions and treat the topics from other points of view.

BIBLICAL PERSPECTIVES

The basic biblical material about the Sabbath is reviewed at several points in later papers. The two (somewhat technical) essays explicitly concerned with the Sabbath in the Hebrew Bible treat its origin and importance. Samuel A. Meier asks, Why was the seventh day special for the ancient Israelites? He answers by looking at seven-day purification rites that restore cleanness and result in holiness; he suggests that, for the writer of Genesis 1–2, the seventh day of creation shared in the significance that adhered to seven-day purification cycles in general. While allowing for the later institution of a seventh-day rest for humans, Genesis 1–2 really emphasizes the sacred character of the seventh day. Heather A. McKay raises questions about the character and antiquity of the Sabbath. She observes that the biblical evidence for the Sabbath as a day of worship is sparse and that the new moon had greater significance for some biblical writers. She concludes that the Sabbath was the latest of all the Jewish holy days to come to prominence in Israel's religious life.

RABBINIC AND NEW TESTAMENT PERSPECTIVES

In his treatment of the Sabbath in rabbinic Judaism, Robert Goldenberg notes two basic elements: avoidance of labor and joyful rest. He shows that the rabbinic tradition gave more attention to joy than to restriction and to the meal and other pleasures of the day than to formal worship services. He suggests that despite the weakened observance of religious law in modern Judaism, the Sabbath remains the central axis of Jewish religious life. Using Matthew 12:1–14 as a starting point, Daniel J. Harrington shows that Matthew and his predominately Jewish-Christian community observed the Sabbath and experienced tensions with other Jews in their debate over what may and may not be done on the Sabbath. He looks at other Sabbath tensions in biblical times and within the early church, such as Sabbath or Lord's Day, and today's trend toward secularization.

In response to Goldenberg, Dennis MacDonald suggests that ethnic distinctiveness is an important element in Jewish Sabbath observance and wonders how joyful and restful the Sabbath is for Jewish women. In reply to Harrington, he observes that the evidence for Jesus' alleged Sabbath liberalism is absent from some very early sources and questions whether the Sabbath controversy was of central importance to Matthew and Christians in the second and third centuries. In response to Goldenberg, George E. Rice affirms that the seventh-day Sabbath is not simply a Jewish institution but is open to Christians too in the light of what the New Testament says about Jesus and the Father. Concerning Harrington's paper, Rice states that the Scripture knows only one Sabbath (the seventh day) and that the other New Testament writers observed the Sabbath and felt its tensions much as Matthew did.

HISTORICAL PERSPECTIVES

Samuele Bacchiocchi judges unsuccessful various attempts at tracing the origin of the Sabbath to astronomical or socioeconomic factors in Moses' time, the settlement period, or the exile. He maintains that the biblical view of the origin of the Sabbath (in the very structure of creation according to Genesis 2:1–3) has been dominant in Jewish and Christian writings throughout the centuries. He gives particular attention to the controversies surrounding the alleged moral and ceremonial aspects of the Sabbath commandment and to the relation between Sunday and the Sabbath commandment. He urges the recovery of the seventh-day Sabbath as a creation ordinance for all humankind. John H. Primus examines the Sabbath views of the Protestant Reformers: Martin Luther (Sunday as a day of worship), John Calvin (Sunday as a day of worship and cessation from labor), and the English Puritans represented by Nicolas Bound (Sunday as fulfilling the biblical Sabbath command in every respect). He then calls for a serious theological reconsideration of the Sabbath by Protestants today, along the lines suggested by Karl Barth.

In response to the historical papers, Craig Blomberg argues that in the light of the New Testament and early church tradition the biblical Sabbath cannot be transferred from Saturday to another day. He concludes that recovering the goals of the biblical Sabbath does not require a mandated seventh day in which Christians do or do not do things differently from the other six days of the week. Dennis Kennedy places the historical-theological controversies over the Sabbath and Sunday in a broad context by letting the Sabbath poems of Wendell Berry capture some contemporary meanings of the Sabbath and by linking the Sabbath with social and ecological concerns.

THEOLOGICAL PERSPECTIVES

Without denying the significance of the alternative view, Walter S. Wurzburger contends that the acknowledgment of God as creator outweighs the liberation of humankind as the dominant motif of the Sabbath experience for Jews. The Sabbath celebrates God's creation, revelation, and redemption; it is "God's sanctuary in time." In his reflection on the Sabbath from a Seventh-day Adventist perspective, Jacques B. Doukhan considers the Sabbath as a sign of remembrance pointing to the past event of creation, a sign of hope referring to the future redemption, and a sign of the Absolute, witnessing to the divine "Other." In an excursus he treats the four key biblical passages on the Sabbath (Genesis 2:1–3; Exodus 20:8–11; Deuteronomy 5:12–15; Exodus 31:12–18). In response to Doukhan, Kenneth Hein seeks to explain why Catholics and Seventh-day Adventists do not arrive at the same conclusion regarding the place of the Sabbath in Christian life. He does so by reflecting on creation theology, biblical interpretation, and divine positive law, and he concludes that Sabbath observance as a universally binding positive law is problematic. Marva J. Dawn proposes that a systematic ordering of the biblical narratives and Jewish-Christian traditions about the Sabbath yields the following categories: ceasing, resting, embracing, and feasting. Under each heading she explores subcategories (ceasing work, ceasing productivity and accomplishment, etc.), and shows how they lead to a holistic lifestyle.

LITURGICAL PERSPECTIVES

In treating the Christian celebration of Sunday, John F. Baldovin proposes that the eucharistic assembly makes the Christian Sunday and Sunday makes the eucharistic assembly. He argues that the Christian church was free to choose Sunday as its day of worship, shows how the Sunday liturgy as a whole shaped the contours of the Christian community in the patristic period, and reflects on the present shape and significance of

Christian Sunday worship. As a way of discerning how "modern" men and women make sense of the Jewish Sabbath, Lawrence A. Hoffman applies the notion of language games to three episodes in Jewish History: seventeenth- and eighteenth-century Salonika (the game of limits), Reform Jews in the nineteenth and twentieth centuries (the game of truth), and today (the game of meaning). He urges synagogues and churches to deal positively with modernity's success as the affirmer of pluralism and personal choice.

William H. Shea points to developments in Seventh-day Adventist attitudes toward the Sabbath that parallel to some extent the three "games" applied by Hoffman to Jewish history. As a supplement to Baldovin's paper he calls attention to developments in Christian worship between the second and fourth centuries and to the second-century controversy over the date of Easter. Frederick E. Greenspahn offers further reflections on the reasons for a decline of interest among some Jews and Christians regarding Sabbath observance today. He warns against too easy an identification of the problems facing institutionalized religion and the decline of religion among people today.

LEGAL AND ECUMENICAL PERSPECTIVES

In reviewing American legal history, Mitchell A. Tyner gives many instances in which Seventh-day Adventists and other Sabbatarians have been economically disadvantaged by more than three centuries of Sunday legislation. He then calls on all Sabbatarians to renew and coordinate their efforts to strengthen legislatively and judicially the accommodation requirement. Writing from a Jewish perspective, Saul F. Rosenthal focuses on the community-relations aspects of Sabbatarianism and urges Sabbatarians to be up-front and consistent about their religious practice. He also warns against the dangers that religious extremists today pose for Sabbath-keepers. Michael E. Lodahl shows how the issue of Sabbath observance can serve as a lens for viewing important issues in Christian–Jewish dialogue: the doctrine of creation and God's covenant with Israel, Christian claims to have superseded Israel as God's people, and the Christian tradition of Sunday worship and its relation to the Jewish Sabbath.

This road map of contents cannot convey fully what the participants in the symposium experienced as they met at the University of Denver: the opportunity to make new friends and renew old acquaintances, to learn about and struggle with our assumptions concerning God and the human condition, and to feel the passion of faith and hear different religious rhetorics.

As the papers clearly testify, the theological, intellectual, spiritual, and practical significance of the Sabbath continues to animate and challenge. It is the hope of the editors that this volume will stimulate Jews and Christians elsewhere to continue the conversation that began in Denver and to probe and appreciate the meanings of the Sabbath in their lives and traditions.

Tamara C. Eskenazi
Daniel J. Harrington, S.J.
William H. Shea

I

BIBLICAL PERSPECTIVES

1

THE SABBATH AND
PURIFICATION CYCLES

Samuel A. Meier
Ohio State University

The universal human quest for the answer to the question why is a
feature of the Bible no less than other literature. Why do women suffer
pain in bringing forth the fruit of their wombs? Because the first woman
ate forbidden fruit. Why do snakes have no legs? It was God's curse for
misleading humanity. Why do Israelites not eat certain sinews of the thigh?
Because the ancestor Jacob wrestled with a divine being who dislocated
Jacob's bone at that point.

Rarely does the biblical text provide the question itself. Among the
exceptional cases is Exodus 12:26: "When your children say to you, 'What
does this rite [Passover] mean to you?' then you shall say. . . ." Apart from
such rare explicit queries (cf. Joshua 4:21–22; 22:24), one must generally
reconstruct the question that lies behind the answer the text gives. Thus,
the account of the serpent in the Garden of Eden may answer the question
why serpents have no legs, but it is possible that the question presupposed
was larger in scope: Why should Israelites not tolerate the veneration of
serpentine figures in the cult? Why does the snake periodically shed its skin
in a continual rebirth? Why is there a natural revulsion against snakes
among humans? Where the questions are not articulated in the text itself
caution must be exercised, for the questions that a reader might like to have
answered may not be the questions of driving significance for any given
narrative.

Such an answer with no clearly articulated question appears in the creation account in Genesis 1–2. When the cosmos is complete, Genesis 2:2–3
summarizes:

And on the seventh day God completed his work which he had done, and he
rested on the seventh day from all his work which he had done. Then God

3

blessed the seventh day and sanctified it, because in it he rested from all his
work which God had created and made.

It is tempting to see this simply as the precursor of the Sabbath, specifically
answering the implied question, Why do Israelites cease activities on the
Sabbath?[1] But this question is too narrow a focus for the text, which
actually is concerned with a much larger issue.[2] The question to which this
text provides an answer is not, Why do Israelites cease activity on the
Sabbath? but rather, Why are cycles of seven-day periods so special?

We must first underscore that there is no clearly articulated single reason
in the Bible for the observance of the Sabbath. The motivation provided
in Exodus 20:8-11 is that since God rested at creation on the seventh day,
so Israelites are to do the same, but Deuteronomy 5:12-15 claims that the
reason for the Sabbath is that it is to commemorate the release from the
bondage in Egypt. It is apparent that the question, Why do Israelites rest
on the Sabbath? was very early susceptible to multiple responses. One may
even suggest that this was a question over which the community was
divided—not only because the Sabbath is the subject of the single greatest
explanatory expansion in the decalogue but because whatever reason one
accepts for Sabbath observance will eventually determine legislative
responses to how the day is to be kept. In this regard, Deuteronomy does
not answer the question of why it is specifically on the seventh day that the
Sabbath occurs. Deuteronomy presupposes the seven-day cycle without
comment, for a seventh-day rest cannot be derived from the reason Deuteronomy provides for the observance, namely, a four-hundred-year bondage
in Egypt followed by forty years in the wilderness. In contrast, Exodus 20
aggressively aims to answer the question of why rest occurs on the seventh
day as opposed to some other day, grounding the explanation in the seven-
day week of creation.

Our focus will be on the text in Exodus, which locates the Sabbath
rationale in creation itself, clearly resonating with the passage in Genesis
1-2. There is little question that the reason provided in Exodus 20 for the
Sabbath is the narrative of Genesis 1-2, a passage that is presupposed by
Exodus 20 and even verbally proximate. But this is not to say that Genesis
2:2-3 was penned primarily with the issue of the Sabbath in mind. There
is, first, the fact that the word "sabbath" occurs nowhere in Genesis.
Although the verb form *wayyišbōt* ("and he ceased") does appear in
Genesis 2:2-3, pointing to the writer's apparent awareness of the existence
of the Sabbath with which he makes this illuminating pun, the absence of
the term "sabbath" from Genesis 1-2 is peculiar. Indeed, when Exodus 20
employs the language of Genesis 2 to defend creation as a reason for Sabbath observance, the writer uses the word "sabbath" in place of the term
"seventh day," which appears in Genesis 2:

Genesis 2:3 *wybrk 'lhym 't ywm hšby'y wyqdš 'tw*
Exodus 20:22 *brk yhwh 't ywm hšbt wyqdšhw*

The failure of Genesis 2 to identify the seventh day of creation as the Sabbath is curious and deserves further attention. Three times in two verses the day is called "the seventh day" (*yôm haššĕbî'î*) with no attempt to provide the usual aesthetically pleasing variations so common to poetry or artistic prose. In a section where the naming of the various components of creation is forefront (1:5: "God called the light 'Day,' and the darkness he called 'Night'"; 1:8: "God called the expanse 'Heaven'"; 1:10: "God called the dry land 'Earth' and the gathering of the waters he called 'Seas'"), it is an unusual oversight to neglect the fact that the seventh day has a name. Yet although God ceases activity (*wayyišbōt*) on the seventh day, he does not name it *šabbāt*. The many opportunities for the writer to identify the seventh day of creation as a Sabbath rest are not exploited.

There are good reasons to avoid calling the seventh day a Sabbath in Genesis 2. Most important is that although the seventh day is a rest for God, it marks a day of labor for humans. In this respect, Israel reflects a general consensus that emerges in ancient Near Eastern accounts of the origins of the cosmos. A major concern among Israel's neighbors in accounting for the origins of the cosmos was the centrality of labor and its relief. In each case, it is the gods who seek relief from labor by designating a substitute laborer in the form of humanity.[3] When one moves from these traditions to the biblical accounts in Genesis, the narrative terrain remains familiar. In Genesis 2:15, "the Lord God took the man and put him into the garden of Eden to work it and keep it," and the motivation for the creation of Eve begins as a search for someone to assist the man in his task (Genesis 2:18): "Then the Lord God said, 'It is not good for the man to be alone; I will make a helper suitable for him'" (*'ēzer kĕnegdô*). Both man and woman are defined as laborers in God's garden. Similarly in Genesis 1, humans are commissioned with a task (v. 28): "and God said to them, 'Be fruitful and multiply, and fill the earth, and subdue it (*wĕkibĕšûhā*), and rule over the fish of the sea and over the birds of the sky and over every living thing that moves on the earth.'"

God's rest is made possible because there is a substitute in his image delegated to maintain the world order and ensure the fruitfulness of the earth. The day in which God rests in the Bible—as in other ancient Near Eastern traditions—is therefore the first day of humanity's labor. The seventh day is God's rest and the day on which humanity begins to work. God can cease from his activity because humanity is now bearing the burden. This point, clear in extrabiblical texts,[4] is obscured in Genesis 1–2 only because there is a tendency to assume that much if not all of the later traditions with respect to the Sabbath was already *in nuce* at creation.[5] But

Genesis 2:2-3 clarifies that it is only God who rests on the seventh day: "And on the seventh day *God* completed *his work* which *he* had done. And *he rested* on the seventh day from all *his* work which *he had done.* Then God blessed the seventh day and sanctified it, because in it *he rested* from all *his work* which *God had created* and made." The persistent repetition affirms emphatically that it is God who rests while the remainder of creation is pictured as operating under the care of a new supervisor delegated to assume God's management while God rests. It is for this reason that the writer of Genesis 1 studiously avoids using the noun "sabbath" anywhere in this text. This is not a rest for creation, much less for humans; this is a rest for God.

Instead, what is emphatic is the fact that this day is the seventh day. The day on which God rests is identified three times in rapid succession, each time called "the seventh day." Instead of answering the question, Why is the Sabbath a special day for Israelites? the text is presupposing the broader question, Why is the seventh day special? The latter is a more encompassing question, for although every Sabbath day is a seventh day, not all seventh days are Sabbath days.

When one turns to literature that is usually identified closely with Genesis 1:1-2:4 (the Priestly tradition), the centrality of the seventh day apart from the Sabbath becomes evident. In the priestly legislation, the standard purification period with few exceptions is a seven-day period that is independent of the weekly cycle and the Sabbath.[6] When a Nazirite, for example, is in the presence of a person who dies, he must undergo a ritual cleansing process which culminates with his purification on the seventh day following the defilement (Numbers 6:9). The sequence of seven days is reckoned from the day of the appearance of the impurity and is entirely independent of the predictable Sabbath-day cycle. Impurity that results from contact with bones, graves, or corpses in general can be counteracted only on the seventh day following the initial act (Numbers 19:11-22).[7] A menstruant requires seven days for purification (Leviticus 15:19, 28), a period that is necessary also for a new mother.[8] A man lying with a menstruant must undergo a seven-day cleansing (Leviticus 15:24), and a man with a discharge must wait for seven days for purification also (Leviticus 15:13). Seven days pass in numerous scenarios of leprosy quarantine for humans (Leviticus 13:4-7, 21, 26, 31, 33), garments (Leviticus 13:50, 54), and houses (Leviticus 14:38-39).[9] The ordination of Aaron and his sons into the priesthood required a seven-day period (Leviticus 8:33-35).[10]

In all of these rites of purification, the passage of seven days is an essential part of the restoration of the unclean and a means of achieving holiness. According to the priestly legislation, Israel is holy and those in Israel who become unclean must take steps to become clean once again and so preserve the sanctity of Israel. During the seven-day cleansing process in which the unclean are once again made clean and holiness is restored, other ritual components are blended with the passage of these days (peculiar sacrifices, sprinkling of blood, lustrations, etc.). But the cleansing process is incomplete without both the passage of the seven days and the accompanying cultic acts. When the seventh day is reached and the proper steps have been taken, the result is the restoration of holiness and the transformation of the unclean to the clean, death to life, isolation to community, sterility to fruitfulness.

The paradigm for this transformation which the cult facilitates is Genesis 1. The creation week is the template for the passage from sterility to fruitfulness. The utter lifelessness and associations with the realm of the dead in the opening verses of Genesis (the sterile *tōhû wābōhû,* the watery environment reminiscent of Sheol, the darkness that characterizes the underworld) contrast with the persistent drive of creation to "be fruitful and multiply" — plants bearing seed (vv. 11–12), the seas swarming with life (vv. 20–22), birds multiplying in the sky (vv. 20–22), animals and humans filling the earth (v. 28). The "very good" that God pronounces is not simply an aesthetic appraisal, for it certainly bears a moral overtone in the light of the moral dissonance that appears when the beginning of the creation week is characterized by the sea and darkness. These poles are echoed in the similar boundaries that characterize the purification in the cult: contact with death and the reminders of mortality require that members of the community undergo a process of revivification and reentry into life. A seven-day progression at creation from sterility to fertility, from dark chaos to a state of "very good," corresponds to the dominant purification cycle where seven days mark the transfer from death to life.

The seventh day in this scheme is of indisputable preeminence. Had God ceased at any point prior to the seventh day, creation would have been incomplete. Earth would not have been a life-giving whole, for the transfer from formless sterility to an ordered whole would have been short-circuited. In the cult, likewise, cessation of ritual purification at any point prior to the seventh day does not effectively transfer one from contact with death to new life. In both the creation week and in the purification in the cult, it is the seventh day which affirms that wholeness and holiness have been achieved.

The peculiarities of the cult often elicit inquiries as to why certain actions are necessary or characteristically performed. Reference has already been made to a hypothetical question from Israelite children, What does this rite [Passover] mean to you? which elicited an appropriate explanatory response regarding this sacrificial meal. Genesis 32:32 [Hebrew 32:33] explains why "to this day the sons of Israel do not eat the sinew of the hip which is on the socket of the thigh, because he touched the socket of Jacob's thigh in

the sinew of the hip." An encounter between the ark of God and Dagon
is employed to explain in 1 Samuel 5:5 why "neither the priests of Dagon
nor all who enter Dagon's temple tread on the threshold of Dagon in
Ashdod to this day." Such articulations are the very essence of cultic
praxis, for they identify the immediate relevance of timeless activities.

Why then is a seven-day cycle so persistent in purification ritual in
Israelite tradition? This is in fact a question that certainly occupied the
attention of ancient Israelites. Since one of the most prominent aspects of
the priestly legislation in the Bible is the seven-day cycle employed for
purification—indeed, far more prominent than the Sabbath—it would not
be extraordinary to find somewhere an attempt to explain or justify this
persistent cyclical pattern.

Genesis 1:1–2:4 provides this rationale. There is not only a parallel of
thought and thematic correspondence between this account and seven-day
purification cycles, as we have just noted. In fact, the writer of Genesis 1
explicitly sought to connect the two concepts—indeed, even grounding the
sacred character of seven-day purification cycles in the activity that God
pursued in Genesis 1–2. This explicit correlation appears in a potent term
employed in Genesis 2:3: God "made holy" the seventh day. Nothing else
in the creation week is similarly treated. Nowhere else in the entire book
of Genesis does God make anything holy, for the *piel* of *qaddēš* appears
only in this verse in Genesis. In contrast, the frequency of the word in the
Priestly legislation of Exodus, Leviticus, and Numbers underscores the
conceptual congruence between Priestly concerns and the theology of
Genesis 1, a fact long noted.

The priestly legislation, where holiness is elaborated at length, provides
a context by which one may explicate the unique appearance of sanctification in Genesis. If one assumes the priestly legislation as the background
for the concept of holiness articulated in Genesis 2:3, it becomes clear that
a closely circumscribed sphere of connotations is being invoked by the nar-
rator of the creation week. Specifically, one finds in the Priestly legislation
that whatever is sacred is capable of transmitting its quality in a diminished
and less potent form to those with whom it comes in contact. Thus, the
holy sacrifices (animal and grain alike) which are to be eaten by the priests
alone will make anyone who touches them holy (Leviticus 6:18, 27 [Hebrew
6:11, 20]). Similarly, the furniture of the tabernacle is made holy with the
result that anyone who comes in contact with these articles will become
holy (Exodus 30:29). The principle of Haggai 2:11–13 is well known;
holiness cannot be transmitted through intermediaries but requires immediate contact.[11] Furthermore, the correspondence in the Priestly legislation
between purity and holiness provides further illustration of the same concept.[12] Purity is achieved by contact with sacred and purifying elements

which transmit their own quality to (or, from another perspective, remove uncleanness from) the person or object with which they come in contact.

When God made the seventh day holy, he by that act invested the day with a quality that could be as contagious as other items also designated holy by God. How is the sacred character of the seventh day attainable so that its holiness may affect humans? It is the ritual of the cult which activates the seventh day's potency. Any day of the week may be someone's seventh day for purification, a process that is set in motion for each individual when that person submits to the appropriate responses of seclusion, sacrifice, lustration, and priestly oversight. A purification process is enacted where new temporal boundaries become significant for the individual. The seven-day process of purification in Israelite ritual, when connected by Priestly writers with Genesis 1–2, becomes a microcosmic replay of creation, both of which begin in alienation and conclude with holiness.

It cannot be denied that among the questions that Genesis 1:1–2:4 addresses is the significance of the Sabbath; however, as was noted above, the Sabbath in this chapter is deliberately obscured by a much larger question on which the writer focuses. The Sabbath is a subcategory of seven-day phenomena in Israel, and by answering the larger question the writer has solved two problems for the price of one: Why are seven days potent for purification and why is the Sabbath a special day? For the writer of Genesis 1–2, the significance of the Sabbath partakes of the significance that adheres to seven-day purification cycles in general.

Whether or not there is a genetic relationship between seven-day purification cycles and the Sabbath is a subject that is now shrouded in obscurity; however, a close reading of Genesis 1–2 indicates that priestly interpretation of the two phenomena subsumed the two under a common explanation. For those involved in the Temple cult, there was a real connection between the predictable Sabbath and the unpredictable seven-day cleansing cycles, which varied from person to person. Such an early theological perspective which saw a unity between the two is worthy of attention in contemporary searches for meaning in the Sabbath, for it emphasizes the function of the Sabbath as a conductor of holiness and as a feature of worship which periodically restores purity.

We began this discussion with an investigation of what question or questions were presumed by the narrative of Genesis 1–2. It became apparent that although there are traditions in the Bible that derive Israel's Sabbath day from the notion of God's rest at creation, the description of creation itself in Genesis 1–2 only hints at this connection. It allows for the later institution of a seventh-day rest for humans but does not specifically endorse it. Instead, the chapter focuses emphasis on the seventh day and its sacred character. Where else do these two concerns find expression in

biblical literature? They find their ready counterpart in Priestly Legislation, where both the tangible reality of holiness and the seven-day cycle for
purification merge as in Genesis 1-2. By reading only a Sabbath significance in Genesis 1-2, modern exegesis may be succumbing to a temptation to discern only issues that are of contemporary import, ignoring or
minimizing as arcane lore the ritual concerns of biblical literature. If one
can recapture the vision of ancient Israelite priests, in which purification
cycles were as prominent as Sabbath observances, the sanctification of the
seventh day in Genesis 2:3 is a tangible reality that allows both individual
Israelites to be restored to the holy community and Israel as a nation to
be resanctified before God when Israel observes the Sabbath.

NOTES

1. This perspective, articulated already in H. Gunkel (*Genesis* [Göttingen:
Vandenhoeck & Ruprecht, 1901] 115) is not uncommon: the Sabbath "connection
with the creation in Genesis 2:2f. is an etiological myth" (Millar Burrows, *An
Outline of Biblical Theology* [Philadelphia: Westminster, 1946] 273).

2. A. R. Hulst, "Bemerkungen zum Sabbatgebot," in *Studia Biblica et Semitica,
Th. C. Vriezen Dedicata* (Wageningen: H. Veenman en Zonen, 1966) 159; Claus
Westermann, *Genesis 1-11* (Trans. John J. Scullion; Minneapolis: Augsburg,
1984) 171.

3. The first tablet of the *Atrahasis* myth and the sixth tablet of the *Enuma Elish*
(especially lines 7-8: "I will create *lullu*-man; upon him shall the services of the gods
be imposed so that they may rest."). A newly published text reaffirms a similar
scenario (1.5'-9'): "The labor of the gods is bit[ter] for them . . . so let us make an
image of clay that we might impos[e upon it this labor,] let us relieve their exhaus-
tion for ev[er]" (Werner Mayer, "Ein Mythos von der Erschaffung des Menschen
und des Königs," *Orientalia* 56 [1987] 55–68; cf. 1.29: "He commanded that the
labor of the gods be assigned to him," i.e., newly created *lullu*-man). Sumerian
antecedents point to a very old tradition (W. G. Lambert, "A New Look at the
Babylonian Background of Genesis," *Journal of Theological Studies* 16 [1965]
287–300).

4. Even the book of *Jubilees*, with its desire to ground ritual regulations in
antecedent acts of God in history (e.g., 3:8–14), acknowledges that the Sabbath is
first observed at Mount Sinai (50:1) and is to be observed only by Israel and no
other nation (2:31). The angels who observe the Sabbath in heaven (2:17–18, 21)
did so before any humans ever did (2:30).

5. Niels-Erik A. Andreasen, for example, notes that there is no command to
humanity in Genesis 2 to rest, but humanity nevertheless participated in the
Sabbath (*Rest and Redemption* [Berrien Springs, MI: Andrews University Press,
1978] 75–77).

6. Exceptions are Leviticus 12:4–5; Numbers 19:12, 19; 31:19. Note that in these

cases, where an alternate purification period is in view, a seven-day cycle is still included.

7. The Midianite war (Numbers 31:19) is followed by a seven-day cleansing period for all who killed or touched a corpse in the battle. Ezekiel 44:25-27 specifies that a priest defiled by a corpse requires seven days for cleansing.

8. A seven-day period passes for the mother of a boy (Leviticus 12:2) and a fourteen-day period (twice seven) for the mother of a girl (Leviticus 12:5). In this case the seven-day sequences must be supplemented by further purification.

9. When the leper is cleansed, he remains outside his tent for seven days before he may reenter (Leviticus 14:8-9); a narrative example occurs in the case of Miriam (Numbers 12:14).

10. Ezekiel 43:25-26 in similar fashion requires seven days before the newly dedicated altar may be used.

11. Carol L. Meyers and Eric M. Meyers, *Haggai, Zechariah 1-8* (AB 25B; Garden City, NY: Doubleday, 1987) 55-56.

12. E.g., Leviticus 10:10; 11:44. "What is new here is the equation of purity with holiness, a theme virtually absent in the narrative, prophetic, and sapiential materials we have just examined. . . . The priestly code equates purity with holiness" (Jacob Neusner, *The Idea of Purity in Ancient Judaism* [Studies in Judaism in Late Antiquity 1; Leiden: Brill, 1973] 18, 25).

2

NEW MOON OR SABBATH?

Heather A. McKay
University of Sheffield, England

It is a commonplace in biblical studies that the Sabbath in ancient Israel was a day of rest *and* a day of worship.[1] But this assumption is not often carefully examined in the light of what the texts themselves say. Nor is it made clear who was actually worshiping, and of what their worship consisted. It is similarly assumed that new moon was a day of festivity and worship but secondary to the Sabbath. I will take a closer look at the impact of these two feast days in the lives of the Israelite community.

To set an effective framework for the discussion, a wide canon of literature will be surveyed here, including apocryphal, deuterocanonical, and Qumran texts along with Philo and Josephus. This approach will allow us to try to understand the Sabbath institution from the opposite standpoint of that usually adopted, that is, to begin with texts that are definitely late and to work back toward the cluster of exilic and preexilic texts.

THE IMPORT OF SABBATH AND NEW MOON

A stance that is frequently encountered in studies on the Sabbath is that the "biblical view is unequivocal: the Sabbath originated in Israel as God's special institution for His people."[2] This view can be sustained only if the biblical texts are read as measured factual accounts of the history of a religion and its practices. The reader has to amalgamate all texts that deal with the Sabbath into one picture, without making any attempt to distinguish between those which speak of Sabbath observance and those which speak of Sabbath worship. By Sabbath observance we understand the cessation of work and trading, which is plainly and frequently enjoined throughout the literature. But the picture about worship is less clear. It is generally believed that psalm singing was a part of worship and that it took place, therefore, on the Sabbath day. Yet the evidence for that in the Bible is meager, only one psalm having as its title "Song for the Sabbath Day," and no other psalm referring to the Sabbath at all. Further, even if psalm singing were a regular feature of worship on holy days (including the Sabbath), it is not clear who was singing. There is evidence that there were teams of Temple singers (1 Chronicles 6:31; 9:33; Nehemiah 7:1, 44; 11:22), but whether others could listen or join in is never made explicit in the biblical sources. Prayer, another common form of worship on the Sabbath, is rather a personal activity that can take place anywhere, not excluding a holy site—for example, Hannah's prayer at the shrine in Shiloh (1 Samuel 1, 2), which took place on Elkanah's annual visit to worship and sacrifice there. But this tells us nothing about activities on the Sabbath.

We might look to details about sacrifices to fill out the content of worship, but when we do we find that only priests were actually involved in sacrificing. It is not clear whether the people (or their prince acting in a representative capacity) were present at the sacrifice session in any meaningful way. Ezekiel 46:3, the only text in the Hebrew Bible that refers to Sabbath worship for the ordinary worshiper, states only that "the people of the land shall worship at the entrance of the gate before the Lord on the Sabbaths and on the new moons."

By worship, then, we mean a purposive activity whereby people of similar beliefs carry out similar rites and rituals in order to pay homage, with adoration and awe, to a particular, named deity. Worship may be carried out individually or in groups, silently or aloud, with singing, dancing, music, reading or reciting of sacred texts, hymns, prayers and blessings, or by sacrificing plants and animals. Instructions for or descriptions of these types of activity in the texts will be regarded in this paper as evidences of worship either expected or carried out by the Israelite community.

An abrasive approach to Sabbath worship is provided by Menahem Haran, who reads the Sabbath texts with a seasoning of skepticism and concludes that the pattern of rites and observances (including the Sabbath and new moon) reported by the Priestly source "cannot originate with the common people, but of necessity is an esoteric prerogative of the priestly family."[3] He implies that it is this priestly group that concerns itself with the preservation and recording of all religious rites and supposes that priestly "ritual takes place in the arcana of the house of God, unseen by the people as a whole."

Agnosticism is expressed by A. S. Herbert, who says of the new moon that "little is known" and that "the origin of Sabbath is also obscure."[4] He assumes the Sabbath to have been a genuine institution in Israel, but he complains that the infrequency with which it is mentioned and the lack of information about its manner of observation in the preexilic histories and prophets add to our difficulty.

Hans-Joachim Kraus makes mention of the association between the terms "new moon" and "sabbath."[5] Kraus notes that there is a lack of stipulation for worship of any kind on the Sabbath as opposed to on the new moon, for which there are ritual practices (Numbers 10:10; 1 Samuel 20; Ezekiel 46:6).[6] Kraus considers the new moon to have been a monthly feast, established early on in the religious life of the families of Israel. Attempting unsuccessfully to isolate the origin and nature of the Sabbath, he concludes from the different explanations of the Sabbath commandment that "both the explanations are secondary, but they show how the Old Testament tradition attempted to anchor the Sabbath day in the fundamental mighty acts of Yahweh."[7] Kraus sees editors or narrators at work here trying to incline the reader toward particular understandings of the Sabbath. He makes a valiant attempt to understand the cultic calendars of the Old Testament and tries to see if the Sabbath can occur in a hebdomadal pattern throughout the year, in concert with the three major feasts, but he cannot find a consistent or coherent system and feels that readers are often driven to conclude that "Israel introduced the 'sacred number' into the calendar."[8]

The weekly Sabbath can be given more substance by a search through the textual evidence of the Dead Sea Scrolls.[9] In the *Psalms Scroll* from Qumran cave 11 we find listed the categories of psalms and songs supposedly composed by David, namely, 364 daily psalms and 52 for the Sabbath. And in the liturgical fragments known as "The Words of the Heavenly Lights," there is a unit called "Hymns for the Sabbath Day."[10] There is also the text known as "Songs of the Sabbath Sacrifice," in which songs are designated to be used on a particular Sabbath, e.g., "the seventh Sabbath on the sixteenth of the second month."[11] These writings imply that the Qumran community kept a weekly Sabbath which included psalm singing and offering of "sacrifices" by members of the community.

Direct evidence for the Sabbath can be found in the *Damascus Document* (cols. 11–12), which contains injunctions concerning the purity and cleanliness of men offering sacrifice on the Sabbath, including elaborate guidelines for proper behavior on the Sabbath. These guidelines, in which there are eighteen references to the Sabbath, seek to preserve the believer from defiling the Sabbath by thoughts about the morrow's work or by any actions that deal with commerce, travel, or work of any sort. Additional guidelines concern the cleanliness necessary before entering the house of worship when a holy service of worship is taking place (but it is not explicitly clear that this also refers to the Sabbath).

These texts from the Dead Sea indicate an accepted progression of weeks through the religious year punctuated by Sabbaths, which were held in considerable regard as days that involved worship and sacrifice.

EVIDENCE AND ARGUMENT

Sabbath

The holy day Sabbath appears in only fifteen books of the Hebrew Bible and in 1 and 2 Maccabees, *Jubilees,* and the *Damascus Covenant.*[12]

Exodus refers to the Sabbath fourteen times. All these references are to the cessation of work on the Sabbath; they say nothing about worship. The picture is similar in Leviticus, with fourteen sections concerned with appropriate Sabbath observance. The Sabbath is mentioned in a cultic calendar in chap. 23 but without any directions for worship or sacrifice on the Sabbath. There are also six references to the Sabbaths kept by the land in chaps. 25 and 26. The book of Numbers has one reference to the Sabbath regarding an infringement of Sabbath laws, and in chaps. 28 and 29 the Sabbath appears in another cultic calendar to which we shall return later. In Deuteronomy the Sabbath is mentioned only in the fourth commandment (Deuteronomy 5:12–14).

The next book to mention the Sabbath is 2 Kings with three references regarding guard rotas at the king's house and their changeover on the Sabbath and one reference to the covered way from palace to Temple for the Sabbath. In addition, in the story about the Shunammite woman, the husband links new moon and Sabbath as days worth visiting a shrine in search of the holy man, who likely would be there. 1 Chronicles mentions the Sabbath twice in connection with Sabbath preparations by the Kohathites, and once in a list of days for burnt offerings (23:31). 2 Chronicles has three references to the guard duty on the Sabbath (// 2 Kings 11), this text giving a clearer indication that the king went to the Temple—possibly on the Sabbath, as a double guard could be mustered then. There are also two references to the land keeping Sabbaths and two lists of days (including Sabbath) suitable for burnt offerings (2 Chronicles 2:4; 8:13; 31:3).

Nehemiah 9 speaks of the Sabbath as God's gift to Israel. Then twice in chap. 10 and ten times in chap. 13, the Sabbath is spoken of in terms of restrictions on business transactions. In the book of Psalms only Psalm 92 is designated by its title as "a song for the Sabbath day." In the prophetic books, between texts dealing with sacrifice and prayer, Isaiah 1:13f. links new moon, Sabbath, assemblies, and appointed feasts as occasions when Yahweh is displeased by what goes on. Isaiah 66:23 implies that worship before Yahweh on new moon and Sabbath will be part of the delights of the New Age. Again, no details of this worship are given. Isaiah 56 has three references dealing with profanation of the Sabbath, and Isaiah 58 has two about proper behavior on the Sabbath, although these do not include any specific references to worship. Jeremiah 17, in a section on business practice on the Sabbath, contains all six references in that book. Lamentations 2:6

has one retrospective and mournful comment on the loss of the Sabbath and appointed feasts. Ezekiel 20–23 has nine references to "my Sabbaths" with respect to their profanation. Chapter 46 has two references to the Sabbath. One concerns the people of the land who worship Yahweh at the gate of the inner court of the Temple; the other offers details about the burnt offerings to be made by the prince on that day (these being in the second cultic calendar, which we will discuss later). There are four additional references to the Sabbath in Ezekiel linked with other holy days (44:24; 45:17; 46:1, 3). In Hosea the Sabbath appears once (2:11) in a list of holy days that are going to be obliterated by Yahweh. Amos has one reference to Sabbath and new moon in connection with the suspending of trading on these days (8:5).

In summary, only three times is the Sabbath mentioned in the Hebrew Bible in terms of actual worship to be carried out on that day: (1) in details of the Sabbath sacrifice in Numbers 28:9f.; (2) in the title of Psalm 92, which indicates that a particular song should be sung on the Sabbath day; and (3) in Ezekiel 46, where the people of the land in a future age are directed to worship (with no further details) at one of the Temple gates and where the burnt offerings to be made on the Sabbath by the prince are detailed. There are no details of Sabbath worship for the ordinary worshiper as opposed to Sabbath observance as rest.

New Moon

New moon is mentioned on its own (without any association with other holy days) in only one book, 1 Samuel, in the story of the celebration to which Saul invites David (20:5–34). This solitary account is interesting when one realizes that new moon occurs in twenty-two other places linked with one or more other holy days; evidently, it was a reasonably well-known feast in Israelite society. However, only in that one narrative is new moon described as an important religious occasion, from which absenting oneself was a serious matter, and only in that narrative does it hold center stage as the sole religious event described. Instructions for rituals to be employed at the beginnings of months are detailed at Numbers 10:10; 28:11–15; 29:6. Trumpet blowing and a sacrifice several times larger than that of the Sabbath are features of new moon celebrations. Leviticus 23:24 describes the first day of the seventh month as a day of solemn rest with trumpet blasts and an offering by fire (unspecified). Psalm 81:3 also indicates that trumpet blowing was traditional at the new moon. Ezekiel 46:6 instructs the future prince to make a burnt offering on both Sabbath and new moon—the new moon sacrifice including one bull more than on Sabbath—and says that the people of the land should worship at the entrance of the gate on the Sabbaths and the new moons. It appears therefore that, compared with the Sabbath, new moon had a greater importance in the minds of some of the biblical writers.

Lists and Sequences of Holy Days

By studying the lists of holy days we might be able to discover how the compiler of the text viewed Sabbath in relation to the other days.

(a) Four-name lists are as follows:

Numbers 28–29	*Ezekiel 45:17*	*Hosea 2:11*
Sabbaths	feasts	feasts
new moon	new moons	new moons
Passover	Sabbath	Sabbath
Weeks	appointed feasts	appointed feasts

1 Maccabees 10:34	*Jubilees 1:14*	Philo *Special Laws* 1.168–69
feasts	new moons	daily
Sabbath	Sabbaths	seventh day
new moon	jubilees	new moons
appointed feasts	ordinances	fasts
		three festal seasons

Note that Sabbath and new moon change places between the lists in Hosea and Ezekiel compared with 1 Maccabees. Could this be an indication that the status of the Sabbath was changing?

(b) Three-name sequences occur nine times in the Bible:

1–2 Chronicles	Sabbath	new moons	appointed feasts (4 times)
Nehemiah 10:33	Sabbath	new moons	appointed feasts
Judith 8:6	Sabbath	new moon	the Israelite feasts
1 Esdras 5:52	Sabbaths	new moons	all solemn feasts
Psalm 81:3	new moon	full moon	feast day
Colossians 2:16	festival	new moon	Sabbath

(c) There are thirteen two-name sequences in the Bible:

2 Kings 4:23; Isaiah 1:13; 66:23; Amos 8:5	new moon	Sabbath
Ezekiel 46:1, 3	Sabbath	new moon
Lamentations 2:6; Ezekiel 44:24	appointed feasts	Sabbath
1 Maccabees 1:45; 2 Maccabees 6:6	Sabbath	feasts
Ezra 3:5; Isaiah 1:14	new moon	appointed feasts

It is instructive to note the relative positions of new moon and Sabbath and the similar numbers of occurrences of the two named days; however, if we consider only the text of the Hebrew Bible we find that new moon appears eighteen times compared with fifteen references to the Sabbath. Plainly, there is no evidence that Sabbath dominated the religious scene.

(d) Cultic Calendars

The three lengthiest texts that discuss holy days and their required practices and that could reasonably be expected to express their authors' understandings of these matters are Leviticus 23:2–43; Numbers 28:1–29:39; and Ezekiel 45:13–46:15. The passages share a more or less common understanding of the three annual feasts, similar to that in Deuteronomy 16, but they differ in the order in which they deal with the days, the sacrifices prescribed, and even the selection of the holy days they present.

In Numbers 28–29 the sequence runs as follows: Sabbaths, beginnings of months, feast of Unleavened Bread, feast of Weeks, Day of Atonement, feast of Booths. The holy days and their rituals are described.

Leviticus 23 has a similar sequence, except that the holy days are arranged in order of their progression through the year, with a statement about the Sabbath interpolated in v. 3 between the general introduction to the appointed feasts and the details for the Passover, and an ambiguous reference to the Sabbath in v. 38. The sequence is (Sabbath), feast of Unleavened Bread, feast of Weeks, first day of the seventh month, Day of Atonement, (Sabbath), feast of Booths.

Ezekiel 45–46 contains another set of instructions for the observance of holy days, though set in the future, and examines them in the following order: Passover, Sabbath, new moon, and appointed feasts; the other two annual feasts are not mentioned by name, although the general term "feast" is there. It is a bit surprising that the same section is also preceded by a list naming feasts, new moon, Sabbath, and all appointed feasts (45:17), but that sequence is ignored in the section that follows. There is obviously no harmonizing of these two sections, because the list does not function in any way as an announcement of the substance to follow in the rest of the section.

Leviticus 23	*Numbers 28–29*	*Ezekiel 45–46*
appointed feasts	daily	Day of Atonement
Sabbath	Sabbath	Passover
appointed feasts	new moon	feast (? Weeks)
Passover	Passover	Sabbath
Firstfruits/Weeks	Weeks	new moon
day of solemn rest	Day of Atonement	appointed feasts
Day of Atonement	Booths	daily
Booths		
appointed feasts		
(Sabbath)		
Booths		

More can be understood if the lists of sacrifices and special instructions given are detailed. Certainly the three calendars are not in agreement about what should happen on the feasts.[13]

The presentation in Numbers has all the appearance of being the most regular of the three, following a system of decreasing frequency of occurrence and containing seven sections. It is worth noting that the new moon offering is many times more lavish than the Sabbath offering. This block of material apparently reveres the new moon a great deal more than the Sabbath as a festal day similar in importance to the three pilgrim feasts. The Sabbath has, in fact, no particular listing of sacrifices but merely has an implicit doubling of the daily offering. The question of rest on the day of the new moon is not addressed.[14]

The listings in Ezekiel can again be seen to fall into seven sets of instructions. Again it looks as if Sabbath and new moon were days similar in importance to the writer of this material, but more animals were slaughtered for the new moon than for the Sabbath. Again there is no mention of rest at new moon.[15]

A close look at the material in Leviticus reveals two references to the Sabbath (but without any content of detail or prescription) which look as if they have been added to an existing cultic sequence, and no reference at all to the new moon as such. (On the first day of the seventh month, rest, ritual acts, and sacrifices are laid down, but it is not clear that this is expected to happen on every new moon.) In this list of feasts the only one clearly detailed by amounts of sacrifices is the feast of Weeks.

Joseph M. Baumgarten reports the rabbinic question about the intrusion of Sabbath details at two places in this section of Leviticus, "What place has the Sabbath in the chapter dealing with festivals?"[16] The two mentions of the Sabbath seem to jar with the rest of the material and seem like later additions to the text. Why should the Sabbath intrude itself in a list of feast days? The rabbi who raised the question must have considered the Sabbath to be other than a feast day. Further, in whose interests would it have been to make the insertion? We are forced to consider the possibility that there was a Sabbath-honoring group in Israelite society. Certainly Kraus recognizes the increase in importance of the Sabbath in the community that produced the book of Ezekiel.[17] A possible conclusion is that the Sabbath was of great importance to the final editors of this text and that they inserted it clumsily. The new moon was of no importance to them, for it is certainly not given a place in this list.

CONCLUSIONS ABOUT THE SABBATH

The evidence presented in this paper encourages the view that the Sabbath was the latest of all the holy days to be given pride of place in the religious life of Israel. Even if the Sabbath was observed from earlier times, it only rose to prominence and acquired a set of rituals at a later date and with the influence of a backing party. In particular, a survey of all the occurrences of the word "sabbath" in the Hebrew Bible and apocryphal and deuterocanonical works shows that the Sabbath was not of equal interest to the writers of the different books. Those to whom it was of the greatest importance were the writers of Exodus 16–20; Leviticus 16–26; Deuteronomy 5; Nehemiah 10, 13; Isaiah 56; Jeremiah 17; Ezekiel 22, 23; 1–2 Maccabees and *Jubilees*. This grouping suggests that the Sabbath was important to certain groups in the later history of Israel.

The picture from the Hebrew Bible alone is of a faithfully observed and revered Sabbath of rest and of a new moon feast day of more extravagant proportions. The Sabbath is, however, in transition through the later texts of the apocryphal and deuterocanonical works. Evidence of this can be found in the books of the Maccabees. Here the phrase "the Sabbath" is used in places where it is not essential for the sense of the narrative, almost as a refrain or with a quasi-formulaic quality (1 Maccabees 2:32–41; 2 Maccabees 8:26–29). Yet in 2 Esdras, Baruch, and Sirach "the Sabbath" is not mentioned at all. Thus, the late date of a book's compilation does not guarantee that it will concern itself with the Sabbath or even include the Sabbath. That seems to depend on something in the ethos of the book itself; the same holds true for the Hebrew Bible.

Let us now explore the slightly different understanding and presentation of the Sabbath that occurs in the apocryphal works. In some texts the day seems to have a rather different value, in that it is no longer a day set aside for rest, but is a day with some quality of holiness that it possesses intrinsically. This quality causes Sabbath to affect other things and to be able to attract further reverence from the community. This can be seen in the book of Judith, where the Sabbath is a day when the pious widow in the midst of her mourning rites is free of the obligation of fasting (8:6). In the more impassioned writing of 1 Maccabees, there are three references to the Sabbath in chap. 1, describing the profanation of the Temple on the Sabbath, the first reference being a quotation of Amos 8:10. In chap. 2 and chap. 9 the Sabbath is mentioned six times in the discussion of whether Jews should fight on the Sabbath or not. It appears also in 10:34 in the list of holy days which attract to themselves extra days of immunity. In a similar heightened mode of writing, 2 Maccabees contains several references to the Sabbath, each indicating the extreme reverence with which the day of rest was regarded.

1 Esdras 5:52 has a list of occasions on which sacrifices were made by the priests: "on sabbaths and at new moons and all solemn feasts." In *Jubilees* 2 there is a long section on the significance of the Sabbath as sign, day of rest, and day on which the people are to eat and drink and bless the

creator. There are also Sabbath laws which prescribe even the death penalty for working or defiling the Sabbath. Near the beginning of the book, Sabbath occurs in a list of days special to Yahweh: "new moons, Sabbaths, festivals, jubilees and ordinances" (1:14).

Of note in the books where the Sabbath is most honored is the fact that each one extends the Sabbath's thrall in a different way. Judith and Maccabees extend its numinous quality *through time* to adjacent days, via the extension of the time span over which one's behavior was conditioned. For Judith, the Sabbath day of freedom from fasting was extended to the previous day as well, and in 1 Maccabees the days of immunity from obligations were extended around each holy day (Sabbaths, new moons, and appointed days) by three days on either side. In *Jubilees* there is a *widening of the sphere of influence* of the Sabbath to the cosmic domain and further applications of the death penalty for breaking the Sabbath. The *Damascus Document* extended the *strictness* of the rules by which the clearly established hebdomadal Sabbath was observed. Later still, Philo made a somewhat illogical extension of Sabbath rest to plants (since they could only be involved in a passive sense or at the most complicitly!) by recommending that his readers spare *even the plant kingdom* from involvement with work on the Sabbath by refraining from plucking fruit from the resting trees (*Life of Moses* 2.21–22). With regard to the new moon, Philo indicates that the new moon was still a very important holy day for Jews, although it had a rather ambiguous status. He makes a clear and pejorative contrast between the celebration of the day of the new moon by "some states," and the "sacred seventh day" of the Jewish nation (*Decalogue* 96).[18] Yet elsewhere in his works he devotes a large section of apologetic material (around four hundred words) to arguing the propriety of celebrating the day of the new moon on the grounds that "it is the beginning of the month, and the beginning, both in number and in time, deserves honour"; and "when it arrives, nothing in heaven is left without light"; and "the moon traverses the zodiac in a shorter fixed period than any other heavenly body" (*Special Laws* 2.140–44). However strange Philo's justifications might seem to us, they make it plain that at this time new moon still had some importance—although secondary to that of the Sabbath.

In spite of all the later elaboration of the status of the Sabbath, these texts with one exception are concerned only with Sabbath rest, not worship. Only the Qumran Songs of the Sabbath Sacrifice and the Psalms scroll from cave 11 point to a Sabbath on which communal worship took place.

Clearly there was no longstanding stability in the views held about the Sabbath, whether as a powerful day of rest or as a day of worship. But its influence was growing and extending. This perception prompts us to look back in time to an era when the Sabbath did not hold this enormous sway in the religious life of Israel, during which the new moon celebrations played a larger role in celebration and worship. Whether the new moon had priority over the Sabbath at any time or place in Israel's history cannot easily be uncovered — nor can it be totally ruled out.

SYNAGOGUES AND SYNAGOGUE WORSHIP

If the Sabbath was not the dominant holy day in Old Testament times, or even a day of communal worship, when did it begin to acquire those aspects which are in continuity with the Sabbath of today? Since organized Sabbath worship would require a location and the developed form of worship that has continued until today took place in buildings called synagogues, it would seem likely that some of the answers might be found by research into the earliest synagogues.

In a compelling article Lester Grabbe reviews the evidence for the existence of synagogues in Israel during the Second Temple period (515 B.C.E.–70 C.E.).[19] He is quite convinced about the reality of synagogues in the Diaspora from the second century B.C.E., but he finds the archaeological evidence for synagogues in Palestine to be slender before the first century of the common era, a time for which the corroborative literary evidence of the New Testament also is pertinent.[20] Literary and archaeological evidence have to be considered separately, and the information they supply cannot be conflated willy-nilly. This is especially important because the same word, *synagōgē*, can be used to mean the assembly of people or the building in which they met.

Philo of Alexandria would seem a likely source of literary evidence for synagogues and Sabbath worship, but a search through Philo's writings for details of Sabbath *worship* in synagogues turns out to be less than rewarding. He often refers to the *proseuchē*, the prayer house or meeting-house at which the Jews met weekly to read and study their laws (*Embassy to Gaius* 132-37, 156-57; *Flaccus* 41-50), and also uses another word for what appears to be the same institution, *proseuktērion*, place of prayer (which he describes in terms similar to the philosophical schools of the Greeks, both in function and outlook). However, he does not use the term "synagogue" in any descriptions of usual Jewish Sabbath activities. In spite of calling the locations "prayer houses," he does not describe any prayer taking place. That the Sabbath day meeting places were not primarily concerned with worship as we know it is corroborated by Philo's statement that "each seventh day there stand wide open in every city thousands of schools of good sense . . . in which the scholars sit . . . with full attention" (*Life of Moses* 2.216; *Special Laws* 2.59-64). To help his readers form a clearer picture of what happened at these assemblies, Philo says that those present sat "together in a respectful and orderly manner" and heard "the laws read so that none should be ignorant of them." They sat in silence except for adding something to signify approval of what was read. A priest or elder who was present read and expounded the holy laws to them (*Hypothetica* 7, 9–13). The Sabbath had become a day of study and contemplation as well as a day of rest, but not, apparently, a day of worship.

There is a more detailed description of religious activities on the Sabbath constituting what we would recognize as worship in Philo's description of the Sabbath of the Therapeutae. According to him, they not only read the holy Scriptures but also "composed psalms and hymns to God" and on the seventh day assembled together sitting quietly in the proper attitude, the right hand between the breast and chin and the left hand along the flank, and listened to a discourse. The sanctuary in which they met had a double enclosure, with the women separate but within earshot (*Contemplative Life* 27–33). This is rather like the popular image of the synagogue of "the Jews" at the beginning of the Christian era, but here Philo attributes it solely to the Therapeutae.

Resembling Philo's description of the Sabbath of the Therapeutae is the picture he draws of the Essenes, who went on the Sabbath to sacred spots which, he says, *they called synagogues* (*Every Good Man Is Free* 81–83). There they listened to books read aloud and discourses. Evidently, the word "synagogue" is not his word; rather, he describes their institution by the name they give it. It looks, therefore, as if the term "synagogue" and the activities carried out in the synagogue derived from these more religious-minded groups of Jews (Therapeutae and Essenes) in Alexandria, who widened and elaborated the activities of the prayer houses.

Further evidence of the flexibility with which the names for religious meetings and religious meeting places were applied is provided by the use of yet another term for the meetings of the Jews. Philo writes of Jews in Egypt assembling in *synagōgia* (gatherings), which were schools of temperance and justice. This agrees with his description of Jews congregating in Alexandria and also opening their doors to outsiders, but in the same section he describes these Jews as having the unusual posture of the right hand tucked inside (the cloak) and the left hand held close to the flank, which he elsewhere attributed to the Therapeutae (*On Dreams* 123–28).

We may conclude that the name for the gatherings of Jews on the Sabbath and the name for the building in which they gathered were not applied unequivocally when Philo was writing. Similarly, the practices on the Sabbath day were still varied (*Embassy to Gaius* 311–12). Thus there were three different names for their gatherings, and these names may or may not have referred to the buildings as well. There were also different descriptions of what happened at the gatherings on the Sabbath.

In the New Testament, the word "synagogue" does not occur in the Pauline corpus. Since Paul was a contemporary of Philo, this absence is worth noting, especially because the word occurs in the Gospels and Acts sixty-five times. In these later texts the word means a building in which Jews met together on the Sabbath to read Scripture and listen to teaching on it. Other activities also took place in these synagogues: teaching, preaching, reading, almsgiving, praying, scourging, sitting, beating, disputing, speaking, and imprisoning. The building was not used purely as a quiet house of worship!

This picture of the synagogue is shared toward the end of the first century C.E. by Flavius Josephus, the final source for investigation of Sabbath worship. Josephus describes an incident in the synagogue at Caesarea. The Jews were taunted by the local people who deliberately slaughtered birds at the entrance to the synagogue on the Sabbath, once they had discovered the Jews would be offended (*Jewish War* 2.284-93). He also describes a synagogue in Antioch as having enough prestige to receive from Antiochus the returned plundered votive brass vessels from the Jerusalem Temple (*Jewish War* 7.39-50). Elsewhere Josephus says that on the Sabbath Jews abstained from work and gathered to listen to the law and learn it thoroughly (*Jewish Antiquities* 16.40-46). He also refers to the prayer house (*proseuchē*) at Tiberias as a large meeting place—in terms and context similar to the descriptions of prayer houses in Philo (*Against Apion* 173-77, 277-87; *Life* 272-82). Thus there are signs that, in contrast to the situation in Philo (and possibly Paul), toward the end of the first century C.E. the word "synagogue" had acquired a more definite meaning in the Gospels and in the works of Josephus. Both the building and the institution represent the forerunner of the modern synagogue.

One piece of architectural evidence demands our consideration, and that is the Theodotus inscription, which is often referred to as proof for the existence of a synagogue in Jerusalem in the first century C.E.[21] At the same time this is taken to be proof of weekly worship services close to the Temple. The inscription commemorates a man who ruled the synagogue and also his grandfather, who had built the synagogue and acted as its ruler before him. It describes a building in which the reading of the law took place and the teaching of the commandments. It is also mentioned that the synagogue had a hospitality suite, with water fittings, for the use of travelers. This description is in accord with the picture in the works of Josephus, Philo, and the New Testament, where a synagogue is a place where teaching and expounding took place, but with the addition of the idea of a hostel as well. However, in common with the other sources studied, there is no mention of any practices—apart from reading and preaching—that are normally included in the term worship.

One New Testament text does refer to prayer in the synagogue: in Matthew 6:5 the hypocrites are described as praying in the synagogues and on the street corners so that they may be seen. ("And when you pray, you must not be like the hypocrites; for they love to stand and pray in the synagogues and at the street corners, that they may be seen by men.") This does not make clear that prayer was a commonplace action in synagogues and may even point to the reverse conclusion, that is, that praying did not normally take place in the synagogue. What is noticeable about the hypocrites in this saying? Could it be that their *standing* as they pray is what is remarkable? In Mark 11:25 there is a saying of Jesus referring to "whenever you stand praying," so it must be something other than their stance that draws the eye. The three other New Testament references to praying in a religious building describe the location as the Temple (Luke 1:10; 18:10; Acts 22:12). Perhaps praying in a synagogue was just as ostentatious and odd as praying on a street corner, and not at all the normal practice of the true worshiper. Thus, the name "synagogue" and the forms of worship with which we are familiar were not exclusively attached to the assemblies of the Jews until after 70 c.e. and at the time of the writing of the Gospels.

THE SABBATH AS A DAY OF WORSHIP

If we limit our discussion to the common era, we can be very clear about the Sabbath as a day of rest, meeting, listening, expounding Scriptures, and reading or singing psalms, for mainstream Judaism and for Christianity. Before that time, there is a much more equivocal picture, and the clearest evidence in favor of the traditional understanding of the Sabbath comes from the community at Qumran or from the Essenes and Therapeutae as Philo describes them. The development of synagogues as buildings and of synagogue worship seems to have been accelerated at the time of the emergence of the early Christian groups, possibly influenced by their custom. Perhaps the existence of rival factions sharpened distinctions and hardened patterns and praxis. Certainly the intensity of the descriptions of synagogue controversies in the Gospels would suggest that they were a great focus of attention in the community at that time.

In trying to chart the development of Sabbath worship we must bear in mind that descriptions of prayer in the synagogue are reserved to the Gospels and Acts, and descriptions of singing hymns to God belong only to the Sabbath of Philo's Therapeutae and the Qumran community. It is necessary to conclude that our knowledge of exactly when and where, and under whose auspices, the gathering on the Sabbath took on the role of worship as distinct from study remains opaque.

NOTES

1. See the overview in Gerhard F. Hasel and W. G. C. Murdoch, "The Sabbath in the Prophetic and Historical Literature of the Old Testament," in *The Sabbath in Scripture and History,* ed. Kenneth A. Strand (Washington, DC: Review and Herald, 1982) 44–56.

2. Harold H. P. Dressler, "The Sabbath in the Old Testament," in *From Sabbath to Lord's Day: A Biblical, Historical, and Theological Investigation,* ed. D. A. Carson (Grand Rapids: Zondervan, 1982) 21–42, esp. 23.

3. Menahem Haran, *Temples and Temple Service in Ancient Israel* (Oxford: Clarendon, 1978) 224, 291, 292, 348.

4. A. S. Herbert, *Worship in Ancient Israel* (Ecumenical Studies in Worship 5; London: Lutterworth, 1959) 45–46.

5. Hans-Joachim Kraus, *Worship in Israel* (Oxford: Blackwell, 1966) 76–88, esp. 79, 80, 86.

6. Similar conclusions are noted by Hasel and Murdoch ("Sabbath in the Prophetic and Historical Literature"); see also Sakae Kubo, "The Sabbath in the Intertestamental Period," in *The Sabbath in Scripture and History,* 57.

7. Kraus, *Worship in Israel,* 79.

8. Ibid., 85.

9. J. A. Sanders, *The Psalms Scroll of Cave 11* (Discoveries in the Judaean Desert of Jordan 4; Oxford: Clarendon, 1972) 9, 91–93.

10. Geza Vermes, *The Dead Sea Scrolls in English* (Harmondsworth, Middlesex: Penguin, 1962) 202, 208, 210; Maurice Baillet, *Qumrân Grotte 4, III (4Q482–4Q520)* (Discoveries in the Judaean Desert 7; Oxford: Oxford University Press, 1982) 137, 150–51.

11. J. Strugnell, "The Angelic Liturgy at Qumran—4QSerek Šîrôt 'Ôlat Haššabāt," in *Congress Volume, Oxford, 1959* (Supplements to Vetus Testamentum 7; Leiden: Brill, 1960) 318–45 (320); also Carol Newsom, *Songs of the Sabbath Sacrifice: A Critical Edition* (Harvard Semitic Studies 27; Atlanta: Scholars Press, 1985) 211.

12. Exodus, Leviticus, Numbers, Deuteronomy, 2 Kings, 1 Chronicles, 2 Chronicles, Nehemiah, Psalm 92 (title), Isaiah, Jeremiah, Lamentations, Ezekiel, Hosea, Amos. The reference in 1 Esdras 1:58 is a quotation of 2 Chronicles 36:21. Sabbath is not mentioned at all in seventeen books of the Hebrew Bible: Genesis, Joshua, Ruth, Ezra, Esther, Job, Proverbs, Ecclesiastes, Song of Solomon, Daniel, Joel, Obadiah, Jonah, Habakkuk, Haggai, Zechariah, Malachi (also Baruch, Sirach, Tobit, 2 Esdras).

13. *Numbers 28–29*

daily	2 lambs
Sabbath	2 lambs as well as the daily offering
new moon	2 bulls, 1 ram, 7 lambs, and 1 goat
Passover	exactly as new moon and do no work
Firstfruits	exactly as Passover
1st day of 7th month	as above but blow trumpets and kill only 1 bull
10th day	as 1st day and also afflicting oneself
15th day	do no work, keep a feast for seven days and make an offering

(? Booths)	13 bulls, 2 rams, 14 lambs, and 1 goat
2nd day of 7	12 bulls, 2 rams, 14 lambs, and 1 goat
and so on	decreasing by 1 bull till the 7th day, then
8th day	1 bull, 1 ram, 7 lambs, and 1 goat

14. *Ezekiel 45–46*

for Atonement	the prince has to make offerings on the feasts, the new moons, the Sabbaths, and all appointed feasts
1st day of 1st month	1 bull
Passover	1 bull, then 7 bulls, 7 rams, and 1 goat for 7 days
15th day of 7th month	the same as Passover
Sabbath	6 lambs and 1 ram
new moon	1 bull, 6 lambs, and 1 ram
appointed feasts	general instructions
daily	1 lamb

15. *Leviticus 23*

appointed feasts	general heading
Sabbath	no mention of sacrifice
appointed feasts	general heading
Passover	unspecified offering by fire for 7 days
Firstfruits	offer 1 lamb
Weeks	offer 7 lambs, 1 bull, 2 rams, 1 goat, 2 lambs
day of solemn rest (1st day of 7th month)	blow trumpets, do no work, make an offering by fire
Day of Atonement	unspecified offering by fire
Booths	unspecified offerings by fire

16. Joseph M. Baumgarten, "The Counting of the Sabbath," *Vetus Testamentum* 16 (1966) 277–286 (277).

17. Kraus, *Worship in Israel,* 87.

18. Quotations from Philo are taken from *Philo,* ed. F. H. Colson and G. L. Whitaker (Loeb Classical Library; London: Heinemann, 1937).

19. L. Grabbe, "Synagogues in Pre-70 Palestine: A Re-Assessment," *Journal of Theological Studies* 39 (1988) 401–10.

20. Joseph Gutman ("Synagogue Origins: Theories and Facts," in *Ancient Synagogues: The State of Research* [Chico, CA: Scholars Press, 1981] 1–6) and Marilyn Chiat ("First-Century Synagogue Architecture: Methodological Problems," in *Ancient Synagogues,* 49–60) reach similar conclusions.

21. Marilyn Chiat, *Handbook of Synagogue Architecture* (Brown Judaic Studies 29: Chico, CA: Scholars Press, 1982) 202. The Theodotus inscription reads: "Theodotus, son of Quettenos (Vettenos), priest and archisynagogus, son of an archisynagogus, grandson of an archisynagogus, built this synagogue for the reading of the Law and for the teaching of the Commandments, and the hostel and the chambers and water fittings for the accommodation of those who [coming] from abroad have need of it, of which [synagogue] the foundations were laid by his fathers and by the Elders and Simonides."

II

RABBINIC AND
NEW TESTAMENT
PERSPECTIVES

3

THE PLACE OF THE SABBATH
IN RABBINIC JUDAISM

Robert Goldenberg
State University of New York at Stony Brook

N o understanding of Jewish religious life is complete unless it includes
an account of the joy and peace of the seventh day. Jews over history
have celebrated the Sabbath in quite varied ways, but this celebration in
all its variety offers the key to the meaning of Jewish life. The Sabbath is
the punctuation of Jewish existence, marking Jewish life off into intervals
of seven days; it determines the rhythm of Jewish life more decisively than
any of the annual festivals and more pervasively than any of the once-in-a-
lifetime rites of passage by which the life span of a Jew can be divided. This
paper cannot provide a thorough examination of all features of this great
Jewish institution, but it will offer some insight into the role of the Sabbath
in shaping Jewish life.

We begin with two stories, the first from the Bible and the second from
the Babylonian Talmud. The biblical story, from the book of Numbers,
reads as follows:

> The Children of Israel were in the desert when they found a man gathering
> wood on the Sabbath day. Those who had found him gathering wood brought
> him up to Moses and Aaron and the whole congregation, and they put him
> under guard, for it had not been clearly stated what should be done to him.
>   The Lord said to Moses, "The man must be put to death; let the entire con-
> gregation stone him outside the camp." The entire congregation took him out-
> side the camp and stoned him so he died, as the Lord had commanded Moses.
> (Numbers 15:32–36)

The phrase *mĕqōšēš 'eṣîm* is unclear; modern translators give "gathering
wood" or "gathering sticks." Whatever its precise nuance, however, the
implications of this story for the present purpose are quite unambiguous.
A man was found doing something on the Sabbath that was considered

31

improper; on inquiry it was determined that his infraction had been a capital crime, so he was put to death. It seems that the people whose lives are reflected in this narrative took the Sabbath very seriously and that they understood the Sabbath to be a day on which certain activities were strictly forbidden.

The story from Numbers can now serve as background for a tale from the Babylonian Talmud, tractate *Shabbat:*

> Caesar [i.e., the Roman emperor] said to R. Joshua b. Hananiah, "Why is this Sabbath food so fragrant?" He said, "We have a certain spice named Shabbat that we put into it and it renders the dish fragrant." He said, "Give us some of it." He said to him, "The spice is effective for anyone who keeps the Sabbath, but will not work for anyone who does not keep the Sabbath." (*Shabbat* 119a)

This is a very different picture of what the Sabbath meant. Here the seventh day is a day of such pleasantness and joy that even the emperor of Rome envies the Jews for possessing such a treasure. It should be kept in mind that on the Sabbath observant Jews will not cook, that even keeping already cooked food hot on the Sabbath can be accomplished only under very restricted conditions. All cooked food eaten on the Sabbath is thus in some sense leftover food, and to say of such food that even Caesar wished he could have some is to make a remarkable claim. Whether any Roman would really have expressed such a wish is neither here nor there; the point of this story is that the Jews who told and retold it believed that he would have. They believed that the food prepared for their Sabbath table was by virtue of that very circumstance fit for a king.

The spice that so provokes the emperor's desire is itself called "Shabbat," that is, Sabbath. This little pun reflects the point just made that food prepared for the Sabbath — food containing Sabbath flavor, so to speak — is always very tasty, and it allows as well for another translation of the rabbi's final response. This translation ignores the point of the remark in context but greatly expands its general significance, for it can now be imagined that the rabbi's real point was this: Not only a certain spice but the Sabbath altogether only works for those who keep it; those who do not keep the Sabbath will never enjoy, will never even comprehend, its benefit. Understood in this way, the rabbi's quip reveals the heart of the Jewish Sabbath, a secret place, so to speak, where strict regulation of behavior and the rigorous enforcement of taboo were combined with a kind of serenity and gratification of body and spirit that would have been the envy of the world if only the world had discovered it. The modern observer too will not understand the Sabbath at all until it has been seen as the union of two themes: the Sabbath as a day of avoidance of labor and the Sabbath as a day of heavenly rest.

The example of grim legalism was drawn from Scripture and the example of playful spirituality from the Talmud largely to poke fun at the usual stereotypes associated with these two texts. In fact, although the Talmud dates from a period when Jews no longer enjoyed the power to execute Sabbath-breakers, it is quite full of extremely complex rules and regulations. On the other hand, the very idea that the Sabbath should be made a day of joy is derived from Scripture (see Isaiah 58:13). The whole point is that joy and abstention from labor together make the Sabbath what it is. This is the point the Roman monarch had such trouble understanding.

Others throughout history have had similar difficulty. Nehemiah had to station soldiers at the gates of Jerusalem to keep the people from widespread violation of the Sabbath (Nehemiah 13:15–22), whereas five hundred years later the Christian apostle Paul, or someone writing in his name, apparently agreed with Nehemiah's contemporaries and condemned Sabbath observance as a kind of superstitious slavery (Romans 14:5–6; Galatians 4:10; Colossians 2:16). The rabbinic rules and traditions concerning the Sabbath must be understood as attempting to achieve a state of joyful rest. It is sometimes hard to understand them that way, but the challenge to the modern inquirer who approaches these texts from outside their own cultural framework is to keep this reality in mind.

The biblical texts, while reminding their readers over and over again that the Sabbath was very important, never say much at all about what it was like. From the meager details Scripture supplies one would never have anticipated that the Mishnah and Talmud would devote two entire tractates, one among the largest and one among the most complex, to detailed regulation of Sabbath rest.[1] Indeed, while the sages who compiled the Mishnah probably did not mean for it to serve as a functioning code of Jewish law, there is no denying that the Mishnah's treatment of the Sabbath consists largely of a very great accumulation of legal details. Where Jeremiah was content to plead that his hearers (or readers) abstain from carrying burdens on the Sabbath day (17:21–27), the Mishnah devotes three chapters in tractate *Shabbat* to the task of defining how much of any conceivable substance constitutes a burden in terms of this law. Whereas Exodus simply rules that every man must remain in his place on the Sabbath (16:29), tractate *'Eruvin,* the other of the two Mishnaic Sabbath tractates, devotes several chapters to defining the limits of a person's "Sabbath resting-place" and detailing procedures available to those who wish to expand those limits or shift that place from its natural location.

To be sure, the Mishnah does offer a generalized list of forbidden activities, which is the closest thing it has to a definition of forbidden labor. Even this list, however, appears to contain only random details; it is not even found where one would expect it, at the beginning of tractate

Shabbat. The location of this list in the middle of things (7:2) seems only to compound the general confusion. This list reads as follows:

> The main categories of labor are forty less one: sowing, plowing, reaping, binding sheaves, threshing, winnowing, sorting,[2] grinding, sifting, kneading, baking; shearing wool, washing it, beating it, dyeing it, spinning, weaving, making two loops, weaving two threads, separating in order to sew two stitches; trapping a deer, slaughtering it, skinning it, salting it, curing its hide, scraping it, cutting it up, writing two letters, erasing in order to write two letters; building, tearing down, putting out a fire, kindling a fire, striking with a hammer, taking anything from one domain into another. These are the main categories of labor, forty less one.

At first glance, this seems to be a random assortment of activities, all of them no doubt forbidden on the Sabbath but otherwise connected by no common feature. The list is also noteworthy for its omissions, for there is no mention here of some of the activities that Jews avoided most carefully of all: there is no mention here of commercial activity, of buying or selling or lending or paying off debts, and there is no mention here of the avoidance of judicial proceedings on the Sabbath, even though Josephus repeatedly informs us that Jews cared so much about such avoidance that it had to be confirmed by numerous Roman authorities in the face of Greek harassment (see esp. *Jewish Antiquities* 14.10; also 16.6). What then does this list really mean?

The Talmud itself assumes that the list details the activities that were needed to build the portable desert sanctuary that is described toward the end of the book of Exodus. It bases this assumption on the fact that one of the Sabbath prohibitions in the Torah (Exodus 35:1–3) is inserted into the midst of the section describing the building of that sanctuary. This idea, however, is not convincing. The linkage is artificial; some of the inclusions and some of the omissions are surprising; and there is too much uncertainty in the Talmud itself about how the sanctuary was actually built, on the one hand, and what items this list should in fact contain, on the other.[3]

The nature of this list therefore cries out for further exploration. On more careful examination, it turns out to contain an early rabbinic enumeration of the fundamental activities of civilized life. The first portion of the sequence has to do with the preparation of food, using bread as the food *par excellence.* This part of the list starts with sowing, ends with baking, and identifies nine intermediate activities that are needed for the production of bread. The catalogue proceeds to the preparation of clothing, starting in the same way with the shearing of wool and ending with "tearing in order to sew two stitches." Food and clothing are followed by the preparation of parchment for writing (not meat as might at first appear the case). The enumeration concludes with the preparation of shelter, a category that includes the use of fire and the division of the world into units of property. Food, clothing, writing, and shelter—these are the indispensable foundations of civilized life as the early rabbis understood them. These are also, it turns out, the materials that one must prepare before the Sabbath sets in, so that the sacred day itself can be devoted to the higher activities which these preparations make possible.

Food, clothing, and shelter are universal necessities of life, as every schoolchild learns, but this list is distinctive for the other category it includes, writing. The only writing the authors of this list could possibly have considered a necessity of life is the writing of the Torah. If the writing of the Torah must be done before the Sabbath, however, then the Sabbath must be a day for the study of the Torah thus prepared; the jumble of rabbinic law thus conceals a vision of the Sabbath that is not so distant from that of the first-century philosopher Philo:

> [Moses] forbade bodily labor on the Sabbath, but permitted the nobler labors, those that concern the principles and teachings of virtue. . . . Moses does not allow any of those who use his sacred instruction to remain inactive at any time, but since we consist of body and soul he assigned to the body its proper tasks and to the soul what falls to it, so that each might be waiting to relieve the other. (*Special Laws* 2.61, 64)

To associate the Mishnah with Philo is not to suggest that all Jews in late antiquity devoted their Sabbath rest to arcane philosophical inquiry, nor should it be thought that the Mishnah itself is a philosophical treatise in disguise. This linkage does however reinforce the previous suggestion that the key to understanding the rabbinic Sabbath is to see how abstention from labor has somehow been connected with striving for a certain mental state or discipline. Another story from the Talmud carries this conception still further:

> A certain pious man once went into his vineyard on the Sabbath and saw there a break in its wall. He decided to repair it when the Sabbath was over, but afterward he said, "Since I decided on the Sabbath that I would repair it, I shall never do so at all." What did the Holy One, blessed be He, do for that man? He prepared a caper-bush which grew into the opening, and the man supported himself off that bush for the rest of his life. (Jerusalem Talmud, *Shabbat* 15:3, 15a–b)

It is clear that the "pious man" of whom this story is told never considered actually performing the indicated repair on the Sabbath; this is not a story designed to dissuade people from doing actual labor on the Sabbath. The question in the mind of the "pious man," and therefore the only question this story seeks to discuss, was whether even thinking about a forbidden activity is itself somehow blameworthy. The story thus suggests that actual

Sabbath breaking was not a serious issue in the rabbinic narrators' community and instead reflects an effort to turn the Sabbath into an escape from everyday reality, into what A. J. Heschel in our own century termed a "palace in time."[4] This little tale seeks to convey the message that conscious refusal to pay attention to ordinary concerns on the Sabbath should not be confused with impractical neglect; on the contrary, those who act thus "impractically" on the Sabbath can expect a lavish and quite material reward from heaven.[5]

The rabbinic Sabbath was thus an attempt to blend elevated religious consciousness with the strict, detailed regulation of behavior. The rabbis' assumption was that each of these modes of self-discipline enhances the other, that the two together form the framework for a life of piety, even saintliness. The Pauline idea that detailed behavioral rules are somehow a block to true religious fulfillment ("the burden of the law") could not have differed more dramatically from this point of view.

* * *

The preceding general remarks provide a framework for the following comments about specific aspects of rabbinic Sabbath observance. This discussion will concentrate on certain customs and rituals that over the centuries have been preserved in many Jewish homes. This focus is designed to combat the natural tendency for Americans to think that it is in the nature of a holy day that people will celebrate it primarily in a house of public worship and that its most important features can be discovered by examining what the worshipers do once they are assembled. Furthermore, the rabbinic synagogue liturgy for the Sabbath is not in the end so very different from that for weekdays. There are some differences to be sure: the prayers are recited a little more slowly and some are rather longer; in keeping with the studied "impracticality" of the Sabbath, the most materially petitionary sections of the liturgy are dropped; and, of course, the public reading of the Torah assumes a far greater role in the Sabbath morning service than it does on weekdays. However, the structure of the synagogue services for weekdays and for the Sabbath and many portions of the actual liturgical texts are very similar indeed.

On the other hand, the onset of the Sabbath dramatically changes the atmosphere in a traditional Jewish home. This has something to do with the need to carry out so much preparation in advance and the deep, quite sudden relaxation that follows when the preparations are done (it has already been mentioned, for example, that all food has to be cooked before the Sabbath has begun). It also reflects the fact that already in ancient times certain foods and certain activities had special meaning and special character on the Sabbath, so that Sabbath meals were different from others, Sabbath lighting different from weekday lighting, and so forth. Among mystics of later centuries even sexual intercourse on Sabbath nights acquired a special character, which received varied and quite graphic symbolic expression.[6]

No later than the first century, the physical materials of the customary Sabbath meal began to acquire some of the holiness of the day. The following enigmatic description by the first-century Roman satirist Persius offers an image of Jewish Sabbath observance that conveys contempt, dread, and fascination all at the same time:

> But when the day of Herod is come, and the lamps, put in greasy windows along with violets, emit their oily clouds of smoke; and when the tail of a tuna fish floats curled round in a red dish, and the white jar is bulging with wine, you move your lips in silence and turn pale at the circumcised Sabbath. (*Satire* 5.179-84)

Many of the aspects of Sabbath observance familiar from later times through our own are already here, though quite strangely described: the burning lights, the wine, the fish, the whispered prayers. With due allowance for the hostility of the Roman writer and for his unfamiliarity with the activities being described, it is not so hard to imagine that the Roman Sabbath of which he writes was very like the Sabbath of the Mishnah, the Talmud, and the Middle Ages that followed them in turn.

In current practice, the Sabbath begins shortly before sunset with the kindling of special Sabbath candles; this act is preceded by a benediction that praises God as the one "who has sanctified us with your commandments and instructed us to light the Sabbath lamp." The kindling of the Sabbath lamps apparently began as a utilitarian act; the Torah as already noted forbids the making of fire once the Sabbath has begun (Exodus 35:3).[7] Therefore, if people wanted light or heat on Sabbath nights they had to make sure a fire was burning before the sun went down and the holy day began. By reciting a liturgical formula, however, this simple practical act was turned into a ritual—in fact, one of the most emotionally resonant in the entire tradition.[8]

At an earlier time, when gender roles in Jewish life were more sharply distinguished, the Sabbath lights were usually kindled by the woman of the house after the men had gone off to the synagogue for the evening prayers; this assignment seems at least as old as the time of the Mishnah (*Shabbat* 2:6; see also 2:7). Even now, in fact, and even in homes where no one goes to the synagogue on Friday evening, it remains the case that this particular ritual is considered the task or as some prefer to say the privilege of the mother of the home.[9]

The first Sabbath meal then begins when those who have gone to the synagogue return home. This meal begins with a special recitation called *Kiddush* that is pronounced over a cup of wine. The term *kiddush* means "sanctification"; it is a slightly different form of the word used in Genesis 2:3 to describe the Creator's original sanctification of the seventh day. Here, of course, the word denotes not a divine act transforming the day but a human act acknowledging this divine transformation. The association of wine with this act of proclamation is a mystery; in fact, the ritual drinking of wine in Jewish life is altogether a perplexing matter. It has no roots in the Bible. The Bible knows that renouncing wine might be a sign of special devotion to holiness. The Torah instructs that every sacrifice in the sanctuary be accompanied by a libation of wine onto the altar. Scripture is also aware that wine can make you feel good (an attractive but a dangerous feature at the same time), but nowhere in Scripture do people drink wine as a ritual act.[10] On the other hand, when one examines post-biblical Judaism one discovers the drinking of wine everywhere: at weddings, at circumcisions, at the onset and the conclusion of every sacred day, in connection with the Grace after meals at any especially solemn or formal occasion. Judging from the New Testament stories of the Last Supper, this use of wine was already taken for granted by the time of Jesus, and rabbinic materials confirm this impression for just a little later on. The passage from Persius, dating from about the same period, gives the same report for contemporary Rome. No one really knows how this happened. Erwin Goodenough thought that the custom must have been learned by ancient Jews from the pagan customs that surrounded them, and no more convincing proposal has come to this writer's attention.[11]

The *Kiddush* prayer, in the standard Ashkenazi version, begins with Genesis 2:1-3, a passage that describes the original institution of the Sabbath as the climax of creation. It then goes on as follows:

> You are blessed, O Lord our God, King of the universe, who creates the fruit of the vine.
> You are blessed, O Lord our God, King of the universe, who has sanctified us by your commandments, taken delight in us, and in love and favor has allowed us to inherit the Sabbath as a remembrance of the deed of Creation. For it is the first day of holy convocations, a reminder of the Departure from Egypt. For you have chosen us and sanctified us from among all the nations, and have allowed us to inherit your holy Sabbath in love and in favor. You are blessed, O Lord, who sanctifies the Sabbath.

This brief prayer summarizes the importance of the Sabbath in later Jewish thought. The link with creation is here, along with the link to the Exodus and its reminder that a free people should stop every now and then for rest and spiritual refreshment. The importance of the Sabbath as a marker of Jewish identity is also acknowledged, though here it is theologized as a token of divine love, and not simply noted for its social or cultural significance.

The special Sabbath part of this text is preceded by a shorter blessing that refers only to the wine. According to rabbinic law this blessing is to be recited whenever wine is drunk and is therefore not strictly a Sabbath prayer at all. The Mishnah reports that rabbinic authorities of the first century disagreed on whether the special Sabbath portion of the text should be recited first, since after all this part identifies the occasion for reciting the prayer altogether, or last, as the culmination of the whole (*Berakhot* 8:1; *Pesaḥim* 10:2).

In the course of time, this dispute expanded into one of the perennial themes of rabbinic discussion of the Sabbath: To what extent should the Sabbath be like all days only lovelier, and to what extent should it be made distinct, as different from other days as possible? It has been noted that certain portions of the synagogue service for the Sabbath are quite indistinguishable from their weekday counterparts, but others are entirely unique, especially the central portion of the '*Amidah* prayer (in rabbinic parlance "the" prayer *par excellence*) and the practice of reading through the entire Pentateuch over the course of the year. The same blend of similarity and difference that was noted in the *Kiddush* prayer at the beginning of the meal can be found at its end, in the Grace. With the exception of a single interpolated paragraph, this fairly lengthy prayer is virtually unchanged on the Sabbath, but in traditional homes it is then sung out loud, with leisurely tunes, rather than simply recited in an undertone, as would be the case during the week.[12]

This uncertainty over the uniqueness of the Sabbath is nicely captured in a story concerning two early masters:

> It was taught concerning Shammai the Elder that all his days he would eat in honor of the Sabbath. Having found a handsome animal he would say, "Let this be for the Sabbath." Having then found one more handsome, he would put aside the second [for the Sabbath] and eat the first [right away].
>
> Hillel the Elder had a different rule . . . as it is said, "Blessed be the Lord each day" (Psalm 68:20).
>
> The House of Shammai say, "From the first [day] of the week [direct your efforts] toward the Sabbath," but the House of Hillel say, "Blessed by the Lord each day." (Babylonian Talmud *Beṣah* 16a)

This looks like a story about trust in divine providence and seems related to remarks attributed to Jesus about not worrying about what one will eat tomorrow (Matthew 6:25–33; Luke 12:22–31), but this story has more to do with the question of the Sabbath. Shammai, along with the school bearing his name, is described as believing that the entire week exists for the sake of the Sabbath—one gets ready for the Sabbath; one makes sure one will be able to celebrate the Sabbath as one ought; and only after this is accomplished does one enjoy the rest of the week with any resources that are left. Shammai's Hillelite opponents will not allow one's relationship with the Creator to be focused so narrowly on just one day a week. The Sabbath has its own rules and its own special character, but these are embedded in a larger system that holds the Sabbath and the other days side by side.

In the home, the chief Sabbath ritual has always been the meal. Even the number of Sabbath meals marked off the day as special: in a culture where most people ate two meals a day, custom and eventually religious law required that on the Sabbath one eat three (Mishnah *Shabbat* 16:2; Babylonian Talmud *Shabbat* 118–119). These meals provided a fixed structure for the Sabbath, and synagogue services, like everything else, had to accommodate themselves to the schedule they created. As early as the time of Josephus it was considered a firm religious custom to begin one's midday meal on the Sabbath no later than noon (Josephus *Life* 54 § 279). These meals had to be fancier and more leisurely than workday meals, and at least since the Middle Ages it has been the custom to prolong them by the singing of table songs devoted to various themes of the Sabbath celebration.[13]

The third of these meals, usually held just as the Sabbath is about to end, eventually developed a special character of its own. This, after all, was an emotionally difficult time; even the world seems mournful at the twilight hour when the so-called third meal takes place, and the Jew's brief escape from an often oppressive economic, social, and political reality was about to end. The holy day was about to give way once again to ordinary reality, but this unhappy consideration was offset by another. By tradition, the Messiah will not arrive on a Sabbath or a Sabbath Eve (Babylonian Talmud *'Eruvin* 43b); on those days, after all, the Jews will be too busy or too restricted to be able to receive him as he ought to be received. The end of the Sabbath, therefore, even though by itself it was a sad time, came to bring with it a kind of consolation: now it was once again possible to hope that the Messiah might be on the way. Under the influence of kabbalistic messianism, the "third meal" came to be a time of serene, meditative song, a time for quiet communal waiting for redemption. The *Havdalah* ("division") ceremony that formally ends the Sabbath came to be associated with the prophet Elijah, who since pre-Christian times has been considered the Messiah's herald. Perhaps in connection with these themes, we already find in the Talmud a prediction that the Messiah would in fact not arrive until all Israel had fully and properly observed two Sabbaths in a row (Babylonian Talmud *Shabbat* 118b). Perhaps as well this is why one early rabbi is reported to have said that observance of the Sabbath is like a foretaste of the pleasures of the world to come (Babylonian Talmud *Berakhot* 57b).

The biblical sources on which later conceptions of the Sabbath were built contributed two main ideas to those conceptions: on the one hand, the idea that the Sabbath ought to be marked by avoidance of the ordinary activities of life,[14] and, on the other, the idea that such restrictions ought to be joyous (see, e.g., Isaiah 58:13). The various possible combinations of these two ideas, which could easily have been considered contradictory (and have been so considered from time to time), have formed the matrix of Jewish Sabbath observance throughout history. From the ancient world there are Sabbath laws found in the book of *Jubilees,* the *Damascus Document* associated with the Dead Sea Scrolls,[15] and the two Mishnaic tractates *Shabbat* and *'Eruvin* together with their talmudic elaborations. From the Middle Ages we have the enormous halakhic literature of the rabbinic tradition along with a parallel literature produced by the Karaites. Modern Jewish thought has given huge amounts of attention to the problem of maintaining this unstable combination under vastly altered circumstances.

It seems fair to say that the rabbinic tradition by and large gave more weight in this mixture to the element of joy and less to the element of restriction than did most of the other types of Jewish religion just listed. This is only a relative statement, to be sure, but still it is important to remember that, while other traditions demanded that people eat unheated food on the Sabbath in unlit rooms, the rabbinic tradition developed admittedly complex legal fictions that turned observance of the Sabbath into a much more comfortable, even enjoyable, experience. The complexity of these arrangements eventually came to be considered a fault, but to discuss that subject it is necessary to consider the question of Jewish Sabbath observance in the contemporary world.

Modern Jewish life has been characterized by a wholesale repudiation by many Jews of their previous loyalty to the religious law of the Torah. There are many reasons why this has taken place, and despite the apparently negative term, simple description is intended here, with no value judgment implied. Even as many Jews have rejected the authority of the religious law, however, they have remained eager to preserve some link to their ancestral culture. The Sabbath was an important part of that culture, and so the place of the Sabbath in Jewish life has somehow been preserved, even as Jewish life as a whole has undergone revolutionary change over the last two hundred years.

Examples of this phenomenon can be found everywhere. The State of Israel is dominated by a thoroughly secularized conception of Jewish life, yet on the seventh day of the week newspapers do not publish, mail goes undelivered, schools and offices stay closed, and buses in most places do not run. Here in America (and in Europe previously) the leaders of Reform Judaism got their followers to accept all sorts of radical changes in the prayer book, and they instituted alterations in synagogue ritual that made it almost unrecognizable to those familiar with more traditional services. They managed, nevertheless, to retain the allegiance of their laity.

However, when the effort was made to shift the main service of the week (in most Reform Temples the only service of the week) to Sunday morning, the effort failed: that somehow felt wrong. Today there are fewer than a dozen synagogues in all of North America where the Sunday service is the main religious event of the Jewish week.

Many important factors have contributed to this result. Economic pressure on Jewish wage earners to go to work on Saturday has been declining for decades, and American society has in general been moving toward the five-day workweek. Therefore, the percentage of American Jews who would like to attend a synagogue but feel compelled to go to work on Saturday morning continues to decrease. Moreover, even Jews who must or choose to work on Saturday are usually free on Friday evening to attend services; fewer and fewer Jews work such long hours or come home so tired that they cannot get out of the house after dinner for a fairly brief visit to the synagogue. Cultural or economic need for a Sunday service, in other words, has virtually disappeared. By shifting the main service of the week from Saturday morning to Friday night, liberal movements in American Judaism have been able to achieve the same gains that the Sunday service aimed for, but without going the extra step that so many people found unacceptable. The Sabbath remains as it has been, the central axis of Jewish religious life.

To be sure, the people who attend these Friday evening services are by no means Sabbath observers in the traditional sense of the term. On Saturday afternoon these people go shopping or sailing or driving into the country, and even on Friday night many of them have their pre-synagogue dinner or post-synagogue dessert in a nearby restaurant. The point is simply that the shape of the Jewish week has been imprinted on their consciousness and will not go away.

That imprinting has become a little smudged, of course. Under the pressure of modern life the combination of joy through restriction that was for so long the distinctive feature of Jewish Sabbath observance has become harder to keep balanced than it used to be. Many Jews claim that the restrictions have grown to the point that they interfere with the joy. Some, though fewer, respond that joy without the restrictions is a false joy, a kind of forgery that entirely misses the true heavenly satisfaction that even the emperor of Rome knew enough to envy. This increasingly sharp dispute explains the battles in Israel over the question of movies on Friday night, along with all the other similar issues receiving widespread if sometimes uncomprehending coverage in the American press.

Still, people throughout the Jewish world who feel no obligation to observe the old rules of Sabbath observance have nevertheless found ways to make that day the "Jewish" day of the week. Secularists and Yiddishists have opened schools that meet on Saturdays to transmit to the young their distinctive conceptions of Jewish life, and even synagogues run Saturday afternoon cultural programs for those who have no interest in attending the morning worship services. A new cultural institution, the *Oneg Shabbat,* has come into being, a gathering on Friday evening or Saturday afternoon where people come together primarily to enjoy relaxed fellowship and some sort of cultural enrichment. Modern Jewish life thus continues to confirm the observation of the great essayist Ahad Ha'am that the Sabbath has preserved the Jews over the centuries even more than the Jews have preserved the Sabbath.[16] For many Jews all over the world, the Sabbath remains the Jewish day of the week, the day for Jewish books, Jewish prayers, Jewish food, Jewish songs, Jewish peoplehood. As was the case many centuries ago, so it remains today: the regular celebration of the seventh day is one of the hallmarks of Jewish life. Through the lens of the Sabbath we can glimpse the Jewish vision of eternity.

NOTES

1. This is why a famous passage in Mishnah *Ḥagigah* 1:8 describes the rules of Sabbath rest as "mountains hanging by a hair."

2. That is, grain from chaff.

3. See Yitzhak D. Gilat, "The Thirty-Nine Classes of Work Forbidden on the Sabbath," *Tarbiz* 29 (1960) 222–28 (Hebrew).

4. See A. J. Heschel, *The Sabbath: Its Meaning for Modern Man* (New York: Farrar, Straus and Giroux, 1951) 12–24.

5. For a modern treatment (chiefly for children) of this same theme, see S. Y. Agnon, "A Story about a Coin," in A. E. Millgram, *Sabbath: The Day of Delight* (Philadelphia: Jewish Publication Society of America, 1959) 128–30.

6. See the new study by Elliot K. Ginsburg, *The Sabbath in the Classical Kabbalah* (Albany: State University of New York Press, 1989).

7. Recall as well the Mishnaic list of forbidden activities that was quoted previously.

8. See B. M. Levin, "On the History of the Sabbath Lamp," in *Essays and Studies in Memory of Linda R. Miller* (New York: Jewish Theological Seminary of America, 1938) Hebrew section, 55–68. According to Levin, the reasons for this transformation have to do with the great struggle between the rabbis of the early Middle Ages and their opponents the Karaites, but the excerpt from Persius already quoted suggests that some sort of special Sabbath lamp was known long before the rise of Karaism.

9. This paper has not considered the question whether women and men have over the centuries experienced the Sabbath in a fundamentally different way. Although women throughout Jewish history have no doubt derived great enjoyment from Sabbath rest, it should be noted as well that in many cases the burden of cleaning and cooking has fallen largely onto their shoulders.

10. Renunciation as a mark of holiness (Numbers 6:24); libation onto the altar

(Numbers 15:5, 7, 10); wine as source of joy (Judges 9:13; Psalm 104:14; but see also Proverbs 21:17; 32:4-5, and many other such warnings). "Nowhere in Scripture," needless to say, means nowhere in the Jewish Scriptures.

11. See Erwin Goodenough, *Jewish Symbols in the Greco-Roman Period* (New York: Pantheon, 1956) 6:219-20. This brief passage summarizes a discussion that has gone on for two hundred pages.

12. For sample liturgical texts, see Philip Birnbaum, *Daily Prayer Book* (New York: Hebrew Publishing Company, 1949) 71-97 (the core of the weekday morning service), 335-59 (Sabbath), 191-211 and 257-73 (evening services), and 760-69 (Grace after Meals).

13. For samples of these hymns, see Birnbaum, *Daily Prayer Book,* 291-97, 425-35.

14. Scripture calls these "labor," but until very recently no one thought that strenuous effort was really at the heart of the concept. In recent times, a powerful incentive to adopt this understanding has been the desire to justify setting the restrictions aside with the claim that everything nowadays is easier to do.

15. See the discussion by Lawrence Schiffman, *The Halakhah at Qumran* (Leiden: Brill, 1975) 77-133.

16. Ahad Ha'am, *Collected Works* (reprint, Tel Aviv: Dvir, 1965) 286 (Hebrew).

4

SABBATH TENSIONS: MATTHEW 12:1–14 AND OTHER NEW TESTAMENT TEXTS

Daniel J. Harrington, S.J.
Weston School of Theology

"Remember the Sabbath day, to keep it holy" (Exodus 20:8; see Deuteronomy 5:12). I liked the Sabbath commandment the very first time I heard it, and I have liked it ever since. Having a day off in the name of religious obligation has always struck me as having the best of both worlds. Of course it was explained to me by my Catholic teachers that for us the Sabbath was Sunday and on Sundays we Catholics were obliged to go to Mass. But after that we were on our own, provided we avoided "servile" work. Forty years ago Sunday differed much more from other days than it does now. We dressed up to go to Church as a family, had a big Sunday dinner together, and frequently went for a ride in the car.

Forty years later I still like the Sabbath commandment in its Catholic application. I sleep a little later, take a long time reading the Sunday paper, go for a very long walk that is usually my special time for prayer and meditation, visit relatives, watch a game on television, preach and preside at a Sunday liturgy in a local parish, eat dinner with my community, and go to bed a little early. Nothing but prayer and relaxation. I love Sunday, and it does wonders for me.

Yet as I observe this day of prayer and relaxation I am aware that even in Catholic Boston and socially conservative New England, my Sunday behavior becomes more peculiar every year. Not that my routine has changed. But the world around me has changed. Many Catholics now go to Mass on Saturday evening. Few younger Catholics "dress up" for church, at least not in such a way that I can recognize it. The Sunday family dinner has disappeared in most cases. The stores that had been firmly locked on Sundays in Massachusetts for over three hundred years by the "blue laws" of the Puritans are now open for business by noontime. Sunday is a good time to shop and watch football games. Prayer seems to be optional and seldom thought of.

As a theologian I have also learned an important distinction: Sunday is not really the same as the Sabbath. Even though our Puritan forefathers and their Catholic Jansenist cousins made that equation and surrounded Sunday with rules pertaining to the Jewish Sabbath, I now regard their theological instincts in this matter to be incorrect. Sunday is not the Sabbath.[1]

"Sabbath Tensions" is the title of my presentation. As I continue to enjoy Sunday as my day of prayer and relaxation, I recognize the tensions inherent in my practice. On the one hand, there is the quick and rather dramatic secularization of Sunday. On the other hand, there is the theological recognition that Sunday is not the Sabbath.

"Sabbath tensions" are not new. I would like to move from the present back to New Testament times and explore some of the tensions that early Christians experienced with regard to the Sabbath. I have chosen to focus on Matthew's Gospel, especially the two Sabbath episodes in Matthew 12:1–14. Matthew seems to have composed his Gospel in the late first century in an area in which Jewish influence was strong. Matthew and most of his community were Jewish Christians. They found themselves in the middle of a Jewish debate about what one may or may not do on the Sabbath.

The aim of this paper is to expose some of the tensions that Matthew and other early Christians experienced with regard to the Sabbath. First I will lead you through a close reading of two Sabbath texts in Matthew – the story of Jesus' disciples eating grain on the Sabbath (12:1–8) and Jesus' healing a man with a withered hand on the Sabbath (12:9–14). Then I will reflect on some tensions that emerge out of these texts: the need that Matthew felt to rewrite Mark 2:23–3:6, the tensions surrounding the biblical passages about the Sabbath, and the differing attitudes toward the Sabbath displayed by Matthew, other Jews, and other early Christians.

A CLOSE READING OF MATTHEW 12:1–14

It seems likely that Matthew and his predominantly Jewish-Christian community observed the Sabbath. As they tried to position themselves in the Jewish debate about what one may or may not do on the Sabbath, they searched for criteria among their traditions about Jesus. Their fundamental conviction was that the Son of Man whom they identified as Jesus is lord of the Sabbath. And so they appealed to his example. Their fundamental criterion for Sabbath observance was expressed in the maxim: "Therefore it is allowed to do good on the Sabbath" (Matthew 12:12).

With the two Sabbath controversies — plucking grain (12:1-8) and healing (12:9-14), Matthew rejoins the series of controversies found in Mark 2:1-3:6. In Matthew 9:1-17 Matthew had given his versions of the first three Markan controversies (Mark 2:1-22). After a long interruption (Matthew 9:18-11:30) he returns to give his versions of the final two Markan controversies (Mark 2:23-3:6). By placing the two Sabbath controversies after Jesus' declaration regarding his own identity and the nature of his teaching ("My yoke is easy, and my burden is light" [Matthew 11:30]), Matthew presents the incidents as examples of Jesus' authority as a teacher and his approach to the Pharisees' traditions.

The first episode (Matthew 12:1-8) concerns the disciples' picking grain on the Sabbath and eating it. The debate concerns whether they were allowed to do this on the Sabbath or whether it constitutes the equivalent of reaping — something forbidden as work on the Sabbath day. That the disciples were permitted to pick the grain in someone else's field is not disputed (see Deuteronomy 23:25). The issue is their doing it on the Sabbath.

> 1. In that time Jesus went on the Sabbath through the grain fields. His disciples were hungry, and they began to pick the heads of wheat and to eat. 2. But the Pharisees saw this and said to him: "Behold your disciples are doing what is not allowed to do on the Sabbath." 3. He said to them: "Have you not read what David did when he and those with him were hungry? 4. How he went into the house of God, and they ate the bread of the presence, which it was not lawful for him to eat nor for those with him, except for the priests alone. 5. Or have you not read in the Law that on the Sabbath the priests in the temple profane that Sabbath and are without guilt? 6. But I say to you that there is greater than the temple here. 7. If you had known what this is — 'I wish mercy and not sacrifice' — you would not have condemned those who are without guilt. 8. For the Son of Man is lord of the Sabbath."

In that time: The temporal indicator, not present in Mark 2:23 or Luke 6:1, may look back to Matthew 11:25 ("In that time") and thus link this passage with the preceding. If this is so, the two Sabbath pericopes in Matthew 12:1-8, 9-14 may be put forward by Matthew as examples of the "light burden" imposed by Jesus (see 11:30). *his disciples were hungry:* Only Matthew supplies a motive for the disciples' behavior (see Mark 2:23; Luke 6:1), though he does not go so far as to suggest that there was any danger of death. *to pick the heads of wheat and to eat:* The disciples' action follows Deuteronomy 23:25: "When you go into your neighbor's standing grain, you may pluck the ears with your hand, but you shall not put a sickle to your neighbor's standing grain." Such humanitarian legislation (see

Deuteronomy 23:24) was intended to sustain the needy without giving them permission to pile up supplies. There is, however, no mention of the Sabbath in these cases. *what is not allowed to do on the Sabbath:* The Pharisees' complaint against Jesus' disciples interprets their action as infringing on Exodus 34:21 ("on the seventh day you shall rest"). In Mishnah *Shabbat* 7:2 there is a list of thirty-nine labors that are prohibited on the Sabbath. The labor that best corresponds to what the disciples did is "reaping" (*haqqoser*). Matthew has turned the Pharisees' question in Mark 2:24 into a direct statement. *what David did:* The incident of David and his men eating the bread of the presence from the sanctuary at Nob is narrated in 1 Samuel 21:1-6. There is no mention of the Sabbath in that text. The point in common between 1 Samuel 21:1-6 and Matthew 12:3-4 is satisfying the hunger of the followers of David/Son of David. Matthew has excised the name of the high priest Abiathar (Mark 2:26), since the priest's name according to 1 Samuel 21:1-6 was Ahimelech. *the house of God:* The expression could suggest that it was the Jerusalem Temple. Of course, the Temple had not yet been built. The "house of God" is the shrine of the ark of the covenant then at Nob, in the territory of Benjamin. Nob developed as a cultic center in the late eleventh century B.C.E., after the destruction of Shiloh. *the bread of the presence:* The ritual surrounding the bread of the presence (or "shewbread") is described in Leviticus 24:5-9. Twelve cakes were set out in the sanctuary. They were finally consumed by the priests ("Aaron and his sons"). Other references to the bread of the presence appear in Exodus 25:30; 39:36; 40:23. Not being from the sons of Aaron, David had no right to consume these breads. *the priests in the temple profane the Sabbath:* There are rules in the Torah itself that allow priests to do work in the Temple on the Sabbath: setting out the bread of the presence (Leviticus 24:8), and doubling the daily burnt offering (Numbers 28:9-10). By finding precedents within the Torah Matthew places the activity of Jesus' disciples on the Sabbath within the confines of Jewish law. *there is greater than the temple here:* The reasoning is from "light" to "heavy" (*qal wāhômer*)—from the case of the priests in the Temple to the case of Jesus' disciples. This is an extraordinary claim about the community surrounding Jesus! The "greater" is a matter of dispute: Is it Jesus, or the kingdom of God inaugurated by Jesus, or the community around Jesus? All three aspects are probably present, the idea of Jesus' community being most prominent. *"I wish mercy and not sacrifice:"* The quotation from Hosea 6:6 was used previously in Matthew 9:13. Given the Temple context set up in Matthew 12:5-6, the reference to "sacrifice" is appropriate here but leads into a wider framework of ritual behavior, including strict Sabbath observance. The "mercy" is demanded from humans, as in showing compassion toward those in need on the Sabbath day. *the Son of Man:* Though it is possible that at some point in the saying's tradition history (see Mark 2:28; Luke 6:5) "Son of Man" may have been a generic term for humankind, in Matthew 12:8 it was surely meant by Matthew as a title for Jesus. The radical saying of Mark 2:27 ("The Sabbath was made for man, and not man for the Sabbath") is omitted by both Matthew and Luke. Matthew 12 continues:

9. And he went from there and came into their synagogue. 10. And behold there was a man having a withered hand. And they asked him, saying: "Is it allowed to heal on the Sabbath?.," in order to bring charges against him. 11. But he said to them: "Which one of you who has one sheep and if it falls into a pit on the Sabbath will not take hold of it and raise it up? 12. How much more is a human being superior to a sheep! Therefore it is allowed to do good on the Sabbath." 13. Then he said to the man: "Stretch out your hand." And he stretched it out, and it was restored as healthy as the other. 14. And the Pharisees went out and took counsel against him in order to destroy him.

Their synagogue: Mark 3:1 and Luke 6:6 simply have "the synagogue." Matthew's expression probably reflects his own time, where there was a division between "their synagogue" and "our synagogue" (Christian). By this expression the evangelist set up a continuity between Jesus and the Matthean community, on the one hand, and Jesus' opponents and the opponents of the Matthean community, on the other hand. *withered hand:* The Greek term is *xēros* ("dry" as in Xerox). The man's hand was stunted in growth and paralyzed. We are to assume that this was a long-term condition (perhaps even from birth) and not a life-threatening illness that demanded immediate action on the Sabbath. *Is it allowed to heal on the Sabbath?:* All the evangelists note that the opponents' question was a trap set for Jesus ("in order to bring charges against him"), but only Matthew gives the question. The rabbinic approach to this question appears in Mishnah *Yoma* 8:6: "A case of risk of loss of life supersedes the Sabbath (law)." Since the withered hand was presumably a long-term, non-life-threatening condition, the rabbinic principle is not followed by Jesus. *it falls into a pit on the Sabbath:* The case is taken up in *Damascus Document* 11:13–14: "if (a beast) falls into a cistern or into a pit, let it not be lifted out on the Sabbath." An opinion more in line with that of Jesus is found in the rabbinic writings (Babylonian Talmud *Shabbat* 128b; *Baba Meṣiʿa* 32b). Jesus assumes that his questioners agree with him on this matter and do not hold the stricter view of the Essenes. Only Matthew includes this case (see Mark 3:3; Luke 6:8). *how much more:* The argument again takes the *qal wāḥômer* structure: If so with a sheep, by how much more with a human being! The case is then turned into the rationale for Jesus' doing good on the Sabbath in healing the man with the withered hand (and for the Matthean community's own attitude toward Sabbath observance). The general principle is that it is permitted to do good on the Sabbath. This principle assumes that the Sabbath is still observed by the Matthean Christians but that Sabbath regulations can be overridden by the need to "do good" (there may be an allusion to the love commandment of Matthew 22:40). *it was restored:* The healing of the withered hand comes almost as an afterthought, since Matthew has placed the debate about Sabbath observance at the center of attention. Only Matthew has the vivid phrase "as healthy as the other (hand)." *the Pharisees:* Only at the end of the pericope are we told that Jesus' opponents were Pharisees (see 12:2). They control "their synagogue" (12:9). Unlike Mark 3:6, there is no mention of the "Herodians" plotting with the Pharisees. Jesus' free attitude toward the Pharisees' Sabbath traditions provokes opposition and leads to a plot against Jesus' life.

SABBATH TENSIONS

In broad outline, Matthew 12:1–8 follows Mark 2:23–28. The disciples' action sets the scene for the Pharisees' objection and Jesus' appeal to the precedent set by David in 1 Samuel 21:1–6 and his concluding claim about the Son of Man as lord of the Sabbath. But there are loose ends in the Markan account—the chief one being the fact that 1 Samuel 21:1–6 makes no mention of the Sabbath.

Matthew has tightened up Mark's account by explaining the reason for the disciples' action (they were hungry [12:1]), turning the Pharisees' statement into a direct assertion rather than a question ("your disciples are doing what is not allowed"), deleting the erroneous mention of the high priest Abiathar (see Mark 2:26; Matthew 12:4), and adding the example about kinds of work allowed in the Temple on the Sabbath (Matthew 12:5–7). It is possible also that Matthew has deleted the radical saying about the Sabbath being made for man and not man for the Sabbath (Mark 2:27), though its omission in Luke 6:5 makes one wonder if that radical saying appeared in the version of Mark used by the other two evangelists. If it was so present, its omission by Matthew would have been part of his more conservative attitude toward the Sabbath and Jewish institutions in general.

In the episode of Jesus healing the man with the withered hand on the Sabbath (Matthew 12:9–14), Matthew has pushed what in Mark 3:1–6 is part debate and part healing story even further in the direction of a debate. The Matthean debate takes place in "their synagogue" (12:9). The opponents put the question directly: "Is it allowed to heal on the Sabbath?" Jesus uses a case that was debated in his time—the case of an animal that falls into a pit on the Sabbath—and argues according to the *qal wāḥômer* pattern ("from the light to the heavy") that it is allowed to heal on the

Sabbath (12:11-12). Finally he notes that the Pharisees (without the Herodians; see Mark 3:6) plotted to destroy Jesus. Thus Matthew has preserved the basic structure of the healing story (Matthew 12:10a, 13) but shifted the focus even more than in Mark 3:1-6 to the debate about healing on the Sabbath. He has not only sharpened the issue under debate and supplied an argument (Matthew 12:10b-12) but also narrowed Jesus' opponents down to the Pharisees (12:14) and connected them with those who frequent "their synagogue" (12:9).

Was the Sabbath made for man or man for the Sabbath? Even though Matthew has omitted (or perhaps did not know) the radical saying in Mark 2:27 in which Jesus asserts that the Sabbath was made for man, there remain tensions regarding the Sabbath. In fact, those tensions reach back to the earliest biblical texts about the Sabbath.[2] In Exodus 23:12 the command to rest on the seventh day is placed in a "humanitarian" context: "that your ox and your ass may rest, and the son of your bondmaid, and the alien, may be refreshed." In Exodus 34:21 the same commandment ("on the seventh day you shall rest") appears in the context of various cultic obligations suggesting that man was made for the Sabbath, that is, that the Sabbath observance was part of Israel's worship of God.

The Sabbath commandments in the Decalogue (Exodus 20:8-11; Deuteronomy 5:12-15) agree that the seventh day is a Sabbath to the Lord for the entire household. But they disagree regarding the theological root of the Sabbath. Whereas according to Exodus 20:11 the Sabbath is a remembrance of creation ("for in six days the Lord made heaven and earth, the sea and all that is in them and rested on the seventh day"), in Deuteronomy 5:15 it is a remembrance of the Exodus from Egypt ("you were a servant in the land of Egypt, and the Lord your God brought you out thence with a mighty hand and an outstretched arm"). The "creation" motif for Sabbath observance, of course, underlies the Priestly creation story in Genesis 1:1-2:4a, in which the Sabbath is said to be woven into the very fabric of creation.

Although references to Jewish observance of the Sabbath can be found in almost every phase of Israel's history, there seems to be no doubt that Sabbath observance became especially prominent before, during, and after the exile in Babylon. Deprived of its Temple, capital city, and homeland, the Jewish exiles emphasized the Sabbath as a very important religious obligation (see Isaiah 56:2; 58:13-14; Jeremiah 17:21-27; Ezekiel 20:11-21). Observance of the Sabbath was not dependent on the existence of the Temple. While not a rival to the Temple cult, Sabbath observance was at least something of a substitute for the Temple cult when the Jerusalem Temple lay in ruins or was not accessible to Jews. The Sabbath along with circumcision and dietary regulations made Jews different from the peoples around them and helped to nourish Jewish identity.

The biblical texts about the Sabbath are surrounded by tensions: Is the Sabbath made for human beings, or is it for the worship of God? Is the Sabbath a remembrance of creation or of the Exodus? Is the Sabbath part of or a rival to worship in the Jerusalem Temple? Despite these tensions it is clear that by New Testament times the Sabbath was such an essential part of Jewish life and piety that the chief concern was trying to determine what constituted "work" on the day of rest. A major innovation by Mattathias (the father of the Maccabees) and his friends around 167 B.C.E. made it possible for Jews to undertake defensive warfare on the Sabbath day: "Let us fight against every man who comes to attack us on the Sabbath day" (1 Maccabees 2:41). On the other hand, the Essenes represented by *Damascus Document* 10:14–11:18 laid down very strict rules for observing the Sabbath—far stricter than those later codified by the rabbis. A similar strictness is present in *Jubilees* 50. The Mishnaic tractates—*Shabbat* and *'Eruvin*—reflect an even later, more refined stage in the debate. But the basic question is the same: What may and may not be done on the Sabbath?

Matthew knew well the shape of the Sabbath debate in his own time. He seems also to have known that Jesus had taken a somewhat free attitude regarding what may and may not be done on the Sabbath. The other Gospels agree that Jesus healed on the Sabbath, as in the case of the woman "who had a spirit of infirmity for eighteen years" (Luke 13:10–17) and the paralytic at the Bethesda pool (John 5:1–18). These were long-term illnesses, and both healings presumably could have been deferred until after the Sabbath. The incident recounted in Mark 2:23–28/Matthew 12:1–8 suggests that Jesus did not stop his disciples from doing what some Jews regarded as reaping on the Sabbath.

As a follower of Jesus, Matthew was obliged to defend this rather free attitude toward Sabbath observance. It is important to remember that this topic was very much under debate in the first century and that the clarity arrived at in the Mishnah still belonged to the future.[3] Besides defending Jesus' attitude Matthew had also to address the concerns of his largely Jewish-Christian community that by and large observed the Jewish Sabbath. The ways in which Matthew reshaped his Markan sources show how he managed to enter into the larger Jewish debate of his day, remain faithful to the example of Jesus, and minister to his own community.

Matthew entered into the larger Jewish debate by sharpening the debating partners. They are Pharisees (according to Matthew 12:2, 14) who are prominent in "their synagogue" (12:9). Thus Matthew has drawn a direct line between the opponents of Jesus and the rivals of his own community some fifty or sixty years later. He has also strengthened greatly the weak argument found in Mark 2:25–26 about David and his men eating the bread of the presence. That precedent was irrelevant to the Sabbath, and

Matthew knew it. So he added the consideration about the "work" done by priests in the Temple on the Sabbath (Matthew 12:5).

In the second incident (12:9–14) Matthew has Jesus cite a case that was debated among Jews of Jesus' and his own day. The Essenes had a strict view on this matter: "If (a beast) fall into a cistern or into a pit, let it not be lifted out on the Sabbath" (*Damascus Document* 11:13–14). The way in which Jesus speaks in Matthew 12:11 seems to presume that the Pharisees and he agreed over against the Essenes that it is allowed to raise an animal out of a pit on the Sabbath.

Matthew appears also to remain faithful to Jesus' own attitude toward the Sabbath. In his own day Jesus seems to have been more liberal on this matter than even the relatively liberal and flexible Pharisees were. And so Matthew presents Jesus as allowing his disciples to feed themselves on the Sabbath and as healing someone in no danger of death on the Sabbath. But Matthew also breaks out of the Jewish debate by giving the two stories a christological dimension.

Jesus is the authoritative teacher; his teaching and example are to be followed. Jesus is the healer; he has authority over the Sabbath regulations. The saying that links the two episodes together is the assertion "The Son of Man is lord of the Sabbath" (Matthew 12:8). With his presence something "greater than the temple is here" (12:6). So when Matthew's Jewish rivals criticize the Matthean community's laxness regarding the Sabbath, the response is rooted in the example of Jesus, who for the Matthean Christians is the authoritative teacher.

Matthew also sought to minister to his own largely Jewish-Christian community on the matter of Sabbath observance. It would appear that the Matthean community continued to observe the Sabbath.[4] At least there is no indication to the contrary, and Sabbath observance would have been quite natural for a largely Jewish-Christian group. The question for the Matthean community—and the pastoral problem that Matthew had to address—was the manner in which the Sabbath was to be observed. The principles derived from the two episodes in Matthew 12:1–14 are compassion toward others ("I wish mercy and not sacrifice" [12:7]) and doing good ("it is allowed to do good on the Sabbath" [12:12]). The second principle ("it is allowed to do good on the Sabbath") served as the basis for the Matthean community's behavior on the Sabbath. That principle may well have carried an allusion to the summary of the Torah as loving God and neighbor (Matthew 22:34–40). At any rate, the criterion placed before the Matthean community as it struggled to deal with the complicated discernment of what one may or may not do on the Sabbath is doing good.

With regard to the Sabbath the Johannine community found itself in a similar position. In the late first century some of its Jewish-Christian members had been or were about to be expelled from the synagogue (see

John 9:22; 12:42; 16:2). Nevertheless, they looked upon their brand of Jewish Christianity as the most appropriate response to the destruction of the Jerusalem Temple in 70 C.E. The narrative in John's Gospel proceeds on two levels: the time of Jesus, and the time of the Johannine community. While taking the institution of the Sabbath as a "given," the evangelist focuses on the identity of Jesus as lord of the Sabbath, thus contributing to his basic christological purposes in writing the Gospel.

The first Sabbath incident in John's Gospel is the healing of a paralytic at the pool of Bethesda (John 5:1–47). The observation in 5:9 that the healing took place on the Sabbath brings about a three-sided controversy among the "Jews," the man, and Jesus. Here the quarrel of the "Jews" with Jesus concerns his loose attitude toward work on the Sabbath (5:16) — his own in healing a non-life-threatening illness, and the man's in carrying his mat from place to place. Jesus' basic response to his opponents is expressed in John 5:17: "My Father is at work until now, so I am at work." He takes for granted the Jewish belief that on the Sabbath God continues to preserve creation and carry on the work of redemption. As lord of the Sabbath (see Mark 2:28; Matthew 12:8; Luke 6:5) Jesus can and must do what God does. Therefore it is appropriate to call Jesus the Son of God and equal to the Father (5:18). Thus Jesus' free attitude toward work on the Sabbath serves as an argument for his divine sonship and equality with God.

The second Johannine controversy about the Sabbath (7:19–24) takes its start from the Sabbath healing of chap. 5: "I did one deed, and you all marvel at it." Jesus' defense takes the form of a scriptural argument. According to Genesis 17:12 and Leviticus 12:3 a male child was to be circumcised on the eighth day after his birth. If the boy was born on a Sabbath, he was to be circumcised on a Sabbath. Thus circumcision overrides the Sabbath rest. From this scriptural premise Jesus argues that, if what pertains to one part of the body can be done on the Sabbath, what pertains to the health of the whole person (as in 5:1–47) can surely be carried out. This reasoning is described as "judging with right judgment" (7:24).

The third Sabbath incident concerns the healing of the man born blind (9:1–41): "Now it was a Sabbath day, when Jesus made the clay and opened his eyes" (9:14). The reason for Jesus' healing on the Sabbath is given in 9:4: "We must work the works of him who sent me while it is day; night comes when no one can work." The present time is "day," and the "light" of the world must work while he is in the world. In the debate among the Pharisees (John 9:13–17) some claim that Jesus could not be from God because he leads people astray by not keeping the Sabbath (see Deuteronomy 13:1–5), whereas others argue that only a good person could perform such signs. Here as in chap. 5 (and practically everywhere else in John's Gospel) the major theme is the identity of Jesus. What is disputed is the manner, not the fact, of Jesus' Sabbath observance. The third Sabbath incident adds to the evangelist's picture of who Jesus really is.

The tensions that the Matthean community experienced regarding the Sabbath may not have come only from the members of "their synagogue." They may have also come from other Christians. There were objections from Paul in Galatians 4:10 and from the Pauline admirer who wrote Colossians (see 2:16) to Gentile Christians being forced to observe the Jewish calendar and its Sabbaths. Moreover, as the first century C.E. progressed, the Lord's Day—Sunday—became a more important and more distinctively Christian institution. The first day of the Jewish week, which began at sundown on Saturday after the Sabbath, was linked from the first Easter with the resurrection of Jesus (see Matthew 28:1 and parallels). The first day of the week was a special time for Christians to gather in order to take up collections for the Jerusalem community (1 Corinthians 16:2) and to break bread and hear an edifying sermon (Acts 20:7). In Revelation 1:10 it is called "the Lord's Day," the only occurrence of this expression in the New Testament.

The Apostolic Fathers add to our picture of "the Lord's Day" as a special time for Christian celebration. The *Didache,* which was probably composed in Syria in the late first century—the same place and time customarily assigned to the composition of Matthew, speaks of the Lord's Day as a time for Christians to gather and break bread and give thanks (14:1). Ignatius, bishop of Antioch in Syria in the early second century, urged that Christians put aside Sabbath observance and keep the Lord's Day instead: "No longer observing Sabbaths but fashioning their lives after the Lord's Day" (*Magnesians* 9:1).

There is no explicit evidence in Matthew's Gospel of a rivalry between proponents of the Sabbath and proponents of the Lord's Day. Matthew and his community may have seen no conflict at all and may have observed both the Sabbath and the Lord's Day. Nevertheless, there are hints within the New Testament of a growing interest in the Lord's Day among some Christians. Even more striking is the fact that both the *Didache* and Ignatius of Antioch, representing the same geographical area as Matthew but a little later, are among the strongest pieces of evidence for a firm Lord's Day tradition and a rivalry with the Sabbath.

What are Christians today to make out of Matthew's Sabbath teachings? After all, Matthew and his community celebrated the Sabbath, while most of us take the Lord's Day (Sunday) as our time of prayer and rest. Matthew 12:1–14 is fascinating on several counts. It shows how Jewish Christians struggled to integrate their new faith in Jesus with their Jewish traditional observances. It shows how Christian convictions about Jesus as lord of the Sabbath and the principle of doing good on the Sabbath shaped Matthew's presentation.

The framework of the Jewish debate about the Sabbath—what one may or may not do on the Sabbath—was narrow, what Christians are in the unfortunate habit of calling "legalistic." The narrowness of the debate in Matthew's time ought not to obscure the fact that Jews by and large enjoyed the Sabbath as a time of prayer and rest. While it is problematic to equate the Jewish Sabbath and the Christian Sunday and to surround Sunday with Sabbath regulations, at least the Christian day of prayer and rest should have reference to Jesus as lord of the Sabbath and whatever works are done on it should be measured by the criterion of doing good.

CONCLUSION

"Sabbath tensions"—a paradoxical title. After all, the point of the Sabbath is to rest and worship God, to put tensions aside. Nevertheless, all of us experience tensions with regard to the Sabbath today. The thrust of my paper has been to show that for early Christians like Matthew the Sabbath also carried with it tensions, though not exactly the same as our own. Matthew felt the need to clarify and bolster the position of Jesus as set forth by Mark. He also sought to enunciate a Jewish-Christian position regarding Sabbath observance while remaining faithful to Jesus' teaching and offering pastoral advice to his own community. "Sabbath tensions" have been with us for a long time—way back into ancient Israel's history. "Sabbath tensions" will probably be with us for a long time to come.

NOTES

1. W. Rordorf, *Sunday: The History of the Day of Rest and Worship in the Earliest Centuries of the Christian Church* (Philadelphia: Westminster, 1968); idem, *Sabbat und Sonntag in der Alten Kirche* (Zurich: Theologischer Verlag, 1972).

2. R. Bartelmus, "Mk 2,27 und die ältesten Fassungen des Arbeitsruhegebotes im AT: Biblisch-theologische Beobachtungen zur Sabbatfrage," *Biblische Notizen* 41 (1988) 41–64.

3. See Michael Hilton with Gordian Marshall, *The Gospels and Rabbinic Judaism* (Hoboken, NJ: Ktav, 1988) 95–118.

4. In the eschatological discourse Jesus says: "Pray that your flight may not be in winter or on a Sabbath" (24:20). Matthew's insertion of "on a Sabbath" presupposes that the Matthean community was still observing the Sabbath.

5

A RESPONSE TO R. GOLDENBERG
AND D. J. HARRINGTON, S.J.

Dennis MacDonald
The Iliff School of Theology

The origin of the seven-day week is no longer visible to us, but it surely was exceedingly ancient, much earlier than the Bible and by no means unique to Jews. What was unique to Judaism was the significance attached to the seventh day, which Jews articulated in at least three ways: (1) rest for human welfare, (2) holiness for honoring God, and (3) covenantal fidelity for distinguishing a social entity. In fact, it would appear that Jewish Sabbath reflection developed in this very order.

Our earliest witness to Sabbath observance appears in a source of the Pentateuch dating no earlier than the mid-tenth century (J). The text demands a seventh day of rest in order to mitigate exploiting the labor of resident aliens, slaves, and beasts of burden. There is nothing here of the seventh day of creation or of worship or of holiness.

Later, during the Babylonian exile, as Professor Harrington said, when the Temple lay in ruins, priestly families apparently put more investment into holy time than into the holy place, and the Sabbath was filled with intensified and perhaps even new cultic content. It is from such exilic circles that we have received the idea that the Creator rested on the seventh day and that violations of the Sabbath showed contempt for Israel's election and therefore could be punished with death.

Later yet, with the return of the exiles to Judah, the Sabbath formulations from Mesopotamia were forced on the Jewish residents of the region by Nehemiah and others, not just for cultic reasons, it would seem, but also to establish the distinctiveness of the Jews in the Diaspora. This third aspect of the Sabbath became progressively important as Jews found themselves increasingly surrounded by Persians, Greeks, and Romans, even in Palestine.

These three Sabbath concerns of human welfare, holy time, and sociological distinctiveness balance and yet compete in the interpretations of the
Sabbath throughout Jewish history. At the beginning of rabbinic Judaism,
when the Temple had again been demolished, holy time and Jewish self-
definition became exceedingly important, as is evident from the complicated halakic debates in the Mishnah and later in the Talmud.

In the light of this overview, I would ask the following of Dr. Goldenberg. Your paper emphasizes "the avoidance of labor and receiving of
joyful, heavenly rest," what I have called "human welfare," more than
matters of holiness and social distinctiveness. You treat the Sabbath as the
calendrical equivalent to the health spa. While I sincerely appreciate this
correction of the view that Jewish concerns for the Sabbath are merely the
casuistic nit-pickings of Bible-reading killjoys, it seems to me that your
approach is too rationalistic, too modern, too in step with yuppie, New
Age religion. My impressions from extended visits to Israel, which include
working in a kibbutz for a summer, were that Israelis welcomed Saturday
night with greater joy than they did Friday night. My first question is this:
In spite of what you have said (with which I agree for the most part), is
not the key to understanding the Sabbath really ethnic distinctiveness
based on a desire to be faithful to God's law or holiness? Is not the issue
less a matter of stress management than of taboo?

Second, is the Sabbath as observed in accordance with dominant
Judaism as joyful and restful for Jewish women as it is for men? The
kibbutz in which I worked was careful about the Sabbath; nevertheless,
some work needed to be done, work that is often assigned to women in
traditional societies, such as looking after chickens, setting table, presenting the meals (even more elaborate than usual), doing dishes, and chasing
after children. In your opinion, is there a disparity on the basis of gender
about which tasks were considered to be work? Christians too, of course,
are guilty of the same prejudices concerning work.

My other questions are for Professor Harrington and concern the role
of the Gospels of Matthew and John in the history of the Sabbath. His
paper states on the following: (1) Jesus was unusually liberal about Sabbath observance. (2) The controversy between Jesus, his followers, and
other Jews who observed stricter Sabbath codes became christological: that
is, it later became framed as a controversy concerning Jesus' authority.

In these respects Professor Harrington conforms to scholarly consensus,
but I suspect both he and the consensus might be wrong, or at least overly
confident. I too suppose that Jesus interpreted Torah more liberally than
most Jewish teachers, but I cannot convince myself that we know what
Jesus thought concerning the Sabbath, except that he presumably kept the
Sabbath in some manner. For example, if Paul knew of Jesus' putative
liberality on the Sabbath, why did he not mention it, when one might most

expect him to, in Galatians 4 where he objects to the observances of "days, and months, and seasons, and years"? Likewise, in Romans 14 he claims, much as the Sabbath controversy stories in the Gospels, that living with a clear conscience matters more than treating one day above the rest. The Synoptic Sayings Source, or Q, also puts no Sabbath legislation on the mouth of Jesus, even though it contains a long discourse against Pharisaic interpretations of the law. The *Gospel of Thomas,* a collection of Jesus' sayings, to some extent independent of the canonical Gospels, surprisingly has Jesus say, "Unless you keep the Sabbath as Sabbath you will not see the Father." Matthew and Luke do not mention Sabbath controversies in passages that form-critically can be attributed to Jesus or even in undeniable prewritten tradition, as I have tried to show in a recent article! As is often the case, Mark is our earliest—and, in this instance, our only—independent witness to the stories of the plucking of grain on the Sabbath and the healing of the man with the withered hand, the subject of Professor Harrington's paper. No critic I know—including, I am sure, Dr. Harrington—would ascribe the healing of the man with the withered hand to the earliest stratum of Jesus' memory. The plucking of grain story is a pronouncement story whose *raison d'être* and generative feature is the aphoristic ending: "The Sabbath was made for the human, not the human for the sabbath, so the Son of Man is lord even of the Sabbath." Only here or in documents clearly dependent on Mark does one find these radical statements. Only here in all of early Christian literature. In my view, this is the only plausible prewritten testimony to Jesus' attitude toward the Sabbath, and it could as easily be attributed to Jewish-Christian apocalyptists as to Jesus himself. In my view Jesus did not speak of himself or of another as Son of Man; rather, this was an early Christian title based on Daniel 7. Therefore, if one is to argue for Jesus' Sabbath liberalism, one must do so on the basis of absolutely no help from Paul, Q, or the *Gospel of Thomas,* or on prewritten traditions of Jesus' teachings, but solely on extrapolation from later Christian debates with Jews back into the lifetime of Jesus. This seems to me methodologically risky.

Furthermore, if the saying "The Son of Man is lord even of the Sabbath" is the earliest saying attributed to Jesus relevant to the Sabbath controversy, one cannot assume that Sabbath controversies later became christological controversies. One might better argue, as I would at this point—though without conviction—that it was controversy over the meaning of Jesus' career and death that spawned a reevaluation of Jewish law and Sabbath.

My first question to Dr. Harrington, therefore, has to do with Jesus' putative Sabbath liberalism and subsequent christologizing.

I have additional questions to Professor Harrington: I agree that the Matthean community seems to have observed the Sabbath, though I do so mostly on the basis of the Matthean addition in 24:20 "Pray that your flight may not be in winter or on a Sabbath." I also agree with your exceedingly clear presentation of the case that the issue for Matthew was lenient versus strict Sabbath observance and that Matthew's position, while more liberal than liberal Jewish interpretations, nudged the tradition toward conservatism. In this respect I am surprised you said nothing in favor of your argument about the passage that Matthew places immediately before his reuse of Mark's Sabbath disputes. Here is my overly tendentious rendition. "Come to me, all who labor and are heavy-laden, and I will give you rest. Take my yoke upon you and learn from me — not from the Pharisees — and you will find rest for your souls. For my yoke — unlike theirs — is easy and my burden light." Surely this reading would support your analysis.

My more important question is this: How important do you think the Sabbath controversy really was to Matthew? I tend to think it was rather minimal. The alterations of Mark are relatively minor here, and Matthew does not bring up Sabbath disputes elsewhere where one might most expect him to. For example, in the Sermon on the Mount, Jesus addresses himself to almsgiving, prayer, and fasting, but says nothing about the Sabbath. In chap. 23, the woes to the Pharisees that bristle with hostility, Jesus says, nothing about the Sabbath. Why?

Allow me to say something about Sabbath disputes after the New Testament. The first disputes about the Sabbath, such as we find in Mark, Matthew, Luke, John, and Paul, obtain to whether strict Sabbath observance really did serve human welfare or were instead oppressive. Thus the saying "The Sabbath was made for the human, not the human for the Sabbath." By the end of the first century, however, the issue was no longer human welfare but sociological distinctiveness. The issue no longer is the distinctiveness of Judaism but Christian distinctiveness from Judaism; for example, Ignatius: "no longer living for the Sabbath, but for the Lord's Day" (*Magnesians* 9:1).

Another reason for the devaluation of the Sabbath had to do with a new location for holiness, no longer primarily time, and certainly not a geographical place, but, in good Greek fashion, the soul. Christians of the second and third centuries, including Gnostic Christians, were consumed by bodily purity for the welfare of the soul's holiness. So, for example, the *Gospel of Truth,* produced by ascetically oriented Gnostics:

> Even on the Sabbath, he [Christ] labored for the sheep which he found fallen into the pit. He gave life to the sheep, having brought it up from the pit in order that you might know interiorly — you, the sons of interior knowledge — what is the Sabbath, on which it is not fitting for salvation to be idle, in order that you may speak from the day from above, which has no night, and from the light which does not sink because it is perfect. Say then from the heart that you are the perfect day. (32:18–33)[2]

This notion is not unique to Gnostics. Everywhere in early Christian literature, from Paul to Augustine one finds a preoccupation with bodily sanctity, but rather little about calendrical sanctity. This is why Christians like Augustine could not understand how Jewish Sabbaths could be holy when Jews drank so much wine, ate so much food, and "their women danced in their homes." It seems to me that weekly celebrations sound like more fun than such ascetic sanctity. Dr. Goldenberg is perhaps right, after all.

A friend of mine was babysitting for a Jewish family, and he and the seven-year-old began talking about religion. When the boy discovered that my friend was Protestant, he asked, "Don't you really want to be Jewish?" My friend asked why he should convert, and the boy answered, "Isn't it obvious? Jews have more holidays."

NOTES

1. D. MacDonald, "From Audita to Legenda: Oral and Written Miracle Stories," *Forum* 2 (1986) 15–26.

2. Harold W. Attridge and George W. MacRae in *The Nag Hammadi Library in English,* ed. James W. Robinson (San Francisco: Harper & Row, 1978) 46.

6

A RESPONSE TO R. GOLDENBERG
AND D. J. HARRINGTON, S.J.

George E. Rice
General Conference of Seventh-day Adventists

RESPONSE TO ROBERT GOLDENBERG

As one reads Robert Goldenberg's description of how the seventh-day Sabbath impacts upon Jewish religious life, one cannot help but imbibe some of the peace and serenity that the Sabbath brings to the Jewish experience. The reader is again aware of the "palace in time" pictured by Rabbi Heschel and wishes that all persons living in this troubled world might for one Sabbath—one period of twenty-four hours—share in this peace. An experience that might, perhaps, lead some to seek the eternal peace of which the seventh-day Sabbath is but a foretaste.

Why should we not talk in terms of all persons entering into the "sanctuary in time," regardless of ethnic background? After all, the Sabbath was introduced into the experience of humanity when planet earth boasted a population of two. By a descriptive metaphor, a "sanctuary in time," Heschel captures the truth of Jesus' words, "The Sabbath was made for man, not man for the Sabbath" (Mark 2:27).

We tend to speak of the seventh-day Sabbath as a Jewish institution, but in reality it was made for Adam, Eve, and all of their descendants. That this is so is established by the fact that the sacred day of rest was introduced on the last day of creation (Genesis 2:1–3), and not at Sinai. True, the Jewish people were entrusted with God's Sabbath, as they were entrusted also with his oracles (Roman 3:2). Their responsibility is to inform all mankind that they have a right to the "sanctuary in time," because this gift was shared by God with humanity at creation. The seventh-day Sabbath is God's institution, for He repeatedly calls it "My Sabbath" (Exodus 31:13; Leviticus 19:3, 30; 26:2; Isaiah 56:4; Ezekiel 20:12, 13, 20; 22:8, 26).

From the perspective of the New Testament, the seventh-day Sabbath has a special significance for Christians, for the New Testament presents Jesus as the Creator through Whom God worked. John opens his Gospel with a christological statement in which the Word is proclaimed as the Creator, "All things were made through him," John says, "and without him was not anything made that was made" (John 1:3).

The apostle Paul supports John's proclamation, "For in him all things were created, in heaven and on earth, visible and invisible, whether thrones or dominions or principalities or authorities—all things were created through him and for him. He is before all things, and in him all things hold together" (Colossians 1:16, 17). The Letter to the Hebrews, speaking of God's Son, says, "Whom he appointed the heir of all things, through whom also he created the world . . . upholding the universe by his word of power" (Hebrews 1:2, 3).

Thus, on the basis of the New Testament, Genesis 2:1-3 is to be understood in the light of Jesus' solidarity with his Father. The choice of the seventh day as a special day, to be a day of peace, serenity, and for spiritual reflection and blessing was made by Jesus, the Creator, in cooperation with His Father. The words of Jesus, "The Son of Man is lord even of the Sabbath" (Mark 2:28), reflect the relationship of the Creator to the created. As far as the New Testament is concerned, it is in this vein that the Lord's Day of Revelation 1:10 is to be understood.

Jesus' divinity, Sonship, and solidarity with the Father—thus His creatorship and its resultant authority—run throughout the New Testament and become the New Testament basis for understanding the Sabbath tensions found in the four Gospels. In these Sabbath episodes the Creator can be seen teaching His creatures the meaning of the gift—this "sanctuary in time"—which He has given them. If Jesus is seen by the people of His generation as breaking the Sabbath, it is because they had lost the true spirit of the Sabbath. "The Sabbath was made for man, not man for the Sabbath" (Mark 2:27), Jesus said. "I desire mercy, and not sacrifice" (Matthew 12:7); "Of how much more value is a man than a sheep! So it is lawful to do good on the Sabbath" (Matthew 12:12).

RESPONSE TO DANIEL HARRINGTON, S.J.

Daniel Harrington has correctly stated that Sunday is not the Sabbath. Therefore, none of the stipulations or regulations given in Scripture regarding the seventh-day Sabbath of God can be imposed on Sunday. This has also been recognized in some of the essays prepared by evangelical Protestant scholars which appear in the book *From Sabbath to Lord's Day*.[1] As A. T. Lincoln suggests in his polemic against transfer theology, neither can the sacredness and holiness of the seventh-day Sabbath be transferred to Sunday.

The continuity of the Sabbath throughout the New Testament period is exhibited by a historical *inclusio* in the writings of John. Both his Gospel and Revelation were written toward the conclusion of the final decade of the first Christian century. We have already noted that John proclaims Jesus the Creator in the introduction to his Gospel, and on the basis of Jesus' creative act the term "Lord's Day" of Revelation 1:10 is to be understood. Within the parameters of this historical *inclusio* – that is, creation and John's vision on the Lord's Day – Scripture knows only one Sabbath – the seventh day. The book of Revelation, however, then carries us down through history to the time of the final judgment, when God's final appeal is made to the inhabitants of this world. Within this appeal is a call to return to the worship of the Creator:

> Then I saw another angel flying in midheaven, with an eternal gospel to proclaim to those who dwell on earth, to every nation and tribe and tongue and people; and he said with a loud voice, "Fear God and give him glory, for the hour of his judgment has come; and worship him who made heaven and earth, the sea and the fountains of water." (Revelation 14:6, 7)

This call to worship the Creator cannot be separated from the day set aside for this purpose by Jesus at the time of creation. Thus the message of the first of the three angels in Revelation 14 is a call, which is contained within the proclamation of the eternal gospel, to observe the seventh-day Sabbath while offering worship to the Creator.

Harrington also makes us aware that Matthew and his Jewish-Christian community were Sabbath observers. Therefore, the tensions found in his Gospel reflect not only Jesus' attitude toward the Sabbath and the debate between Jesus and His opponents but also the experience of Matthew's community, which was caught in the middle of a "Jewish debate" about what is proper and what is not proper for Sabbath observance.

Harrington says that he detects a growing interest among some New Testament Christians, however, in Sunday as the Lord's Day. He sees this reflected in Paul's writings and in the writings of some "Pauline admirers." Because Paul's ministry was directed toward the Gentiles, we would then expect a move toward Sunday to be reflected in Paul's ministry and among his Gentile converts. However, Luke, the only Gentile convert, companion, and fellow worker of Paul to write for the New Testament, reflects the opposite.

In Luke's Gospel we see the same Sabbath tensions that are reflected in Matthew. If Luke and Theophilus were moving away from the seventh-day Sabbath toward Sunday under the influence of Paul, the debate over how the seventh-day Sabbath should be observed would have little interest for them. However, Luke records more Sabbath episodes than any of the other Gospel writers. It is Luke, the Gentile, who tells his Gentile reader that it was Jesus' practice to be in the synagogue for religious services on the Sabbath (Luke 4:16) and that Jesus' followers rested the Sabbath day from burial preparations according to the commandment (Luke 23:56).

In Acts, Luke presents Paul's ministry among the Gentiles as that of a Sabbath observer. For example, within the context of Paul's labor in Corinth, Luke tells Theophilus how every Sabbath Paul preached Christ to both Jews and Greeks. When Paul was denied access to the synagogue, he continued his work in the house of Titus Justus, a worshiper of God. Thus Paul's labors continued on for a year and a half in Corinth (Acts 18:1-11).

Galatians 4:10 and Colossians 2:16, which are cited as Paul's objection to Sabbath observance, must be read and understood within the broader context of Jesus' creatorship and His solidarity with His Father. That is, if Jesus remains Creator, Paul's comments in these verses must be understood in a way other than referring to the abolition of the sacred day that Jesus established at creation. Paul Giem discusses "catchphrases" that were tied to the ancient sanctuary system and demonstrates that "the weight of evidence indicates that what Paul actually had reference to was the sacrifices on the seventh-day sabbath prescribed in Num 28:9-10, which pointed forward to Christ and are no longer binding on the Christian since his death."[3] The basic principle of catchphrases may also be applied in understanding "days, and months, and seasons and years" in Galatians 4:10.

The Sabbath tensions, as they are seen in the Gospels—including Luke, a Gentile writing to a Gentile—are an accurate reflection of Jesus' experience. Whatever tension may have been experienced by the later followers of Jesus simply points out the truth of Jesus' words "The disciple is not above his master, nor the servant above his lord" (Matthew 10:24). According to Acts, Paul, who recognized the divinity of Jesus and His solidarity with the Father, continued to be a Sabbath observer and taught his Gentile converts to be observers as well.

NOTES

1. *From Sabbath to Lord's Day: A Biblical, Historical, and Theological Investigation,* ed. D. A. Carson (Grand Rapids: Zondervan, 1982). In this volume, see the following articles: A. T. Lincoln, "Sabbath, Rest, and Eschatology in the New Testament" ("As opposed to such a view we would reiterate that the theology of the New Testament writers in relation to the Sabbath rest and the Lord's Day did not include the transference of the rest of the seventh day to the rest on the first day" [p. 216]); D. A. Carson, "Jesus and the Sabbath in the Four Gospels" ("There

is no hint anywhere in the ministry of Jesus that the first day of the week is to take on the character of the Sabbath and replace it" [p. 85]); R. J. Bauckham, "The Lord's Day" ("Our study of the origins of the Lord's Day has given no hint of properly sabbatical associations; for the earliest Christians it was not a substitute for the Sabbath nor a day of rest nor related in any way to the fourth commandment" [p. 240]).

2. Lincoln, "From Sabbath to Lord's Day: A Biblical and Theological Perspective," in *From Sabbath to Lord's Day*, 389-90.

3. Paul Geim, "Sabbatōn in Col 2:16," *Andrews University Seminary Studies* 19 (1981) 195-210.

III

HISTORICAL PERSPECTIVES

7

REMEMBERING THE SABBATH: THE CREATION-SABBATH IN JEWISH AND CHRISTIAN HISTORY

Samuele Bacchiocchi
Andrews University

The principle and practice of Sabbath keeping both unite and divide Judaism and most branches of Christianity. Both religions recognize the vital role of a weekly "Sabbath day" of worship and spiritual renewal for the survival of their respective religions. Ahad Ha'am aptly expresses the vital function of the Sabbath in Jewish history: "We can affirm without any exaggeration that the Sabbath has preserved the Jews more than the Jews have preserved the Sabbath."[1]

The same can be said of the impact of Sabbath keeping on Christianity. The essence of Christianity, like that of Judaism, is a relationship with God. Such a relationship grows especially through the time and opportunities for worship and meditation provided by the observance of the Sabbath day. In a speech delivered on 13 November 1862, President Abraham Lincoln emphasized the vital function of the Sabbath: "As we keep or break the Sabbath day, we nobly save or meanly lose the last and best hope by which man arises."[2] Obviously Lincoln was thinking of Sunday as the Christian Sabbath. This does not detract from the fact that one of America's outstanding presidents viewed Sabbath keeping as the last and best hope that can renew and elevate human beings.

The survival of both Judaism and Christianity as dynamic religions may well depend on the survival of the observance of their respective "Sabbaths." In Western European nations, where only 10 percent or less of the Christian population attends church services on the day traditionally regarded as the "Lord's Day," the survival of Christianity is threatened. Social analysts already speak of the "post-Christian" era in Western Europe.

Sabbath keeping, however, not only unites but also divides Judaism from most branches of Christianity. The division is caused not only by the different day of the week on which Jews and most Christians observe their respective "Sabbaths" but also by their different understandings of the origin and nature of the Sabbath. Most Sunday-keeping Christians have historically viewed seventh-day Sabbath keeping as a Jewish institution, deriving from Moses and abrogated by Christ at the cross. The tendency has been to attach a negative stigma to seventh-day Sabbath keeping, by identifying it with the Jewish dispensation allegedly based on salvation through legal obedience. Sunday keeping, on the other hand, has been associated with the Christian dispensation allegedly based on salvation through faith by grace. Thus, Sabbath keeping historically has been perceived as a trademark of Judaism. Within Christianity itself those Christians who have retained seventh-day Sabbath keeping have often been stigmatized as Judaizers, holding onto an outdated Jewish superstition.

The historical process that led the majority of Christians to view seventh-day Sabbath keeping as a negative Jewish practice is a complex one. I have devoted considerable attention to this question, especially in my dissertation *From Sabbath to Sunday* (1977). In this paper I shall focus on one aspect of this process, namely, the question of the origin and nature of the Sabbath, which has been debated both in Jewish and Christian history.

Special attention will be given to the attempts made by Catholics and Protestants to differentiate between a *moral* (creational) and a *ceremonial* (Mosaic) aspect of the Sabbath commandment in order to sanction the observance of Sunday as the Christian Sabbath. The thesis of this paper is that the controversy over the origin and nature of the Sabbath not only has widened the gulf between Judaism and Christianity but also has left many Christians confused about why they should observe Sunday as a holy Sabbath day. The paper closes offering some suggestions on how to resolve this existing confusion.

THE ORIGIN OF THE SABBATH

The question of the origin of the Sabbath has been debated on and off throughout Christian history and especially during this past century.[3] The discovery of alleged Babylonian parallels to the biblical Sabbath over a century ago stimulated a fresh quest for Sabbath origin.[4] A major reason why the question of the origin of the Sabbath has attracted much attention is that it is bound with the larger question of whether or not the principle and practice of seventh-day Sabbath keeping are binding upon Christians.

Those who believe that the Sabbath was established by God at creation for the benefit of humanity accept its observance as a creation ordinance binding upon all, Jews and Christians. On the other hand, those who hold that the Sabbath originated at the time of Moses or after the settlement in Canaan because of socioeconomic or astrological-astronomic considerations regard the Sabbath as a Jewish institution not applicable to Christians. In view of these implications, it is important to examine briefly how the question of the origin of the Sabbath has been debated in Jewish and Christian history. We shall begin by looking at the leading theories espoused during this past century.

The leading theories date the origin of the Sabbath (1) before or at the time of Moses, (2) after the settlement in Canaan, or (3) during or after the exile. The main reasons adduced for these origins can be labeled respectively as (1) astrological-astronomic, (2) socioeconomic, and (3) magical-symbolic.[5]

Pre-Mosaic/Mosaic Origin of the Sabbath

The theory that the Sabbath originated by the time of Moses rests primarily on the supposed influence of such factors as the planet Saturn, the lunar phases, and the existence of a Mesopotamian seven-day period.

Kenites' Saturn day. Some derive the Old Testament Sabbath from the superstitious observance of the day of Saturn by the Kenites, a tribe with whom Moses came in close contact by marriage when he fled to Midian (Judges 4:11, 17).[6] It is speculated that the day of Saturn was an ancient taboo day for the Kenites, forgers of the desert, on which they would not light their smelting ovens. The Israelites allegedly adopted this Kenite taboo day and extended its regulations to normal household chores. Support for this hypothesis is sought in the prohibition of fire making on the Sabbath (Exodus 35:3; Numbers 15:32-36), which is made dependent on the supposed ancestral worship of Sakkuth and Kaiwan (Amos 5:26), alleged names for Saturn.[7] The primary weakness of this hypothesis is that it rests on the assumption that the Kenites had a seven-day week in which a day was dedicated to Saturn. To the best of our knowledge it is only with the introduction of the planetarian week toward the beginning of the Christian era that a weekly *dies saturni* first appears.[8] Moreover, there is no indication in the Old Testament or in ancient Jewish literature that the Sabbath was ever regarded as sacred to Saturn.[9] For these and other reasons the Kenite hypothesis is now discredited by practically all scholars.[10]

Lunar origin. The lunar theory links the origin of the Sabbath with the days associated with the four phases of the moon. An Assyrian calendar found in 1869 among the cuneiform tablets in the British Museum marks the 7th, 14th, 19th, 21st, and 28th days of the month as *ume lemnuti,* that is, evil or unfavorable days.[11] The origin of these evil days is attributed by some to the four phases of the moon, which recur approximately every seven days.[12] The Hebrews would thus have derived their Sabbath from an ancient Mesopotamian lunar-phases cycle.[13] This theory has three main weaknesses: (1) The lunar month (lunation) consists not of twenty-eight days (4 x 7) but of just over twenty-nine days—a period that is not divisible by weeks of seven days each.[14] (2) If the Babylonians employed the evil days in a civil "weekly" cycle (which apparently they never did), the cycle would be interrupted at the beginning of every month, since its first evil day would occur after eight or nine days from the last evil day (twenty-eighth day) of the previous month.[15] (3) Nothing in the cuneiform texts indicates that the Babylonians ever employed the recurring evil days as a "weekly" division of time for civil purposes.[16]

Full moon/Sabattu. Somewhat similar to the lunary-phases theory is the full-moon theory. The term *sabattu,* which looks and sounds much like the Hebrew word *šabbat* (Sabbath), occurs in several Akkadian documents of ancient Mesopotamia. The term apparently designated the fifteenth day of the month, that is, the day of the full moon.[17] In several tablets *sabattu* is defined as *um muh libbi,* usually translated as "day of rest of the heart" or "day of appeasement."[18] *Sabattu,* then, was the day of the full moon, when presumably the gods were propitiated or appeased.[19] The similarity of the look and sound between the Akkadian *sabattu* and the Hebrew *šabbat* (Sabbath), as well as the association in the Old Testament between the Sabbath and the new moon, has led some scholars to conclude that the Sabbath was originally not a weekly but a monthly festival connected with the day of the full moon. The transformation of the Sabbath from a monthly to a weekly festival would have occurred much later, under Ezekiel in response to a demand for rest.[20] The full-moon theory fails to explain how an alleged "monthly Sabbath" came to be observed as a weekly seventh-day Sabbath. If for centuries the Israelites had observed the day of the full moon as their Sabbath, it is surprising that no memory of it can be found at later times. For example, the day of the full moon in Hebrew is called *keseh* (Psalm 81:3), a term that is not etymologically related to the Akkadian *sabattu.*[21] The theory also ignores the fact that there is nothing in Ezekiel of a new mode of observing the Sabbath.[22] On the contrary, Ezekiel complains that Israel failed to observe the Sabbath in the old sense (Ezekiel 20:12ff.; 22:8, 26; 23:38; 44:24).

Seven-day period. Another theory traces the origin of the Sabbath to seven-day celebrations mentioned in some ancient Mesopotamian documents.[23] In the Mesopotamian flood stories, for example, the duration of the storm was seven days and the first bird was sent out seven days after the ship came to rest upon a mountain.[24]

The few references to seven-day periods offer meager evidence for an early Babylonian week, as S. H. Horn points out:

especially in view of the hundreds of thousands of cuneiform records recovered in the Mesopotamian valley. If the ancient Sumerians, Babylonians, or Assyrians possessed a week like that of the Hebrews in Biblical times, or gave to the seventh day of such a week special sanctity, they would certainly have left us a clearer record of it.[25]

Settlement Origin of the Sabbath

The failure of extrabiblical sources to provide a satisfactory explanation for the origin of the Sabbath has driven scholars to search for its roots within Old Testament texts. Such a study has led some to conclude that the Sabbath was first introduced after the occupation of Canaan.[26] The reasons given for its introduction are based primarily on social and economic considerations. The need to give a day of rest to laborers and the necessity of a market day in which to sell and buy produce would have induced the introduction of the Sabbath as a "day off."[27] In time, it is argued, the Sabbath underwent an evolution from a social to a religious institution, that is, from a day for the sake of slaves and of marketing to a day for the sake of Yahweh. Credit for such a transformation is given to the prophets and priests who by the time of the exile developed a theology of the Sabbath to promote its religious observance.[28]

What militates against this theory is the fact that no trace has been found of regular market weeks in Palestine, much less at seven-day intervals. Moreover, the prophetic denunciation of the trading done by some on the Sabbath suggests that the day at times deteriorated into a market day rather than originated from it (Nehemiah 13:14–22; Jeremiah 17:19–27; Amos 8:5).

Exilic Origin of the Sabbath

The period of the Jewish exile in Babylon (605–539 B.C.E.) is generally regarded as crucial for the history of the Sabbath. For some scholars the exile represents the very time of the origin of the Sabbath.[29] For others, the exilic and postexilic periods are the turning point in the theological and cultic development of the Sabbath.[30] The first view need not detain us because it is openly contradicted by such preexilic passages such as 2 Kings 4:23 and 2 Kings 11:4–12, which speak of the Sabbath over two centuries before Ezekiel's time. The second view deserves some consideration. The exile, it is claimed, contributed in at least two ways to transforming the Sabbath from a social institution (a day for the sake of slaves and cattle) to a religious festival (a day for God's sake). First, the loss of the homeland and of dependent workers would have eliminated the social reasons for the

Sabbath and at the same time induced the search for theological justifications. Second, it is argued that the loss of a holy place (Jerusalem temple
in 586 B.C.E.) made *holy time* (the Sabbath) of utmost importance, especially since it could be celebrated even in exile.[31]

The information provided by the Old Testament for this period lends no
support to this Sabbath-transformation theory. The exilic prophets do not
present an innovative theology and practice of the Sabbath. Ezekiel, for
example, prescribes no new manner or motivation for the celebration of
the Sabbath. On the contrary, the prophet goes so far as viewing the past
profanation of the Sabbath as a major cause for the calamities which had
befallen Israel (Ezekiel 20:15–16, 21, 36; 22:26, 31). To promote a return
of proper Sabbath keeping, Ezekiel appeals not to a *new* theological
rationale but to the *old* historical meaning of the Sabbath, namely, its
being a "sign" or pledge of Israel's covenantal relationship with God
(Ezekiel 20:12, 20). This covenantal function of the Sabbath was most
relevant during the exile experience, for the threat of national disinte-
gration or even disappearance was an ever-present reality.[32]

Did the Sabbath develop into holy time as a result of the loss of a holy
place (the Jerusalem temple)? Again, this is hardly suggested by Ezekiel,
who frequently associates the Sabbath with holy things (Ezekiel 22:26;
23:38) and with service in the future temple (Ezekiel 45:17; 46:1–4, 12).[33]
The exilic period, with its deportation and cultic deprivation, seems to have
contributed not to radical ideological or practical *innovations* but rather
to the *consolidation* of institutions such as the Sabbath. This is suggested
also by the messages given and the measures adopted by Jeremiah during
the exile and by Nehemiah after the exile, to stop trading activities in
Jerusalem on the Sabbath (Jeremiah 17:19–27; Nehemiah 10:31, 33;
13:15–22). Their efforts were aimed not at transforming the Sabbath
institution but at reforming its abuses.

The attempts to trace the origin of the Sabbath to the time of Moses, or
the settlement or the exile because of astronomical or socioeconomic considerations have proved to be unsuccessful. More and more scholars have
come to recognize that it is preferable to seek the origin of the Sabbath in
the biblical record rather than in extrabiblical sources.[34]

THE CREATION ORIGIN OF THE SABBATH

Old Testament

The biblical view of the origin of the Sabbath is unequivocal: the
Sabbath, as seventh day, originated at the completion of the creation week
as a result of three divine acts: God "rested," "blessed," and "hallowed" the
seventh day (Genesis 2:2–3).

Twice Genesis 2:2-3 states that God "rested" on the seventh day from all his work. The Hebrew verb *šābat,* translated "rested," denotes cessation, not relaxation. The latter idea is expressed by the Hebrew verb *nwḥ,* which is used in Exodus 20:11, where the divine rest fulfills an anthropological function: it serves as a model for human rest. In Genesis 2:2-3, however, the divine rest has a cosmological function. It serves to explain that God, as Karl Barth puts it, "was content to be the Creator of this particular creation. . . . He had no occasion to proceed to further creations. He needed no further creations."[35] To acknowledge this fact, God stopped.

Genesis 2:3 affirms that the Creator "blessed" (*brk*) the seventh day just as he had blessed animals and man on the previous day (Genesis 1:22, 28). Divine blessings in the Scripture are not merely "good wishes," but assurance of fruitfulness, prosperity, and a happy and abundant life (Psalm 133:3).[36] In terms of the seventh day, it means that God has promised to make the Sabbath a beneficial and vitalizing power through which human life is enriched and renewed.[37] In Exodus 20:11 the blessing of the creation seventh day is explicitly linked with the weekly Sabbath.

Genesis 2:3 also affirms that the Creator "hallowed" (RV, RSV) the seventh day, "made it holy" (NEB, NAB), or "sanctified it" (NASB). Both here and in the Sabbath commandment (Exodus 20:11) the Hebrew text uses the verb *qiddēš* (*piel*), from the root *qdš,* "holy." In Hebrew the basic meaning of "holy" or "holiness" is "separation" for holy use. In terms of the Sabbath, its holiness consists in God's separation of this day from the six working days. The holiness of the Sabbath stems not from humanity's keeping it, but from God's choice of the seventh day to be a channel through which human beings can experience more freely and fully the awareness of his sanctifying presence in their lives.

The great importance of the creation Sabbath in the Old Testament is indicated by the fact that it provides the theological motivation for the commandment to observe the seventh day (Exodus 20:11) and the theological justification for serving as a covenant sign between God and Israel (Exodus 31:17). The theological reasons given for the command to observe the seventh-day Sabbath "to the Lord your God" (Exodus 20:10) is "for in six days the Lord made heaven and earth, the sea, and all that is in them and rested the seventh day; therefore the Lord blessed the Sabbath day and hallowed it" (Exodus 20:11). The tie between the creation Sabbath and the Sabbath commandment is so close that the former provides the basis for the latter. To keep the Sabbath holy means (1) to follow the divine example given at creation, (2) to acknowledge God as Creator, and (3) to participate in God's rest and blessings for humankind.

The creation Sabbath serves also as "a sign" (*'ôt*) of the covenant relationship between God and his people: "It is a sign for ever between me and the people of Israel that in six days the Lord made heaven and earth, and on the seventh day He rested, and was refreshed" (Exodus 31:17). The very nature of a sign is to point to something beyond itself, to mediate an understanding of a certain reality and/or to motivate a corresponding behavior.[38] As a covenant sign, rooted in creation, the Sabbath mediates an understanding of redemptive history (i.e., covenant history) by pointing retrospectively and prospectively. Retrospectively, the Sabbath invites the believer to look back and memorialize God as the creator of an original, perfect creation (Genesis 2:2-3; Exodus 20:8, 11; 31:17). Prospectively, the Sabbath encourages the believer to look forward and trust God's promise to fulfill his "everlasting covenant" (Exodus 31:16; Hebrews 4:9) to restore this world to its original perfection. Thus, the Sabbath stands as a sign of an "everlasting covenant" between creation (Genesis 2:2-3; Exodus 20:11; 31:17) and redemption (Deuteronomy 5:15; Isaiah 56:1-4). It directs us to the past perfect creation and it points constantly to the future ultimate restoration.

New Testament

The New Testament takes for granted the creation origin of the Sabbath. A clear example is found in Mark 2:27 where Christ refutes the charge of Sabbath breaking leveled against the disciples by referring to the original purpose of the Sabbath: "The Sabbath was made for man, not man for the Sabbath." Christ's choice of words is significant. The verb "made" (*ginomai*) alludes to the original "making" of the Sabbath[39] and the word "human" (*anthrōpos*) suggests its human function. Thus, to establish the human and universal value of the Sabbath, Christ reverts to its very origin, right after the creation of people. Why? Because for the Lord the law of the beginning stands supreme.

The importance of God's original design is emphasized in another instance when in reporting the corruption of the institution of marriage that occurred under the Mosaic code Christ reverted to its Edenic origin, saying "From the beginning it was not so" (Matthew 19:8). Christ then traces both marriage and the Sabbath to their creation origin in order to clarify their fundamental value and function for humanity.

Some authors interpret this famous pronouncement of Christ as meaning that the "well-being of man is superior to the Sabbath rest" and since the Sabbath "no longer spelt blessings but hardship, it had failed in its divine purpose, and as a consequence rebellion against it or disregard of it was no sin."[40]

The least that can be said of this interpretation is that it attributes to God human shortsightedness for having given a law that could not accomplish its intended purpose and which he was consequently forced to abolish. By this reasoning, the validity of any God-given law is determined not by its intended purpose but rather by the way human beings use or abuse it. Such a conclusion would make a person rather than God the ultimate arbitrator who determines the validity of any commandment. Furthermore, to interpret this saying as meaning that the "well-being of man is superior to the Sabbath rest" would imply that the Sabbath rest had been imposed arbitrarily upon humanity to restrict their welfare. But this interpretation runs contrary to the very words of Christ. "The Sabbath," he said, "was made on account of (*dia*) man and not man on account of the Sabbath." This means that the Sabbath came into being (*egeneto*) after the creation of humans, not to make them slaves of rules and regulations but to ensure their physical and spiritual well-being.

This welfare of humanity is *not restricted* but *guaranteed* by the proper observance of the Sabbath. By this memorable affirmation, then, Christ does not abrogate the Sabbath commandment but establishes its permanent validity by appealing to its original creation, when God determined its intended function for the well-being of humankind.

Another explicit reference to the creation Sabbath is found in the Letter to the Hebrews. In the fourth chapter, the author establishes the universal and spiritual nature of the Sabbath rest by welding together two Old Testament texts, Genesis 2:2 and Psalm 95:11. Through the former, Hebrews traces the origin of the Sabbath rest back to creation, when "God rested on the seventh day from all his works" (Hebrews 4:3; cf. Genesis 2:2-3). By the latter (Psalm 95:11), Hebrews explains that the scope of this divine rest includes the blessings of salvation to be found by entering personally into God's rest (Hebrews 4:3, 5, 10). Our immediate concern is not the meaning of the rest mentioned in the passage,[41] but rather to note that the author traces its origin not to the time of the settlement in Joshua's days (Hebrews 4:8),[42] but back to the time of creation, when "God rested on the seventh day from all His works" (Hebrews 4:4).

The context clearly indicates that the author is thinking of the "works" of creation, since Hebrews explains that God's "works were finished from the foundations of the world" (Hebrews 4:3). The probative value of this statement is heightened by the fact that the author is not arguing for the creation origin of the Sabbath but rather takes it for granted in explaining God's ultimate purpose for his people. Thus, in Hebrews 4, the creation origin of the Sabbath is not only accepted but is also presented as the basis for understanding God's ultimate purpose for his people.

Jewish History

Outside the biblical sources, one finds widespread recognition of the creation origin of the Sabbath in both Jewish and Christian history. The Jews developed two differing views regarding the origin of the Sabbath.

Broadly speaking, the two views can be distinguished linguistically and geographically. Palestinian (Hebrew) Judaism reduced the Sabbath to an exclusive Jewish ordinance linked to the origin of Israel as a nation at the time of Moses. As stated in the book of *Jubilees,* "He [God] allowed no other people or peoples to keep the Sabbath on this day, except Israel only; to it alone he granted to eat and drink and keep the Sabbath on it" (2:31; see also 2:20–22). If the patriarchs are sometimes mentioned as keeping the Sabbath, this is regarded as an exception "before it [the Sabbath] was given" to Israel (*Genesis Rabbah* 11:7; 64:4; 79:6).

This view represents not an original tradition but a secondary development which was encouraged by the necessity to preserve a Jewish identity in the face of Hellenistic pressures (especially at the time of Antiochus Epiphanes [175 B.C.E.]) to abandon Jewish religion. This is indicated by the fact that even in Palestinian literature there are references to the creation origin of the Sabbath. For example, while on the one hand the book of *Jubilees* (about 140–100 B.C.E.) says that God allowed "Israel only" to keep the Sabbath (*Jubilees* 2:31), on the other hand it holds that God "kept the Sabbath on the seventh day and hallowed it for all ages, and appointed it as a sign for all His works" (*Jubilees* 2:1).

In Hellenistic (Greek) Jewish literature, the Sabbath is unmistakably viewed as a creation ordinance for all humanity. Philo, for example, not only traces the origin of the Sabbath to creation but also delights to call it "the birthday of the world" (*Creation* 89; *Life of Moses* 1.207; *Special Laws* 2.59). Referring to the creation story, Philo explains: "We are told that the world was made in six days and that on the seventh God ceased from his works and began to contemplate what had been so well created, and therefore he bade those who should live as citizens under this world-order to follow God in this as in other matters" (*Decalogue* 97). Because the Sabbath exists from creation, Philo emphasizes that it is "the festival not of a single city or country but of the universe, and it alone strictly deserves to be called public, as belonging to all people" (*Creation* 89).

Early Church

The recognition of the creation origin of the Sabbath is found in several documents of the early church. For example, in the *Syriac Didascalia* (ca. 250 C.E.) Sunday is presented as "greater" than the Sabbath because it preceded the latter in the creation week. As the first day of creation, Sunday represents "the beginning of the world.[43] In the treatise *On the Sabbath and Circumcision,* found among the works of Athanasius (ca. 296–373), the superiority of Sunday over the Sabbath is argued on the basis of creation versus recreation: "The Sabbath was the end of the first creation, the Lord's day was the beginning of the second in which He renewed and restored the old."[44] The fact that both Sabbath- and Sunday-keepers would defend the legitimacy and superiority of their respective days by appealing to their roles with reference to creation shows how important the latter was in their view.

In the so-called *Constitutions of the Holy Apostles* (ca. 380), Christians are admonished to "keep the Sabbath and the Lord's day festival; because the former is the memorial of the creation, and the latter of the resurrection" (7.23).[45] Several other references to the creation Sabbath are found in the same document. For example, a prayer commemorating Christ's incarnation begins with the words "O Lord Almighty, Thou hast created the world by Christ and hast appointed the Sabbath in memory thereof, because on that day Thou hast made us rest from our works for the meditation upon Thy laws" (*Constitutions* 7.36).[46]

The theme of the creation Sabbath, as noted by Jean Danielou, is also "at the center of Augustinian thought."[47] For Augustine (354–430), the culmination of the creation week in the Sabbath rest provides the basis to develop two significant concepts. The first is the notion of the progress of the history of this world toward a final Sabbath rest and peace with God. In other words, the realization of the eternal rest represents for Augustine the fulfillment of "the Sabbath that the Lord approved at the beginning of creation, where it says, 'God rested on the seventh day from all his works'" (*City of God* 22.30).[48]

The second Augustinian interpretation of the creation of Sabbath may be defined as the mystical progress of the human soul from restlessness into rest in God. A fitting example is found in one of the most sublime chapters of his *Confessions,* where Augustine prays:

> O Lord God, Thou who hast given us all, grant us Thy peace, the peace of rest, the peace of the Sabbath, the peace without an "evening."[49] For this very beautiful order of things will pass away when they have accomplished their appointed purpose. They all were made with a "morning" and an "evening." But the seventh day is without an "evening" and it has no setting, because Thou has sanctified it so that it may last eternally. Thy resting on the seventh day after the completion of Thy works, foretells us through the voice of Thy Book, that we also after completing our works through Thy generosity, in the Sabbath of eternal life shall rest in Thee. (13.35–36)[50]

This mystical and eschatological interpretation of the creation Sabbath shows what a profound appreciation Augustine had for its significance, in spite of the fact that he failed to accept the literal observance of the fourth commandment.[51]

The Middle Ages

The Augustinian spiritual interpretation of the creation Sabbath continued to some extent during the Middle Ages.[52] But a new development occurred following the Constantinian Sunday Law of 321. In order to give a theological sanction to the imperial legislation demanding rest from work on Sunday, church leaders often appealed to the Sabbath commandment, interpreting it as a creation ordinance applicable to Sunday observance. Chrysostom (ca. 347–407) anticipates this development in his exposition of Genesis 2:2, "God blessed the seventh day and hallowed it." He asks, "What do the words 'He hallowed it' actually mean? . . . [God] is teaching us that among the days of the week one must be singled out and wholly devoted to the service of spiritual things" (*Homily* 10.7; *In Genesim*).[53]

The reduction of the creation Sabbath from the specific observance of the *seventh day* to the principle of resting *one day in seven* in order to worship God made it possible to apply the Sabbath commandment to the observance of Sunday. Peter Comestor, for example (died ca. 1179), defends this application, arguing on the basis of Genesis 2:2 that "the Sabbath has been always observed by some nations even before the Law" (*Historia scholastica: Liber Genesis* 10).[54] This recognition of the Sabbath as a creation and thus universal ordinance was motivated, however, not by the desire to promote the observance of the seventh day, but by the necessity to sanction and regulate Sunday keeping.

In late medieval theology the literal application of the Sabbath commandment to Sunday keeping was justified on the basis of a new interpretation which consisted in distinguishing between a moral and a ceremonial aspect within the fourth commandment. Thomas Aquinas (ca. 1225–1274) offers the most articulated exposition of this artificial distinction in his *Summa Theologica*. He argues that "the precept of the Sabbath observance is moral . . . in so far as it commands man to give some time to the things of God . . . but it is a ceremonial precept . . . as to the fixing of the time."[55]

How can the fourth commandment be *ceremonial* for specifying the *seventh day* but *moral* for enjoining one to set apart *a day* of rest for worship? Basically because for Aquinas the moral aspect of the Sabbath is grounded on natural law, that is to say, the principle of a regularly stated time for worship and rest is in accordance with natural reason.[56] The ceremonial aspect of the Sabbath, on the other hand, is determined by the symbolism of the seventh day commemoration of "creation" and prefiguration of the "repose of the mind in God, either in the present life, by grace, or, in the future life by glory."[57]

One wonders how the Sabbath can be ceremonial (transitory) for symbolizing God's perfect creation and the rest to be found in him both in the present and future life. Is it not this reassurance that provides the basis for setting aside *any time* to worship God? To reject as *ceremonial* the original message of the seventh-day Sabbath, namely, that God is the perfect Creator who offers rest, peace, and fellowship to his creatures, means to destroy also the very *moral* basis for devoting any time to the worship of God.

Apparently Aquinas himself recognized the inadequacy of his reasoning, since he makes a distinction between the Sabbath and other symbolic Old Testament festivals such as Passover, "a sign of the future Passion of Christ." The latter, Aquinas explains, were "temporal and transitory . . . consequently, the Sabbath alone, and none of the other solemnities and sacrifices, is mentioned in the precepts of the decalogue."[58]

Aquinas's uncertainty about the ceremonial aspect of the Sabbath is reflected also in his comment that Christ annulled not the precept of the Sabbath, but "the superstitious interpretation of the Pharisees, who thought that man ought to abstain from doing even works of kindness on the Sabbath; which was contrary to the intention of the Law."[64] Aquinas's uncertainty, however, was largely forgotten and his moral/ceremonial distinction of the Sabbath became the standard rationale for defending the church's right to introduce and regulate the observance of Sunday and holy days. This resulted in an elaborate legalistic system of Sunday keeping akin to that of the rabbinical Sabbath.[60]

Lutheranism

The sixteenth-century reformers reproposed with new qualifications Aquinas's distinctions between the moral (creational) and ceremonial (Mosaic) aspects of the Sabbath. Their position was influenced by their understanding of the relationship between the Old and the New Testaments as well as by their reaction against the legalistic and superstitious observance not only of Sunday but of a host of holy days as well.

Luther and some radicals, in their concern to combat legalistic Sabbatarianism, which was promoted not only by the Catholic Church but also by left-wing reformers such as Andreas Karlstadt,[61] attacked the Sabbath as a Mosaic institution "specifically given to the Jewish people."[62] Sunday was retained by Luther not as the Christian Sabbath but as a convenient day "ordained by the Church for the sake of the imperfect laity and the working class,"[63] who need "at least one day in the week to rest . . . and attend divine service."[64] This position was largely determined by a radical distinction between the Old and New Testaments.

In the *Large Catechism* (1529) Luther explains that the Sabbath "is altogether an external matter, like other ordinances of the Old Testament, which were attached to particular customs, persons, and places, and now have been made free through Christ."[65] This view is stated even more emphatically in Article 28 of the *Augsburg Confession* (1530): "Scripture has abrogated the Sabbath-day; for it teaches that, since the Gospel has been revealed, all the ceremonies of Moses can be omitted."[66] Luther's radical distinction between the Old and New Testaments and between law and gospel was adopted and developed to extremes by radicals such as

Anabaptists, leftist Puritans, Quakers, Mennonites, Hutterites, and many modern antinomian denominations.[67] These have generally claimed that the Sabbath is not a creation ordinance but a Mosaic institution which Christ fulfilled and abolished. Consequently, believers in the Christian dispensation are free from the observance of any special day.

Sabbatarians

Radical reformers promoted two opposing views regarding the Sabbath. One group, mentioned earlier, pressed to its logical conclusion the Lutheran distinction between the Old and New Testaments, rejecting the observance of the Sabbath or of any day, as part of the Mosaic dispensation which Christ had fulfilled and replaced with the dispensation of grace. Another group, however, pursued the logical implications of the Calvinistic unity between the two Testaments, accepting and promoting the observance of the seventh-day Sabbath as a creation ordinance meant for all time and people. We shall call the latter "Sabbatarians," a name frequently given to them by their opponents.[68]

Recent studies have shown that Sabbatarians constituted a respectable group at the time of the Reformation, especially in such places as Moravia, Bohemia, Austria, and Silesia.[69] In fact, in some Catholic catalogues of sects, they are listed immediately after the Lutherans and Calvinists.[70] Erasmus (1466–1536) mentions the existence of Sabbatarians in Bohemia: "Now I hear that among the Bohemians a new kind of Jews are springing up, whom they call *Sabbatarii,* who serve the Sabbath with great superstition."[71] Similarly, Luther reports on the existence of Sabbatarian groups in Moravia and Austria.[72] In fact, in 1538 Luther wrote *Letter Against the Sabbatarians (Brief wider die Sabbathers),* arguing from the Bible against their observance of the seventh-day Sabbath.[73]

Oswald Glait, a former Catholic priest who became first a Lutheran and then an Anabaptist minister, began in 1527 or 1528 successfully to propagate his Sabbatarian views among Anabaptists in Moravia, Silesia, and Bohemia.[74] He was supported by the learned Andreas Fisher, also a former priest and Anabaptist.[75] Glait wrote *Booklet on the Sabbath (Buchlein vom Sabbath,* ca. 1530), which is not extant. From a refutation of Glait's book by Caspar Schewenckfeld we learn that Glait maintained the unity of the Old and New Testaments, accepting the validity and relevance of the Decalogue for the Christian dispensation.[76] Glait rejected the contention of his critics that the Sabbath commandment is a ceremonial law like circumcision. He held instead that the "Sabbath is commanded and kept from the beginning of creation."[77] God enjoined "Adam in paradise to celebrate the Sabbath."[78] Therefore "the Sabbath . . . is an eternal sign of hope and a memorial of creation, . . . an eternal covenant to be kept as long as the world stands."[79] On account of this teaching, Glait faced expulsions, persecutions, and finally death by drowning in the Danube (1546).[80]

The death of Glait, perhaps the most prominent leader of the Sabbatarian Anabaptists, did not stop the propagation of the Sabbath doctrine. This is indicated by the existence of seventh-day Sabbath keepers at the time of the Reformation in several European countries such as Poland, Holland, Germany, France, Hungary, Russia, Turkey, Finland, and Sweden.[81] In the seventeenth century the presence of Sabbatarians became particularly felt in England. This is noted by R. J. Bauckham:

> An impressive succession of Puritan and Anglican spokesmen addressed themselves to combating the seventh-day error: Lancelot Andrews, Bishop Francis White, Richard Baxter, John Bunyan, Edward Stillingfleet, John Owen, Nathanael Homes, John Wallis. Their efforts are a tacit admission of the attraction that the doctrine exercised in the seventeenth century, and seventh-day observers (who then usually also advocated Sunday work) were harshly treated by Puritan and Anglican authorities alike.[82]

The Seventh Day Baptists became the leading Sabbatarian church in England.[83] Their first church in America was founded at Newport, Rhode Island, in December 1671.[84] Seventh-day Adventists gratefully acknowledge their indebtedness to Seventh Day Baptists for bringing to them the knowledge of the Sabbath in 1845.[85] Later on, the Sabbath was accepted as a creation ordinance by the Church of God Seventh Day, the Worldwide Church of God, and a score of smaller denominations.[86]

Reformed Tradition

Churches in the Reformed tradition, such as English Puritans, Presbyterians, Congregationalists, Methodists, and Baptists, adopted what might be called a "compromise position," on the one hand acknowledging the Sabbath as a creation ordinance, while on the other hand defending Sunday as a legitimate substitution of the Sabbath accomplished by the church. They generally distinguished between the temporal and the spiritual observance of Sunday. Calvin can rightly be regarded as the pioneer and promoter of this view, which exerted far-reaching influence, especially in Anglo-American Puritan Sabbatarianism. The basis of Calvin's teaching regarding the Sabbath is to be found in his rejection of Luther's antithesis between law and gospel. In his effort to maintain the basic unity of the Old and New Testaments, Calvin christianized the law, spiritualizing, at least in part, the Sabbath commandment.[87]

Calvin tried to reconcile his acceptance of the Sabbath as a creation ordinance for humanity with his view that "on the advent of our Lord Jesus Christ, the ceremonial part of the commandment was abolished" by

reproposing a new version of Aquinas's distinction between the moral and
ceremonial aspects of the Sabbath. He argues that at creation the Sabbath
was given as a perpetual ordinance but "afterwards in the law a new precept
concerning the Sabbath was given, which should be peculiar to the Jews,
and but for a season."[88]

What is the difference between the "Jewish" (ceremonial) seventh-day
Sabbath and the "Christian" (moral) first-day Sabbath? The difference is
not easy to detect, especially for someone not trained to distinguish theological nuances. Calvin describes the Jewish Sabbath as being "typical"
(symbolic), that is, "a legal ceremony shadowing forth a spiritual rest, the
truth of which was manifested in Christ."[89] The Christian Sabbath [Sun-
day] on the other hand is "without figure."[90] By this he apparently means
that it is more a pragmatic institution, designed to accomplish three basic
objectives: first, to allow God to work in us; second, to provide time for
meditation and church services; and third, to protect dependent workers."[91]

Calvin's attempt to resolve the tension between the Sunday Sabbath as
a perpetual creation ordinance and the Saturday Sabbath as a temporary
ceremonial law can hardly be considered successful. Do not both fulfill the
same pragmatic functions? Moreover, by teaching that for Christians the
Sunday Sabbath represents "self-renunciation" and the "true rest" of the
Gospel,[92] did not Calvin also attribute to the day a "typological-symbolic"
significance, much like the type he assigned to the Jewish Saturday Sabbath?

This unresolved tension can be followed in the teaching of Calvin's suc-
cessors and has been the cause of endless controversies. For example,
Zacharias Ursinus, the compiler of that important Reformed confession
known as *Heidelberg Catechism* (1563), teaches that "the Sabbath of the
seventh day was appointed of God from the very beginning of the world,
to declare that men, after His example, should rest from their labours,"
and "although the ceremonial Sabbath has been abolished in the New
Testament, yet the moral still continues and pertains to us as well as to
others."[93] This position was later defended tenaciously in the monumental
work *The Doctrine of the Sabbath,* written in 1595 by the famous English
Puritan Nicolas Bownde [Bound],[94] as well as in other confessional documents such as the Synod of Dort of 1619 and the *Westminister Confession
of Faith* of 1647.[95]

These and similar documents fail to offer a rational explanation for the
artificial and arbitrary distinction between the so-called *moral* (one-day-in-
seven) aspect of the Sunday Sabbath and the ceremonial (specification of
the seventh day) aspect of the Saturday Sabbath, supposedly annulled
by Christ.

There is no trace of such an artificial distinction in Scripture. If such a
distinction existed in the Old Testament, we would expect the alleged moral
aspect of the Sabbath commandment, that is, the principle of one-day-in-

seven, to be applied to such people as the priests (who had to work on the Sabbath) by granting them a day off at another time during the week. The absence of such a provision constitutes a most direct challenge to those who uphold the one-day-in-seven principle. Donald Carson acknowledges:

If the Old Testament principle were really "one-day-in-seven for worship and rest" instead of "the seventh day for worship and rest," we might have expected Old Testament legislation to prescribe some other day off for the priests. The lack of such confirms the importance in Old Testament thought of the *seventh* day, as opposed to the one-in-seven principle so greatly relied upon by those who wish to see in Sunday the precise New Testament equivalent of the Old Testament Sabbath.[96]

To contend that the specification of the *seventh day* is a ceremonial element of the Sabbath, because it was designed to aid the Jews in commemorating creation and in experiencing spiritual rest, means to be blind to the fact that Christians need such an aid just as much as the Jews; it means to leave Christians confused as to the reasons for devoting one day to the worship of God. R. J. Bauckham acknowledges the existence of such a confusion when he notes that most "Protestants in the mid-sixteenth century had as imprecise ideas about the basis of Sunday observance as most Christians at most times have had."[97]

The unresolved contradiction between the moral and ceremonial aspects of the fourth commandment has aroused recurrent controversies over the relationship between Sunday and the Sabbath commandment. Truly the Sabbath has had no rest. The moral/ceremonial distinctions regarding the Sabbath have led to two main opposing views of Sunday. In the Netherlands, for example, the two views were hotly debated during more than a decade after the Synod of Dort (1619). On the one side, Dutch theologians such as Willem Teellinck, William Ames, and Antonius Walaeus wrote major treatises defending the creation origin of the Sabbath and thus the legitimate application of the fourth commandment to the observance of Sunday.[98] On the other side, a leading professor, Franciscus Gomarus, produced a major response entitled *Enquiry into the Meaning and Origin of the Sabbath and Consideration of the Institution of the Lord's Day* (1628), in which he argues for a Mosaic origin of the Sabbath and consequently for an independent ecclesiastical origin of Sunday.[99]

The debate over these two conflicting positions has flared up time and again in different countries, and no reconciliation appears yet to be in sight.[100] A fitting example is provided by some of the recent publications. On the one side, there is the symposium edited by Donald Carson, *From Sabbath to Lord's Day* (1982) and Willy Rordorf's *Sunday: The History of the Day of Rest and Worship in the Earliest Centuries of the Christian Church* (1968). Both of these studies espouse the thesis that seventh-day Sabbath keeping is not a creation ordinance binding upon Christians but a Jewish institution annulled by Christ.[101] Consequently, Sunday is not the Christian Sabbath, but is an exclusive Christian creation, introduced to commemorate Christ's resurrection through the Lord's Supper celebration.[102]

By severing all ties with the Sabbath commandment, Rordorf follows the Lutheran tradition in reducing Sunday to an *hour* of worship, which could be scheduled in accordance with the demand of modern life. The practical implications of this position are obvious. If fully carried out, it could prove to be "the death certificate of Sunday,"[103] since in time even the hour of worship could readily be squeezed out of the hectic schedule of modern life.

On the other side, there is the study of Roger T. Beckwith and William Stott, *This is the Day: The Biblical Doctrine of the Christian Sunday* (1978), which follows the Reformed tradition by defending the Sabbath as a creation ordinance accepted and clarified by Christ. The apostles allegedly used the Sabbath to frame Sunday as their new day of rest and worship.[104] Consequently they conclude that "in the light of the New Testament as a whole, the Lord's day can be clearly seen to be a Christian Sabbath — a New Testament fulfillment to which the Old Testament Sabbath points forward."[105] The practical implication of their conclusions is that Sunday should be observed not merely as an hour of worship but as "a whole day, set apart to be a holy festival . . . for worship, rest and works of mercy."[106]

CLOSING OBSERVATIONS

The above survey has shown that the controversy over the origin and nature of the Sabbath has been largely inspired by the need that arose after the Constantinian Sunday Law of 321, to give a biblical sanction to the observance of Sunday as the new Christian day of rest and worship. The absence of any command of Christ or the apostles to observe Sunday made it necessary for church leaders to defend its observance by appealing to the fourth commandment. This was done, as we have seen, by arbitrarily and artificially differentiating between the moral and ceremonial aspects of the Sabbath commandment. The *moral* aspect was understood to be the creation ordinance to observe one-day-in-seven, whereas the *ceremonial* was interpreted to be the Mosaic specification of the seventh-day.

The different understanding of the relationship between the *moral* and *ceremonial* aspects of the Sabbath commandment has resulted in two different historical views of Sunday keeping. On the one hand, the Catholic and Lutheran traditions have emphasized the alleged *ceremonial* aspect of the fourth commandment, which was supposedly abolished by Christ. Consequently, they have largely divorced Sunday keeping from the Sabbath commandment, treating Sunday as an ecclesiastical institution ordained primarily to enable the laity to attend weekly the Mass or the divine service. On the other hand, the churches of the Reformed tradition have given prominence to the *moral* aspect of the Sabbath commandment, viewing the observance of a day of rest and worship as a creation ordinance for humanity. Consequently, they have promoted Sunday keeping as the legitimate substitution and continuation of the Old Testament Sabbath.

The confusion generated by this controversy has undoubtedly contributed to the secularization of Sunday. The reason is simple. Those Christians who divorce Sunday from the Old Testament Sabbath—viewing the latter as a ceremonial, Mosaic institution abrogated by Christ—see nothing wrong in pursuing on Sunday such secular activities as buying, selling, dancing, playing, or watching a ball game, doing maintenance or repair work around the house. On the other hand, those Christians who view Sunday as the legitimate substitution of the Sabbath are hard pressed to justify its observance on the basis of the Sabbath commandment, since the latter enjoins the observance of the seventh day and not of the first day. The result of this confusion is that most Christians today, as in the past, have no clear ideas why they should observe Sunday as a holy day, and consequently they end up treating it as a holiday.

How can the prevailing confusion regarding the justification for Sunday keeping be resolved? My proposal, which to most Sunday-keeping Christians may appear radical and unacceptable, is rather simple. It consists of three main steps.

First, it is necessary to recognize that the historical attempt to ground Sunday keeping on the alleged *moral* aspect of the Sabbath commandment represents a well-meaning but unwarranted interpretation. The Sabbath commandment specifies the observance of the seventh day and not of one-day-in-seven.

Second, it is important to understand the historical process that led to the adoption of Sunday and the abandonment of the Sabbath. In my dissertation (*From Sabbath to Sunday*) I endeavored to identify some of the political, social, pagan-religious, and Christian contributary factors. A major political factor was Emperor Hadrian's policy (about 135) of radical suppression of the Jewish religion in general and of Sabbath keeping in particular. These circumstances, as well as the conflict between Jews and Christians, encouraged the development of a "Christian" theology of separation from and contempt for the Jews. A practical outcome of this development was the substitution of weekly Sunday and Easter Sunday for characteristic Jewish festivals such as the Sabbath and Passover.

A recognition of the factors that influenced the adoption of Sunday observance instead of the Sabbath is essential before considering the implementation of the third step, namely, the recovery of the seventh-day Sabbath as a creation ordinance for all humankind, Jews and Christians alike. Such a recovery should be facilitated by the fact that our quest has shown that the creation origin of the Sabbath is clearly taught in the Scripture and has been widely accepted both in Jewish and Christian history. Such a recovery could have far-reaching positive effects. It would bring Jews and Christians closer together by eliminating the negative Jewish stigma that has been historically associated with seventh-day Sabbath keeping, as well as the radical distinction and discontinuity between the Old and New Testaments maintained by many. Further, a recovery of the Sabbath would provide Christians with a biblical meaning, authority, and conviction for observing the Sabbath as a holy day rather than a holiday. Finally, a recovery of the Sabbath can offer a basis for a cosmic faith, since the themes of the Sabbath encompass creation, redemption, and final restoration; the past, the present, and the future; humanity, nature, and God; this world and the world to come.

We no longer live in the *perfect beginning* but in an *imperfect middle:* an age characterized by injustice, greed, violence, corruption, suffering, and death. In the midst of the chaos and disorder of our age, we seek for certainty, meaning, and hope. A recovery of the Sabbath can bring us weekly reassurance and hope. It reassures us that our origin and destiny are rooted in God. It provides us with a sense of continuity with the past and a hope for the future. It invites us to rest in God while living in a restless *middle* and waiting for that endless rest and peace that awaits the people of God (Hebrews 4:9).

NOTES

1. Quoted by Augusto Segre, "Il Sabato nella Storia Ebraica," in *L'uomo nella Bibbia e nelle culture ad essa contemporanee* (Brescia: Paideia, 1975) 166.

2. Quoted by R. H. Martin, *The Day: A Manual on the Christian Sabbath* (Pittsburgh: National Reform Association, 1933) 184.

3. See the informative surveys by T. J. Meek, "The Sabbath in the Old Testament," *Journal of Biblical Literature* 33 (1914) 201-12; E. G. Kraeling, "The Present Status of the Sabbath question," *American Journal of Semitic Languages and Literature* 49 (1932-33) 218-28; R. North, "The Derivation of Sabbath," *Biblica* 36 (1955) 182-201; R. de Vaux, *Ancient Israel: Its Life and Institutions* (London: Darton, Longman & Todd, 1961) 476-79; C. W. Kiker, "The Sabbath in the Old Testament Cult" (Th.D. diss., Southern Baptist Theological Seminary, 1968) 5-39; W. Rordorf, *Sunday: The History of the Day of Rest and Worship in the Earliest Centuries of the Christian Church* (Philadelphia: Westminster, 1968) 19-24; N.-E. Andreasen, *The Old Testament Sabbath* (SBLDS 7; Missoula, MT: Scholars Press, 1972) 1-16; N. Negretti, *Il Settimo Giorno* (Rome: Gregorian University Press, 1973) 31-108; G. Robinson, *The Origin and Development of the Old Testament Sabbath* (Hamburg: Hawthorne, 1975) 6-24.

4. G. Lotz appears to have been the first to seek the origin of the Sabbath from Babylonian sources in *Questiones de historia Sabbati libri duo* (Leipzig, 1883) 57, 58, 106).

5. For a fuller treatment of these theories, see Samuele Bacchiocchi, *Divine Rest for Human Restlessness: A Theological Study of the Good News of the Sabbath for Today* (Rome: Gregorian University Press, 1980) 24–41.

6. The Kenite theory is traced back to Abraham Kuenen, *The Religion of Israel* (1874) 274. It has been revived by Bernardus D. Eerdmans, "Der Sabbath," in *Vom Alten Testament: Festschrift Karl Marti,* No. 41 (Leiden: Universitaire Pers, 1925) 79–83; Karl Budde, "The Sabbath and the Week: Their Origin and Their Nature," *Journal of Theological Studies* 30 (1930) 1–15; H. H. Rowley, "Moses and the Decalogue," *Bulletin of the John Rylands Library* 34 (1951–52) 81–118; L. Koehler, "Der Dekalog," *Theologische Rundschau* 1 (1929) 181.

7. The identification of Sakkuth and Kaiwan as names of Saturn has been challenged recently by Stanley Gevirtz, "A New Look at an Old Crux: Amos 5:26," *Journal of Biblical Literature* 87 (1968) 267–76; cf. William W. Hallo, "New Moons and Sabbaths: A Case-study in the Contrastive Approach," *Hebrew Union College Annual* 48 (1977) 15.

8. On the question of the origin of the planetarian week, see Bacchiocchi, *From Sabbath to Sunday: A Historical Investigation of the Rise of Sunday Observance in Early Christianity* (Rome: Gregorian University Press, 1977) 241–47.

9. Jacob Z. Lauterbach points out that "when in later Jewish works an astrological connection between Saturn and the Jews is mentioned, it is emphasized that the Jews observe the Sabbath rather to demonstrate their independence of Saturn, that they need no help whatever from him, but rely on God alone" (*Rabbinic Essays* [Cincinnati: Hebrew Union College Press, 1951] 438). It is noteworthy also that Jewish rabbis called Saturn *Shabbti,* which means "the star of the Sabbath." This name represents, as noted by Hutton Webster, "not a naming of the day after the planet, but a naming of the planet after the day" (*Rest Days: A Study in Early Law and Morality* [New York: McMillan, 1916] 244).

10. See Kraeling, "Sabbath Question," 218–19; J. J. Stamm and M. E. Andrew, *The Ten Commandments in Recent Research* (London: SCM, 1967) 91–92; de Vaux, *Ancient Israel,* 480.

11. See George Smith, *Assyrian Discoveries* (London, 1883) 12. Webster suggests that the original calendar possibly belonged to the age of Hammurabi (*Rest Days,* 223). Hallo also argues that the Neo-Babylonian lunar festival represents a survival of the older Sumerian tradition ("New Moons," 8). The nineteenth day has been taken to represent the forty-ninth day from the first of the preceding month, or seven evil days—*ume lemnuti.* However, since a lunar month lasts just over twenty-nine days, the "weekly" cycle between the last evil day (twenty-eighth day) and the first evil day (seventh day) of the next month would be eight or nine days, depending on whether the last month was of twenty-nine or thirty days.

12. Each quarter of the moon represents 7¾ days, which makes it impossible to obtain an exact cycle of seven days.

13. See Paul O. Bostrup, *Den israelitiske Sabbats: Oprindelse og Karakter i Foreksilsk* (Copenhagen, 1923) 50–55.

14. The period between two successive new moons (lunation) averages 29 days, 12 hours, 44 minutes, and 2.8 seconds.

15. It is generally recognized that the Babylonian evil days had a religious, but not a civil, function. Webster points out that "nothing in the cuneiform records indicates that the Babylonians ever employed them for civil purposes. These periods seem to have had solely a religious significance" (*Rest Days,* 230). Similarly, Siegfried H. Horn remarks, "The cuneiform records do not say that anyone should rest on those five particular days of the month, or refrain from work, or worship the gods. They simply admonish certain persons—kings, physicians, et cetera—to avoid doing certain specified things on those five 'evil days'" ("Was the Sabbath Known in Ancient Babylonia? Archeology and the Sabbath," *The Sabbath Sentinel* [December 1979] 21-22). In a Neo-Babylonian calendar and in its Kassite original published by Rene Labat, the majority of the days are unfavorable and multiples of seven can be either good or bad ("Un calendrier cassite de jours fastes et nefastes," *Sumer* 8 [1952] 27; idem, "Un almanach babylonien," *Journal of Theological Studies* 30 (1930) 6.

16. Karl Budde notes that there are frequent instances in cuneiform texts of the "division of the month into six parts, involving a five-day week" ("The Sabbath and the Week," 6).

17. E. A. Speiser, "The Creation Epic," in *Ancient Near Eastern Texts,* ed. J. B. Pritchard (Princeton: Princeton University Press, 1950) 68. Cf. W. F. Lambert and A. R. Millard, *Atra-hasis: The Babylonian Story of the Flood* (Oxford: Oxford University Press, 1969) 56f.; Theophilus G. Pinches, "Sabattu, the Babylonian Sabbath," *Proceedings of the Society of Biblical Archeology* 26 (1904) 51-56.

18. For examples, see *Cuneiform Texts from Babylonian Tablets in the British Museum* XVIII, 17c d.

19. M. Jastrow argues that *sabattu* was primarily a day of pacification of a deity's anger and the idea of rest applies to gods rather than to humans (*Hebrew and Babylonian Traditions* [New York: Block, 1914] 134–49).

20. This theory was initially developed by Johannes Meinhold, *Sabbath und Woche im Alten Testament* (Göttingen, 1905) 3ff. In an early study (*Sabbat und Sonntag* [Leipzig, 1909] 9, 34), Meinhold attributed the change from monthly full-moon day to the weekly Sabbath to Ezekiel. In a later essay, however ("Zur Sabbat-frage," *ZAW* 48 [1930] 128–32), he places the process in postexilic times, in conjunction with Nehemiah's reforms. This theory has been adopted with some modifications by several scholars. See Samuel H. Hooke, *The Origin of the Early Semitic Ritual* (London: Oxford University Press, 1938) 58–59; Adolphe Lods, *Israel: From its Beginning to the Middle of the Eighth Century* (New York: Knopf, 1932) 438; Sigmund Mowinckel, *Le Decalogue* (Paris: Librairie Felix Alcan, 1927) 90; Robert H. Pfeiffer, *Religion in the Old Testament: The History of a Spiritual Triumph* (New York: Harper & Brothers, 1961) 92–93.

21. This is true also of the Jewish month names, which, as N. H. Tur-Sinai points out, do not follow the Babylonian ones ("Sabbat und Woche," *Bibliotheca Orientalis* 8 [1951] 14).

22. Budde registers his regret for such an unfounded theory by pointing out that there is not a "single word in Ezekiel which prescribes a new mode of celebration

for the Sabbath. On the contrary Ezekiel complains constantly (20:12ff.; 22:8, 26; 23:38; 44:24) that for long years . . . Israel has failed to observe the Sabbath in the old sense" ("The Sabbath and the Week," 9); see also Kraeling, "Sabbath Question," 222.

23. Friedrich Delitzsch, *Babel und Bibel* (Leipzig, 1903) 38. Cf. A. S. Kapelrud, "The Number Seven in Ugaritic Texts," *Vetus Testamentum* 18 (1968) 494–99; H.-J. Kraus, *Worship in Israel* (Richmond: John Knox, 1966) 85–87; Negretti, *Il Settimo Giorno*, 31–109; S. E. Loewenstamm, "The Seven Day-Unit in Ugaritic Epic Literature," *Israel Exploration Journal* 15 (1965) 121–33.

24. *Ancient Near Eastern Texts*, 44, 94.

25. Horn, "Was the Sabbath Known," 21.

26. For example, J. Morgenstern confidently asserts, "All available evidence indicates unmistakably that the sabbath can have originated only in an agricultural environment. Actually the Hebrews became acquainted with the sabbath only after they had established themselves in Palestine and had settled down there alongside their Canaanite predecessors in the land, whom in some measure they displaced, and had borrowed from them the techniques of tilling the soil, and with this various institutions of agricultural civilization, of which the sabbath was one" ("Sabbath" in *The Interpreter's Dictionary of the Bible* [ed. G. A. Buttrick; Nashville: Abingdon, 1962] 4:135).

27. Rordorf articulates this view emphatically but not convincingly (*Sunday*, 12).

28. The reason Rordorf gives for this transformation is "the fact that from the time when the Jews were no longer in their own country they no longer had any slaves, and so they scarcely knew what to make of the motivation of Sabbath observance on the ground of social ethics" (*Sunday*, 18).

29. See above n. 20.

30. Kraus, *Worship*, 87; Morgenstern, "Sabbath," 139; M. Jastrow, "The Original Character of the Hebrew Sabbath," *American Journal of Theology* 2 (1898) 324.

31. See Rordorf, *Sunday*, 18; Eduard Lohse, "Sabbaton," in *Theological Dictionary of the New Testament* (Grand Rapids: Eerdmans, 1971) 7:5.

32. That Ezekiel is not transforming the Sabbath from a social to a religious institution is indicated also by the fact that he associates the profanation of the Sabbath with the disregard for social obligations toward parents, strangers, and the underprivileged (Ezekiel 22:7–8). The social and religious aspects of the Sabbath are viewed by the prophet as interdependent.

33. N.-E. A. Andreasen underscores this point: "To be sure, the prophet Ezekiel who lived in captivity during this period mentions the Sabbath repeatedly, but he nearly always speaks of it in connection with the Jerusalem temple and its holy things (Ezekiel 22:8, 26; 23:38), or in connection with the future temple for which he fervently hoped (Ezekiel 44:24; 45:17; 46:1–4, 12)" (*Rest and Redemption* [Berrien Springs, MI: Andrews University Press, 1978] 29).

34. Kiker, "Sabbath in the Old Testament Cult," 67–187; Robinson, *Origin*, 6–24.

35. *Karl Barth, Church Dogmatics* (Edinburgh: T. & T. Clark, 1956) vol. 3., part 2, p. 62.

36. C. A. Keller and G. Wehmeier, "brk segnen," in *Theologisches Handwörterbuch zum Alten Testament* (Munich: Kaiser, 1971) 1:353-76.

37. See S. R. Driver, *The Book of Genesis* (London: SCM, 1943) 18; J. Skinner, *Genesis* (Edinburgh: T. & T. Clark, 1930) 38; A. Simpson, "The Book of Genesis," in *The Interpreter's Bible,* ed. G. A. Buttrick (Nashville: Abingdon, 1952) 1:490.

38. F. J. Helfneyer, "oth," *Theological Dictionary of the Old Testament* (Grand Rapids: Eerdmans, 1977—) 1:171.

39. Numerous scholars recognize that Christ's saying alludes to the original (creation) function of the Sabbath. For example, Charles E. Erdman, *The Gospel of Mark* (1945) 56; H. B. Swete, *The Gospel According to St. Mark* (London: McMillan, 1902) 49; J. A. Schep, "Lord's Day Keeping from the Practical and Pastoral Point of View," in *The Sabbath-Sunday Problem* (Geelong: Hilltop, 1968) 142-43; Roger T. Beckwith and W. Stott, *This is the Day: The Biblical Doctrine of the Christian Sunday in its Jewish and Early Christian Setting* (London: Marshall, Morgan and Scott, 1978) 11; Francis Nigel Lee, *The Covenantal Sabbath* (London: Lord's Day Observance Society, 1966) 29.

40. Rordorf, *Sunday,* 63.

41. For my analysis of the meaning of the rest in Hebrews, see *Divine Rest,* 137-40.

42. See above nn. 26 and 27.

43. *Didascalia Apostolorum. The Syriac Version Translated and Accompanied by the Verona Latin Fragments,* ed. R. Hugh Connolly (Oxford: Clarendon, 1929) 233.

44. Athanasius, *De sabbatis et circumcisione* 4 (J. Migne, *Patrologia graeca* [Paris, 1857-66] vol. 28, col. 138 B.C.). For additional examples and discussion, see Bacchiocchi, *Sabbath to Sunday,* 273-78.

45. *The Ante-Nicene Fathers,* ed. A. Roberts and J. Donaldson (Edinburgh, 1866-72) 7:469.

46. *Ante-Nicene Fathers,* 7:474; cf. 2.36.

47. Jean Danielou, *The Bible and Liturgy* (South Bend, IN: University of Notre Dame Press, 1956) 276.

48. Trans. Henry Bettenson (Oxford: Oxford University Press, 1972) 1090.

49. The fact that in the creation story there is no mention of "evening . . . morning" for the seventh day is interpreted by Augustine as signifying the eternal nature of the Sabbath rest both in the mystical and in the eschatological sense.

50. Cf. *Sermon* 38 (J. P. Migne, *Patrologia latina* [Paris, 1844-64] vol. 58, col. 1242); *De Genesis ad litteram* 4, 13 (Migne, *Patrologia latina,* vol. 34, col. 305).

51. In his *Epistula 55 ad Ianuarium 22,* Augustine explains: "Therefore of the ten commandments the only one we are to observe spiritually is that of the Sabbath, because we recognize it to be symbolic and not to be celebrated through physical inactivity" (Corpus scriptorum ecclesiasticorum latinorum 34:194). One wonders how it is possible to retain the Sabbath as the symbol of mystical and eschatological rest in God while denying the basis of such a symbol, namely, its literal Sabbath rest experience. For a discussion of this contradiction, see below.

52. Eugippius (ca. 455-535), for example, quotes *verbatim* from Augustine, *Adversus Faustum* 16, 29 (*Thesaurus* 66 [Migne, *Patrologia latina,* vol. 62, col. 685]). Cf. Bede (ca. 673-735), *In Genesim* 2.3 (Corpus christianorum. Series latina 118A, 35); Rabanus Maurus (ca. 784-856), *Commentaria in Genesim* 1.9 (Migne, *Patrologia latina,* vol. 107, col. 465); Peter Lombard (ca. 1100-1160), *Sententiarum libri quatuor* 3.37.2 (Migne, *Patrologia latina,* vol. 192, col. 831).

53. Migne, *Patrologia graeca,* vol. 53, col. 89.

54. Migne, *Patrologia latina,* vol. 198, col. 1065. On the development of the principle of "one day in seven," see discussion in Wilhelm Thomas, "Sabbatarianism," in *Encyclopedia of the Lutheran Church,* ed. Julius Bodensieck (Minneapolis: Augsburg, 1965) 3:2090.

55. Thomas Aquinas, *Summa Theologica,* part I-II, Q. 100, 3, 1947, p. 1039 (trans. Fathers of the English Dominican Province; New York: Benziger, 1947).

56. Aquinas subdivided the Mosaic law into moral, ceremonial, and judicial precepts. The moral precepts of the decalogue are viewed as precepts also of the natural law, that is to say, they are precepts binding upon all because they are discoverable by all through human reason without the aid of special revelation. See Aquinas, *Summa,* part I-II, Q. 100, 1 and Q. 100, 3, pp. 1037, 1039.

57. Aquinas, *Summa,* part I-II, Q. 100, 5, p. 1042.

58. Ibid.

59. Aquinas, *Summa,* part I-II, Q. 107, 3, p. 1111.

60. See L. L. McReavy, "'Servile Work': The Evolution of the Present Sunday Law," *Clergy Review* 9 (1935) 279ff. A brief survey of the development of Sunday laws and casuistry is provided by Paul K. Jewett, *The Lord's Day: A Theological Guide to the Day of Worship* (Grand Rapids: Eerdmans, 1971) 128-69. A good example of the adoption of Aquinas's moral-ceremonial distinction can be found in the *Catechism of the Council of Trent.*

61. Karlstadt's conception of the Sabbath rest contains a strange combination of mystical and legalistic elements. Basically he viewed the day as a time to abstain from work in order to be contrite over one's sins. For a clear analysis of his views, see Gordon Rupp, *Patterns of Reformation* (London: Epworth, 1969) 123-30; idem, "Andrew Karlstadt and Reformation Puritanism," *Journal of Theological Studies* 10 (1959) 308-26; cf. Daniel Augsburger, "Calvin and the Mosaic Law" (Doctoral diss., Strasbourg University, 1976) 248-49; J. N. Andrews and L. R. Conradi, *History of the Sabbath and First Day of the Week* (Washington, DC: Review and Herald, 1912) 652-55.

62. Luther, *Against the Heavenly Prophets, Luther's Works* (1958) 40:93. A valuable study of Luther's views regarding the Sabbath is to be found in Richard Muller, *Adventisten-Sabbat-Reformation* (Studia Theologica Lundensia; Lund, 1979) 32-60.

63. Luther, *Treatise on Good Works* (1520), *Selected Writings of Martin Luther* (St. Louis: Concordia Publishing House, 1957) 174.

64. *Concordia or Book of Concord, The Symbols of the Evangelical Lutheran Church* (St. Louis: Concordia Publishing House, 1957) 1974.

65. Ibid.

66. *Augsburg Confession* (*Concordia or Book of Concord,* p. 25); cf. Philip

Schaff, *The Creeds of Christendom* (New York: Harper, 1919) 3:69.

67. Winton V. Solberg, *Redeem the Time* (Cambridge, MA: Harvard University Press, 1977) 15-19; A. G. Dickens, *The English Reformation* (London: Batsford, 1964) 34; George H. Williams, *The Radical Reformation* (Leiden: Brill, 1962) 38-58, 81-84.

68. See n. 70 below.

69. A valuable survey of the ideas and influences of these Sabbatarians is provided by G. F. Hasel, "Sabbatarian Anabaptists," *Andrews University Seminary Studies* 5 (1967) 101-21; 6 (1968) 19-28. On the existence of Sabbath keepers in various countries, see Andrews and Conradi, *History of the Sabbath*, 633-716. Cf. Muller, *Adventism*, 110-29.

70. In a list of eleven sects by Stredovsky of Bohemia, "Sabbatarians" are listed in the third place after Lutherans and Calvinists. The list is reprinted by Josef Beck, ed., *Die Geschichts-Bücher der Widertaufer in Osterreich-Ungarn* (Fontes Rerum Austriacarum; Vienna, 1883) 43:74. For an analysis of this and three other lists, see Hasel, "Sabbatarian Anabaptists," 101-6. Cf. Henry A. DeWind, "A Sixteenth Century Description of Religious Sects in Austerlitz, Moravia," *Mennonite Quarterly Review* (1955) 51; Williams, *Radical Reformation*, 676, 726, 732, 848, 408-10, 229, 257, 512.

71. Desiderius Erasmus, "Amabili ecclesiae concordia," *Opera Omnia* V:505-6; trans. Hasel, "Sabbatarian Anabaptists," 107.

72. Luther reports: "In our time there is a foolish group of people who call themselves Sabbatarians [Sabbather] and say one should keep the Sabbath according to Jewish manner and custom" (*D. Martin Luthers Werke*, Weimer ed. 42:520). In his *Lectures on Genesis* (4:46) Luther furnishes similar information: "I hear that even now in Austria and Moravia certain Judaizers urge both the Sabbath and circumcision; if they should boldly go on, not being admonished by the work of God, they certainly might do much harm" (cited in Andrews and Conradi, *History of the Sabbath*, 640).

73. J. G. Walch, ed., *Dr. Martin Luthers sammtliche Schriften* (1910), 20:1828ff. Cf. D. Zscharnack, "Sabbatharier," *Die Religion in Geschichte und Gegenwart* (1931) 5:8.

74. On Oswald Glait, see Muller, *Adventisten*, 117-25. Cf. Hasel, "Sabbatarian Anabaptists," 107-21.

75. On Andreas Fisher, see Muller, *Adventisten*, 125-30; Petr Ratkos, "Die Anfänge des Wiedertaufertums in der Slowakei," in *Aus 500 Jahren deutsch-tschechoslowakischer Geschichte*, ed. Karl Obermann (Berlin: Rutten & Loening, 1958) 41-59. See also the recent study by Daniel Liechty, *Andreas Fischer and the Sabbatarian Anabaptists* (Scottdale, PA: Herald, 1988).

76. Caspar Schwenckfeld's refutation of Glait's book is found in *Corpus Schwenckfeldianorum*, ed. S. D. Hartranft and E. E. Johnson (Leipzig: Breitkopf & Hartel, 1907) 4:451ff.

77. Ibid., 458; the translation is by Hasel, "Sabbatarian Anabaptists," 119.

78. *Corpus Schwenckfeldianorum*, 491.

79. Ibid., 457-58.

80. An Anabaptist (Hutterian) chronicle provides a moving account of Glait's

final days (*Die älteste Chronik der Hutterischen Brüder,* ed. A. J. F. Zieglschmid [1943] 259, 260, 266; trans. Hasel, "Sabbatarian Anabaptists," 114–15).

81. A brief historical survey of seventh-day Sabbath keepers from the fifteenth to the seventeenth century is found in Andrews and Conradi, *History of the Sabbath,* 632–759. A more comprehensive and critical study of Sabbath keeping through the ages is the symposium *The Sabbath in Scriptures and History,* ed. Kenneth A. Strand (Washington, DC: Review and Herald Publishing Corporation, 1982). About twenty scholars have contributed chapters to this study.

82. R. J. Bauckham, "Sabbath and Sunday in the Protestant Tradition," *From Sabbath to Lord's Day: A Biblical, Historical and Theological Investigation,* ed. D. A. Carson (Grand Rapids: Zondervan, 1982) 333.

83. See W. Y. Whitley, *A History of British Baptists* (London: Kingsgate, 1932) 83–86; A. C. Underwood, *A History of the English Baptists* (1947) chaps. 2–5.

84. Seventh Day Baptist General Conference, *Seventh Day Baptists in Europe and America* (Plainfield, NJ, 1910) 1:127, 133, 153; see also Winton V. Solberg, *Redeem the Time,* 278.

85. Raymond F. Cottrell notes: "The extent to which pioneer Seventh-day Adventists were indebted to Seventh Day Baptists for their understanding of the Sabbath is reflected in the fact that throughout the first volume [of *Advent Review and Sabbath Herald*] over half of the material was reprinted from Seventh Day Baptist publications" ("Seventh Day Baptists and Adventists: A Common Heritage," *Spectrum* 9 [1977] 4).

86. The Church of God Seventh Day traces its origin back to the Millerite movement. The 1987 *Directory of Sabbath-Observing Groups,* published by The Bible Sabbath Association, lists over 180 different denominations or groups observing the seventh-day Sabbath.

87. A comprehensive study of Calvin's understanding of the fourth commandment is provided by Daniel Augsburger, "Calvin and the Mosaic Law," 248, 284.

88. John Calvin, *Commentaries on the First Book of Moses Called Genesis,* trans. John King (Grand Rapids: Eerdmans, 1948) 106.

89. Ibid.

90. John Calvin, *Institutes of the Christian Religion,* trans. Henry Beveridge (Grand Rapids: Eerdmans, 1972) 1:343.

91. Ibid.

92. John Calvin, *Commentaries on the Four Last Books of Moses Arranged in the Form of a Harmony,* trans. Charles William Bingham (Grand Rapids: Eerdmans, 1950) 435–36.

93. Zacharias Ursinus, *The Summe of Christian Religion* (Oxford, 1587) 955.

94. On the enormous influence of Nicolas Bownde's book, *The Doctrine of the Sabbath,* see Winton U. Solberg, *Redeem the Time,* 55–58.

95. In the 163rd session of the Synod of Dort (1619) a commission of Dutch theologians approved a six-point document in which the traditional ceremonial/moral distinctions are made (Gerard Brandt, *The History of the Reformation and Other Ecclesiastical Transactions in and about the Low Countries* [London, 1722] 3:320; cf. 3:28–29, 289–90).

The Westminster Confession, chapter 21, article 7, reads: "As it is of the law of nature, that in general, a due proportion of time be set apart for the worship of God; so, in His Word, by a positive, moral, and perpetual commandment, binding all men in all ages, he hath particularly appointed one day in seven for a Sabbath, to be kept holy unto him: which, from the beginning of the world to the resurrection of Christ, was the last day of the week; and, from the resurrection of Christ was changed into the first day of the week" (Philip Schaff, *The Creeds of the Christendom,* 3:648-49).

96. Donald A. Carson, ed., *From Sabbath to Lord's Day,* 66-67.

97. R. J. Bauckham, "Sabbath and Sunday," 322.

98. Willem Teellinck, *De Rusttijdt: Ofte Tractaet van d'onderhoudinge des Christenlijken Rust Dachs [The Rest Time: Or a Treatise on the Observance of the Christian Sabbath]* (Rotterdam, 1622). William Ames provides a theoretical basis for Sunday observance (*Medulla Theologica* [Amsterdam, 1623; trans. John D. Eusden, *The Marrow of Theology* (1968) 287-300]). Antonius Walaeus, *Dissertatio de Sabbatho, seu Vero Sensu atque Usu Quarti Praecepti [Dissertation on the Sabbath, Or the True Meaning and Use of the Fourth Commandment]* (Leiden, 1628).

99. An earlier treatise against Sabbatarianism was produced by Jacobus Burs, *Threnos, or Lamentation Showing the Causes of the Pitiful Condition of the Country and the Desecration of the Sabbath* (Tholen, 1627). Andreas Rivetus refuted Gomarus's contention that the Sabbath was a Mosaic ceremony abrogated by Christ in his *Praelectiones [Lectures]* (1632). Gomarus replies with the voluminous *Defensio Investigationis Originis Sabbati [A Defense of the Investigation into the Origin of the Sabbath]* (Leiden, 1633).

100. The controversy flared up again in Holland in the 1650s. Gisbertus Voetius and Johannes Cocceius were the two opposing leaders in the new round. For a brief account, see Solberg, *Redeem the Time,* 200.

101. Rordorf's book was first published in 1962 in German. Since then it has been translated into French, English, and Spanish. Its influence is evidenced by the many and different responses it has generated.

102. Rordorf's denial of any connection between Sunday and the fourth commandment can be traced historically in the writings of numerous anti-Sabbatarian theologians, such as Luther (*Treatise on Good Works; Concordia or Book of Concord*); William Tyndale, *An Answer to Sir Thomas More's Dialogue* (1531), ed. Henry Walter (Cambridge, 1850) 97-98; the formulary of faith of the Church of England known as *The Institution of A Christian Man* (1537); Franciscus Gomarus (*Defensio Investigationis*); Francis White, *A Treatise of the Sabbath-Day: Concerning a Defence of the Orthodox Doctrine of the Church of England against Sabbatarian Novelty* (London, 1636); James A. Hessey, *Sunday: Its Origin, History, and Present Obligation* (London, 1866); C. S. Mosna, *Storia della domenica dalle origini fino agli inizi del V. secolo* (Rome: Gregorian University Press, 1969); *From Sabbath to Lord's Day,* ed. D. A. Carson.

103. This concern is expressed, for example, by P. Falsioni, in *Rivista Pastorale Liturgica* (1967) 311, 229, 97, 98; (1966) 549-51.

104. See Beckwith, *This is the Day,* 26; cf. pp. 2-12.

105. Ibid., 45-46. Beckwith and Stott's view of the Sabbath as an unchanging

creation ordinance upon which the observance of Sunday rests can be traced historically in the writings of theologians such as Aquinas (partly; see n. 55 above); Calvin (partly; see nn. 88, 90, 92 above); Richard Hooker, *Laws of Ecclesiastical Polity* (Cambridge, MA: Belknap Press of Harvard University, 1957) V:70, 3; Nicholas Bownde [Bound], *Doctrine of the Sabbath;* William Teellinck, William Ames, and Antonius Walaeus (see n. 98 above); formularies of faith such as the *Westminster Confession* and the Synod of Dort (see n. 95 above); E. W. Hengstenberg, *Über den Tag des Herrn* (1852); recently by J. Francke, *Van Sabbat naar Zondag* (Amsterdam: Van Bottenburg, 1973); Karl Barth, *Church Dogmatics* (Edinburgh: T. & T. Clark, 1956, 3:47-72; Paul K. Jewett, *The Lord's Day* (partly); Francis Nigel Lee, *Covenantal Sabbath.*

106. Beckwith and Stott, *This is the Day,* 141, 143.

8

SUNDAY: THE LORD'S DAY
AS A SABBATH – PROTESTANT
PERSPECTIVES ON THE SABBATH

John H. Primus
Calvin College

When John Pocklington, chaplain to the bishop of Lincoln in England, preached a sermon before the bishop in August 1635, he entitled it "Sunday No Sabbath."[1] The alternative for Pocklington, however, was not a Saturday Sabbath; his plea was for no Sabbath at all. He was, nevertheless, completely in favor of divine worship on Sunday. One could hardly expect otherwise from a chaplain to a bishop of the Church of England. Pocklington does not hesitate to call Sunday *dies Dominicus,* the Lord's Day, and he applauds the decision of the early church "that the first day of the weeke should be set apart for the religious and solemne service of God, because our Redeemer arose on that day. . . ." Sunday is a day when people should "leave all worldly businesse" and "betake themselves wholly to the Lord's service," and yet he asserts emphatically that Sunday is no Sabbath![2]

What then was Pocklington's concern? Part of his agenda was undoubtedly political, for in the 1630s the Puritans in England were mounting an offensive that was perceived to be an attack on both church and state and it was the Puritans who were increasingly identified with "Sabbatarian" notions.[3] They did not hesitate to call Sunday the New Testament Sabbath. They saw the Sabbath commandment in the Decalogue as essentially binding on the Christian church. This is what Pocklington disputed. He writes:

> we Christians are not commanded to observe the Sabbath after the letter by
> a strict rest, as did the Jews, nor the Lords Day after the maner of the Jewish
> Sabbath: for of all the ten Commandments, the third, which concerneth the

Sabbath . . . is to be understood figuratively. For this Commandement was given for no other end but onely for a signe.

Why then was he so insistent about worship on the Lord's Day? We keep that day, he says, "by vertue of Apostolical constitution and tradition of Holy Church, and not the Sabbath by force of the fourth Commandement," for that commandment is to be understood as *solutum*, that is, "dissolved." The Sabbath of the Decalogue is essentially a Jewish ceremony that has been fulfilled and ended in Christ, and "when the Sabbath lost his force it forfeited the name, therefore ought not so to be called: and so having lost both force and name, is become nothing at all but a meere Idoll."[4]

Chaplain Pocklington illustrates the subtlety of the differences within early Protestant thought on the Sunday–Lord's Day–Sabbath issue. Some said that the Lord's Day is the Christian Sabbath. Christians keep the Sabbath commandment on Sunday. Others said that the only relevance of the Sabbath commandment is that one day a week ought to be set aside for the worship of God. Christians should keep the commandment but not on the seventh day, and not even necessarily on the first day of the week. Finally, still others said that keeping a weekly day of rest and worship, although spiritually beneficial, is not obligatory at all. At one level, therefore, the differences among the early Reformers were purely theoretical in nature; they were differences of understanding and interpretation of the relationship between the Lord's Day and the Sabbath commandment. In practice nearly all Protestants were united, for they observed the Lord's Day as the weekly day of worship for Christians. Were the differences then truly significant, and are they still worth exploring today? They were, and are, at least in this sense: they reveal some distinctive theological emphases that are broadly characteristic of several important and lasting Protestant traditions. In an effort to expose these underlying emphases, let us go on to examine more carefully the Sabbath views of Luther, Calvin, and the English Puritans. Let us, finally, consider some contemporary Protestant approaches as well.

I

When Martin Luther in his Small Catechism answers the question about what it means to remember the Sabbath day to keep it holy, his answer is surprising for it seems not to deal with the Sabbath question at all. He says that the Sabbath commandment means this: "We should fear and love God, and so we should not despise his Word and the preaching of the same, but deem it holy and gladly hear and learn it."[5] Luther simply uses the commandment as a springboard from which to launch an admonition about one of his favorite themes: the Word of God and its proclamation.

When he hears the Sabbath commandment his mind leaps to a single thought: communal worship centered in the Word of God. For Luther, this is the gospel intent and New Testament application of the law of the Sabbath. He expands on this interpretation in his Large Catechism. There Luther says that, as far as the "outward observance" of the Sabbath commandment is concerned, it was "given to the Jews alone." In the Old Testament era, God's people were to abstain from work "so that both man and beast might be refreshed." In this "literal and outward sense," the Sabbath "does not concern us Christians."[6] It is one of those Old Testament ordinances from which Christians have been set free in Christ. Elsewhere, in a discussion of the proper date for Easter, Luther says, "Moses is dead and buried by Christ, and days and seasons are not to be lords over Christians, but rather Christians are lords over days and seasons, free to fix them as they will or as seems convenient to them. For Christ made all things free when he abolished Moses."[7]

Christian freedom was one of Luther's most passionately held beliefs, and the distinction between law and gospel his most fundamental hermeneutical device.[8] The Bible is filled with demands and promises, law and gospel, and the gospel frees us from the law. These themes are evident in his approach to the Sabbath commandment. He employs the medieval scholastic distinction between moral, judicial, and ceremonial law, and he expressly refers to the Sabbath commandment as "ceremonial." If Christians were to keep the Sabbath law of Moses *as a law of Moses,* then they would be required to keep all laws of the Old Testament, including circumcision itself. Luther's single-minded conviction about the freedom of the Christian from any semblance of legal, works salvation accounts for his radical reinterpretation of the Sabbath command. His fear of a Christian reentry into a religion of law is reflected also in these words: "If anywhere the day is made holy for the mere day's sake, then I order you to work on it, to ride on it, to feast on it, to do anything to remove this reproach from Christian liberty."[9]

Although the Sabbath commandment *as law* has been abrogated, it is not irrelevant for the Christian community. In fact, Luther offers what he calls a "Christian interpretation of what God requires in this commandment." It is what "nature" requires, and whatever nature requires must still be observed. Consequently, there is continuing social and cultic significance in the Sabbath, namely, that "man-servants and maid-servants who have attended to their work and trades the whole week long" should have a day for rest and refreshment, and that people be given the time and opportunity for public worship. Christians need periodically to assemble in order to "hear and discuss God's Word and then praise God with song and prayer." Luther insists that these exercises should be tied to no particular day, "for in itself no day is better than another." Ideally, in fact, worship should be performed daily, but "since this is more than the common people can do, at least one day in the week must be set apart for it." The church since ancient times has set Sunday apart for worship and "we should not change it," for it is good to establish common order and "unnecessary innovation" would only lead to disorder.[10]

His heavy emphasis on freedom from law does not keep Luther from declaring that "God insists upon a strict observance of this commandment." For Christians, however, this strict observance is part of the life of the gospel, not the law. It is defined in terms of the Word of God. As God once punished Sabbath-breakers for breaking the Sabbath rest, now he "will punish all who despise his Word and refuse to hear and learn it, especially at the times appointed." We do not sanctify that appointed day "when we sit behind the stove and refrain from external work, or deck ourselves with garlands and dress up in our best clothes, but . . . when we occupy ourselves with God's Word and exercise ourselves in it." The Sabbath commandment is "violated" by those who frivolously "neglect to hear God's Word or lie around in taverns dead drunk like swine," as well as by those who only appear to listen to the Word but do not do so seriously with an earnest attempt to learn and retain that Word. He issues a solemn warning that indicates how important his reinterpreted Sabbath remains: "It is the commandment of God, and he will require of you an accounting of how you have heard and learned and honored his Word."[11]

In the light of his abhorrence of special holy days, Luther makes some surprising statements in his commentary on Genesis 2:3, "So God blessed the seventh day and hallowed it, because on it God rested from all his work which he had done in creation."[12] He begins with a disclaimer: "But Moses says nothing here about man; he does not say in so many words that the Sabbath was commanded to man; he says that God blessed the Sabbath and that He sanctified it for himself." And yet, since God sanctified only the Sabbath and nothing else in heaven or earth, it is to be understood that "the seventh day in particular should be devoted to divine worship." That he sanctified the Sabbath means that it was "set aside for sacred purposes, or for the worship of God." There was a Sabbath in paradise. "Unspoiled human nature would have proclaimed the glory and the kindnesses of God in this way: on the Sabbath day men would have conversed about the immeasurable goodness of the Creator; they would have sacrificed; they would have prayed, etc." In this manner, humanity was to share in the eternal rest of God himself. There is gospel in the Sabbath of Genesis 2, for it was established that Christians might keep a sure hope of eternal life. All the things God wanted done on the Sabbath are signs of "another life after this life," for it is a day of special communion between God and humanity, a day "on which God speaks with us through His Word and we, in turn speak with Him through prayer and faith." The Genesis Sabbath points to "that rest of God which God, through the sanctifying of the Sabbath, wished not only to symbolize for men but also to grant to them." It is apparently in this sense that Luther can say that "the Sabbath command remains for the church," that is, because "it denotes that spiritual life is to be restored to us through Christ."

Then, as though to deflect the possible charge that he may be slipping into a sort of Sabbatarian exaltation of the day, Luther goes on to speculate that the original fall into sin occurred on the Sabbath. Adam was created on the sixth day, Eve toward the evening of that day while Adam was sleeping. Early on the seventh day God spoke with Adam, giving him directions for worship and forbidding him to eat of the tree of knowledge of good and evil. In other words, the Word of God came to Adam, and this "is the real purpose of the seventh day: that the Word of God be preached and heard." This conversation between Adam and God took place early on the seventh day along with divine orders about how to manage his household and "world affairs." But Satan was upset about all of this—about the new creation and the hope of eternal life which he had lost. He therefore approached Eve with the fatally effective temptation "perhaps about noon." Luther observes, "So it is wont to be to this day. Where the Word of God is, there Satan also makes it his business to spread falsehood and false teaching; for it grieves him that through the Word, we like Adam in Paradise, become citizens of heaven. And so he successfully incites Eve to sin." Luther is persuaded that all these events took place on the first Sabbath, on the very day intended for teaching, preaching, and reflection on the Word and the works of God!

It is Luther's passion for the Word of God, with, in turn, its themes of law and gospel and freedom, that controls his interpretation of the Sabbath commandment. The Word is the one holy thing in humanity's possession, and in it lies the power to give life and to sanctify all that is jaded by sin in this world.

> The Word of God is the true holy thing above all holy things. Indeed, it is the only one we Christians acknowledge and have. Though we had the bones of all the saints or all the holy and consecrated vestments gathered together in one heap, they could not help us in the slightest degree, for they are all dead things that can sanctify no one. But God's Word is the treasure that sanctifies all things. By it all the saints themselves have been sanctified. At whatever time God's Word is taught, preached, heard, read, or pondered, there the person, the day, and the work are sanctified by it, not on account of the external work but on account of the Word which makes us all saints. Accordingly, I constantly repeat that all our life and work must be guided by God's Word if they are to be God-pleasing or holy. Where that happens the commandment is in force and is fulfilled.[13]

II

In many ways, the interpretation of the Sabbath by the Genevan reformer John Calvin is similar to Luther's. He emphasizes, like Luther, the ceremonial character of the Sabbath commandment; he warns against a legalistic approach; and he avoids turning Sunday into a Christian Sabbath. Yet there are certain nuances that distinguish his view — seemingly small differences with nonetheless significant theological implications. In his *Institutes of the Christian Religion,* Calvin's opening statement on the Sabbath commandment reveals his fundamental theme, the centrality of grace. He writes, "The purpose of this commandment is that, being dead to our own inclinations and works, we should meditate on the Kingdom of God, and that we should practice this meditation in the ways established by him."[14] For Calvin as for Luther, salvation is the gracious act of a sovereign God. The Sabbath is given as a reminder of this grace, for it calls Christians to rest from their works. In Calvin's view, the call to a Sabbath rest is a call to abandon the works of the law as the basis for humanity's relationship to God, for that relationship is grounded in grace. Moreover, instead of making the Word the focus of the day's meditation, Calvin introduces the more cosmic, creational concept of the kingdom of God. At the center of Calvin's Sabbath stands the kingdom of God. The Sabbath can be seen as a symbol of God's rule, both in creation and in redemption.

Calvin agrees with Luther that the "outward keeping of the day" has been abolished with the coming of Christ. At the same time, there are a number of elements embedded in the Sabbath commandment that have continuing significance for the Christian community. Calvin's view of the Sabbath commandment is three-dimensional.

> First, under the repose of the seventh day the heavenly Lawgiver meant to represent to the people of Israel spiritual rest, in which believers ought to lay aside their own works to allow God to work in them. Secondly, he meant that there was to be a stated day for them to assemble to hear the law and perform the rites, or at least to devote it particularly to meditation upon his works, and thus through this remembrance to be trained in piety. Thirdly, he resolved to give a day of rest to servants and those who are under the authority of others, in order that they should have some respite from toil.

All three of these elements also appear in Luther, but the first is much more pronounced in Calvin. The Sabbath represents spiritual rest. In Christ, this element has been fulfilled so that there is, consequently, a diminished emphasis on precise Sabbath observance in the New Testament. Nevertheless, although the outward sign of the strict observance of a particular day has been abolished by Christ, the "inward reality" of the Sabbath remains for the Christian community. This inward reality is, once again, the reality of grace. "We must be wholly at rest," says Calvin, "that God may work in us; we must yield our will; we must resign our heart; we must give up all our fleshly desires. In short, we must rest from all activities of our own contriving, so that, having God working in us, we may repose in him as the apostle also teaches." Rest and repose are, however, a perpetual duty for the Christian, not restricted to one day in seven. It is a redemptive rest, an "eternal cessation" from dependence on works, that is symbolized by the Sabbath. As such it remains important for sanctified people, for it is a sign of God's covenant relationship, a "sign of God's separating of his faithful Church from all the rest of the world."

By the "ceremonial" element of the Sabbath Calvin apparently has reference to the strict observance of a particular day each week as a type of redemptive, eternal repose in God. Since this redemptive rest, represented by the Sabbath day in the history of Israel, finds its fulfillment in Christ, the external observance as a redemptive symbol is in Christ abolished. Calvin states emphatically, "He is, I say, the true fulfillment of the Sabbath." What was in the old order represented by the observance of the Sabbath is in the new order represented by the living Christ, namely, spiritual life and redemption. Calvin concludes, "Christians ought therefore to shun completely the superstitious observance of days." By this he apparently means the keeping of holy days as a means of salvation. Christians are to find their eternal rest in Christ, not in a holy day.

Like Luther, Calvin emphasizes that there is a cultic element in the Sabbath commandment that is applicable to all ages, for it implicitly suggests that a special time should be set aside for communal worship. In the church, good order must be upheld, and if there is no "arrangement and regulation" to set aside some specific time for worship, "immediate confusion and ruin threaten the church." The need of the ancient Israelites for such regulation was one of the reasons why God established the Sabbath. Since Christians today are subject to the same necessity, they should continue to observe this aspect of the Sabbath institution. "For our most provident and merciful Father willed to see to our needs not less than those of the Jews." In a perfect world, Calvin goes on to say in terms reminiscent of Luther, God's people would meet daily for worship "so as to remove all distinction of days." But the world has fallen into sin and the Sabbath commandment reflects God's concession to humanity's weakness. To set aside one day a week for worship involves the risk of a "distinction of days," but that risk must be run. In fact, Calvin's Geneva was criticized for a legalistic "observance of days," but Calvin defends Genevan practice by arguing that although the observance of a weekly day of worship continues, the reason for and spirit of this observance have been transformed. "For we are not celebrating it as a ceremony with the most rigid scrupulousness," he argues. "Rather, we are using it as a remedy needed to keep order in the church."

So Calvin subtly distinguishes between a "distinction of days" — which he opposes — and the "lawful selection that serves the peace of the Christian fellowship" — which he supports. The early Christians selected a new day for worship: Sunday, the first day of the week. Is there something special about that day, something that makes it inherently a better day for worship than the other days, and is it consequently a day established by divine authority? Calvin answers the first part of this question with the familiar assertion that the first day of the week is peculiarly appropriate for worship because it was the day of the Lord's resurrection in which the purpose and fulfillment of true rest are to be found. "Hence, by the very day that brought the shadows to an end, Christians are warned not to cling to the shadow rite." He argues that the day was changed "to demonstrate the liberty of Christians" won by Christ in his resurrection.[15] At the same time he states explicitly that the church is not bound to the first day by divine authority, nor even to the rhythm of one day in seven. He criticizes the legalistic "fixing of one day in seven," but nevertheless links this work and worship rhythm to the creation account in Genesis 1.

Calvin does not explicitly state that the Sabbath commandment is a creation ordinance. He does say that "it may be probably conjectured that the hallowing of the Sabbath was prior to the Law," and that the observance of the seventh day of rest "seems to have had its origin from a well-known and received custom." He asserts somewhat cryptically that the Sabbath was first instituted "when God revealed the rite of sacrifice to the Holy Fathers," apparently a reference to the early patriarchs. He believes that "in the depravity of human nature" the Sabbath became "extinct among heathen nations" and "almost obsolete with the race of Abraham." It was therefore reestablished in the Decalogue.[16]

Calvin says considerably more than Luther does about Christians "keeping the Sabbath." Two lengthy sermons from his series on the ten commandments in Deuteronomy 5 are dedicated to the Sabbath commandment, and in both of them there is heavy emphasis on Christian observance of this law of God.[17] In these sermons he expands on each of the three aspects of the Sabbath: spiritual rest, public worship, and physical rest for servants.

In the new order ushered in by grace, "keeping the Sabbath" means first of all a constant, daily resting from sinful deeds. Christians must continue to observe the "substance" of the commandment by suppressing their own will and works and by opening themselves to the will and work of God. Whenever, therefore, God's people are full of "envy, spite, ambition, cruelty and fraud" they break the Sabbath commandment. Conversely, when they commit themselves to God and to the guidance and governance of his Holy Spirit, then they are faithfully observing the substance of the Sabbath. Renunciation of self and total dedication to God are called by Calvin the "spiritual" keeping of the Sabbath. This is far more demanding than the mere external observance of a day. Anyone can rest from labor, but only when empowered by the grace and spirit of God can people rest from their sinful works and allow God to work redemptively in them (*Sermons,* 101–3).

Calvin believes that the ancient Israelites were required to observe the Sabbath with a view to this underlying spiritual meaning also. That is why punishment for Sabbath breaking was so severe according to Calvin. Why punish someone with death for chopping wood? Surely not because God takes such great pleasure in idleness, but because the Sabbath commandment embraces "all the service of God." Simply to rest from daily work and yet in the meantime to indulge their own wicked inclinations would have been a mockery of God and his law (*Sermons,* 103–4).

For Calvin, a Christian "keeping of the Sabbath" requires secondly a literal, physical cessation of daily labor on the Lord's Day, not as an end in itself but to provide time for worship of God. He urges that shop windows be shut on the Lord's Day, that travel be curtailed and recreation avoided so that there be sufficient time and freedom to meet together and make confession of faith, to hear God's word, to pray, and to use the sacraments. Like Luther, Calvin bemoans the neglect of worship in his day. For "though the bell tolls the sermon," many "seem only to have time for their own affairs," and shut themselves up in their houses where they remain "aloof from the church of God" (*Sermons,* 109).

Calvin takes an additional step in this second part of his Sabbath ethics. He argues that the Sabbath was instituted "in order that we might devote all the rest of time to praising God." Worship on Sunday becomes the catalyst that stimulates reflection on God and his works throughout the rest of the week.

> Thus we ought to observe Sunday as if from a tower in order that we might climb high upon it to contemplate the works of God from afar, in a way in which we are neither impeded by nor occupied with anything else, so that we might be able to extend all our senses to recognize the benefits and favors with which he has enlarged us. And when Sunday is able to help us practice that . . . we will surrender to him all the rest of time. (*Sermons,* 110)

God's people, therefore, should come to hear the sermon on Sunday and then should privately "ponder these things" in order to apply the word to the totality of their lives. Calvin's emphasis, however, is on public, corporate worship. He argues that "it is not enough for each in his own way to think of God and his work, but it is essential for us to gather on that particular day in order to make a public confession of our faith." For this purpose, some day or days, "whether one or two," must be set aside. "But all of that can be left up to the liberty of Christians" (*Sermons,* 111).

In the third part of his Sabbath ethics, Calvin deals with those parts of the commandment that refer to six days of labor and to the provision of rest for hired servants. First, he rejects the view that the phrase "Thou shalt work six days" should be regarded as a divine command to labor. Rather, God has included those words simply as a reminder that he has given his people plenty of time for their own affairs, so that it is not unreasonable for him to require one day of seven for worship. Calvin alludes again to a day that should be "fully reserved" for God's service and to God's requirement of "the seventh part of time." It is evident that while Calvin was not absolutely committed to the one-in-seven rhythm, he does take it very seriously and assumes it as a normal and typical routine for the Christian community (*Sermons,* 116–17).

Calvin then elaborates on the social implications of the requirement that rest be granted to servants, beasts of burden, and sojourners. He clearly regards this obligation as applicable to the Christian community as well as to ancient Israel. On the day of worship, servants, sojourners, and beasts of burden are to be given the opportunity for physical rest. This will also be of benefit to God's people, for when the stables and stalls are closed there is a "reminder before their eyes" of the day of rest and worship. Twice in this context Calvin refers to the Sabbath as a sacrament (*Sermons,* 119–20).

The social aspect of the commandment is secondary, for the primary intent of the Sabbath is the service of God and growth in holiness and obedience. Yet the command to give servants rest is important, for it is a reminder that God's people are to deal compassionately with the poor and with "all who are not in authority or esteemed, all subjects who are not deemed worthy in the eyes of the world." In spite of differing social and economic stations in life, humankind is "united together in one flesh." All are created in the image of God (*Sermons,* 121–26).

Calvin's passion for grace and for the sovereign God of grace are clearly reflected in his approach to the Sabbath commandment. These are also fundamental Lutheran concerns, of course, but Calvin draws more deeply from the commandment the sweeping conclusion that Christians truly keep the Sabbath only when God works in them by his Spirit so that they may rest from their evil works all the days of their lives. Nevertheless, Calvin and Luther are in fundamental agreement in their interpretation of the Sabbath, especially in their emphases on its ceremonial character and its realized fulfillment in the coming of Jesus Christ. Theologically, neither Calvin nor Luther is a Sabbatarian or even semi-Sabbatarian: for them the Christian Sunday is not to be identified with the Old Testament Sabbath. On the other hand, when Calvin discusses the implications of the Sabbath commandment for the Christian community, his emphasis is markedly different from Luther's. Luther reduced the whole matter to the word of God. The church is faithful to what God requires when the word of God is faithfully proclaimed and heard. Calvin, in his more detailed emphasis on Sabbath keeping, verges on what might be labeled a "practical Sabbatarianism." In Calvin, the tensions between law and gospel are not as severe as in Luther. There is gospel, or grace, in law. He is, therefore, not averse to introducing a disciplined keeping of the Sabbath that might be regarded as somewhat legalistic relative to Luther's approach. But even here the differences are subtle. Essentially, on the crucial issues, Calvin and Luther agree.

III

Although there has been some recent debate about whether the expression "Puritan Sabbath" is historically appropriate, it certainly remains the most convenient label for the strict Sabbath-Sunday views that developed within English Protestantism in the last part of the sixteenth century. This is yet another Protestant perspective on the Sabbath — indeed, a very important one — for it continues to have impact and significance both in England and in America. There is at least some latent "Sabbatarianism" in the Keep Sunday Special campaign in England, and there are remnants of the Puritan Sabbath in Sunday work issues that federal courts in the United States are called on to deal with from time to time.

In my description of the Puritan Sabbath, I shall use as prototype Nicholas Bound, who wrote extensively on the Sabbath in the late sixteenth century. He published two volumes of detailed commentary on the fourth commandment, the second of which must approach talmudic dimensions with its staggering 459 pages.[18]

Two theological positions relative to the Sabbath commandment are articulated by Bound, and they became henceforth the hallmarks of Sabbatarian theology. First, the Sabbath is rooted in creation and therefore antedates both the fall and the Mosaic law. The fourth commandment, no less than the other commandments, is a creation ordinance. It is a natural, perpetual moral law binding on all humanity, not a ceremonial law binding only on ancient Israel. This means, furthermore, that the Christian observance of the Lord's Day is not simply a practical regulation established by the church, but is an observance that is based directly and immediately on the fourth commandment in the Mosaic law, which is traced, in turn, to creation itself.

The second theological position concerns the shift of the day of rest and worship from the Jewish seventh day to the Christian first day. The view spelled out by Bound is that the adoption of Sunday as the New Testament Sabbath is based not on an early ecclesiastical decision, but on a divine mandate which came ultimately from Christ himself and was transmitted through the apostles. The first day of the week, moreover, is distinct from and superior to the other days, and no other day may be substituted out of convenience for the church. The Sabbath—first the Jewish and now the Christian Sabbath—was sanctified by God.

Before explicating these two positions, Bound declares that the fourth commandment is the key commandment in the whole Decalogue, "for in the practice of it, consisteth the practice of all the other, and in the neglect of it is the neglect of all religion." It stands out among the commandments in four ways. First, it begins with "remember" or "observe," whereas all the other commandments simply command this or forbid that. Second, in all the other laws God forbids the sins and assumes the virtue, whereas in the fourth commandment he both commands the good and forbids the evil. Third, the Sabbath commandment has more reasons affixed for keeping it "because our nature is most against the observation of it." No fewer than three reasons are given to support it: the six days of labor, God's creation example, and his sanctification of this day. Bound's Sabbatarianism begins to emerge when he says, "God hath bestowed an especiall blessing upon this day distinct from the rest." The fourth way in which the Sabbath commandment stands out in excellence above the rest is found in its concern with others in our charge—beasts of burden, servants, and strangers—a concern absent from the other commandments in the Decalogue (*Doctrine,* 1-4).

With regard to the first premise of Sabbatarian theology—that the fourth commandment is rooted in creation—Bound is unequivocally clear. Sabbath keeping is traced to Adam. "Adam and his posteritie, if they had continued in their first righteous estate, should have kept that day holie above the rest" (*Doctrine,* 5). Bound claims that the fourth commandment "was first delivered by lively voyce, namely to Adam and Eve in Paradise" (*Sabbathum,* 11). The other nine commandments were naturally engraved on the heart of humans, but the fourth commandment came by the express word of God. This commandment, therefore, "hath so much antiquitie, as the seventh day hath being: for so soone as the day was, so soone was it sanctified . . . and as it was in the beginning of the world, so it must continue to the ending of the same" (*Doctrine,* 6). Bound only very reluctantly disagrees with the position that "this commandment should be placed first in the Decalogue, because it is most ancient, and was first given out in expresse words" (*Sabbathum,* 7-8). He quotes with approval Jerome Zanchius who opines that when God created the Sabbath "the Sonne of God taking upon him the shape of man, was occupied that whole seventh day in most holy colloquies with Adam . . . instructing our first parents, and in exercising them in the worship of God . . ." (*Sabbathum,* 19-20).

In Bound's view, therefore, the fourth commandment is "naturall, morall, and perpetuall," and he offers as evidence the fact that even the Gentiles who were without the law kept some days holy (*Doctrine,* 7). The law of the Sabbath is etched on the human heart, and as part of the natural creation order must be universally observed. To ensure that it is, Bound demands that this commandment be incorporated into the laws of the land. He writes, "it behoveth al Princes and Magistrates, that be in highest authoritie, to provide that lawes bee enacted for the preservation of this rest, with civill punishments to be inflicted upon them that shall break it . . ." (*Doctrine,* 94).

The Sabbath commandment is so fully moral and perpetual that it should not be regarded as even partly ceremonial according to Bound. Just as a human cannot be human and beast at the same time, so a commandment cannot be both moral and ceremonial at the same time. Bound is concerned that if the fourth commandment is regarded as even partly ceremonial, it will lose its force. People must feel just as obligated to the Sabbath today as ancient Israel was. Bound asserts that his contemporaries "are as precisely to rest as the Jews were" (*Doctrine,* 260).

The second theological pillar of the Puritan Sabbath is its Sunday absolutism, that is, the insistence that the first day of the week has been appointed and sanctified by God to be the Christian day of rest and worship. In a long and involved discussion of this matter, Bound begins by stressing the absolute character of the seventh day in the Old Testament. It was the seventh day on which God rested; it was the seventh day which God sanctified. The pope has sanctified the other "holy days," but God himself sanctified this one (*Doctrine,* 32). Indeed, Bound's argument about the seventh day is such that one wonders how he will be able to go on to justify the shift from the seventh to the first in the Christian tradition. His emphasis on the uniqueness of the seventh day, however, arises precisely from his concern to make Christian Sabbath keeping a direct and immediate response to the fourth commandment. He glorifies the seventh day in that commandment because he believes it comprehends not only the Jewish Sabbath but also the Christian's Lord's Day, "as genus comprehendeth both his species" (*Sabbathum,* 71).

Bound's explanation of the shift to the first day of the week takes fifteen pages of intricate argument, and the paragraph that opens the discussion reveals the sleight of hand necessary to make the case.

But now concerning this very speciall *seventh day,* that now we keepe in the time of the Gospell, that is well knowne, that it is not the same, as it was from the beginning which God himselfe did sanctifie, and whereof hee speaketh in this Commandment, for it was the day going before ours, which in latine retaineth his ancient name, and is called the *Sabbath,* which we also grant, but so that we confesse, it must alwaies remaine, never to be changed anymore, and that all men must keepe holie this seventh day, and none other, which was unto them not *the seventh,* but the first day of the weeke, as it is so called many times in the new testament, and so it still standeth in force, that we are bound unto *the seventh day,* though not unto that very seventh. (*Doctrine,* 35)

Apparently Bound is using "seventh day" in two senses here: first, in the sense of the seventh day of the week or Saturday; and, second, in the sense of "every seventh day," which could be any day of the week but which Bound links specifically with Sunday.

It is the practice of Christ's apostles that provides the foundation for the argument concerning the change of the day. Using typical Puritan biblical methodology, Bound argues that not only the apostolic word but also the practice of the apostles is normative and binding, for it is based either on the direct command of Christ or on the work of the Holy Spirit within them. Moreover, since the apostle John in Revelation 1:10 calls Sunday the "Lord's Day," it is certain that the day has been authoritatively changed. It is a change analogous to several other Old to New Testament shifts: from priest to apostle, sacrifice of animals to sacrifice of self, sacrament of Passover to Lord's Supper, and circumcision to baptism.

The apostolic choice of the first day was determined by the resurrection event on that day. Because the first day of the week was the day of Jesus' resurrection, the climax and end of the Lord's work of redemption and the fulfillment of all the ceremonies of the Jews, the apostles "were directed by the . . . Spirite advisedly to chuse *this day* (which we now keepe, and must keepe to the end of the world). . . ." Bound boldly declares that "not so much the Apostles, as Christ himselfe brought in this chaunge, and was the author of this day." The first day of the week, therefore, must be recognized as "ordained by speciall advice, and no one but *this day* could be chosen to be the Sabbath and day of Rest, in which Christ Jesus the Creator of the new world, rested from his work of the new creation . . ." (*Doctrine,* 42–46).

That the church has discretionary power to name some other day as the day of worship is unthinkable for Bound. The day must not be changed "unto the ende of the world," and "it must not so much as enter into men's thoughts to goe about to change it." To change the Christian day of rest and worship and "to keep it upon Munday, Tuesday, or any other day, the Church hath no authoritie; for it is not a matter of indifferencie, but a necessarie prescription of Christ himselfe . . ." (*Doctrine,* 48).

The name "Lord's Day" must always be used, for it gives added stature to the day. It "breeds reverence" for the day and "maketh the day more highly to be esteemed." In fact, the name "Sunday" should be abandoned, for by origin that name is heathenish and profane. The name "Sunday" could have been arbitrarily attached to any day of the week, but because of the distinctiveness and uniqueness of the first day of the week, that day alone can be called the Lord's Day, "for as by it can bee ment no other day, but that which wee keepe for our Sabbath, so the name cannot be imparted to any other day without sacriledge." Given this strong emphasis, it is curious that Bound throughout both of his works refers to the Christian day of worship as "the Sabbath" more frequently than as "the Lord's Day" (*Doctrine*, 48–49).

Bound states unabashedly that the Lord's Day is holy in a way in which the other days are not. He argues that everything used in the service of God is sanctified and made distinctive, such as the water of baptism and the bread and wine of the Lord's Supper. God has blessed these elements in such a way that He "made them so wholly to differ from all other, as though they were not of the same nature and kinde, and so, from that they were before, as though they were not the same anymore" (*Doctrine*, 151). Similarly, the Lord's Day has been sanctified so that it has become a unique day among the days. It is a holy day, the one holy day that remains in the Christian era.

Bound does not ignore the practical, ethical implications of his Sabbath theology. Nearly one half of each book is devoted to rather precise and detailed instructions on Sabbath keeping. The fourth commandment requires *rest*. Bound emphasizes that this is a literal, physical rest, not a spiritual rest that entails cessation from ordinary daily work and play, "a most carefull, exact and precise rest" (*Doctrine*, 53). Everyone must rest. There are no exceptions. Schoolmasters and students, lawyers and clients, and even "the Physitian from the studying of the Anatomie." All people "even from him that sitteth upon the throne to the maid servant that is at the Mill, and the captive that is in prison, must rest from their ordinarie workes . . ." (*Doctrine*, 78–79).

Contributing to the climate that eventually produced King James's famous *Book of Sports*, Bound plunges headlong into the debate concerning Sabbath recreation. He concedes that recreation contributes to the human condition, but it is not absolutely necessary. If rest from daily labor is required on the Sabbath, therefore, then surely rest from recreational pursuits is doubly mandatory, for recreation serves "but *for pleasure*, without the which mankind may continue, though not so well continue." The purpose of rest from recreation is to eliminate another distraction from our basic Sabbath duty—the duty to worship. It is clearly impossible for people to "both be at Church serving God" and "in their houses sporting themselves with their companions" at the same time (*Doctrine*, 131).

In his discussion of the worship service, Bound reveals the chaotic conditions that prevailed in the English churches in the late sixteenth century. He complains about preachers who cannot or will not preach and charges them with primary responsibility for desecration of the Sabbath. But he complains about distractions among the hearers as well. He warns hunters that proper Sabbath keeping means leaving their bows and arrows, falcons and dogs at home. Worshipers should not come to church "with their bowes and arrowes in their hands" nor "with their hawkes upon their fists" (*Doctrine,* 132). He also laments the disorderly traffic conditions in church. Bound finds it necessary to insist that the people come on time and remain until the end of the service.

> For all the people, nay the severall housholds come not together, but scattered, and one dropping after another in a confused manner: First comes the man, then a quarter of an houre after his wife, and after her, I cannot tell how long, especially the maid servants, who must needes bee as long after her, as the menservants are after him: Whereby it cometh to passe that either halfe the service of God is done before all be met, or else if the minister tarrie till there be a sufficient congregation, the first commers may be wearie, and sometimes cold with tarrying, before the other shall bee warme in their seates. (*Doctrine,* 268)

Additional disorder surrounded the mechanics of almsgiving during the worship service. The picture Bound paints is reminiscent of the money changers in the Temple. During the worship service in many churches, Bound complains, "you shall see men go up and down asking, receiving, changing, and bestowing of money, wherein many times you shall have them so disagree, that they are louder than the minister; and the rest stand looking, and listning unto them, leaving the worship of God (as though it did not concerne them) and thus all is confused." Consequently, he urges that alms be gathered at "some other time of the day . . . to bestowe at the end of the service upon the needie. . ." (*Doctrine,* 193). Such worship conditions invited the development of a stricter and more orderly Sabbath observance. The total discipline which characterized the Puritan Sabbath must have been an attractive option by which to overcome the disorderly abuses common in that day.

The worship of God is the purpose of the Puritan Sabbath, and while communal worship is regarded by Bound as "the chiefest poynt," Christian worship must extend far beyond the hours for public assembly. The whole day is the Lord's and that day is a full twenty-four hours, extending from morning to morning. Bound declares that "we must spend the morning, evening, and whole day, yea some part of the night, so farre as our necessarie rest and sleepe will permit us in praising and serving the Lord" (*Sabbathum,* 366–74). He recommends that there be careful preparation for communal worship. This includes self-examination, prayer, and reading of Scripture. Another requirement is quiet meditation following the worship service, that is, reflection on what was heard in the sermon and read in the Scripture. Another important home exercise is discussion with others about what was heard or read in the service, for this will help to fix the word or the sermon in the memory. Psalm singing is stressed as another important element in Sabbath activity. The Psalms should be sung at home as well as in church. Such spiritual exercises promote greater thankfulness to God which will enhance Christian living throughout the rest of the week (*Doctrine,* 208–39).

Bound's view of Sabbath keeping also includes a social emphasis. Works of mercy are to be done especially on the Sabbath, for the whole worship of God is ordained to this end—that we be better equipped to show love to others. We must, therefore, feed the hungry, clothe the naked, lodge the homeless, and visit the sick and the imprisoned. The Lord's Day is "the day of shewing mercy" (*Doctrine,* 247). With considerable insight into the human condition, Bound stresses the importance of deliberately going out to *see* the miseries of others as a stimulus to greater compassion (*Sabbathum,* 445).

Bound concludes his Sabbath exposition with still another admonition to those in authority to enact good laws compelling all people to sanctify the Sabbath. Heads of households are included in this admonition, for proper Sabbath observance is the key to family strength as well as to national morality. Sabbath desecration, conversely, is the underlying cause for all manner of evil, including rebellious children, disobedient servants, and unfaithful wives. He sums up the principal purpose of the Sabbath in these words: that "we might be fashioned unto the image of God, and begin that Sabbath here, that shall bee for ever continued in heaven" (*Doctrine,* 272–82).

Theologically, an economic trinity provides the foundation and the structure for the Puritan view of the Sabbath we have described. The essential works related to the Father, Son, and Holy Spirit come quite clearly into view not only in Bound's Sabbath exposition but also in the many others published at this time.[19] The biblical-theological motifs of creation, redemption, and sanctification are essential to the Puritan Sabbath, surfacing regularly in Puritan arguments relative to the three most controversial issues: the institution, the alteration, and the celebration of the Sabbath.

Crucial to the Puritan argument was the creational institution of the Sabbath, for this was the basis of the conviction that the Sabbath is part of the natural moral order—hence not a Jewish ceremony but applicable to all of humankind for all of time. In all of the Puritan Sabbath treatises, the position is clear: the fourth commandment was pre-Mosaic, even pre-lapsarian, delivered to the progenitors of the human race in paradise and therefore etched indelibly on the collective heart of humanity. In the Puritan view the Sabbath was grounded in Genesis 1, in God's example of work and rest when he created the universe, and only reiterated in the Mosaic law. Sabbatarian thought was centered in the creation and in the Creator.

Because of the Puritan insistence on a full and literal application of the fourth commandment to the New Testament Christian community, the alteration of the Sabbath to Sunday became a somewhat problematic issue. The fourth commandment, after all, explicitly designates a certain day for worship—and it is not the first day of the week. Yet one of the marks of the Puritan view was the conviction that Sunday, and no other day, is the Christian's Sabbath. In every Sabbath treatise without exception, the argument for the alteration of the day is pinned to the pivotal event in the Christian history of redemption, the resurrection of Jesus. By grounding the alteration of the day upon this bedrock redemptive miracle, the Puritans substantiated their conviction that the shift from the seventh day to the first has divine, biblical authority and is not merely an ecclesiastical decision made in the early centuries of the church. The Lord's Day stands apart from and above all the other "holy days" of the church, and it is by no means within the power of the church to change this special day of worship. With the alteration linked to the resurrection it could be argued that "Christ himselfe brought in this change, and was the author of this day."[20]

Finally, the heavy Puritan emphasis on proper celebration of the Sabbath is centered in the Puritan preoccupation with sanctification. It was in the context of the quest for personal holiness, as well as for a holier church and commonwealth, that Sabbatarianism developed in England. In the Puritan vision, the Sabbath is the principal means of a three-dimensional sanctification. In creation, God sanctified the Sabbath; in the fourth commandment, the people of God are called to sanctify the day; and through divine and human sanctification of the Sabbath, the Spirit of God sanctifies the world. Nicholas Bound sums up the sanctification purpose of the Sabbath beautifully: "Therefore to conclude, I doe most willingly acknowledge, that this was one principall end, for which the Sabbath was ordained: even that thereby we might be sanctified through the pure use of Gods worship upon that day; and that this should be the fruit of our resting, and sanctification of the day; without the which all that we do is to no purpose."[21] For the Puritans, all of life found its meaning and purpose in the sanctification of the Sabbath.

IV

The Sabbath needs serious reconsideration within Protestantism today. In the twentieth century, justice has not been done to the significance given to the Sabbath in Scripture and in religious history. This neglect, at least within large segments of mainline Protestantism, may be due in part to the efforts of early Protestant theologians to emphasize the ceremonial character of the Sabbath. The inevitable result of such a move is to regard it as an Old Testament ritual that is essentially irrelevant in the life of the Christian Church. Strangely enough, the Puritans may also have contributed to its contemporary neglect, in part because of the backlash resulting from boredom and sheer exasperation with their intricately detailed expositions, and also because their discussions began to focus more and more on purely practical issues so that the Sabbath became a topic for consideration in ethics but not for serious reflection in theology.

There is, however, at least one well-known twentieth-century Protestant and Reformed theologian who has taken the Sabbath with utmost seriousness and who provides us with some fresh and creative insights. This is none other than the theological giant of at least the first half of our century, Karl Barth.[22]

As is typical of Barth, he deals with the Sabbath not simply as a commandment for humanity but as a revelation of God. In almost Puritan tones, he extols the Genesis account of the Sabbath as an essential reminder of the antiquity and divine character of the institution. When the Scriptures are read canonically and not primarily historically-critically, the Sabbath is seen as rooted in God's example and, therefore, far older than the Mosaic Decalogue. Regardless of whether one believes that the Sabbath *commandment* is rooted in creation, there can be no debate about the fact that God's Sabbath is a part of the creation narrative. What does this tell about God and his relationship to creation? Surely, God did not have to recuperate after a busy week. Rather, his adoption of the Sabbath suggests that God was so content and so satisfied with his work of creation that that work could now cease. After God crowned creation with perfect humanity, there was nothing left for him to do. He had no regrets. He had no need to go on to create a still better world, nor to create some creature more wonderful and perfect than the man and woman he had created on the day before. He did not stop being the Creator, but he freed himself from any new work of creation, for his work was finished and his work was good. Moreover, he rested from all that he had made. He did not withdraw from it; he did not depart from it; he did not return to an existence without the creation. The Sabbath is tied to the completion of that creation and suggests "a supremely positive relationship of God to the creaturely world and man as they now confronted Him."[23]

What more does the Sabbath teach about God? Barth says that it points to the freedom of God. In this respect God is sharply distinguished from any kind of inner "world principle" as the source of creation, such as a principle of self-development or evolution. Such a principle is forever tied to the creation, entangled with the ongoing process. But the freedom of God is suggested by the Sabbath fact that he sets limits on his creative activity. Only a being that is separate from creation can be free from creation and can limit his work of creation. He is truly God, standing over against what he has made.

The Sabbath also suggests love as a feature of God. An evolutionary principle caught up in the creative process, a part of the machinery as it were, is not free to love, for it is "never ceasing"; it has no time for a relationship with creatures and cannot love for it is a mechanistic principle. God, however, ended his creative activity because he had "found the object of his love." So Barth asks rhetorically, "When is He God more truly, or more perfectly Himself in the whole course of His work of creation, than in this rest on the seventh day?"[24]

The Sabbath also suggests God's immanence with the world. The Sabbath was a temporal event like the other days of creation. By establishing the Sabbath day, and resting on it, God indicates that he himself enters time, that he enters into ongoing creation history and links himself temporarily "with the being and purpose and course of the world, with the history of man." In this sense, man and woman are not the crown of creation after all; rather, the Sabbath is the pinnacle of the Genesis account, for it is the Sabbath that reveals the true character of the Creator, his freedom, his love, and his desire to continue to associate with what he made. The Sabbath represents the beginning of the history of humankind with God, the beginning of an everlasting covenant relationship. Instead of retiring into eternity, God gives temporal form to his freedom and love by entering into the seventh day.[25]

The Sabbath tells us about humanity as well as about the deity. For "the clear inference is that creation, and supremely man, rested with God on the seventh day" and shared in his freedom and love. In fact, God's Sabbath rest is the first divine event that man and woman are privileged to witness. That they may keep the Sabbath with God is the very first blessing they receive. The Sabbath signifies a unique relationship between the Creator and this creature who images him. The participation of human beings in this first Sabbath rest comes at the beginning, not at the end, of their work. It is solely God's work that precedes this Sabbath, not humanity's. It is God who has worked and accomplished the creation, this occasion for rest and joy. It is initiated solely because of what God has done, not for what the man and woman have done. Hereby the universe of grace is suggested. God has done what was necessary, and humans are simply invited to participate in it. Thus the Sabbath represents the beginning of the history of humankind with God as well as the end. Humanity is not only headed for a Sabbath rest with God; the very beginning of human history is set within this Sabbath rest with God. Barth observes that since the first Sabbath came at the beginning of human work rather than at the end, Sunday, the first day of the week, is a most appropriate Sabbath. Although the Sabbath was the seventh day for God — following his work — it was the first day for man and woman—preceding their work. Human history begins with a Sabbath already sanctified. It begins with the gospel, not with the law. The movement is not from work to rest, but from rest to work, not from service to freedom, but from freedom to service. Each week, "instead of being a trying ascent," is a "glad descent from the high-point of the Sabbath." Furthermore, if the history of the covenant between God and humanity finds its culmination in the resurrection of Jesus, then the early Christians' revolution against the divine order in creation was appropriate. That is, "the first day of this new time had to become literally as well as materially the day of rest which dominates life in this new time."[26]

Barth regards the Sabbath as having a special place of priority among the commandments. Not only is it unusual in its length and detail, but its prominence in the life of ancient Israel suggests that it constituted a peculiarly important test of human obedience to God. Barth believes there is no question about its continued importance in the Christian church. In fact, he comments on how quickly and naturally it was seen to be valid and authoritative in the New Testament. This makes all the more surprising the casual, feeble treatment it receives from most modern theologians.

Barth treats the Sabbath commandment first among the special ethical duties of God's people because they can only understand the rest of life, all ethical responsibility, and the meaning of work, by understanding the significance of the Sabbath. The law cannot be heard before the gospel, and the Sabbath brings God's people into contact with the gospel. They cannot do justice to their work without first pausing, resting, rejoicing, and observing the Sabbath interruption of that work. In the Sabbath is "the true time" which gives meaning to the rest of time. So "we must undoubtedly concern ourselves first with the Sabbath commandment and only then and on this basis with all else that is commanded us."[27]

The Sabbath commandment meant and continues to mean that there must be a weekly interruption of work, a deliberate limiting of work, "a temporal pause, to reflect on God and His work and to participate consciously in the salvation provided by Him and to be awaited from Him." Human work is "bounded by this continually recurring interruption." The key phrase in Barth's understanding of Sabbath observance is "renouncing faith," for on this day people are pointed away from everything that they do and will and achieve, to God and to his will and work and achievements. Without implying that human work is unimportant or impossible, the Sabbath points to God's work and, therefore, makes human work important and possible. Human effort is the most productive when it is limited and relativized by the observance of the Sabbath.[28]

By reminding humanity of the decisive will and activity of God, the Sabbath renounces faith in self. "It forbids him faith in his own plans and wishes, in a justification and deliverance which he can make for himself, in his own ability and achievement." What the Sabbath really forbids is not work, but trust in human work. Human beings are to work with all seriousness and strength, but they are never to believe in their work. "The aim of the Sabbath commandment is that man shall give and allow the omnipotent grace of God to have the first and the last word at every point"; it aims at complete and total surrender to God. In this sense the Sabbath is the key commandment and has as its purpose the fundamental concerns of all the other days of the week.[29]

Not only does the Sabbath determine the significance and meaning of the other days; it also points to the final consummation of all things in history. It points toward God's eternal Sabbath, the establishment of a new age. Because it does this, Barth speaks of "the radical importance, the almost monstrous range of the sabbath commandment." It is a commandment that confronts us with the Creator, with his will and word and work, and with the final goal determined by him.[30]

This "almost monstrous range" of the Sabbath is reflected in the provocative suggestion made more recently by another twentieth-century Protestant theologian, the American Herbert Richardson.[31] He calls for a recognition of the Sabbath as the key to the understanding of a unique American emphasis in Christian theology, the "desire to actualize eschatological holiness in space and time."[32] From the beginning, American Christianity has been captivated by the vision of creating a righteous society on earth and by the goal of having God's purpose for creation realized in this world. Establishing the kingdom of God on earth is a theme that pervades the history of the American church. This entails the sanctification of all things by the presence of God, precisely the meaning of the Sabbath.

In terms somewhat reminiscent of Barth, Richardson argues that Sabbath rest must be defined in terms of God and his activity following creation, not simply in terms of humanity and cessation from work. The Sabbath represents the goal of creation, for it indicates that all that God made, including humanity itself, issues into Sabbath holiness. When the Sabbath is tied to creation, when it is viewed as the terminus of creation, then it is seen as that for which even humankind was created. Again borrowing from Barth, Richardson declares that in this perspective the creation of man and woman is not the crowning achievement of God after all; there is something higher and more wonderful: the Sabbath. Humanity's end and purpose, therefore, are not to be found in itself, but in God, or rather in the holiness of God, which by means of the Sabbath institution becomes the future toward which all of creation is directed. The Sabbath becomes the antidote for the disastrous promethean error of modern humanity: that humanity is the measure of all things.

The Sabbath, moreover, is a sign of the presence of God in the world and thus an anticipation of the incarnation. As such, it is to be regarded as a sacrament, a sign of God's gracious presence within his creation still today. It is also the supreme model of the world to come, the perfected future kingdom of God. The critical question in American Christian theology is not *cur Deus homo,* but *cur creatio* — Why did God create the world? The Sabbath provides the answer! It is the microcosm for the macrocosmic purpose of God: the sanctification of all things.

Contemporary Protestantism needs to recover the doctrine of the Sabbath. There is great power especially in the idea that the Sabbath is a "sacrament," a means by which God can be richly experienced and by which his holiness and glory are realized. In this sacrament is the "real presence" of God. As sacrament, of course, its significance is not limited to creation, but extends to redemption. In it, therefore, the Exodus and Deuteronomy versions of the Sabbath commandment are joined together and the themes of memory and hope are combined. The Protestant observance of Sunday is not a repudiation of this Sabbath sacrament but an extension of it, a testimony that the divine holiness of the Sabbath "overflows" the seventh day and fills the other days as well. The Christian Sunday is the extension of the Sabbath presence of God into all of our space and time.[33]

The Sabbath is no minor article of religion, but is a key to holy worldliness — indeed, a key to the end and purpose of history. It has, therefore, enormously positive associations. The Sabbath is a most precious resource of life in a world of death.

NOTES

1. John Pocklington, *Sunday No Sabbath* (London: Robert Young, 1635).
2. Ibid., 5.
3. The precise relationship between Puritanism and Sabbatarianism is still being debated. See, for example, Kenneth L. Parker, *The English Sabbath: A Study of Doctrine and Discipline from the Reformation to the Civil War* (Cambridge: Cambridge University Press, 1988); and John H. Primus, *Holy Time: Moderate Puritanism and the Sabbath* (Macon, GA: Mercer University Press, 1989).
4. Pocklington, *Sunday No Sabbath,* 16–19.
5. T. Tappert, ed., *The Book of Concord* (Philadelphia: Muhlenberg Press, 1959) 342.
6. Ibid., 375, 376.
7. E. W. Gritsch, ed., *Luther's Works:* Vol. 41, *Church and Ministry III* (Philadelphia: Fortress, 1966) 67.
8. Gerhard Ebeling, *Luther* (Philadelphia: Fortress, 1970) chap. 7; and Paul Althaus, *The Theology of Martin Luther* (Philadelphia: Fortress, 1981) chap. 19.

9. Quoted in Christopher Hill, *Society and Puritanism in Pre-Revolutionary England* (London: Secker & Warburg, 1964) 210.

10. *Book of Concord,* ed. Tappert, 376.

11. Ibid., 376–78.

12. J. Pelikan, ed., *Luther's Works:* Vol. 1, *Lectures on Genesis* (St. Louis: Concordia, 1958) 79–82.

13. *Book of Concord,* ed. Tappert, 377.

14. *Calvin: Institutes of the Christian Religion,* ed. J. T. McNeill (Philadelphia: Westminster, 1960) 394. This citation and those that follow in this section of the paper, unless noted otherwise, are taken from his discussion of the fourth commandment in book 2, chapter 8, sections 28–34.

15. *John Calvin's Sermons on the Ten Commandments,* ed. B. W. Farley (Grand Rapids: Baker, 1980) 111.

16. The quotations in this paragraph are from Calvin's commentary on Exodus 20:8.

17. Sermons 5 and 6 in *Sermons on the Ten Commandments,* ed. Farley.

18. Nicholas Bound, *The Doctrine of the Sabbath* (London, 1595); *Sabbathum Veteris et Novi Testament* (London, 1606).

19. See Robert Cox, *The Literature of the Sabbath Question* (Edinburgh: Maclachlan & Stewart, 1865).

20. Bound, *Doctrine,* 44.

21. *Sabbathum,* 47.

22. His theology of the Sabbath may be found, in English, in *Church Dogmatics* (Edinburgh: T. & T. Clark, 1958) 3/1:213–28; 3/4:47–72.

23. Ibid. 3/1:223.

24. Ibid. 3/1:215.

25. Ibid. 3/1:216–17.

26. Ibid. 3/1:225–28.

27. Ibid. 3/4:49–51.

28. Ibid. 3/4:53–54.

29. Ibid. 3/4:54.

30. Ibid. 3/4:57.

31. H. Richardson, *Toward an American Theology* (New York: Harper & Row, 1967).

32. Ibid., 126.

33. Ibid., 155.

9

THE SABBATH AS FULFILLED IN CHRIST: A RESPONSE TO S. BACCHIOCCHI AND J. PRIMUS

Craig Blomberg
Denver Seminary

The papers by Drs. Bacchiocchi and Primus have been well paired. They advocate two of the three main Christian understandings of the Sabbath. Although I have a much briefer period of time allotted to me than they, I would like to include in my response an advocacy for the third main understanding.

The three main views may be briefly summarized as follows: (1) Some believe that the Sabbath must always refer to the seventh day of the week, that is, Saturday. They believe also that observing the seventh day as a day of rest remains mandatory for Christians today. (2) Some believe that it is legitimate for Christians to transfer the concept of Sabbath from Saturday to Sunday. Because the first day of the week was the day of Jesus' resurrection, it is fitting to worship and rest on that day. This group agrees with the first that Christians must observe one day in seven as a day of rest, even if that particular day need not be Saturday. (3) Proponents of the view that I support agree with view (1) that Sabbath cannot be transferred from Saturday to another day. They agree with view (2) that it is appropriate to worship on Sunday. But they disagree with both these views by maintaining that the Sabbath laws of the Hebrew Scriptures do not apply to Christians without significant qualification. They cannot accept language that calls Sunday the Christian Sabbath. They often prefer to call Sunday the Lord's Day, to make it clear that Sunday and Sabbath are not the same. They further believe that the New Testament teaches that Sabbath laws were fulfilled in Christ in such a way that Christians are not *commanded* to do anything particularly special on one day out of seven, though they may voluntarily choose to do so. Perhaps the best recent volume articulating this perspective is the anthology to which Dr. Bacchiocchi has already referred: *From Sabbath to Lord's Day,* edited by D. A. Carson.

It is obvious that Bacchiocchi's paper vigorously affirms the first of these three views. Sabbath remains Saturday and still applies to Christians. Dr. Primus's paper is more a historical survey than a defense of a particular position, but he seems to support some version of the second position. Barth and Richardson receive his greatest accolades, and these theologians, though significantly broadening the meaning of Sabbath when compared with their predecessors, nevertheless retain the ideas of Sabbath as a "weekly interruption of work" (so Barth) and as "cessation from work" (so Richardson). Primus also apparently supports Sabbath keeping when he concludes that "contemporary Protestantism needs to recover the powerful idea of the Sabbath as a sacrament."

Both Bacchiocchi and Primus, however, do discuss the third view as well. But here some clarifications need to be made. Primus stresses that the understanding of Sabbath as a creation ordinance was crucial to Puritan Sabbatarianism. Bacchiocchi observes that those who believe that Sabbath keeping is not incumbent on Christians usually maintain that the Sabbath is a distinctively Jewish institution, emphasizing its Mosaic rather than its creation origins. To be sure, most of those who have rejected Sabbath keeping down through church history have taken this tack. But Mosaic origin is not a necessary part of the argument. In fact, it might actually weaken the position, as Bacchiocchi has suggested, if the biblical data support a creation origin of Sabbath. It is curious that of the four views Bacchiocchi discusses under "Pre-Mosaic/Mosaic Origin of the Sabbath" none addresses the straightforward reading of Scripture that Sabbath keeping *as a commandment* originated at Sinai and is therefore distinctively Jewish, even though the theological rationale of the commandment clearly goes back to creation. None of the biblical texts Bacchiocchi cites in favor of the creation origin of Sabbath says anything about its origin as *a commandment*.

Nevertheless, the more cogent approach for Christians who reject Sabbath keeping is to argue that *all* of the Hebrew Scriptures need to be interpreted in the light of Jesus' teaching and New Testament doctrine. It is therefore largely irrelevant whether a commandment existed before or only after Sinai. Jesus himself made the claim, according to Matthew 5:17, that he came to fulfill the "Law and the Prophets," an expression which in first-century Judaism referred to the *entire* Hebrew Scriptures. So what is relevant is how the New Testament interprets the Sabbath, not the date of the Sabbath's origin. Circumcision, for example, clearly predated Sinai, yet the apostle Paul minces few words in condemning those who would require

it of Christians (see especially Galatians 5:2–6). Mandatory capital punishment for murder goes as far back as Noah, yet many Christians strenuously
resist its enforcement in the Christian era. And not a few Christians today
would even reject Paul's appeal to the order of creation in 1 Timothy 2:13
as a rationale for the subordination of women to men in favor of his apparently more programmatic declaration of full equality in Galatians 3:28.

What then is the New Testament teaching on Sabbath? I can obviously
touch merely on one or two highlights here. Although Jesus regularly
embroiled himself in controversies with certain Pharisees over Sabbath
halakah, he nowhere clearly broke any portion of Torah. This observation
has often been used to promote Sabbath keeping for Christians, but the
logic is flawed. Jesus obeyed Torah because he understood it to be binding
for the period of history in which he lived. The question that should
concern Christians is what is binding for the new period of history (the age
they believe to be the fulfillment of Jeremiah's prophesied new covenant)
which was not established until the complex of events involving Christ's
death, resurrection, ascension, and the sending of the Holy Spirit at
Pentecost. Most of Jesus' teachings and actions regarding the Sabbath as
recorded in the four Gospels simply do not address the issue of how to
behave at this later date.

At the same time, one need only read the Gospels somewhat cursorily to
detect that the four evangelists' emphases in portraying Jesus vis-à-vis the
law do not depict him as a theological conservative! Time and again he
scandalized the Jewish leaders with his radical views. Bacchiocchi rightly
observes that on one occasion (Mark 2:27 and parallels) Jesus defended his
departure from Pharisaic understanding of the Sabbath by appealing to its
origin as an institution for benefiting humans rather than for enslaving
them. What Bacchiocchi fails to mention is that in the previous verse, Jesus
first justified his behavior by appealing to the precedent in 1 Samuel 21 in
which David clearly disobeyed the written law in eating the consecrated
bread, which was reserved for priests. If all Jesus was trying to say was that
he rejected the oral tradition, then he chose a highly misleading illustration
to make his point. It seems rather that his reference to the creation of the
Sabbath was not trying to reinstate a pristine pre-Sinai form of the institution but to demonstrate that as "lord of the Sabbath" (an equally scan-
dalous implicit equation of himself with the deity) he is now transcendent
over and the sovereign interpreter of the written law. (Examples of similar
incidents from the Gospels could be multiplied; I refer the interested reader
at this point to my article "The Law in Luke-Acts," *Journal for the Study
of the New Testament* 22 [1984] 53–80.)

Turning from the Gospels to the book of Acts, one finds oneself in a
transitional era of the church's history. In thirty short years Christianity
grew from an exclusively Jewish sect to a predominantly Gentile world

religion. Christians, especially Jewish believers, did not abandon any part of Torah overnight. But after a complex series of debates and controversies they did eventually for the most part agree that no law of Moses could be propounded as mandatory for Christians, either Jew or Gentile, simply by virtue of being included in what the letter to the Hebrews called the "old covenant" (Hebrews 8; cf. especially Acts 15 and the entire epistle to the Galatians).

Yet at the same time, Christians continued to condemn murder, adultery, theft, lying, and covetousness, to support love for God and neighbor and in numerous other ways to uphold fundamental concerns of the laws of Moses. The question naturally arose how much of Torah to obey and how much to set aside. Most of Christian theology can be placed on a spectrum of answers to this question. At one end of the spectrum are those, often today from a Calvinist heritage, who emphasize the continuity between old and new covenants. They frequently adopt the hermeneutical rule of thumb of accepting everything in the Hebrew Scriptures which the New Testament does not explicitly set aside. At the other end of the spectrum are those, often today from a Lutheran heritage, who emphasize the dis- continuity between the covenants. They frequently argue that one should set aside everything in the Old Testament which the New Testament does not explicitly reaffirm. The former usually conclude that Sabbath keeping is in some sense still valid; the latter often do not. The New Testament is conspicuous in its explicit reaffirmation of all nine of the Ten Command- ments except the Sabbath command.

In my view, the biblical data are too complex to yield to either of these simplistic extremes. Numerous inconsistencies call into question both systems. For example, most Lutherans would condemn sorcery, witch- craft, and spiritism, even though the New Testament never says anything about them. So too, most Calvinists would be uncomfortable with stoning rebellious children even though the New Testament never revokes that law. So other proposals have been offered. A very popular approach distin- guishes between the moral and ceremonial laws, another between the Ten Commandments and everything else. Yet nowhere in the New Testament do grounds for such distinctions appear; numerous laws are difficult to assign exclusively to either moral or ceremonial categories; and a good case can be made for seeing all of Torah as the legitimate extension of the prin- ciples programmatically enunciated on the Sinai tablets.

What is more, the New Testament itself consistently affirms both that all of Torah is in some sense binding upon Christians and that none of it is binding apart from understanding how it is fulfilled in Christ. When Jesus declared that he did not come to abolish the law, he did not go on to affirm the expected antithesis—something like "I came to uphold it." Rather, he said "I came to fulfill"—to bring to its goal and climax and point out the totality of its intended meaning. When the epistle to the Hebrews declares the old covenant "obsolete" (Hebrews 8:13), it is only after a lengthy quotation of Jeremiah which defines the new covenant in terms of the same laws as the old but now internalized and easier to keep (v. 10). The apostle Paul regularly juxtaposes statements about Christians' freedom from the law with disclaimers that they still uphold the law (e.g., Romans 3:21–31). 2 Timothy 3:16 affirms the inspiration and continuing relevance of all of the Hebrew Scriptures, yet the New Testament writers only rarely cite legal texts from Scripture to reinforce their moral commands. On the other hand, when they do, they range indiscriminately over the entire Mosaic code, including both fundamental principles from the Decalogue and seemingly minor points such as not muzzling oxen while they are treading grain (1 Timothy 5:18).

The appropriate hermeneutical paradigm for Christian interpretation of the law would therefore seem to be as follows. Every passage in the Hebrew Scriptures has some abiding relevance for Christians, but no passage can be properly applied until one understands how it has been fulfilled in Christ. In some instances (e.g., the prohibition of murder), it may carry over relatively unchanged; in others (e.g., offering animal sacrifices), it is set aside once and for all but continues to have value for the Christian by reminding her or him of Christ's atoning, sacrificial death. The problem with attempts to break the law into different categories is not that the law cannot be subdivided but that it is usually not subdivided enough. One needs to look at sacrifices, dietary laws, circumcision, prohibitions against idolatrous, pagan practices, safety laws, laws about periodic festivals, and numerous other categories, each on its own merits, trying to discern what New Testament teaching about each topic mandates for Christians today.

When one adopts this approach, perhaps the single most significant New Testament text for understanding the Sabbath becomes Colossians 2:16–17, a passage that neither Primus nor Bacchiochi discussed. There Paul writes, "do not let anyone judge you by what you eat or drink, or with regard to a religious festival, a new moon celebration or a Sabbath day," an apparently clear reference to the annual, monthly, and weekly holy days of Judaism. Paul continues, "These are a shadow of the things that were to come; the reality, however, is found in Christ." Similar prohibitions against mandating practices with respect to holy days recur in Romans 14:1–8. In his book *From Sabbath to Sunday,* Bacchiochi dismisses the force of Paul's commands first by arguing that the Colossians and Romans were not observing strictly Jewish holy days but a syncretistic mixture of Jewish and pagan festivals and second by arguing from the absence of Pauline polemic against Sabbath keeping to his endorsement of the institution (p. 368).

But neither of these arguments can stand. Evidence for syncretism at Rome is meager and, though more plentiful at Colossae, has been cogently called into question even there by T. N. Wright's recent commentary on Colossians and Philemon in the revised Tyndale series (Leicester: IVP, 1986). But even if some of the Sabbath keeping were syncretistic, nothing in Paul's remarks justifies a distinction between jettisoning the pagan and preserving the Jewish. Second, the absence of Pauline polemic proves precisely the opposite of what Bacchiocchi alleges. Whenever Paul believes a practice is or is not definitely mandated for Christians, he argues far more vigorously than he does here; when it is a matter of *adiaphora,* then he permits diversity of practice.

So in what sense is the Sabbath command authoritative for Christians after its fulfillment in Christ? In many of the ways Bacchiocchi and Primus have discussed — by reminding believers that work is not the summation of human existence, by highlighting the nature of the entire Christian life as resting in God through Christ (recall Jesus' words, "Come to me all you who labor and are heavy laden and I will give you rest" [Matthew 11:28]), by pointing forward to the more perfect rest believers will one day all enjoy (see especially Hebrews 4), by reminding us of God's freedom and love, and so on. I agree wholeheartedly with both writers that Christians need to recover these goals of the Sabbath in contemporary life. But none of these objectives requires a mandated seventh day in which Christians do or do not do certain things differently from the other six days of the week. In an increasingly complex and pluralistic society, it is becoming more and more difficult for people to worship and/or rest following any fixed cycle of days. How liberating it could be for many believers if more churches reassured them that God is equally pleased with his people's worship and rest whenever it occurs!

As a Protestant, my final authority for doctrinal and moral matters is, in theory at least, the Bible — and not church tradition. Nevertheless, it may be worthwhile to notice in closing some support for my view from church history. The two papers have amply surveyed post-Augustinian and post-Reformation thought. Neither has said much about the position of the earliest church fathers, who for the most part supported the abrogation of the Sabbath and who, at least on this issue, may have stood not only most close in time to the New Testament writers but also most close in theology. Consider the following catena of citations: Ignatius (ca. 110) declares that they who walked in ancient customs have come to a new hope "no longer living for the Sabbath, but for the Lord's life (or day)" (*Magnesians* 9:1). Justin Martyr (ca. 170) writes in his *Dialogue with Trypho* (10), "We do not live after the law, we are not circumcised in the flesh, we do not keep the Sabbath." Athanasius (ca. 360) notes, "We keep no Sabbath day; we keep the Lord's Day, as a memorial of the beginning of the second new creation" (*Concerning the Sabbath and Circumcision*). Canon 29 of the Council of Laodicea (363) even goes so far as to pronounce that "Christians must not judaize by resting on the Sabbath, but must work on that day, rather honoring the Lord's Day; and, if they can, resting then as Christians." To be sure, growing anti-Semitism enabled such views to be held comfortably, but I am not persuaded that anti-Semitism can fully account for this earliest Christian theology of the Sabbath.

This last quotation reminds us that although the seeds were being sown during these early centuries for the transfer of Sabbath theology to Sunday, from the earliest it was not so. Most Gentile Christians came from the lower strata of society and even from the slave class; they would have had no option but to work on Sundays in the pre-Constantinian empire of the first three centuries c.e. Christian worship would have regularly occurred before dawn or after dusk on Saturday or Sunday evenings, just as we see in Acts 20:7. Even where cessation from work was possible, the evidence shows it was not necessarily practiced.

In his introduction, Bacchiocchi laments the decline of the church in Western Europe as a product of the demise of Sabbatarianism. I am not sure I can accept this correlation. At least with respect to Great Britain, where I lived for four years of the past decade, Sabbatarianism is culturally much stronger than in the United States, but it seems to me that it has contributed to rather than guarded against the collapse of vibrant Christianity. Conversely, the remarkable growth of the early church, like the astonishing spread of Christianity in China today, frequently occurred when most Christians had no legally authorized day of rest. Perhaps in North America too, the church could be rid of much of its strangling nominalism if true believers had to worship before or after work and were not encouraged by the laws of the land to think that a relatively effortless change in routine one day out of seven bore any material relation to true piety or to God's pleasure with them.

10

A RESPONSE TO
S. BACCHIOCCHI AND J. PRIMUS

Dennis Kennedy
Catholic Archdiocese of Denver

At a conference I attended recently in Washington, D.C., a very secular gathering of elements of the peace movement and the World Federalists, Saul Mendlovitz, a prominent Jewish peace activist, started his talk with these words: "I come this Sabbath morning to profess law." Sabbath in his mind was not just a religious cloaking device, something to dress up his speech, but a seat and source of convicted power.

Jesus taught that Sabbath is not necessarily always the highest or only law—some specifics of the Jewish law he would override at times to cure a leper or feed the hungry. But he firmly embraced the practice of Sabbath—whereas today, as we well know, your boss's whim can overthrow the Sabbath in making you work, or the NFL, or a corporate policy set in New York.

The papers of Drs. Bacchiocchi and Primus were excellent scholarly sources of convicted power. Therefore, I have chosen to forgo scholarly repartee and critique and instead assume the role of admirer, drawing pleasure from the morning's moments, rhapsodizing over the texts, and playing with your attention. I want to share two specific gifts with you: the first is a series of contemporary poems written on our theme by Wendell Berry, a poet, farmer, and theologian of the land.* The second gift is the concept of Environmental Sabbath, celebrated fortuitously the first weekend of June, culminating on the twentieth anniversary of Earth Day, Monday, June 5th.

Interwoven with my comments, then, will be poems and prayers that may sustain us until lunch.

---

* Excerpted from *Sabbaths*, copyright © 1987 by Wendell Berry. Published by North Point Press and reprinted by permission.

I go among trees and sit still.
All my stirring becomes quiet
around me like circles on water.
My tasks lie in their places
where I left them, asleep like cattle.

Then what is afraid of me comes
and lives a while in my sight.
What it fears in me leaves me,
and the fear of me leaves it.
It sings, and I hear its song.

Then what I am afraid of comes.
I live for a while in its sight.
What I fear in it leaves it,
and the fear of it leaves me.
It sings, and I hear its song.

After days of labor,
mute in my consternations,
I hear my song at last,
and I sing it. As we sing
the day turns, the trees move. (1979/I)

* * * * *

To sit and look at light-filled leaves
May let us see, or seem to see,
Far backward as through clearer eyes
To what unsighted hope believes:
The blessed conviviality
That sang Creation's seventh sunrise.

Time when the Maker's radiant sight
Made radiant every thing He saw,
And everything He saw was filled
With perfect joy and life and light.
His perfect pleasure was sole law;
No pleasure had become self-willed.

For all His creatures were His pleasures
And their whole pleasure was to be
What He made them; they sought no gain
Or growth beyond their proper measures,
Nor longed for change or novelty.
The only new thing could be pain. (1979/III)

I read Dr. Bacchiocchi's book *From Sabbath to Sunday* when I was studying for my liturgy degree at Notre Dame. I used it again in my studies at Catholic University in Washington, D.C., and I found it unfailingly scholarly, readable, and convincing. The key point in today's paper is the contrast between the moral or creational aspect of Sabbath and the ceremonial or Mosaic aspect. The Catholic and Lutheran traditions have emphasized the ceremonial aspect, whereas the Reformed tradition has given prominence to the moral aspect of the Sabbath commandments; this has led to the confusion we have today about Sabbath and Sunday keeping.

Since I have known for several months that I would be reacting to these papers, I have tried to pay attention to what goes on around me on Saturdays and Sundays, and I have come to the conclusion that children keep the Sabbath, the seventh day, with great, almost religious, fervor. As I think back on it myself, Saturday was always a much more delicious day than Sunday. As children, for one thing, we didn't have to go to church. The Saturday morning smells, the prospect of forty-eight hours without teachers, and what seemed like an eternity of play stretching before us, gave us much delight and joy. I'm not sure the organization of play that has given birth to Little League, soccer practices, ballet classes, dance lessons, and parental carpooling has improved our sense of keeping the Sabbath any. As a matter of fact, in my tradition, we Catholics have installed a Saturday night Mass (which counts for Sunday, of course) that could add some interesting dynamics to our future understanding of Sabbath. After all, we've used the Jewish measurement of time in celebrating the vigil of a feast or a Sunday. The Eucharist that is celebrated at seven o'clock at night is remarkably different in tone than one celebrated at seven or ten Sunday morning, although pastoral practitioners do not always take that into account. I wonder if we were to come across the notion of Sabbath in someone else's religion, through anthropological investigation, whether we would not find the practice intriguing and persuasive. After all, for six days a week human beings are heavily involved in the act of making, chasing, or transforming the world. It is appropriate to take one solid period of time, twenty-four hours, to change our relationship to the world, to back off from acting on it and stand back and celebrate its grandeur and the mystery of creation. To experience the world free from the need to interfere with it is a liberating experience. But if we are still getting, spending, speeding, and making, we cannot come into contact with that creational reality. That is where our rituals come in.

The particular genius of Judaism is the combined celebration of nature with the simultaneous affirmation of a need to transform the human world, by freeing it of oppression. The Sabbath has a joyful feeling: big celebratory meals, where people sit around dining, singing, arguing the fine points of the law, and sharing good food and wine. I also have a special

affection and longing for the injunction that married people should have
sex on the Sabbath. It is a nice, vicarious custom to a celibate.
Back to Wendell Berry:

> What stood will stand, though all be fallen,
> The good return that time has stolen.
> Though creatures groan in misery,
> Their flesh prefigures liberty
> To end travail and bring to birth
> Their new perfection in new earth.
> At word of that enlivening
> Let the trees of the woods all sing
> And every field rejoice, let praise
> Rise up out of the ground like grass.
> What stood, whole in every piecemeal
> Thing that stood, will stand though all
> Fall—field and woods and all in them
> Rejoin the primal Sabbath's hymn. (1979/VI)

I also enjoyed Dr. Bacchiocchi's comments about the creational interplay
of Sabbath. Sabbath meant cessation rather than relaxation. As he put it,
God, in a sense, blesses the Sabbath, makes it holy, lifting out its innate
holiness. We humans need to experience God's sanctifying presence. So we
keep the Sabbath to (1) follow divine example, (2) acknowledge God as
Creator, and (3) participate in God's rest and blessing. It is a sign of covenant between God and us—we look back to the past perfect creation and
forward to the ultimate salvation.

I would like to suggest that this Sabbath symposium is not some kind
of dusty, scholarly tediousness for a few learned doctors only; rather, it is
an attempt to revise the relationship of Creator to creation and to define
what our part in that creation is to be. Sabbath is meant to refer to rest
for all involved in the process of creation: rest for the earth as well as for
the humans. It is a symbol of a balanced relationship, of a harmony
between God and creation. It is a vision of interconnectedness. The United
Nations environmental program has picked up on this in its program of
Environmental Sabbath, Earth Rest Day. They suggest that we imagine an
infant nursing at its mother's breast. The mother grows weak, but the
infant continues suckling, allowing her no rest until she is dead. Then the
infant must die too. They suggest that humanity is such an infant at the
moment; humanity has become a taker—and a careless taker from the
mother, earth. Every year we burn a hundred thousand square kilometers
of primary tropical rain forest. This is not jungle that grows back in a
month or two but a primeval creation that takes centuries and eons to
create. The United Nations environmental program draws on the religious

traditions of Jewish, Christian, Muslim, Hindu, and Buddhism, as well as the Native American tradition, Quakers, and the Baha'i faith to call us to act in creating the Sabbath again. They cry: "Stop the sacrilege.! Reach the center of change—the human heart." They know that what is at issue here is not some ivory-tower squabble, but a profound spiritual problem. What is our relationship with creation? How are we living up to our reputation of being made in the image of God? The Environmental Sabbath means discovering the fundamental reality of oneness, the interconnectedness of ecosystems, the principles of diversity, autonomy, and communion that underpin every life form. The sacrilege occurs: soil disappears or loses its life force; water is turned to acid and burns the trees as well as our souls; our air is no longer benign, protecting us from harsh rays or carrying pure food for lungs and blood. The lesson for this Sabbath is either we change fundamentally or we will not be around to enjoy the fruits of our efforts. Wendell Berry:

> The year relents, and free
> Of work, I climb again
> To where the old trees wait,
> Time out of mind. I hear
> Traffic down on the road.
> Engines high overhead.
> And then a quiet comes,
> A cleft in time, silence
> Of metal moved by fire;
> The air holds little voices,
> Titmice and chickadees,
> Feeding through the treetops
> Among the new small leaves,
> Calling again to mind
> The grace of circumstance,
> Sabbath-economy
> In which all thought is song,
> All labor is a dance.
> The world is made at rest,
> In ease of gravity.
> I hear the ancient theme
> In low world-shaping song
> Sung by the falling stream.
> Here where a rotting log
> Has slowed the flow: a shelf
> Of dark soil, level laid
> Above the tumbled stone.

Roots fasten it in place.
It will be here a while;
What holds it here decays.
A richness from above,
Brought down, is held, and holds
A little while in flow.
Stem and leaf grow from it.
At cost of death, it has
A life. Thus falling founds,
Unmaking makes the world. (1983/II)

Dr. John Primus, in his paper on Protestant perspectives on the Sabbath, makes it clear that we do not want Sabbath as an idol. Calvin did not want to make the Sabbath an idol; our relationship with God is grounded in grace. Calvin talks about daily resting from sinful deeds, which again would be an excellent text for the notion of Environmental Sabbath. So many of our daily deeds are unthinking, ecological bad habits. Nicholas Bound asks rest for servants, beasts of burden, and sojourners on the Sabbath and says that the Sabbath is etched on the human heart, something that Catholics would find very akin to natural law. Calvin appreciates works of mercy done on the Sabbath and states that people should see the miseries of others in order to stimulate compassion. I think of some parents who on weekends or holy days take their children into less affluent areas, visiting soup kitchens or shelters and talking with their children about who these other children are and how they are their brothers and sisters. I also resonate with Bound's musings on people not coming to the Sabbath with bows and arrows or hawks upon their fists, and how he dislikes disorderly traffic conditions. Any Catholic pastor has the same concerns.

It was eye-opening to me to see Sabbath reaffirmed as the crown of creation—not man and woman, but the Sabbath. I had always described man and woman at the top of creation with the statement that the human brain is the crowning achievement of creation. What is it that tells us that the brain is the crowning achievement of creation, but the human brain? It always seemed a little self-serving. The Sabbath, however, in its revelation, in its sanctification, in its invitation to love, establishes again and again a new age. (I could not very well give a paper within earshot of Boulder, without using the phrase, "New Age.") Human beings are not the measure of all things; rather, the Sabbath is a sacrament that creates a holy worldliness—what a wonderful phrase! A phrase not only for the Sabbath day, but to take back with us into the workweek. Our quest for Sabbath grace and nourishment, our need for reconnection with the earth, is wonderfully summed up by a quote from Chief Seattle:

Teach your children what we have taught our children, that the earth is our mother. Whatever befalls the earth, befalls the children of the earth. If we spit upon the ground, we spit upon ourselves. This we know. The earth does not belong to us; we belong to the earth. . . . One thing we know, which the white man may one day discover, our God is the same God. You may think now that you own God, as you wish to own our land, but you cannot. God is the God of all people, and his compassion is equal for all. This earth is precious to God, and to harm the earth is to heap contempt on its Creator. So love it as we have loved it. Care for it as we have cared for it. And with all your mind, and with all your heart, preserve it for your children, and love . . . as God loves us all." (1855; from "Environmental Sabbath: Earth Rest Day," *United Nations Environment Programme*, p. 14)

Let me close my own rhapsodizing, again, with the words of Wendell Berry. It again returns to his theme of this certain grove of trees that he enjoys and identifies with the Sabbath. We might identify it with the rain forests of Brazil or our own little copse of birches that we remember and cherish.

> A gracious Sabbath stood here while they stood
> Who gave our rest a haven.
> Now fallen, these trees are given
> To labor and distress.
> These times we know much evil, little good
> To steady us in faith
> And comfort when our losses press
> Hard on us, and we choose,
> In panic or despair or both,
> To keep what we will lose.
>
> For we are fallen like the trees, our peace
> Broken, and so we must
> Love where we cannot trust,
> Trust where we cannot know,
> And must await the wayward-coming grace
> That joins living and dead,
> Taking us where we would not go —
> Into the boundless dark.
> When what was made has been unmade
> The Maker comes to His work. (1985/II)

* * * * *

> How long does it take to make the woods?
> As long as it takes to make the world.
> The woods is present as the world is, the presence
> of all its past, and of all its time to come.

It is always finished, it is always being made, the act
of its making forever greater than the act of its destruction.
It is a part of eternity, for its end and beginning
belong to the end and beginning of all things,
the beginning lost in the end, the end in the beginning.

What is the way to the woods, how do you go there?
By climbing up through the six days' field,
kept in all the body's years, the body's
sorrow, weariness, and joy. By passing through
the narrow gate on the far side of that field
where the pasture grass of the body's life gives way
to the high, original standing of the trees.
By coming into the shadow, the shadow
of the grace of the strait way's ending,
the shadow of the mercy of light.

Why must the gate be narrow?
Because you cannot pass beyond it burdened.
To come into the woods you must leave behind
the six days' world, all of it, all of its plans and hopes.
You must come without weapon or tool, alone,
expecting nothing, remembering nothing,
into the ease of sight, the brotherhood of eye and leaf. (1985/V)

* * * * *

So must our Sabbaths come, for us and our earth.

IV

THEOLOGICAL PERSPECTIVES

11

A JEWISH THEOLOGY AND PHILOSOPHY OF THE SABBATH

Walter S. Wurzburger
Yeshiva University

An important caveat must be heeded in any discussion of the philosophy or theology of the Sabbath. Judaism constitutes a way of life rather than the profession of a creed. Because it revolves around the observance of halakah (religious law) rather than the affirmation of articles of faith, precise dogmatic formulations are eschewed. No matter how far theological beliefs may diverge from the mainstream of Jewish thought, they qualify as perfectly legitimate expressions of Judaism, as long as they are compatible with the acknowledgment of the binding authority of the halakah. As Abraham of Posquiere put it in his strictures against Maimonides, one would not be excluded from the community of faith, even if one would veer as far from the dominant theological view as to attribute corporeal attributes to God.[1]

Since Judaism sanctions such enormous latitude in matters of belief, it is impossible to develop a philosophy or theology of the Sabbath that can lay claims to objective validity. All I hope to achieve in this paper is to provide a conceptual framework for what the experience of the Sabbath means to me and to show how the philosophy and theology I read into the Sabbath contributes to the enhancement of my personal appreciation and love of the Sabbath and enables me to treat the Shabbat as the very focus of my existence. My formulations are merely offered as possible interpretations of the postulates underlying the normative teachings of Judaism, which are embodied in the halakah.

In this connection it might be useful to refer to the *Pesiqta De'Rab Kahana,* which notes that the Sinaitic revelation addressed each individual in the voice appropriate for that person (12:25). Similarly, the kabbalists point out that the divine revelation was heard by each individual in a different form. In keeping with this emphasis on the subjectivity that characterizes the realm of Aggadah as opposed to objectively binding halakic norms regulating conduct, my objective is a very limited one: I merely want to develop *a* philosophy or theology of the Sabbath, for which I make no claims except that it satisfies the needs of my personal existential situation.

To be sure, in striking contrast to the many areas of religious practice where classical biblical and rabbinic sources hardly offer any clue to their theological or philosophical meaning, we suffer from an embarrassment of riches in the attempt to explore the spiritual meaning of Sabbath observance. The numerous scriptural references to the Sabbath allude to a variety of themes, ranging from creation to the Exodus from Egypt, from constituting a day of rest for the individual to a summons to a "holy convocation." The Sabbath is portrayed also as a sign of the covenant between God and Israel that God created heaven and earth in six days (Exodus 31:17).

Especially revealing is the difference between the two versions of the Decalogue as presented in Exodus and in Deuteronomy. The former concerns itself exclusively with the creation theme and focuses on the theocentric aspects of the Sabbath, reminding humans that the world does not belong to them but to God. Refraining from work on the Sabbath primarily is interpreted as the acknowledgment of God as the Creator of the universe. A person's right to engage in creative activity is limited to what is explicitly sanctioned by God and contributes to the fulfillment of God's purposes. To be legitimate, human activity must conform to the pattern established by God, who stopped the process of creation on the Sabbath. In sharp contrast to this exclusive emphasis on the surrender to God, which seeks to guard humans against self-deification and the worship of their own powers, the version of the Decalogue in Deuteronomy includes, in addition to the creation theme, a reference to the Exodus from Egypt and dwells upon the benefits accruing to man and woman from the Sabbath as a day of liberation and rest. This humanistic motif is further elaborated in prophetic writings, which mandate that the Sabbath be proclaimed as a day of delight and be treated with the honor due to such a sacred and joyous event. The Tannaim developed these ideas by stressing that the Sabbath should not merely be treated as a commandment but be hailed as a special and unique gift that the Almighty had bestowed upon Israel (Babylonian Talmud *Shabbat* 10b).

Although with reference to the Sabbath, a relatively large number of themes is adumbrated in Scriptures and subsequently developed in rabbinic literature, it appears that, contrary to Hermann Cohen's opinion, acknowledgment of God as the Creator rather than the liberation of humanity constitutes the dominant motif of the Sabbath experience.[2] Notwithstanding the fact that the Torah enjoins the remembrance and the sanctification of the Sabbath as well as the cessation of whatever activity interferes with the observance of a day of rest, the drastic penalties that the biblical legal code provides for desecration of the Sabbath are reserved exclusively for violations of the prohibition against *melakhah* (work). Public desecration of the Sabbath through performance of *melakhah* is deemed the equivalent of the rejection of the entire Torah. According to talmudic law, any individual guilty of such conduct is deprived of many privileges associated with membership in the Jewish community and in some respects is treated as a non-Jew. Although according to many contemporary authorities the upheavals of the post-Emancipation era have for all practical purposes rendered this law inoperative, it is of the utmost importance to bear in mind that traditionally observance of the prohibitions against *melakhah* was a *conditio sine qua non* of membership in the Jewish community. Since the Sabbath functions as sign between God and Israel that God is the Creator of heaven and earth, the desecration of the Sabbath amounts not merely to an act of disobedience but in effect to an outright denial of one of the most central tenets of Judaism—the affirmation of God as the Creator of the universe.

According to the rabbinic interpretation, no matter how strenuous an activity may be it does not fall under the category of biblically prohibited work, unless it constitutes *melekhet machshevet,* that is, an activity performed with design and purpose (Babylonian Talmud *Beṣah* 16a). To do so, it must not only resemble the thirty-nine types of work that according to Jewish tradition were necessary for the construction of the mobile sanctuary that was built in the desert; it must also follow the normal procedures and customary objectives associated with the activity in question. If an activity is carried out in an abnormal fashion (*kele'achar yad*), it is only rabbinically prohibited but does not constitute an infringement of the biblical prohibition against *melekhet machshevet.*

That designful activity rather than toil represents the defining characteristic of work sheds considerable light on the reason why the Sabbath plays such a pivotal role in the Jewish scale of values. It clearly indicates that such "social hygiene" functions as rest or relief from drudgery represent merely secondary considerations. Performing an activity in an awkward manner or without a purposeful, constructive intent would hardly affect the amount of effort expended. Were the suspension of toil and labor the primary goal of the Sabbath as a day of rest, the elements of purposeful activity could not be invoked as criteria determining whether or not a particular activity constitutes *melakhah.*[3]

The halakic definition of *melakhah* not as toil or labor but as purposeful work points to the specifically religious dimension of the Sabbath, which transcends considerations of social or psychological utility. If Isaiah (56:2, 14) and Nehemiah (9:13) single out the Sabbath as the hallmark of faithfulness to the covenant, it was because they saw in the Sabbath the concretization of the most fundamental tenets regarding a person's relationship to God and to nature. Maimonides even declares that the original divine legislation issued at Marah provided only for the Sabbath and ethical laws; no other ritual laws were deemed necessary at that time (*Guide for the Perplexed* 3:32). Small wonder, then, that the Sabbath is regarded as the quintessence of Judaism. As Dayan I. Grunfeld phrased it so aptly, the "Sabbath epitomizes the whole of Judaism."[4] Viewed from this vantage point, the prohibition against *melakhah* emerges as a much-needed reminder to humans that for all their powers of creativity, they too are merely creatures of God.

To be sure, human creativity and dominion over nature represent perfectly legitimate activities. Judaism does not subscribe to the Promethean myth that condemns human creativity as an act of defiance of the heavenly powers.[5] There is really no basis for Eric Fromm's suggestion that the prohibition against work on the Sabbath aims at the reconciliation of humanity with nature and the restoration of the peace that has been disturbed as the result of human efforts to assert dominion over nature.[6] However appealing this explanation may be to an age that is becoming increasingly sensitivized to ecological issues, the Jewish religious tradition can hardly be invoked to justify such an antitechnological bias. According to an often-quoted midrashic statement, even under the idyllic conditions that prevailed in the Garden of Eden it was necessary for man to engage in work and to tend and guard the earth.[7] It is also highly significant that the act of circumcision, which according to numerous commentators symbolizes man's task to become a partner with God in helping perfect the world,[8] takes precedence over the prohibitions against work on the Sabbath. There is therefore scant plausibility to Fromm's suggestion that the Sabbath is intended as a protest against interference with nature. There is really nothing in the Jewish tradition to support the thesis that reconciliation with nature as evidenced by the cessation of human constructive activities constitutes an integral part of the messianic ideal of perfect *shalom*—the ultimate peace of which the Sabbath is the forerunner.

It therefore seems much more likely that the prohibitions against work on the Sabbath are grounded not in antitechnological attitudes but in the realization of the debilitating spiritual hazards posed by human creativity. It is one thing to endorse human creativity as the fulfillment of a God-given mandate to conquer the world and to harness the forces of nature for the satisfaction of human needs and is another to become oblivious to the enormous dangers to the image of God within humanity, which, as we have so painfully discovered in an age of secularization and desacralization, are likely to result from our technological triumphs. We are prone to become so intoxicated with our success in subduing nature that we may succumb to the danger of arrogant self-idolization and forget that the entire universe, including our own creative capacities, is not a self-contained cosmos but God's creation, which must recognize its dependence on him.

The regularity and order prevailing within the realm of nature tend to obscure the divine source of all existence. It is for this reason that it is precisely on the day when according to the biblical account the world began to function in accordance with the laws of nature that it is incumbent upon us to acknowledge God as the owner and master of the universe.

By abstaining on the Sabbath from productive activity in conscious imitation of the Creator, who "stopped" his work of creation on the Sabbath, we affirm that what appear to the secular mind as purely natural phenomena are in actuality manifestations of the divine. Thus the Sabbath reveals what nature conceals. It is interesting to recall in this context that, according to the *Zohar,* the letters of the term *E-lohim* suggest that this name of God reflects the quest for the ultimate meaning of reality, which can be apprehended only when we raise the question *Mi eleh* (Who are these?) (*Zohar* 1:1b). In a similar vein, Rabbi Shneur Zalman Mi'Liadi noted that the numerical equivalent of the term *teva* (nature) is *E-lohim*.[9] It is through the Sabbath experience that we are directed to penetrate beneath the surface to the core of reality and to become aware that the universe is not a self-sufficient cosmos but is created and sustained in its being by the divine Creator, the source of all reality.

Since the experience of the holiness of the Sabbath is the matrix of the formation of proper perspectives on the "secular" domain, it is readily understandable why the Jewish religious tradition looks upon the Sabbath as the very purpose of all of creation. Accordingly, the Sabbath was not primarily intended as a day of rest enabling a person to return refreshed to worldly tasks with renewed vigor and zest. Instead, the liturgy in the Friday evening service extols the Sabbath as "the very goal of the making of the heaven and earth." Jewish life is supposed to be Sabbath-centered. The Jew does not rest on the Sabbath to prepare himself or herself for the tasks awaiting in the following week. Instead, the Jew literally lives for the Sabbath. He or she works six days in preparation for the goal of life—to enter the sacred precincts of the sanctuary in time that the Sabbath represents.

Nachmanides pointed out that the biblical commandment "Remember the Sabbath day to sanctify it" implies that the Sabbath is the only day of the week worthy of being designated by a name (*Commentary to Exodus* 20:8). The rest of the days are defined solely in terms of their relation to the Sabbath. In Hebrew there is no word for Sunday or Monday, etc; they are simply the first or the second day of the week. It is noteworthy that the Midrash interprets the biblical phrase "God finished on the seventh day the work He had made" (Genesis 2:2) as implying not merely that the work was concluded on the seventh day but that the work became perfect only on the seventh day (*Genesis Rabbah* 10:10). As Rashi interpreted it, until the Sabbath was created, the world was without *menuchah* (tranquillity) (Rashi on Genesis 2:2).

Although the exclusively theocentric formulation of the fourth commandment in the book of Exodus in describing the "Sabbath unto God" does not mention the social and psychological benefits accruing to one from its observance, the version of the Decalogue as presented in the book of Deuteronomy adds the themes of liberation and rest to be enjoyed by all creatures. Both Hermann Cohen and Erich Fromm write from a basically humanistic perspective, which frowns on obedience to heteronomous norms as being devoid of all ethical worth.[10] They concentrate on what they regard as the ethical implications of the Sabbath as set forth in Deuteronomy, which are contrasted with what they describe as the mythological features contained in the creation story, which form the core of the fourth commandment in Exodus 19. It appears to me that this approach reflects a dogmatic insistence on forcing Judaism into a Procrustean bed of humanistic categories. The additional references in Deuteronomy to anthropocentric themes do not in any way detract from the theocentric aspects mandating total surrender to God as the Creator and master of the universe. Significantly, it is precisely in the version in which the humanistic benefits are introduced that the Torah stresses that the observance of the Sabbath is in conformity to a divine imperative ("as God has commanded thee").

This being the case, it would be far more appropriate to treat the anthropocentric and the theocentric dimensions of the Sabbath experience as reflections of the dialectical tension between these two components rather than as irreconcilable positions. Contrary to E. Feuerbach and K. Marx, a person's unconditional submission to the Creator does not devalue human existence but adds an extra dimension of meaning and significance, which enables him or her to experience true dignity and freedom. The Sabbath experience makes us aware of the fact that our ontological status is based not on what we make but on what we are. As the bearer of the divine age, persons must not be "thingified" and reduced to self-alienated commodities or tools but must be accorded the dignity due to creatures endowed with infinite, intrinsic spiritual value. Through the observance and experience of the Sabbath, the Jew learns that in the divine economy, a person's worth does not depend upon social utility as an agent of production but derives from the intrinsic sanctity of the human personality.

At first blush it may strike us as strange that the observance of the Sabbath, which cuts a person down to size by mandating that his or her creative powers may be exercised only within the parameters approved by God, simultaneously elevates a person's dignity by providing us with a day of universal rest and liberation, which engenders the experience of *oneg*

Shabbat—the enjoyment of delight, peace, and harmony. But it must be borne in mind that classical Jewish thought has always proceeded from the premise that it is only through submission to the authority of a transcendent God that humans achieve true dignity and inner freedom. In the often-cited formulation of the rabbinic sages, "one attains freedom only when one is engaged in Torah" (*Avot* 6:2).

The dialectical nature of the Sabbath experience is suggested also in a well-known Midrash which states that "every thing pertaining to the Sabbath is double . . . double Omer (of Mannah) . . . , double sacrifices . . . , double penalites . . . , double rewards . . . , double admonitions . . . and the Sabbath Psalm is double" (*Midrash Tehillim* on Psalm 92:1). The two loaves of bread that are *de rigeur* for Sabbath meals (Babylonian Talmud *Shabbat* 117b) reflect this emphasis on the duality characterizing the Sabbath observance. Significantly, the Talmud points out that the two versions of the fourth commandment were simultaneously commanded by God to Israel in one single pronouncement (Babylonian Talmud *Rosh Hashanah* 27a). The emphasis on the twofold nature of the Sabbath also comes to the fore in the rabbinic doctrine that with the arrival of the Sabbath the Jew is endowed with a *neshamah yeterah* (an additional soul), which departs at the conclusion of the Sabbath (Babylonian Talmud *Beṣah* 16a).

Since the Sabbath represents in a sense the bridge between the natural and the transcendent realms, the Talmud took it for granted that the Sinaitic revelation occurred on the Sabbath (*Shabbat* 86b). It seemed obvious to the rabbinic mind that the day which, according to the Bible, symbolized the incursion of the divine upon the world of nature, represented the ideal time for his revelation to Israel.

Another theme that is associated with the Sabbath is that of redemption. Although in the Torah the connection between the Sabbath and liberation is made only with reference to the Exodus from Egypt, rabbinic thought expands the concept by treating the Exodus as the prototype of the divine redemption—a process that will be completed only in the messianic redemption, when the kingdom of God will be acknowledged by all of humanity. The proper observance of the Sabbath, therefore, is regarded not merely as a reminder of the past liberation but also as a promise of the future realization of our eschatological hopes. It is for this reason that, in the opinion of the sages, the meticulous observance of the Sabbath on the part of the entire Jewish people would ensure the arrival of the Messiah (Babylonian Talmud *Shabbat* 118b). Because of the close association between the Sabbath and the redemption, the liturgy for welcoming the Sabbath includes a number of psalms that give vent to the feeling of exhilaration and jubilation that will be precipitated by the establishment of the kingdom of God.[11]

The Sabbath does not merely point to the redemption of the world from moral evil. Since the Sabbath atmosphere is supposed to make us oblivious to unfulfilled wants and unfinished tasks, it provides a foretaste of the world to come. This is why when the prayer of grace is recited after the Sabbath meal, the phrase "May the All-Merciful One cause us to inherit the day which be completely a Sabbath of rest and eternal life" is added to the weekday version.

It is interesting that the Talmud records two distinct modes of preparation that are appropriate for the proper encounter with the Sabbath. One Amora (a talmudic sage) is reported to have urged his disciples to welcome the Sabbath as a queen, whereas another advocated that the Sabbath be greeted as a bride (Babylonian Talmud *Shabbat* 119a). In other words, one opinion emphasized the majesty, awe, and reverence with which the Shabbat should be approached, whereas the other stressed the intimacy with the divine that should be engendered by the encounter with what the liturgy describes as "the most desirable of days." Since the two approaches need not contradict each other, they should be synthesized in the ideal Shabbat experience. Rabbinic authorities till this very day are divided over the question of whether there is a requirement to experience real *simchah* (joy) on the Sabbath or whether one is merely obligated to engage in activities that can be described as *oneg* (pleasant) but do not necessarily lead to the higher level of *simchah* which is mandated for holidays. Be that as it may, there is universal agreement that the Sabbath must be respected not only by refraining from work in the technical sense but by staying away from any activity that interferes with the atmosphere of holiness which ought to prevail on the Sabbath. The dignity of the Sabbath demands that one not only dress and eat differently from the rest of the week, but that one's entire demeanor and conduct reflect the sanctity of the Sabbath. Subjects that disturb the spiritual atmosphere of the Sabbath are to be avoided in conversation (Babylonian Talmud *Shabbat* 69a).

For a proper appreciation of the sanctity of the Sabbath it should be borne in mind that the Sabbath, God's sanctuary in time, commands the kind of reverence that must be accorded to God's sanctuary in space. It is highly significant that the Torah juxtaposes the two types of sanctuary in the twice-repeated verse "Ye shall keep My Sabbaths and reverence My sanctuary" (Leviticus 19:30 and 26:2). Moreover, the Torah harps repeatedly on the overriding importance of the observance of the Sabbath in connection with the demand to build a sanctuary for God. It is precisely this close linkage between the two types of sanctuaries that prompted the sages to define *melakhah* in terms of the categories of work that were needed for the construction of the sanctuary in the days of Moses.

Because the Sabbath is treated as a sanctuary of God, it is readily understandable that Jewish mystics employ spatial metaphors to describe the unique holiness that envelops the world with the arrival of the Sabbath. According to the *Zohar,* "On Friday evening a tabernacle of peace descends from heaven. . . . When Israel invites this tabernacle of peace to their homes as a holy guest, a divine sanctity comes down and spreads its wings over Israel like a mother encompassing her children" (*Zohar* Genesis 48a–b).

It must be realized, however, that the holiness of the Sabbath mandates not merely the cessation of certain types of "secular" activity but also the fulfillment of a number of specific positive obligations. Both the arrival and the departure of the Sabbath must be marked by special ceremonies (*Kiddush* and *Havdalah*). Moreover, according to Nachmanides' interpretation, the inclusion of the Sabbath among the days of "holy convocations" implies that Jews are not merely required to sanctify the Sabbath individually but are supposed to assemble for the purpose of divine worship and the reading of the Torah. In other words, the Sabbath experience is designed not only to impact upon the Jew individually but also to stimulate the formation of a unique sense of religious community. As a Midrash puts it, Israel's loneliness can be overcome only by the realization that it is mated with the Sabbath—the symbol of its unique spiritual destiny (*Genesis Rabbah* 11:8).

It thus can be seen that, properly observed, the Sabbath is not just a day of rest and total inactivity. Notwithstanding the fact that already in the ancient world the Sabbath was maligned by anti-Semitic writers as evidence of the Jewish predilection to lassitude, which exacts a heavy price in terms of loss of productivity and usefulness, the Sabbath represents a day of spiritual creativity,[12] which, in the words of Ahad Ha'am, has made possible the very survival of the Jewish people. That the Sabbath is to be regarded as a day of positive achievement rather than of lack of activity can be seen from the fact that the Torah employs the term *la-'asot* (to make) in conjunction with the admonition to keep the Sabbath (Exodus 31:16 and Deuteronomy 5:16). As Rabbi Kook expressed it so aptly, the Sabbath figures not only as a day of rest but also as a day of holiness.[13] Abstention from activities aiming at the conquest of nature do not exhaust the meaning of the Sabbath. Physical rest must be utilized for all-out spiritual efforts to respond to the challenge posed by the dynamic ideal of holiness which constantly beckons us toward ever greater heights of religious and moral perfection in the never-ending quest of *imitatio Dei.* This is perhaps what was supposed to be conveyed by the daring kabbalistic doctrine that the Sabbath symbolizes the union between the male (active) and the female (passive) metaphysical principles, which, according to Jewish mysticism, provide the foundation of the universe.[14]

NOTES

1. Abraham of Posquiere, *Hasagot Hara'vad Lemishneh Torah ad Hilkhot Teshuvah* 3:7 (Jerusalem, 1984).

2. Hermann Cohen, *Religion der Vernunft* (trans. Ephraim Fischoff; Leipzig: G. Foch, 1919) 180–82.

3. See my article "Sabbath and Creation," in *Yavneh Shiron,* ed. Eugene Flink (New York: Yavneh Students Organization, 1968) 51–53.

4. D. I. Grunfeld, *The Sabbath: A Guide to its Understanding and Observance* (London: Sabbath League of Great Britain, 1956) 11. Dayan Grunfeld has pioneered in popularizing the ideas of Samson R. Hirsch in the English-speaking world. Their influence can readily be perceived in my own treatment of the relationship between the Sabbath and the creation theme.

5. See my article "Orthodox Judaism and Human Purpose," in *Religion and Human Purpose,* ed. W. Horosz and T. Clements (Dordrecht: Nijhoff, 1986) 106–22.

6. Eric Fromm, *The Forgotten Language* (New York: Grove Press, 1985) 488–91).

7. *Avot De'rabbi Natan,* 11:1.

8. See *Sefer Hachinukh,* chapter 2.

9. R. Shneur Zalman Mi'Liadi, *Tanya, Sha'ar Hayichud Ve'ha'emunah* (Brooklyn: Kehot Publication Society, 1953) chap. 6.

10. Cohen, *Religion der Vernunft,* 180–82; Fromm, *Ye Shall Be As Gods* (New York: Holt, Rinehart & Winston, 1966) 193–99.

11. See Yechiel Michel Epstein, *Aruch Hashulchan, Orach Chayim* (New York: Halakhah Publishing, 1950) 277:2.

12. See Normann Lamm, "Ethics of Leisure" in *Faith and Doubt* (New York: Ktav, 1971) 197–98. I have also learned a great deal from Abraham J. Heschel's *The Sabbath: Its Meaning for Modern Man* (New York: Farrar, Straus and Giroux, 1951) as well as from the profound insights of Yitzchak Hutner in his *Sefer Pachad Yitzchak* (Brooklyn: Gur Aryeh Institute, 1982).

13. Abraham Isaac Kook, *Olat Haraya* (Jerusalem: Mossad Harav Kook, 1949) 2:146.

14. See *Zohar* Exodus 135a-b; *Zohar* Genesis 48a-b; and Nachmanides, *Commentary to Exodus* 20:8.

12

LOVING THE SABBATH AS A CHRISTIAN: A SEVENTH-DAY ADVENTIST PERSPECTIVE

Jacques B. Doukhan

When I received this assignment, my first reaction was to change the title into one that would sound more scholarly, more objective, and therefore more respectable. I was wrong, for any reflection on the topic of the Sabbath of necessity implies the involvement of the human subject.

"Loving the Sabbath as a Christian" means that I am expected to approach this question from a Christian point of view, taking into consideration Christian theology, with its emphasis on grace, as well as the reference to its fundamental source — the Bible, that is, the Old and the New Testaments. Yet my task will be more specific. The title of this paper indicates that I am supposed to present a Christian theology of the Sabbath from a Seventh-day Adventist perspective. Therefore, it is as a Christian and as a Seventh-day Adventist that I shall approach this topic of the Sabbath. As history has demonstrated, this association may appear difficult, for throughout the centuries the seventh-day Sabbath and Christianity have not gotten along very well. Because of the keeping of the Sabbath, Seventh-day Adventists have often been, and sometimes still are, suspected of being non-Christian people, even up to the point of being assimilated with Jews.[1]

Further, the paradoxical tone of this presentation will be enhanced because I must add an unexpected third perspective to the two previously mentioned. It is not only as a Christian and as a Seventh-day Adventist that I am approaching this topic. It is also as a Jew who grew up in a Jewish family and lived the Sabbath within the tension of the two great faiths — Christianity and Judaism. I am aware that this personal involvement with the Sabbath will affect the nature of my approach. However, it is with the tools of a biblical scholar, more precisely, as an interpreter of the Bible, that I intend to address this topic.[2]

Since the Sabbath is called a sign in the Bible (Exodus 31:13; Ezekiel 20:12), I have chosen to conduct my reflection in a systematic manner on the basis of that designation. As a sign, that is, as a *sēmeia* category (*'ôt*), the Sabbath is intended to be a language that speaks to believers not only about a reality that involves them now but also about a reality that is beyond themselves.[3]

It is true that we celebrate the Sabbath as a sign of holiness in our *present* existence; however, the Sabbath is also of compelling importance because of what it objectively represents and points to. Thus the Sabbath is a sign of remembrance pointing to the *past* event of creation, a sign of hope refer-ring to the *future* redemption, and a sign of the Absolute, witnessing to the divine "Other." It is within these four dimensions of the Sabbath, as integrated within the larger framework of Seventh-day Adventist theology, that I will present my reflections.

After this deductive theological study, I will bring out in an excursus the four key biblical passages on the Sabbath: in the creation story (Genesis 2:1–3), in the Decalogue (Exodus 20:8–11; Deuteronomy 5:12–15), and in the account of the tabernacle (Exodus 31:12–18). In an inductive manner this excursus will draw out ideas from the observation of the literary struc-ture of the pericopes and will either confirm the concepts already pointed out or indicate new directions of thought.

Obviously, this study is personal and does not necessarily reflect all the nuances of Seventh-day Adventist theology. I have tried, however, to remain as faithful as possible to the main trends of Seventh-day Adventism. Thus, I have accompanied my reflections and observations with specific footnotes containing relevant quotations from the most representative contemporary Seventh-day Adventist theologians of the doctrine of the Sabbath.[4] The influence of Abraham Joshua Heschel has considerably affected the thinking of these writers[5] and is indeed easily discernible in this presentation.

A SIGN OF REMEMBRANCE

The first function of the Sabbath is that it is an act of the memory. In the Ten Commandments this precept is explicitly qualified with the word: "Remember" (Exodus 20:8). It is also implicitly so understood because it refers to an event of the past. In fact, the Sabbath implies the act of remem-brance *par excellence* since it reminds us of the absolute past, that is, the beginning of the world and of humanity—hence, the past of everything and everyone. This "reminding" function of the Sabbath is suggested also by the fact that the Sabbath is juxtaposed to the fifth commandment in the Decalogue. Not only do they immediately follow each other, but they are also the only two commandments to be positively formulated.[6] This correspondence indicates a common concern. Both regulations enjoin the act of remembrance by implying the origins and roots of human beings—the fourth commandment through the creative act of God, and the fifth through the procreative actions of one's own parents.

This "reminding" function is an indication of the nature of the lesson the Sabbath is intended to convey: it is not only of a philosophical nature, a truth to be conceived or meditated on, but rather a reference to a historical event. Remembrance implies essentially history and not just theology. If the "reminding" function of the Sabbath conveys the idea that creation is a historical event, it teaches by implication specific lessons concerning the nature of the universe and the nature of humanity. With regard to the nature of the universe, it means that the universe has no creative power in itself—not only in the pantheistic sense but also in the modern sense of evolution, as in the writings of Henri Bergson or Pierre Teilhard de Chardin, for instance. The Sabbath teaches that creation is a historical event that took place at a particular moment in time, that is, with a beginning and an end. Furthermore, as the last day of the creation week, the Sabbath reminds us that the work of creation had come to an end. Therefore, the idea of creation is in Seventh-day Adventist theology incompatible with the idea of evolution.[7] The Sabbath reminds us that creation is a historical event started and ended in the past, whereas evolution teaches that creation has always been and still is in process. The two beliefs are "mutually exclusive."[8]

With regard to the nature of humanity, it means that, like the universe, human beings have not come about as the result of a process, but "suddenly" as the result of a definite creation. The Seventh-day Adventist rejection of the idea of an innate immortal soul in the human body and, by implication, the emphasis on the unity of being as well as the belief in a healthy life-style are directly related to that theology of creation and are therefore consistent with the lessons of the Sabbath.

Second, the Sabbath in precept and practice is a reminder of the existence of the Sabbath itself; as Exodus 20:8 says, "Remember the Sabbath day." This specification indicates the nature of that remembrance. This is not just an intellectual performance; it is an actual repetition in one's life of the very day. "Remember the Sabbath day" means that I should not ignore or forget in my present existence the passage of the Sabbath day. To "remember" the Sabbath means that I should distinctly mark out the time of the Sabbath from the rest of my time. One of the implications of this task is the necessity of remaining faithful to the true Sabbath day. Since Seventh-day Adventist theology is situated within Christianity, which generally keeps Sunday as the Sabbath, it is expected that this last concern should be important in Adventist apologetics.[9]

A SIGN OF HOPE

Hope is conveyed through the Sabbath on the basis of what the Sabbath recalls, namely, the events of creation and of the seventh day. Drawing our minds back to the event of creation, the Sabbath is a sign of hope, for it tells us of the miraculous process in which existence was brought out of nothing. Therefore, the Sabbath is referred to also as the sign of deliverance from Egypt (Deuteronomy 5:15) and later as the sign of deliverance from the Babylonian exile (2 Chronicles 36:21). Actually the Sabbath is used as a sign for the Exodus and the return from the exile precisely because both events are perceived as a creation (Exodus 15:8;[10] Deuteronomy 4:32–33; Isaiah 43:15–17; 44:24). It seems that the New Testament follows the same line when it reports that most of Jesus' miracles were performed on the Sabbath (Matthew 12:9–14; Mark 1:21–28, 29–31; Luke 14:1–6; John 5:1–6; 9:1–38), especially in order to point out the redeeming function of the Sabbath (Luke 13:16).[11] Because creation and deliverance are related, the Sabbath is the sign for both. Thus, the prophet Isaiah describes salvation as a creation (Isaiah 66:22). Likewise in the New Testament, the redemptory activity of Jesus is related to his creative activity (Hebrews 1:1–3; John 1:1–5; Colossians 1:16, 20). Moreover, the Christian experience is compared to a creation (2 Corinthians 5:17), to the passage from darkness to light (Colossians 1:13; 2:12–13; John 3:1–21).[12]

The Sabbath not only teaches a lesson of hope indirectly through the reference to creation, but it also does so directly as the Sabbath in its own essence. Marking the end of the week, the Sabbath functions as an *eschaton,* thereby pointing to the cosmic *eschaton,* the end of time. This eschatological connotation of the Sabbath can be perceived already in Genesis 2:1–3. The idea of "end" is explicitly indicated twice in the verb *klh* (finish),[13] once in relation to the object: "the heavens and the earth and all the host of them were finished" (Genesis 2:1), and once in relation to the subject "God finished" (Genesis 2:2). The idea of end is also implicitly present in the three occurrences of the word *kôl* (all), to indicate that "all" the work has been "completed."[14] The three repetitions of "seventh day" have a rhetorical significance. As a rhetorical number, seven expresses the idea of perfection (Zechariah 3:9; 4:2; Revelation 4–5; Leviticus 4:6; 8:11; James 3:17; 2 Peter 1:5–8);[15] and in time it generally indicates the conclusion of a cycle (Leviticus 25:8–10; Exodus 29:25–37; Daniel 7:25; Revelation 11:2; Genesis 4; 7:3–4, 10, Ezekiel 3:16–17).

Marking the completion of creation, the Sabbath/seventh day indicates also the cosmic nature of salvation. The event of salvation concerns the universe and is not just subjective and spiritual.[16] The salvation of the individual cannot happen apart from the complete and objective salvation of the world.[17] Further, the prosaic specification "seventh day," because it brings to remembrance the historical character of a day precisely situated in time, points to the historical reality of salvation. Like the event of the Sabbath, salvation is an event that is to take place at a specific time appointed by God himself.

The Sabbath of the creation week was also the first whole day of Adam, the first day of human history, set apart by God, as God's rest in which Adam participated. The Sabbath reminds us then of the first human fellowship with God. As such, the Sabbath points by analogy to the rest of salvation, when human beings will again enjoy fellowship with God. This dimension of the Sabbath is indicated by the prophet Isaiah, who associates the delight of the Sabbath with the delight of the Lord (Isaiah 58:13–14).[18] If you delight in the Sabbath, you will delight in the Lord. The Sabbath is understood as the very place in time of the experience of "God with us." This specific idea is implied in Exodus 40:33–38, where the *shekhinah,* the sign of God's presence, is introduced at the conclusion of the building of the sanctuary with the same technical words *wayekal melakhah* (he finished the work) that introduce the Sabbath at the end of the creation story.[19]

In the New Testament this identification of the Sabbath with God's very presence takes on a particular aspect. Jesus, the one who provides salvation, identifies himself with the Sabbath; he is the one who provides rest (Matthew 11:28–29);[20] he is "God with us."[21] On the other hand, the Letter to the Hebrews refers to the rest of the Sabbath as a type of salvation, when the people of God will enter God's rest (Hebrews 3–4).[22] This reference to the Sabbath may even contain eschatological overtones, if we interpret the "today" of Hebrews 4:7 as a reflection of the Hebrew *hayyôm,* which can also mean "*the* day"; that is, the eschatological Day of the Lord (Ezekiel 7:10, 27; Joel 3:18; Jeremiah 30:7). This eschatological interpretation may be supported in the Bible, since the Sabbath is also called the Day of the Lord (Exodus 20:10; Deuteronomy 5:14),[23] an expression that characterizes the eschatological event of God's coming in history (Isaiah 13:9; Joel 2:31; 1 Thessalonians 5:2; 2 Peter 3:12).[24]

If the two ideas of creation and hope are conveyed together through the Sabbath, it is because they both imply the same rationale and are closely related to each other.[25] They pertain to the same quality of faith. To venture to hope in the kingdom of God, one must dare to believe in creation. For the God who was able to raise the world from nothing, to begin history and to consent to come into human time, will also be able to recreate from chaos, to conclude history, and to come again into human time. Thus, the Sabbath conveys the idea of hope in two ways, by referring to the miracle process of creation and by pointing to the conclusion of history, when God enters into fellowship with humanity.

Biblical hope is a vision of the future which is paradoxically channeled through memory. As the event of creation is remembered, one can think of the event of recreation; therefore, one can hope. This process of association is important, because it places hope not merely within the categories of thought or of imagination as a spiritual concept, but rather within the categories of memory, that is, as a historical reality. The Sabbath conveys hope because of its "reminding" function. Hope is only genuine hope insofar as it has the same historical substance as the event of which the Sabbath reminds us. This is the main lesson of Deuteronomy 5, which associates the Sabbath with the salvation of Israel in the Exodus event. Here also, salvation is perceived as a historical event to be remembered. The salvation to which the Sabbath refers is not just psychological in nature, a kind of spiritual experience of peace; it is more than this—or, rather, it may imply such an experience only because it points to the real historical event of salvation.

It is to be noted that the association of these two truths, creation and hope, is important in Seventh-day Adventist theology. In fact, this association is so essential that it has inspired the very name "Seventh-day Adventist," which relates the remembrance of creation to the hope of the coming of the Lord, "the Advent." This double lesson of the Sabbath is also consistent with a number of specific doctrines which characterize this religious denomination, for example, the emphasis on the eschatological cosmic salvation as an implication of the unity of creation and the resurrection of the dead as a necessary implication of the unity of being. This theology of the Sabbath is consistent with a number of specific liturgical celebrations, including baptism, which points both to the past event of creation and to the future event of re-creation (Romans 6:3-5), and the Lord's Supper, which points both to the past event of the Passover and the crucifixion and to the future restoration of the fellowship with the Lord (1 Corinthians 11:16).[26]

A SIGN OF THE ABSOLUTE

The Sabbath bears witness to the Absolute in that it points to a reality that is free from and beyond any contingency, to the divine law, to God's grace, and ultimately to God himself. Because it is divine law, the Sabbath in essence is a sign that points to the Absolute. It is introduced by an imperative: "Remember."[27] It belongs to the law which has come to human beings as a revelation from outside. Several elements indicate even the very distinctive preeminence of the Sabbath among the rest of the laws. In the levitical list, the Sabbath is referred to in distinction from the other feasts and Sabbaths (Leviticus 23:2–4ff.). In the Ten Commandments, it is the only "feast" day mentioned. Significantly, the Sabbath has been remembered in biblical tradition as the first commandment ever observed by humans. Right after creation, the first human couple started life and thereby the course of human history in obeying that commandment. It was also the first commandment required of Israel right after the event of the Exodus (Exodus 16). In the levitical laws this is actually the only day that is not annual and the only day whose time is not dependent on natural or astronomical cycles. The justification of the Sabbath is then essentially religious.[28] No natural or ethical reason lies behind this observance. In fact, faith happens to be the only reason for the Sabbath. Furthermore:

> respect for the Sabbath as the day which has been determined by the Creator, and not for the other day which has been decreed by human tradition, indicates the loyalty of the believer. It is from above only, from the Absolute, that the believer draws his value system. By keeping the Sabbath, the sign of belonging to God (Exodus 31:12–17; Ezekiel 20:12), the believer, remarkably, becomes a sign himself—a sign that the kingdom to which he belongs is not of the world, but of God. The break of the Sabbath has nothing to do with a weekly vacation; it is the concrete expression of faith in Creation, the sign of one's dependence on heaven. When that is well understood, the keeping of the Sabbath excludes any trend to legalism or formalism. As the absolute sign of faith in the God of heaven, the Sabbath carries in itself the view that salvation is only from above.[29]

In that sense the Sabbath may be considered as the sign of a reference to the absolute criteria from above (Exodus 31:12–17; Ezekiel 20:2), the law *par excellence*.[30]

This last characteristic of the Sabbath would be enough to disqualify it in traditional Christian theology where the law is no longer valid under the economy of grace. In Seventh-day Adventist theology, however, this "tension" between law and grace is assumed. The Sabbath constitutes a good example of that tension.[31] In obeying the fourth commandment, the believer does not negate the value of grace. On the contrary, the awareness of grace is implied. Through obedience to God's law, the believer expresses faith in God's grace. This principle is particularly valid when it applies to the Sabbath, because in it not only the divine law but also divine grace are magnified. Indeed, the Sabbath reminds us of the free act of God toward men and women and thereby witnesses to the Absolute. The idea of grace implies of necessity the idea of "something" having originated from outside, independently—hence, the idea of the Absolute. God did not work out of something or with someone. Humanity was not yet. God's act of creation was not triggered by something or someone outside of himself. It was a free act. It was absolute grace. On the level of the human being, the Sabbath teaches us the fact that we are nothing but God's gift. We are the result of God's grace.[32]

The Sabbath also conveys the idea of grace, for it reminds us of God's rest. God has taken the initiative of this rest and of entering into human time for fellowship. God rested in order to relate to men and women. By remembering God's rest, the Sabbath points to divine grace and love.[33] On the human level the Sabbath is also a pedagogue of grace, in that it teaches us the value of nonaction in relationship with God, a lesson that is echoed in the miracle of the manna (Deuteronomy 8:3). Refraining from working on the Sabbath is an indication of total dependence on God. What one *has* is not a result of work, but a free gift from God. Adam did not enjoy the first rest as a reward for work, but rather as grace, as God's gift. God worked for, and without, Adam and then granted him a rest he did not deserve and that God himself did not need. This is a rest that is "free" grace, a rest, therefore, that carries the mark of the Absolute.

Lastly, the Sabbath is the sign of the Absolute in that it conveys the reference to God, the absolute "Other." It is said to be the day of the Lord (Exodus 20:10; Leviticus 23:3; Deuteronomy 5:14); the day the Lord has made (Genesis 2:1–3); the sign of God (Exodus 31:15; Ezekiel 20:12). The Sabbath day is thus holy in itself, a day "full of objective holiness," as Gerhard von Rad puts it.[34]

A SIGN OF HOLINESS

As we have already pointed out, the Sabbath is set apart and made holy because of what it means, as a sign of an external reality pointing to the past, the future, and the Absolute. But the Sabbath also draws its *raison d'être* and its holiness from within the believer. The Sabbath "exists" also in the present life of the believer. The holiness of that day, indeed, implies the participation of men and women. The Sabbath will not be holy without human beings; the holiness of the Sabbath implies the holiness of men and women. The reason for this prerequisite lies essentially in the Hebrew concept of time. For the Hebrew, time does not exist outside of the human being, as an external threatening reality. The Hebrew concept of time is bound up with its content and even identified with it.[35] The Sabbath is therefore also related to the human person. The Sabbath is not only "made" by God for the human person; it is also a day "made" by the human person for God (Deuteronomy 5:15). The holiness of the Sabbath depends on the participation of both partners. It is a sign of the covenant between God and human beings (Exodus 31:17; cf. Ezekiel 20:20). However, the human "making" of the Sabbath is nothing but a response to the divine one;[36] it is an *imitatio Dei*.[37] Just as the Sabbath is the divine expression of love toward humanity, it is also, on the human level as a response, the expression of human love toward God. This understanding of the Sabbath, as a response, means that humanity has to adjust, and not the reverse. On Sabbath we are urged to refrain from doing our own will (Isaiah 58:13-14). Thus, the Sabbath is not just a theology; it is a praxis, a confrontation with the reality of life. This commitment of love has led many Seventh-day Adventists to run risks at every level of their existence. Their jobs, their promotion in society, and even their lives have often been threatened or sacrificed because of their religious commitment. (This has been my own painful experience, when during military service I was jailed, beaten, and tortured for several months, simply because of faithfulness to the Sabbath.) One must recognize that the observance of the Sabbath day cannot pass by unnoticed. It is visible and disruptive in our well-structured society, which is so concerned with efficiency. These struggles, which have often become the lot of Seventh-day Adventist people,[38] are interpreted in Adventist theology as a part of the ultimate test of faith and therefore as a sign of holiness.[39] By observing the Sabbath, the believer engages in the experience of being set apart, different, holy. In fact, by observing the Sabbath as a sign of holiness, believers learn to become themselves a sign of holiness (Exodus 31:13).

This holiness of the Sabbath, which sets the believers apart, should not however separate them from their neighbors. On the contrary, in the Sabbath the openness to the divine "Other" is complemented with the openness to the human "other." The social dimension of the Sabbath is implied in the reference to the event of creation, which reminds us of the common origin of all men and women. It is also explicitly indicated in the fourth commandment, which refers to the human "other," that is, the servant or the stranger enjoying during that day the same privileges of freedom and rest as the Israelites. This is the day when each one is to remember the neighbor as equal, and hence respectable.[40] The Sabbath is also described by the prophet Isaiah as the place of reunion of all the peoples in God (Isaiah 56:3-8).

This social dimension of the Sabbath is one of the characteristics in the Seventh-day Adventist observance of the fourth commandment. The Sabbath is indeed the day of the Lord, a day of holiness devoted to worship and to the study of the Holy Scriptures. But it is also the day that will turn us to others. This is supposed to be a special day for family reunion, the day when husband, wife, and children have time to listen to each other.[41] During that day it is not forbidden to heal, to help, to love one's neighbor (Mark 3:4). Yet this horizontal movement toward the human other is balanced and controlled by the vertical movement toward the divine Other. Actually the two movements are related and in a certain sense dependent.[42]

EXCURSUS:
THE SABBATH TEXTS: THEIR LITERARY STRUCTURE

The Genesis Creation Story (Genesis 1-2)[43]

Introduction
In the beginning of the Creation . . . (vv. 1-2)
1. light from darkness (vv. 3-5)
2. firmament in heaven (vv. 6-8)
3. plants (vv. 9-13)

4. luminaries to separate (vv. 16-19)

5. animals (vv. 20-23)

6. dominion of man over animals (vv. 24-31)
7. the sabbath (2:1-3)

Introduction
In the day of the making . . . (2:4b-6)

1. man from dust (v. 7)
2. garden on earth (v. 8)
3. dominion of man over the earth (vv. 9-15)
4. tree of knowledge separated (vv. 16-17)
5. concern for companionship for man (v. 18)
6. dominion of man over animals (vv. 19-22)
7. the couple (vv. 23-24)

"thus the heavens and the earth and all the host of them were *finished* (a)

"and God *finished* (a) *on the seventh day His work* (b) which He had done, and He rested *on the seventh day from all His work* (b) which He had done

"then God blessed the seventh day and sanctified it because He rested *in it from all His work* (b) which God had created and made"

Conclusion
These heavens and earth

and Adam said: "*this* (x) is now bone of my bones and flesh of my flesh

"*this* (x) shall be called *woman* because *this* (x) was taken out of *Man* (motif of couple: y)

"therefore *man* shall leave his father and mother and be joined to his *woman* (motif of couple: y), and they shall become one flesh"

Conclusion
these two, man and wife

Technical Observations
Note the parallelism between the section of the Sabbath and the section of the marriage (7th section).
Note the same repetitive pattern (a/abb/b: x/xxy/y).

Theological Implications
The Sabbath and marriage convey common ideas: both are divine institutions, crowning the work of creation; both point to the same type of experience (a social experience, an experience of love, and happiness); and both involve the human factor in the process of creation.

The Decalogue (Exodus 20:1-17)

Prologue (vv. 1-2) I am the Lord . . .

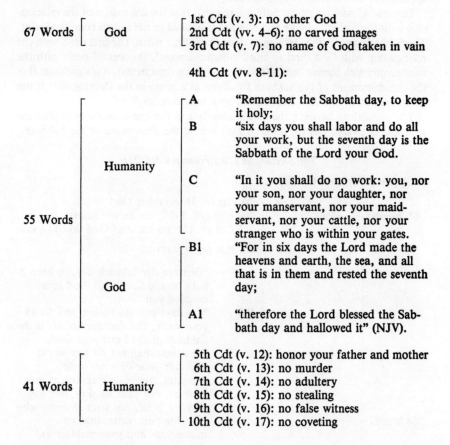

67 Words	God	1st Cdt (v. 3): no other God
		2nd Cdt (vv. 4-6): no carved images
		3rd Cdt (v. 7): no name of God taken in vain

4th Cdt (vv. 8-11):

55 Words	Humanity	A	"Remember the Sabbath day, to keep it holy;
		B	"six days you shall labor and do all your work, but the seventh day is the Sabbath of the Lord your God.
		C	"In it you shall do no work: you, nor your son, nor your daughter, nor your manservant, nor your maid-servant, nor your cattle, nor your stranger who is within your gates.
	God	B1	"For in six days the Lord made the heavens and earth, the sea, and all that is in them and rested the seventh day;
		A1	"therefore the Lord blessed the Sabbath day and hallowed it" (NJV).

41 Words	Humanity	5th Cdt (v. 12): honor your father and mother
		6th Cdt (v. 13): no murder
		7th Cdt (v. 14): no adultery
		8th Cdt (v. 15): no stealing
		9th Cdt (v. 16): no false witness
		10th Cdt (v. 17): no coveting

Technical Observations

Note the significance of the Sabbath commandment, which is emphasized by the centrality of its position and its relative length: the fourth commandment has 55 words (in Hebrew) and is situated between 67 words that come before and 41 words that follow it. Thus it contains about half as many words as the rest of the Decalogue (108) and is placed approximately in the middle of it. Note the alternate movement: God/Humanity/God/Humanity, confirming the central position of this commandment and suggesting the unity of the passage.

Note the chiastic structure of the Sabbath commandment: A, B, C, B1, A1.[44] The human activity (A, B) parallels the divine activity (B1, A1). Note that C, the center of the commandment, has universal application (every human category as well as animals are implied; note the list of seven).[45]

Theological Implications

The alternate movement between God and humanity suggests a reciprocal dependence between the two relationships.

The central position of the Sabbath suggests that the dimension of the relationship with the "other" (divine and human) is implied in the fourth commandment. The Sabbath divides the Decalogue into two distinct parts. The first deals with the relationship with God (first to third commandments), the second deals with the relationship with human beings (fifth to tenth commandments). It is significant that the commandment of the Sabbath functions as a hinge in the Decalogue.[46] It lies in the middle of the unit and implies both relationships.[47]

The parallelism between the divine activity and the human activity implies the principle of *Imago Dei* (or *imitatio Dei*) behind the observance of the Sabbath.

The Decalogue (Deuteronomy 5:6–21)

Prologue (v. 6) I am the Lord . . .

67 Words — God
- 1st Cdt (v. 7): no other God
- 2nd Cdt (vv. 8–10): no carved images
- 3rd Cdt (v. 11): no name of God taken in vain

4th Cdt (vs. 12–15):

64 Words

Humanity

A — "Observe the Sabbath day, to keep it holy, as the Lord your God commanded you.

B — "Six days you shall labor and do all your work, but the seventh day is the Sabbath of the Lord your God.

C — "In it you shall not do any work: you, nor your son, nor your daughter, nor your manservant, nor your ox, nor your donkey, nor any of your cattle, nor your stranger who is within your gates, that your manservant and your maidservant may rest as well as you.

God

B1 — "And remember that you were a slave in the land of Egypt, and that the Lord your God brought you out from there by a mighty hand and an outstretched arm;

A1 — "therefore the Lord your God commanded you to keep the Sabbath holy" (NJV).

49 Words — Humanity
- 5th Cdt (v. 16): honor your father and mother
- 6th Cdt (v. 17): no murder
- 7th Cdt (v. 18): no adultery
- 8th Cdt (v. 19): no stealing
- 9th Cdt (v. 20): no false witness
- 10th Cdt (v. 21): no coveting

Technical Observations

Note the same central position of the Sabbath commandment, which here occupies more space than in Exodus 20: the fourth commandment has 64 words and is situated between 67 words before and 49 words after. That is, it contains more than half the amount of the rest of the words of the ten commandments (128). Note the same alternate movement: God/Humanity/God/Humanity.

Note the same chiastic structure of the Sabbath commandment as in Exodus 20: A, B, C, B1, A1.

In general, the Sabbath commandment is more expanded and explicit in Deuteronomy 5 than in Exodus 20, but the content remains essentially the same. In C, the "cosmic" idea, that every kind of domestic animals is concerned, is more explicit: "nor your ox, nor your donkey, nor any of your cattle"; moreover, the reason for the rest of the servants is made more explicitly—that they "may rest as well as you."

Theological Implications

The fact that the state of slavery (from the root $\sqrt{\,'bd}$) in B1 parallels the six days of labor ($\sqrt{\,'bd}$) in B, indicates that the Sabbath is interpreted as a sign of deliverance: the Sabbath corresponds to the Exodus.

The vertical principle of *Imago Dei* (or *imitatio Dei*) can be recognized in B1 through a hint to C. Just as God freed the Israelites from slavery ($\sqrt{\,'bd}$), the Israelites were to free the servant ($\sqrt{\,'bd}$) on the Sabbath.

The horizontal principle of "you shall love your neighbor as yourself " is implied. The Israelites were to free the slave and the stranger because they themselves had been slaves and strangers (cf. Deuteronomy 15:15; cf. Leviticus 29:34, where this principle is explicitly applied to the treatment of the stranger).

The Account of the Tabernacle (Exodus 31:12-18)

Introduction: And the Lord *spoke* to Moses, saying, Speak also to the children of Israel saying

A   Surely My Sabbaths you shall keep, for it is *a sign between Me and you throughout your generations,* that you may know that I am *the Lord who sanctifies* you.

B   you shall keep the Sabbath, therefore, for it is *holy to you.* Everyone who profanes it shall surely *be put to death;* for whoever does any work on it, that person shall be cut off from among his people.

B1   Work shall be done for six days, but the seventh day is the Sabbath of rest, *holy to the Lord.* Whoever does any work on the Sabbath day, he shall surely *be put to death.*

A1   therefore the children of Israel shall keep the Sabbath, to observe the Sabbath *throughout their generations* as a perpetual covenant. *It is a sign between Me and the children of Israel* forever; for in six days *the Lord made* the heavens and the earth, and on the seventh day He rested and was refreshed.

Conclusion: And when He had made an end of *speaking* with him on Mount Sinai, He gave Moses two tablets of the Testimony, tablets of stone, written with the finger of God.

Technical Observations

Note the place of the Sabbath in the account of the building of the tabernacle. "The first account of the tabernacle closes with the Sabbath command (31:12ff.); the second account of its building begins with the Sabbath command (35:1ff.)."[48]

Note the structure of the commandment. Inserted between the Introduction (v. 12) and the Conclusion (v. 18), which echo each other on the motif of speaking (*inclusio*), the commandment is developed according to a chiastic structure A, B, B1, A1, which echo each other on specific motifs (italicized in text).

Significantly the prescription of the Sabbath preludes the giving of the Decalogue (Exodus 31:18).

Theological Implications

The connection between the Sabbath and the tabernacle shows the role of the Sabbath in the covenant.

> The tabernacle represents the fulfillment of the covenant promise: "I will make my dwelling with you . . . I will be your God and you shall be my people." But the actual sign of the covenant is the sabbath. Therefore, the observance of the sabbath and the building of the tabernacle are two sides of the same reality. Just as the sabbath is a surety of Israel's sanctity (31.13), so the meeting of God with his people in the tabernacle serves the selfsame end (29.43). There can be no genuine tension between these two signs. The witness of the tabernacle and that of the sabbath both testify to God's rule over his creation (31.17).[49]

The structure of the commandment suggests a dialectical tension between life and death (A, life; B, death; B1, death; A1, life), which is one of the characteristic features of the covenant (Deuteronomy 30:11–20).

The parallelism between "holy to the Lord" (B1) and "holy to you" (B) points to the categories of the covenant. Because the Sabbath is holy both to the children of Israel and to the Lord, it becomes a sign between the Lord and the children of Israel, that is, a sign of covenant.

The fact that the prescription of the Sabbath preludes the giving of the Decalogue suggests that the covenant established by the Decalogue implies the faith expressed in the Sabbath commandment.

This inductive study of the four classic texts of the Sabbath confirms the theology of the Sabbath that has been outlined in the systematic essay. The Sabbath is a sign of remembrance pointing to the past event (creation, Exodus, divine rest, blessing, and hallowing of the Sabbath). It is a sign of hope not only through the channel of memory because of what it reminds us of but also because it points to the future as a sign of perpetual covenant. It is a sign of holiness implying a relationship with both God and humanity in the present life of the believer. It is a sign of the Absolute as it witnesses to God, his law, and his actions (creation, salvation, holiness). In Seventh-day Adventist theology all these dimensions of the Sabbath are interrelated. Memory, hope, and faith nurture each other and give meaning to the present life of the Sabbath.

CONCLUSION

In conclusion, I would like to refer briefly to a dimension of the Sabbath that I have not explicitly noted in this presentation, but which was nonetheless implicit in my discussion. As a time of "pausing" and as a time of silence in relationship with the sublime, the Sabbath witnesses to a different quality of time, the dimension of eternity.[50] This dimension has been well rendered by Abraham J. Heschel, but it is often neglected or simply overlooked by most of the students of religion. Beyond all the weight of the words, whether they belong to the apologetic discussion or to the scholarly and theological demonstration, the Sabbath conveys the sense of "something else."

This mystical function of the Sabbath is confirmed also on a more rational level through our deductive and inductive studies. From that standpoint, the Sabbath indeed urges us to move beyond ourselves and brings us into relationship with that which is other than ourselves, that is, with "something else." First, the Sabbath compels us to move out of the confines of our present existence to relate to the remote past and to the distant future—to remember and to hope. Second, the Sabbath obligates us to move out of our own persons to be open to the "other"—to relate to other human beings and to God. Unfortunately, it seems to me, this double function of the Sabbath has often been forgotten. In the present life of the believer, the Sabbath itself has shrunk.

Instead of opening the believer to the past and to the future, the Sabbath has become either a mere ritual, which provides the present religion with its dramatic scenery and folklore or simply a day of rest that provides one with immediate happiness. Thus the Sabbath has simply been interpreted and lived as a psychological need. This function should not be denied. It holds some truth. Yet there is more to the Sabbath than the mere existential experience. The reference to the past and to the future conveyed by the Sabbath is vital, not only because it gives the Sabbath its historical meaning but also because it resituates the religious person in the historical perspective, namely, between creation and recreation.

In regard to the second function, instead of bearing witness to the universal Absolute that is beyond all particularism, and of being a place of love and fellowship, the Sabbath has become the occasion of division and exclusiveness among religious groups, a mere sociological datum within the present world. It is noteworthy that each of the three religions arising out of the Bible (Judaism, Christianity, and Islam) observes a different Sabbath. The sociological aspect of the Sabbath also has some value. The Sabbath does indeed express an actual belonging (Exodus 31:12–17; Ezekiel 20:12). Yet instead of causing separation and opposition among different communities, the Sabbath should teach all of us because of what it means in its essence — and, more particularly, Jews and Seventh-day Adventists, because of what it implies historically in the life and the destiny of those two communities — a lesson of openness and tolerance, of attention and love.[51]

NOTES

1. This is the case, for instance, in Africa, where "Adventists were described by their foes as modern Jews because they kept the Jewish Sabbath. Because the Jews killed Jesus Christ, Adventists were labelled antichrist" (David Agboola, *The Seventh-day Adventists in Yoruba Land* [Ibadan, 1987] 46). This is also the case in many Arabic countries, where Adventists have often been suspected of being spies for Israel.

2. Critical questions of the origin of the Sabbath will not be addressed here. The biblical document will be referred to in its totality and in its finished state. For a critical study of the origin of the Sabbath, see Niels-Erik A. Andreasen, "The Old Testament Sabbath: A Tradition-Historical Investigation" (Ph.D. diss., Vanderbilt University, 1971); cf. Gerhard F. Hasel, "The Sabbath in the Pentateuch," in *The Sabbath in Scripture and History,* ed. Kenneth A. Strand (Washington, DC: Review and Herald, 1982) 21–43.

3. Hasel states: "The very nature of a 'sign' is that it points to something beyond itself" ("The Sabbath in the Pentateuch," 34).

4. See for instance M. L. Andreasen, *The Sabbath, Which Day and Why?* (Washington, DC: Review and Herald, 1969); *The Sabbath in Scripture and History,* ed. Strand; *Festival of the Sabbath,* ed. Roy Branson (Takoma Park, MD: Association of Adventist Forums, 1985); Sakae Kubo, *God Meets Man* (Nashville: Southern Publishing, 1978); N.-E. Andreasen, "The Old Testament Sabbath"; idem, *Rest and Redemption* (Berrien Springs, MI: Andrews University Press, 1978); Samuele Bacchiocchi, *Divine Rest for Human Restlessness: A Theological Study of the Good News of the Sabbath for Today* (Rome: Gregorian University Press, 1980); idem, *From Sabbath to Sunday: A Historical Investigation of the Rise of Sunday Observance in Early Christianity* (Rome: Gregorian University Press, 1977); John C. Brunt, *A Day for Healing* (Washington, DC: Review and Herald, 1981); Charles Scriven, *Jubilee of the World: The Sabbath as a Day of Gladness* (Nashville: Southern Publishing, 1978); Richard M. Davidson, *A Love Song for the Sabbath* (Washington, DC: Review and Herald, 1988).

5. See Kenneth A. Strand, "Introduction," in *The Sabbath in Scripture and History,* 16; see also N.-E. A. Andreasen, "Jubilee of Freedom and Equality," in *Festival of the Sabbath,* 97; Kubo, *God Meets Man,* 5; Davidson, *A Love Song for the Sabbath,* 19, 27, etc.

6. See also Leviticus 19:3, where the two commandments are associated.

7. It is noteworthy that highly rated scientists, specializing in various disciplines, are working at the Geoscience Research Institute (founded in 1957) at Loma Linda University. Their specific purpose is to provide scientific support for the creation theory. They publish a semiannual journal, *Origins,* that deals basically with creation-evolution issues. Geologist Ariel A. Roth is the editor of this journal and also the director of the Institute.

8. M. L. Andreasen states: "It is clear . . . that there can be no agreement between belief in the Bible and belief in the evolutionary theory. The one is destructive of the other. No man can believe in the Word of God and also believe in evolution. They are mutually exclusive. It is impossible to straddle the question as many attempt to do. It must be either, or. It cannot be both" (*The Sabbath, Which Day and Why?* 25).

9. See especially M. L. Andreasen, *The Sabbath, Which Day and Why?;* Paul Nouan, *Le Septième jour, signe de Dieu pour l'homme d'aujour d'hui* (Paris: *Sdt,* 1979); Gustav Tobler, *Unser Ruhetag* (Zurich: Advent-Verlag, n.d.). It is noteworthy that for the last few years Seventh-day Adventist scholars have been more interested in "the meaning of the Sabbath experience" than in apologetics. See Branson, *Festival of the Sabbath,* 7.

10. Note the association of the two words *tehom* (abyss) and *ruaḥ* (wind, spirit), which belong to the technical language of the creation story (Genesis 1:2).

11. See Brunt, *A Day for Healing;* Bacchiocchi states: "Not only did Jesus announce His mission as the fulfillment of the sabbatical promises of redemption (Luke 4:18-19), but also on the Sabbath, He intensified His work of salvation (John 5:17; 9:4)" ("A Memorial of Redemption," in *Festival of the Sabbath,* ed. Branson, 63).

12. Sakae Kubo states: "While the Sabbath memorializes the once-for-all redemptive activity of Christ, the redemption of each person is considered a 'new creation.' 'Therefore, if any one is in Christ, he is a new creation, the old has passed away, behold the new has come' (II Cor. 5:17). . . . As the Sabbath memorializes the completed activity of creation, so it now also memorializes the finished redemptive activity of the new creation in Christ" ("The Experience of Liberation," in *Festival of the Sabbath,* ed. Branson, 50).

13. G. Gerleman, *"klh zu Ende sein,"* in *Theologisches Handwörterbuch zum Alten Testament* (Munich: Kaiser, 1971) 1:831-33.

14. The Sabbath belongs also to the work of creation since the completeness of the work comes only with the appearance of the Sabbath. See Oswald Loretz, *Schöpfung und Mythos: Mensch und Welt nach den Anfangskapiteln der Genesis* (Stuttgarter Bibelstudien 32; Stuttgart: Katholisches Bibelwerk, 1968) 70.

15. See M. H. Pope, "Seven, Seventh, Seventy," in *Interpreter's Dictionary of the Bible,* ed. G. A. Buttrick (Nashville: Abingdon, 1962) 4:294-95.

16. See Donald E. Gowan, *Eschatology in the Old Testament* (Philadelphia: Fortress, 1986) 122-23.

17. This universal dimension of the Sabbath is implied in the fourth commandment, which concerns every category of creation (Exodus 20:10; cf. Deuteronomy 5:14; see Excursus), and is also hinted at by the structure of Genesis 8-9, which

parallels Genesis 1:1–2:4a, thereby relating the rainbow (seventh section) to the Sabbath; see Jacques B. Doukhan, *Daniel, the Vision of the End* (Berrien Springs, MI: Andrews University Press, 1987) 133 n. 106; see also Warren A. Gage, *The Gospel of Genesis: Studies in Protology and Eschatology* (Winona Lake, IN: Carpenter Books, 1984) 16–20.

18. On the meaning of this passage, see Gerhard F. Hasel and W. G. C. Murdoch, "The Sabbath in the Prophetic and Historical Literature of the Old Testament," in *The Sabbath in Scripture and History*, 47–49.

19. The only other time that the same echo occurs is at the end of the record of the building of the Temple, where it is also followed by the appearance of the *shekhinah* (2 Chronicles 5:14; cf. 2 Chronicles 7:12; see Peter J. Kearney, "Creation and Liturgy: The P Redaction of Exodus 25–40," *Zeitschrift für die alt-testamentliche Wissenschaft* 89 [1977] 375–87; see also Jacques B. Doukhan, *The Genesis Creation Story: Its Literary Structure* [Berrien Springs, MI: Andrews University Press, 1978] 81–83, 162).

20. For the allusion to the Sabbath in this passage, see Robert M. Johnston, "The Eschatological Sabbath in John's Apocalypse: A Reconsideration," *Andrews University Seminary Studies* 25 (1987) 40.

21. Kubo states: "In the coming of Jesus Christ, who lived among us and who was called—'God with us'—we find a re-Sabbatization. . . . The time Christ lived on earth represents a kind of long Sabbath day" (*God Meets Man*, 17).

22. See Charles Scriven, "Gladness in Hope," in *Festival of the Sabbath*, ed. Branson, 81.

23. See Kenneth A. Strand, "Another Look at 'Lord's Day' in the Early Church and in Revelation 1:10," *New Testament Studies* 13 (1966–67) 174–81.

24. Perhaps also Revelation 1:10; see Bacchiocchi, *From Sabbath to Sunday*, 123ff.; Doukhan, *Daniel, the Vision of the End*, 131 n. 98.

25. On the theological relationship between these two ideas, see Doukhan, *Daniel, the Vision of the End*, 93–98.

26. Branson states: "As baptism and the Lord's Supper refer to the past and anticipate the future, so the Sabbath points to God's past and future fellowship with mankind" ("Festival of Fellowship," in *Festival of the Sabbath*, ed. Branson, 76).

27. For the use of the infinitive absolute as "an emphatic imperative," see E. Kautzsch, ed., *Gesenius' Hebrew Grammar* (2nd ed.; Oxford: Clarendon, 1910; reprint, 1970) §113 bb.

28. Fritz Guy states: "Unlike the single day, the month and the year, the seven-day cycle has no 'natural' basis. No astronomical, agricultural or physiological period gives it 'practical' significance. This means that both its origin and its significance are distinctively religious: it is a commandment—and a gift—of God. In short, it is a way of saying 'Yes' or 'No' to the Creator. The 'seventh-day-ness' of the Sabbath has this special meaning: it symbolizes God's ultimacy as reality and power and as goodness and value" ("The Presence of Ultimacy," in *Festival of the Sabbath*, ed. Branson, 37).

29. Doukhan, *Daniel, the Vision of the End*, 71.

30. Raymond Cottrell states: "The fourth commandment is not an inherently moral law in the strict sense of the word—like the commands against murder,

adultery and theft, whose rationale is self-evident to conscientious people—but a positive precept that could not be known except by revelation" ("A Common Heritage," in *Festival of the Sabbath,* ed. Branson, 22).

31. On this question, see Davidson, *A Love Song for the Sabbath,* 33-46.

32. Kubo states: "The Sabbath itself is a sign of God's grace, of the fact that salvation comes by nothing that man does but by everything that God does" ("The Experience of Liberation," 43).

33. See Guy, who describes the Sabbath as "a sign of God's total and permanent commitment to human being[s]" ("Presence of Ultimacy," 33).

34. G. von Rad, "Les Idées sur le Temps et l'Histoire en Israel et l'Eschatologie des Prophètes," in *Hommage à Wilhelm Vischer* (Montpellier: Causse Graille Castelnau, 1960) 201.

35. E. Jenni, "Time" in *Interpreter's Dictionary of the Bible,* 4:646; see also Gerhard von Rad, "The Theology of Israel's Prophetic Traditions," in *Old Testament Theology,* trans. D. M. G. Stalker (2 vols.; New York: Harper & Row, 1962-65) 2:99, 100.

36. As Guy puts it: "A covenant with God is a special kind of covenant. It is never made *a priori;* it is never the first word, the initiation of a relationship. Any covenant with God is made, rather, *a posteriori;* it is always a second word, so to speak, a consequence of a relationship that has already been established by God's own initiative and commitment. And this is the way it is with the covenant symbol of the Sabbath" ("Presence of Ultimacy," 33).

37. See Mircea Eliade: "The Judaeo-Christian Sabbath is also an *imitatio dei.* The Sabbath rest reproduces the primordial gesture of the Lord" (*The Myth of the Eternal Return,* trans. Willard R. Trask [New York: Pantheon Books, 1954] 23; see also Hasel, "The Sabbath in the Pentateuch," 24.

38. Hence the importance of the Department of Religious Liberty of the Seventh-day Adventist Church.

39. Richard Rice states: "Adventists believe that it will become a decisive religious issue just before Christ returns" ("The Mission of the Church, Eschatology, and the Sabbath," *The Journal of Adventist Education* 51 [1989] 30). "Historically, Seventh-day Adventists have interpreted their work as a continuation of the Protestant Reformation, which began the process of returning to the faith of the Bible. They believe that they have a specific mission to complete this work of reform by recovering the biblical Sabbath during the closing days of human history. So Sabbath observance has important eschatological significance for Adventists. This is particularly evident in the description of the Sabbath as the 'seal of God.' Several biblical passages describe God's people receiving a seal, or mark, in the forehead (Ezekiel 9:4, 6; Revelation 7:3; 14:1)" (Ibid., 28).

40. See N.-E. A. Andreasen, "Jubilee of Freedom and Equality," 99ff.

41. For a beautiful example of how Adventists like to live the Sabbath in the family, see Davidson, *A Love Song for the Sabbath,* 51.

42. Guy implies the same tension as he describes the Sabbath "invested with the relatedness and the ultimacy of God." He further specifies: "God's relatedness and ultimacy are a theological polarity—a pair of elements or ideas that mutually complement and at the same time mutually limit each other" ("Presence of Ultimacy," 29).

43. See Doukhan, *The Genesis Creation Story*, 41–43, 78–79. (Only the Sabbath commandment is entirely quoted from NJV, except when the clarity of the demonstration requires otherwise.)

44. See N.-E. A. Andreasen, "The Old Testament Sabbath," 197–98; Hasel proposes another structure essentially founded on themes; see "The Sabbath in the Pentateuch," 29.

45. The tenth commandment also has a list of seven, but as object of the commandment and not as subject of the commandment.

46. "The Sabbath is the arch holding together the structure of the law. Coming as it does between the outline of commitment to God and obligations to fellow men, the Sabbath commandment is the hinge of the two tables of stone" (Branson, *Festival of the Sabbath,* 72).

47. This median position of the Sabbath in the Decalogue has led some to think that the Sabbath might have had the same function as the seal in covenant documents (see Meredith G. Kline, *Treaty of the Great King: The Covenant Structure of Deuteronomy. Studies and Commentary* (Grand Rapids: Eerdmans, 1963] 18, 19; idem, *The Structure of Biblical Authority* [Grand Rapids: Eerdmans, 1972] 120).

48. Brevard S. Childs, *The Book of Exodus: A Critical, Theological Commentary* (Philadelphia: Westminster, 1974) 541.

49. Ibid., 541–42.

50. Kubo states: "On the Sabbath, then, in a special way we have eternity breaking into the present. . . . The Sabbath stands in a unique way as a symbol of the blessings of eternity" (*God Meets Man,* 68); see also Gerald Winslow, "Moment of Eternity," in *Festival of the Sabbath,* ed. Branson, 91ff.

51. I thank Ronald A. G. du Preez of Andrews University for reading and editing this paper.

13

A CATHOLIC RESPONSE
TO J. B. DOUKHAN

Kenneth Hein, O.S.B.

M r. Doukhan has shown us the rich significations of the Sabbath and the various reasons why he loves the Sabbath. Now it is my obligation to take his presentation for what it is and what he intended it to be and, within this context, make my observations and remarks, which will raise a number of questions.

SOME MAJOR DIFFERENCES

As the first step in the formulation of my response, I believe it will be useful to address a number of differences between a Seventh-day Adventist and a Roman Catholic that may govern their religious and theological perceptions. I have chosen to proceed in this manner because it will provide a better insight into the reasons why two persons claiming to be Christians do not arrive at the same conclusion about the role of the Sabbath in Christian life.

Creation Theology

When Charles Darwin published his theory of natural selection and evolution in 1859 (just four years before the Seventh-day Adventists were formally organized), he had no intention of upsetting the Christian theological world.[1] But Christians were soon put on the defensive when liberal elements concluded that evolution disproved the alleged truth of the Bible. At first, the nearly universal reaction of the Christian churches was to condemn or belittle the theory of evolution rather than to consider the possibility that their doctrinal positions did not unconditionally exclude it. However, in due time, the Catholic Church learned to live with the idea of evolution just as it and the rest of Christianity learned to live with the idea that the earth is spherical and travels around the sun, even though these concepts contradict the language of the Bible.[2] The Catholic Church maintains, however, that the spiritual soul of each human being is created directly by God (i.e., it is not the result of natural evolution) and that the doctrine of the universality of sin (original sin theory) must not be abandoned in favor of a theory of evolution that cannot be reconciled with these beliefs.

Historical-Critical Method

This term, along with "higher criticism," refers especially to the methods of biblical and theological analysis that sprang from the work of Julius Wellhausen (1844–1918), a German Protestant biblical scholar, who was virtually disowned by his own church for his theory that the Pentateuch was a collection of documents written over a period of centuries. Since then, however, most of the larger Christian denominations have become accustomed to applying the historical-critical methods of theology and biblical studies, especially in Europe.

The purpose of this review of historical criticism lies in its relationship to creation theology. Nature and history are intimately connected, and if there is evolution in nature, then it is also to be expected in history. Therefore, theology and biblical studies have to contend with the question of evolution not only in nature but also in the material of the Bible. To many Christians (and perhaps to many Jews as well), such an admission seems tantamount to denying the truth of the Bible.[3] But others view it simply as God's freely chosen way of presenting us with the material of revelation—that is, packaged in the concepts and language of the human writer, who was culturally still a child of his times even when inspired to write material that eventually, and often after much redaction by later generations, was collected into the material we revere as the Bible.

This latter view sees the Bible as the God-willed and God-inspired witness to divine revelation rather than revelation itself in a pure, simple, and direct form. It also sees divine-biblical inspiration as the grace of God that motivated human writers to record what God wanted them to record, but without removing or overriding the thought processes and human methods of expression of the human writers. Thus, for example, the human writers were free to adopt and adapt a variety of myths taken from their surrounding cultures in order to express a divinely inspired theological concept such as the goodness of creation that is emphasized in Genesis 1.[4] Again, different biblical writers could use some of the same material to arrive at different concepts. This appears to explain how one biblical writer, writing during a period of Israel's history when idolatry was a major threat, could portray the human desire to "be like God"[5] as the root of all sin, whereas a later writer, at a time when Israel was thoroughly committed to monotheism, could jubilantly proclaim that human beings are created in the image and likeness of God (Genesis 1:26). Similarly, the application of higher criticism to the matter of Sabbath observance indicates evolution both in the nature of the observance and in the religious reasoning given for the observance—the association of the Sabbath with the story of creation being relatively late in Israel's history. These conclusions are generally not shared by denominations that tend toward fundamentalism as expressed in their insistence on creationism and in modern-day Bible prophecy.

Divine Positive Law

In the days before Julius Wellhausen, the theological concept of "divine positive law" held a prominent position in Christian theology and biblical studies. For those Christian denominations which style themselves as "fundamentalist" or otherwise fit the definition this continues to be the case. They may not employ the expression "divine positive law," but they make full use of the concept—namely, that God's will in regard to certain matters of human conduct is known only by way of direct revelation rather than through nature or the natural law.

In times before the rise of biblical fundamentalism as a conscious and deliberate choice, divine positive law was invoked to uphold the so-called divine right of kings, papal claims to supreme authority in matters of state as well as church,[6] the stoning or burning of "heretics" (or "witches"), and on and on goes the list. In a Christian denomination where an uncritical concept of divine positive law plays a major role in its theological deductions, there will easily be a tendency to fear that the abuses of the past will repeat themselves in the present—all in the name of "God's holy will." However, if nothing else, modern methods of doing theology have taught the Catholic Church and many other denominations that divine positive law cannot be so glibly invoked or so readily assumed as a matter of fact in any given case.

MAKING SENSE OF THE SABBATH

At this point, I wish to bring together the ideas that I have addressed or developed above and formulate the conclusions to be drawn from them in regard to Mr. Doukhan's paper. I shall begin where I left off—with the matter of divine positive law.

If a command that is placed in the mouth of God in the Bible is a law that we are to observe out of faith for no other binding reason than the fact that God ordered it so, then clearly Sabbath observance is a matter of divine positive law. But the inductive methods of theology as influenced by higher criticism lead to a different view of what constitutes divine positive law. This understanding contrasts strongly with the interpretation found among Christians who eschew the findings and claims of higher criticism as understood by many of the larger Christian denominations and when applied to the material of the Bible. This places me in a rather awkward and difficult position: I am supposed to respond to a paper on the Sabbath, which takes the position that Sabbath observance is a matter of "divine (positive) law." On the other hand, there is no agreement between our two Christian traditions in regard to the nature and role of divine positive law in the case at hand. We may be able to speak of divine positive law to a limited degree in regard to the connection made by biblical writers between the Mosaic covenant and Sabbath observance. But that applies as a law only to the Israelites and their descendants – if we assume, contrary to the conclusions of higher criticism, that God historically associated the covenant with Sabbath observance at the time of Moses. The matter of Sabbath observance as a universally binding divine positive law is even more problematic.

Unless I have misconstrued my sources, Seventh-day Adventist theology views Sabbath observance as a binding obligation because of the divine will as expressed in the creation account and in the account of God's covenant with Israel at the time of the Exodus. Modern Catholic theology sees the connection between the creation account (or, better, accounts) and divine positive law as problematic on several accounts. First, there is the historical-critical contention that the first creation account in Genesis is about four hundred years later than the second account with its setting in the Garden of Eden. Thus, the chronologically earlier account makes no allusion at all to a six-day scheme of creation followed by the Sabbath. Second, neither account of creation, when examined critically in regard to concepts and grammar, presents the notion of *creatio ex nihilo* – an understanding of creation that finds its first explicit written recording only shortly before the time of Jesus of Nazareth in 2 Maccabees 7:28, which is considered a canonical work only in Catholicism. In Catholic theology, the Bible, at least as a finished product, does not apparently intend to give us an accurate, historical,[7] step-by-step account of the events of creation. Yet such would seem to have to be the case if the view that the order of creation as presented in Genesis 1-2:4a contained a binding law in regard to Sabbath observance. But let us assume for the moment that there are not two independent accounts of creation in Genesis and that the Adam and Eve story is just a genuine, historical continuation of and expansion on the six-day creation scheme. In that case, matters still remain problematic from a purely linguistic point of view. An accurate rendering of the Hebrew text does not say, after the creation of light, "the first day," but rather "a first day" or simply "day one" (*yôm 'eḥād*). There is no definite article until "the sixth day," which serves to emphasize the completion of God's creative activity. But the lack of the definite articles in general in regard to the numbering of the days linguistically precludes the contention that the account describes either from a scientific point of view or even from the writer's point of view the absolutely first week of the world's history and existence. The writer has no scientific agenda here, but rather the goal of crowning his carefully worked account, borrowed in part from Babylonian sources, with a theological statement about the sanctity of the Israelite Sabbath.

On the other hand, Roman Catholic theology has always been very conscious of natural law theory. Accordingly, worship of God is inherent in the natural law and therefore is naturally appropriate to and, at least theoretically, morally binding on the human being. But it remains the church's prerogative and obligation to establish the most appropriate times and methods for the *ekklēsia* to gather and worship in the light of the works and person of Jesus Christ. In this way, the natural obligation that a creature with intelligence and free will has to acknowledge its Creator is fulfilled with, in, and through Jesus Christ, who gave us a *new covenant* and who alone can bring this obligation of worship to perfection as the nature of God requires. Consequently, it is at this precise point that I find my greatest difficulties with the paper to which I am responding.

In my estimation, Mr. Doukhan presented an incomplete christological basis for Christian observance of the Sabbath, although there appear to be many good reasons in the Christian Scriptures to prefer Sunday as the preeminent day for worship and for considering Sabbath observance as something else than a binding law on all Christians. The few examples from Christ that Mr. Doukhan does present as support of Christian observance of the Sabbath are really two-edged swords — that is, they can cut either way in favor of either side of the argument. For example, he points out that "Jesus . . . identifies himself with the Sabbath; he is the one who provides rest," etc. One could deduce from this, rightly or wrongly, that Jesus simply gives deeper meaning to the Sabbath. But one can just as readily deduce that it means the Jewish Sabbath is replaced, purely and simply, by conversion of one's life to Jesus.

No objection is being made in my response to the choice of day that a Christian denomination might make in setting aside sacred time for community worship of God. But from the perspective of Catholic theology, I do have to question the implication that Christians do not have a basic freedom in that regard or that, by choosing a day other than the Jewish Sabbath, they are in essence failing to observe the law of God.

Christian theology is or becomes specifically and fully Christian when, guided by the Holy Spirit (see Acts 15:28f.), it subjects all, including the word of God in the Bible, to Jesus of Nazareth as the first and foremost principle of religious interpretation and application. An outstanding example of this is found in Jesus' abrogation of the Mosaic laws concerning divorce (see Deuteronomy 24:1ff. and Mark 10:11f.). This same principle needs to be applied to questions about Sabbath versus Sunday observance.

A Christian treatment of the Sabbath question must thoroughly address Jesus' own liberal attitude toward the Sabbath and especially his contention, upon being accused of breaking the Sabbath, that "My Father is still working, and I am working" (John 5:17),[8] which certainly seems to go counter to a theology of divine positive law that would insist on Sabbath observance for Christians on the basis of the creation stories found in the Hebrew Scriptures.

CONCLUSION

In summary, Mr. Doukhan's presentation seems to me to be insufficient, as presented, to indicate specifically Christian arguments for Sabbath observance as a matter of divine law binding on Christians. Of course, this is not the point of Mr. Doukhan's paper. But the love of the Sabbath that he presented builds on this premise, and I must question its validity. He chose not to address the critical questions. This is certainly his prerogative, but I am compelled to raise these questions since they largely explain how and why the Catholic position does not correspond to the Seventh-day Adventist view of Sabbath observance — even though we can all appreciate and learn from the Adventist reasons for loving the Sabbath.

Finally, I must acknowledge the many outstanding and positive points that Mr. Doukhan made in his presentation. He has performed a valuable service for all who are concerned, or should be concerned, about appropriate worship of God from a Judeo-Christian perspective. He was able to point to so many sacred values that have been tossed by the way in our secular world. And how good it is for even the faithful to hear them so well stated! The questions that I have raised and the observations that I have made do not *per se* negate the virtue of his scholarship or the value of his contribution for an age so much in need of rediscovering its own religious roots, practices, and beliefs.

NOTES

1. Darwin (1809–1881) was studying to be an Anglican churchman when he developed an interest in the origin of species. He never felt his theories were necessarily at odds with his faith, and he avoided all polemics in that regard.

2. Occasionally one comes across the contention that the Bible does indeed view the earth as spherical and as revolving around the sun. Be that as it may, the poor treatment that Galileo received from the Catholic Church and that Kepler received from Protestantism at the time was due to the general belief that geocentrism rather than heliocentrism was taught by the Bible.

3. In Vatican Council II, the Catholic Church clarified its understanding of biblical truth in *De Revelatione* 3.11: ". . . the books of Scripture must be acknowledged as teaching firmly, faithfully, and without error that truth which God wanted put into the sacred writings for the sake of our salvation" (*The Documents of Vatican II,* ed. Walter M. Abbot [New York: Guild Press, 1966] 119.

4. Not all major religions of the world look upon visible reality as something good or the work of a good, loving Creator. For many people, the basic goodness of creation is not immediately clear, and belief in it would be a matter of faith based on revelation.

5. The Hebrew term used here (Genesis 3:15) for God is *'ĕlōhîm,* which is a plural form and often is to be translated "gods." This may well be the case here, since the Yahwistic writer of this passage (according to biblical scholars who employ the methods of historical criticism) wrote about 950 B.C.E., when the average Israelite did not question the existence of many gods.

6. This claim to divinely given supreme authority in secular as well as ecclesial affairs is often referred to as "the doctrine of the two swords." This expression was probably derived from St. Bernard of Clairvaux's (1090–1153) allegorical interpretation of Luke 22:38. See Karl Bihlmeyer and Herman Tüchle, *Church History:* Vol. 2, *The Middle Ages* (Westminster, MD: Newman, 1963) 203f.

7. In high criticism, "historical" can have the meaning of "popular story form"—the meaning that *historisch* has in German, from which academic world so many aspects of higher criticism have been derived. But it is assumed here that Mr. Doukhan is using the term "historical" in its usual English meaning of actual event of the past.

8. Jesus' words (or possibly John's interpretation of Jesus) in John 5:17 were not entirely original. Rabbis had long acknowledged that God continued to work after creation: otherwise, nature would cease to exist. See Raymond E. Brown, *The Gospel According to John (I–XII)* (Anchor Bible 29; Garden City, NY: Doubleday, 1966) 216–21.

14

A SYSTEMATIC, BIBLICAL
THEOLOGY OF SABBATH KEEPING

Marva J. Dawn
Christians Equipped for Ministry

Though one dare not box the mystery and beauty of the Sabbath Queen too tightly into rigid analytical categories, it seems to me that a systematic ordering of Sabbath theology can serve an interfaith purpose. Whereas, on the one hand, Jews, Seventh-day Adventists, Roman Catholics, and Protestants observe many different practices and preserve a wide variety of traditions concerning Sabbath keeping, on the other hand, seven years of exploring the similar patterns of these insights and applications have convinced me that there could be general agreement upon the structural framework of the underlying biblical theology of the Sabbath. Moreover, the elaboration of these foundational theological purposes contributes to a renewal of interest in following the Sabbath-keeping practices of particular faith traditions.

The thesis of this paper is that a systematic ordering of the biblical narratives and Jewish-Christian traditions suggests foundational theological values best understood by means of the categories of Ceasing, Resting, Embracing, and Feasting. Each of these categories, furthermore, must be understood in holistic terms. Though the various dimensions of this theory happen in practice simultaneously, the following separation of elements is intended to deepen our appreciation for the values inherent in our respective observances.

CEASING

Ceasing Work

To cease working is the original meaning of Sabbath, underscored by the expansion of God's instructions concerning the Israelite feasts in Leviticus

176

23. The Sabbath command is proclaimed as follows: "There are six days when you may work, but the seventh day is a Sabbath of ceasing, a day of sacred assembly. You are not to do any work; wherever you live, it is a Sabbath to the LORD" (Leviticus 23:3). Various faith traditions make use of different practices to begin decisively this day of ceasing work, but the important thing about our *Kiddush* rituals is that they point dramatically to the moment when we cease from the work of our week and enter into an entirely different state of existence.

Ceasing Productivity and Accomplishment

The second kind of ceasing for which we are freed by the practice of Sabbath keeping is the delight of quitting the endless round of trying to produce and to accomplish. A strong biblical notion in both the Hebrew and Christian Scriptures is that our worth does not depend on what we accomplish but upon Yahweh's choice of us. These words from Isaiah summarize the point well:

> But now, this is what the LORD says —
> he who created you, O Jacob,
> he who formed you, O Israel:
> "Fear not, for I have redeemed you;
> I have called you by name; you are mine . . .
> For I am the LORD, your God,
> the Holy One of Israel, your Savior; . . .
> Since you are precious and honored in my sight,
> and because I love you. . . ." (Isaiah 43:1, 3a, 4a)

When we celebrate the Sabbath, we join the generations of believers who set aside a day to remember that we are precious and honored in God's sight and loved — profoundly loved — not because of what we produce.

To celebrate God's love on our Sabbaths also transforms us so that we can more deeply value others in the same way. When we are not under the compulsion to be productive, we are given the time for the embracing and feasting that will be explicated in the third and fourth sections.

Ceasing Anxiety, Worry, and Tension

Besides ceasing work and the need to be productive, we also deliberately set aside all worries about our tasks. As we prepare our homes for the Sabbath Queen, we put away not only the elements of our labors but also our tensions concerning it. My *Kiddush* prayers specifically commit my anxieties into God's hands for the Sabbath. This is not to run away from them; instead, the very customs of the day will give not only refreshment but also new perspectives, new priorities, and a new sense of God's presence, which all cause the tensions themselves to assume a less hostile shape during the week to come.

To celebrate the Sabbath is a way to practice these verses from Paul's letter to the Philippians:

> Rejoice in the Lord always. I will say it again: Rejoice! . . . Do not be anxious about anything, but in everything by prayer and petition, with thanksgiving, present your requests to God. And the peace of God, which transcends all understanding, will guard your hearts and your minds. . . . Finally, brothers [and sisters], whatever is true, whatever is noble, whatever is right, whatever is pure, whatever is lovely, whatever is admirable — if anything is excellent or praiseworthy — think about such things. . . . And the God of peace will be with you. (Philippians 4:4, 6-8, 9)

To celebrate the Sabbath is to rejoice in God's presence. Our practices for the day include special times of prayer and petition and extra moments of thanksgiving by which we can lay our anxieties and worries before God so that his peace, which both bypasses and surpasses our understanding, can guard our hearts and minds. Finally, to think about constructive things rather than our concerns ushers us into the presence of the God of peace himself.

Ceasing Our Trying to Be God

When we cease working, we dispense with the need to create our own future. The account of the people of Israel first gathering manna in the wilderness teaches us that God will provide for his people; they do not have to struggle to work things out for themselves. When some of the people went out on the seventh day to gather manna and found none, the LORD said to Moses, "How long will you refuse to keep my commands and my instructions? Bear in mind that the LORD has given you the Sabbath; that is why on the sixth day he gives you bread for two days. Everyone is to stay where he is on the seventh day; no one is to go out" (Exodus 16:28–29). On the Sabbath we do nothing to create our own way. We abstain from work, from our incessant need (and false guilt) to produce and accomplish, from all the anxieties about how we can be successful in all that we have to do to get ahead. The result is that we can let God be God in our lives.

Ceasing Our Possessiveness

In order to keep a longing for God as the focus of our Sabbath celebrations, it is necessary that we cease our possessiveness. The great reformation instituted by Nehemiah after the exiles returned from Babylon to build the walls of Jerusalem included this promise by the people: "When the neighboring peoples bring merchandise or grain to sell on the Sabbath, we will not buy from them on the Sabbath or on any holy day" (Nehemiah 10:31).

Abraham Joshua Heschel begins his book *The Sabbath* by contrasting other religions, in their location of the deity in space, to the Jewish recognition of holiness in time. To deepen our Sabbath experience of the holiness of time, we must cease our acquisition of the things of space.

Ceasing Our Enculturation

Those who cease working to observe the Sabbath are different from the world around them. The liturgy of creation in Genesis 1:1–2:3 emphasizes that humankind is made in the image of God and that God ceased his work on the seventh day. Correlatively, the Exodus version of the Sabbath command posits the motivation for its observance in imitation of God's original ceasing.

The emphasis in Jewish liturgies and hymns on imitation needs to be captured more by Christians, because to imitate God in our life-styles necessarily means to stop imitating the world. We have already considered setting aside our notions of productivity and accomplishment, our worries and anxieties, our striving to be our own god, and our possessiveness. Now we widen that ceasing into all the ways that we have fallen into the patterns of the world and away from the unique nonconformity of faithful divine imitation.

Ceasing the Humdrum and Meaninglessness

One of the worst problems for those who do not observe the Sabbath day—including a large majority of Christians and many nonobservant Jews who dismiss the practice as mere nostalgia—is that life can become so humdrum, every day the same. The pressures of work never let up; there is always something more to do. Our culture's great need to cease working is evidenced by the mass exit from the cities for the weekend—thousands of people trying to "get away from it all." The ironic thing is that these attempts usually cannot be successful because most of those trying to run away from the pressures of their work are not actually doing anything to relieve those pressures or lessen their anxieties. Merely to run away from work, productivity, tensions, striving to be in control, the hassles of buying and selling, and the prevailing cultural values does not work because one must come back to them again.

Celebrating the Sabbath is different from running away. We do not merely leave the dimensions discussed in the preceding six points; we actually cease letting them have a hold on our lives.

Everything is turned around when we keep the Sabbath. Meaningless-ness is counteracted by the divine rhythm. Our culture desperately needs a return to the spiritual dimension that haunts us. In an age that has lost its soul, Sabbath keeping offers the possibility of gaining it back.

RESTING

Spiritual Rest

Both Abraham Heschel and Martin Luther recognized that the founda-tion of our Sabbath resting is a spiritual one. In his "Treatise on Good Works," Luther wrote that "the spiritual rest which God especially intends in the [Sabbath] commandment is that we not only cease from our labor and trade but much more—that we let God alone work in us and that in all our powers do we do nothing of our own."[1] Similarly, Heschel discusses spiritual rest in terms of the word *měnûḥâ*, which, he says, to the biblical mind "is the same as happiness and stillness, as peace and harmony. . . . 'The Lord is my shepherd. I shall not want. He maketh me to lie down in green pastures; He leadeth me beside the still waters' (the waters of *měnû-ḥôt*). In later times *měnûḥâ* became a synonym for the life in the world to come, for eternal life."[2]

Spiritual rest enables us to live even with difficult circumstances because it teaches us that we do not need to rely on our own strength to deal with the tragic or the mysterious. Furthermore, it gives us the ability to live with paradox, to have faith in what we cannot see, to deal constructively with the tensions of contradictions. Finally, the spiritual rest of the Sabbath is a foretaste of eternal life, however that is understood in our various faith traditions. That is why our *Havdalah* prayers include great yearning for the next Sabbath and for the ultimate rest of eternity.

Physical Rest

The importance of physical rest in Sabbath keeping is obvious. That is the thrust of the Sabbath command in Deuteronomy 5. What is difficult in our viciously accelerating and graceless society is truly to rest. Certainly an essential contribution of Jews and Christians to our world is our invitation to others to incorporate a rhythm of work and rest into their life-styles.

Emotional Rest

Not as obvious is the component of emotional rest. That God is con-cerned for our psychological well-being is indicated by such accounts in the Scriptures as the story of Elijah's running from Queen Jezebel after his duel of divine fire with the prophets of Baal. In response to Elijah's awful mixture of fear, exhilaration, terror, confidence, panic, delight, and doubt, God twice put him to sleep and then fed him, after which he met him at Mount Horeb in a quiet, gentle whisper (1 Kings 19:1-12).

Emotional healing is granted to us by our Sabbath, set apart for deepening our relationship with God. The day also gives us the silence to discover ourselves and to recover our integrity and creativity and to deepen our relationships with others, in contrast to the technological nonintimacy fostered by our society. Furthermore, the gathering of the Jewish assembly and the Christian church for worship causes emotional rest as the result of both the spiritual rest in the grace and love of God and the fellowship of the community.

Intellectual Rest

Sabbath keeping offers us the time to gain a larger perspective, to view our fragmented existence in the light of a larger whole—in Jacques Ellul's terms, to view our visible reality in the light of the invisible, and larger, Truth.[3] Our concentration on who God is, as part of our Sabbath traditions, gives us a new framework in which to refocus our thinking in the days to come.

Furthermore, Sabbath keeping enables us to understand the larger purposes of God and to place our intellectual work within that cosmic framework. Instead of the frenzy of the world's activity, the strain for prominence and success, the empty intellectualizing that serves only to elevate the thinker and not to contribute to the well-being of others in the world, the intellectual rest of the Sabbath gives us the courage to give up any senseless thinking or intellectual pride that might thwart God's purposes. The following exhortation from Paul's letter to the Romans describes the connection of spiritual practices and our minds:

> Therefore, I urge you, brothers and sisters, with eyes wide open to the mercies of God, as an act of intelligent worship, to offer your bodies as living sacrifices, holy and pleasing to God. Do not conform any longer to the pattern of this world, but be transformed by the renewing of your mind, so that you may prove in practice that the plan of God for you is good, acceptable, and moves toward the goal of true maturity. (Romans 12:1-2)

Aids to Rest

Various practices in which we engage in our customary Sabbath keeping enable us truly to rest in all the ways described in this section. Our differing faith observances offer many specific disciplines that contribute to spiritual, physical, emotional, and intellectual rest, but surely the most important aid to rest is God's very setting aside of the day. As Abraham Heschel so marvelously emphasizes, the first thing that is called *qādôš* in the Scriptures is time (Genesis 2:3).

Holy time frees us to rest our bodies and souls, our minds and our hearts. Moreover, it enables our Sabbath keeping to effect social rest.

Social Rest

I have never heard the phrase "social rest." Both in our immediate communities and in the larger world, characterized by social unrest, Sabbath keeping leads to very practical consequences. The Mishnah teaches that the Sabbath law against the carrying of any kind of burden in the public domain includes weapons. Similarly, the Christian church in the Middle Ages established "the Truce of God," which prohibited warring peoples from fighting on the Sabbath day and other festival days.

To keep the Sabbath and thus to follow seriously that commandment incites us to pay better attention to the other nine. Genuine Sabbath people cannot be characterized by goyish violence. Rather, Sabbath keeping fosters an increase in our personal and corporate gentleness as it teaches a nonaggressive stance toward others and the ability to dismantle our own power. Furthermore, it exposes our political illusions. The prophet Isaiah warned that the Israelites' efforts to secure military alliances and to trust in weapons were futile; instead, he reminds us all, "in repentance and rest is your salvation; in quietness and trust is your strength" (Isaiah 30:15).

Sabbath rest, *měnûḥâ,* includes harmony with all others, the absence of strife, fighting, fear, and distrust. The extension of the Sabbath day in the Sabbath years and the jubilee reminds us that the elimination of violence is made more possible by the procurement of justice and economic redistribution. This aspect will be considered more thoroughly in the section on embracing God's values.

Ethics of Character

All of the aspects of resting discussed in the previous six points lead to a more comprehensive understanding of the nature of ethics. First, our ethics are founded upon the grace of God. Spiritual rest teaches us that we behave in certain ways not because we have to but out of the freedom of response to a God who loved us and delivered us from bondage in Egypt first before he gave us covenant commands. Second, in contrast to our society, in which work determines the value of everything else, the value of our work is determined by our Sabbath rest. Moreover, the emotional and intellectual rest of the Sabbath keeps us from blocking the work of the

Spirit of God, which transforms our minds and personalities. We become a Sabbath people who are characterized by peace building and justice seeking.

All of this means that the Sabbath rhythm of weekday work and holy day worship leads to an ethics of *becoming* (how our character is being developed) and not of *doing* (how we react to specific situations). Furthermore, the Scriptures, which are the foremost element of our Sabbath traditions, will call us to new faithfulness to their revelation. As we rest in the Sabbath, the practices of the day will increase our desire to follow God's instructions against idolatry, killing, stealing, adultery, false witness, and coveting, and his commands to honor parents and keep the Sabbath.

EMBRACING

Embracing Intentionality

One of the main reasons that Christians desperately need to recover the Sabbath traditions of our Jewish roots is that with the loss of the day has also come a loss of its intentional deliberateness of thought. The typical Christian misunderstanding of such things as Jewish discussions of where to put one's napkin perhaps arises primarily from the church's enculturation. Sabbath keeping proclaims clearly that we are not going to do what everybody else does. We are going to be deliberate about our choices in order to live truly as we want to live as the people of God. Everybody else catches up on yard work on the Sabbath day, but we have chosen to rest from work. Everyone else goes window-shopping at the mall on that day, but we have chosen to cease the American hankering after possessions. We embrace the Sabbath day as a holy time for carefulness.

Jacob Neusner's *Invitation to the Talmud* taught me that the many debates over particulars are a natural outflow of the rabbis' intention to imitate God by using their minds and to carry Torah from heaven to earth.[4] Certainly how we think changes how things are. Though our ways to celebrate this intentionality differ extensively, our customs demonstrate the desire to embrace it.

Embracing the Values of the Jewish or Christian Community

One of the main reasons for being deliberate about how we do what we do is so that we can recover more firmly in our lives the different set of values that we hold because we are God's people. Not only do we need to cease the enculturation that so easily entraps us; we must also positively embrace the values of God—his different purposes, a different ordering of priorities, a different mind-set about what is important in and for our lives. Mark Zborowski and Elizabeth Herzog's *Life Is with People* underscores this sense of the community and its values:

> Not only does each Jew know that all those in the shtetl are sharing his Sabbath experience. He feels, beyond that, a community with Jews who are celebrating the Sabbath all over the world. This is a major strand in the Sabbath feeling—a sense of proud and joyous identification with the tradition, the past, the ancestors, with all the Jewish world living or gone. On the Sabbath the shtetl feels most strongly and most gladly that "it is good to be a Jew."[5]

That same collective sense was first experienced by the early Christians as described in these words from the book of Acts:

> And they were continually devoting themselves to the apostles' teaching and to fellowship, to the breaking of bread and to prayer. And everyone kept feeling a sense of awe; and many wonders and signs were taking place through the apostles. And all those who had believed were together, and had all things in common. And they began selling their property and possessions, and were sharing them with all, as anyone might have need. And day by day continuing with one mind in the temple and breaking bread from house to house, they were taking their meals together with gladness and sincerity of heart, praising God, and having favor with all the people. (Acts 2:42-47)

To a great extent the Christian church has lost this sense of community and this adherence to the values of the community. A deepening of Sabbath keeping among both Christians and Jews would inherently also restore a more intentional community.

Embracing Time instead of Space

Surrounded in our culture by the rapid pace of too much change, a Sabbath day of ceasing, resting, embracing, and feasting enables us to assess our use of time in light of God's eternity, to learn what is important in all those changes and how to prioritize our tasks and desires so that we are not overcome by the tyranny of the urgent. Thus, we spend the day in the deliberate choice of focusing on events in time with persons rather than using time to acquire the things of space or to accomplish tasks.

One of the most important stories of the Christian Gospels about choosing time and persons instead of space and things is the account of Jesus healing a crippled woman on the Sabbath day in Luke 13. David M. Feldman writes that Jesus was in good rabbinical tradition when he responded to those who objected to his healing efforts on the Sabbath by affirming that "The Sabbath is given to man, not man to the Sabbath."

Rabbi Feldman stresses by this discussion from the Talmud that the Sabbath itself teaches us to set it aside in order to choose time and life:

> "How do we know that evidence of a threat to life sets aside the Sabbath?" ask the Talmud (*Yoma* 95b). Rabbi Simon ben Menassia: "We are told: 'You shall keep the Sabbath for it is holy unto you' (Ex. 31:13). That means unto you is the Sabbath given over but you are not given over to the Sabbath," Rabbi Nathan: "We are told: 'The people of Israel shall keep the Sabbath, to observe the Sabbath through the generations' (Ex. 31:16). That means, violate one Sabbath if necessary in order to keep many Sabbaths afterward." Rabbi Yehudah in the name of Rabbi Samuel: "We are told: 'Keep My commandments and ordinances, which if a man do them he will live by them' (Lev. 18:5). That means, live by them and don't die because of them."[6]

Our various Sabbath traditions involve differing methods for choosing time instead of space, but they all are based upon the deliberate intention to embrace that value.

Embracing Giving instead of Requiring

Tragically, our acquisitive society has turned the major holy days of Judaism and Christianity into commercialized holidays, characterized by inordinate desires instead of special times of adoration and worship. Sabbath keeping repels this invasion with a weekly counteroffensive — our Sabbath traditions of giving rather than accumulating, of caring for the needs of others instead of requiring for ourselves, of putting aside our personal pleasure in order to create pleasure for many. Our negative ceasing to possess must be accompanied by a positive choosing to be generous.

In 2 Corinthians 8:11-15 and 9:6-15, the apostle Paul builds on his earlier comment in 1 Corinthians 16:1-2 to set aside a proportionate amount of one's income on the first day every week. The 2 Corinthians passage cites both Exodus 16:18 and Psalm 112:9 in its exhortation to generosity and the freedom of Sabbath giving. Paul emphasizes that the experience of the children of Israel in the wilderness — having exactly what they needed even though they gathered no manna on the Sabbath — teaches us the importance of trusting God to provide not only for our needs but also for our sharing with others. Furthermore, such giving strengthens the bonds of the community of believers.

Our traditions widen this generosity beyond money and invite us to celebrate the Sabbath by bringing gifts. Paul celebrated the Sabbath generosity that could arise even in difficult times with this extraordinary equation:

most severe trial + overflowing joy + extreme poverty = rich generosity.

Embracing Our Calling in Life

Psalm 92, entitled "A song for Shabbat," reveals the following ways in which our Sabbath traditions impress us with the goodness of God and increase our longing to be more faithful in serving God according to the gifts and resources he has given us and the calling he has issued in our lives.

> It is good to praise the LORD
>   and make music to your name, O Most High,
> to proclaim your love in the morning
>   and your faithfulness at night,
> to the music of the ten-stringed lyre
>   and the melody of the harp.
> For you make me glad by your deeds, O LORD;
>   I sing for joy at the works of your hands.
> How great are your works, O LORD,
>   how profound your thoughts!
> The senseless [person] does not know;
>   fools do not understand,
> that though the wicked spring up like grass
>   and all evildoers flourish,
> they will be forever destroyed.
>
> But you, O LORD, are exalted forever. . . .
>
> You have exalted my horn like that of a wild ox;
>   fine oils have been poured upon me. . . .
> The righteous will flourish like a palm tree,
>   they will grow like a cedar of Lebanon; . . .
> They will still bear fruit in old age, . . .
>   proclaiming, "The LORD is upright."

This Sabbath song emphasizes that God's people contemplate his deeds and recognize that their lives are part of God's larger purposes. Tom Sine, a Christian futurist, emphasizes that we ask the wrong question if we search for God's will in our individual lives.[7] Instead, we should see what God is doing in the world and become part of his program. This is the implication of the psalm, too, for, in contrast to those fools whose lives are futile, the people of God are made glad in thinking about his works and purposes.

God's exaltation of the poet's horn and the anointing with oil underscore the commissioning of the individual for God's special purposes. In their assignments, the people of God will flourish like palm trees and cedars. Our Sabbath traditions of worship, Torah study, and fellowship with other believers enable us to discover more thoroughly and embrace with greater commitment our calling in life.

Embracing Wholeness—Shalom

The extraordinary septenary development of Genesis 1:1–2:3, so wonderfully delineated by Samuele Bacchiocchi in *Divine Rest for Human Restlessness*,[8] underscores our belief that we are physiologically, psychically structured in a seven-day rhythm. To be obedient to that rhythm allows us the possibility for wholeness and order in a fragmented and disordered world. Our various Sabbath traditions, in their very repetitiveness, give us the stability of ritual wholeness. This goes back to such biblical customs as the setting out of the twelve loaves of shewbread, which were set out "before the LORD regularly, Sabbath after Sabbath" (Leviticus 24:8).

Furthermore, the Sabbath rhythm gives us the possibility for wholeness even in affliction and sorrow. This is suggested, for example, by the end of the book of 2 Chronicles. Though that book is filled with narratives of the failures of the kings of both Israel and Judah to follow the ways of Yahweh, the book ends with the declaration that, during the time of the exile, the land "enjoyed its Sabbath rests; all the time of its desolation it rested" (36:21) and then the proclamation of Cyrus allowing the Israelites to return to Jerusalem to rebuild the Temple (36:23). The juxtaposition of those two points suggests that Yahweh was with the land.

Since observing the Sabbath implies a sense of the presence of Yahweh, the point seems to be that, in the absence of the people who failed, the land nevertheless continued to experience God's presence. Yahweh was still at work on behalf of the Israelites, and so, after the seventy years of their exile, he called them back to their homeland and to the wholeness of Sabbath rests.

Embracing the World

Though to observe the Sabbath means that we choose values different from those of the world (in embracing intentionality), our very Sabbath traditions enable us more thoroughly to embrace the world itself. As we embrace the values of our faith communities, time instead of space, people instead of things, giving instead of requiring, our own calling to participate in the purposes of God in the world, and the wholeness of God's *shalom,* our Sabbath keeping changes the world. We certainly do serve the world better out of the wholeness, order, revived spirits, empowered emotions, healthy bodies, renewed minds, authentic relationships, and nurtured senses of ourselves that Sabbath keeping creates. We are much more able to be healers in a sin-sick world when we ourselves have experienced the profound healing that is made possible by Sabbath keeping. Furthermore, our Sabbath study and worship make more urgent our desire to reflect the character of our God, who cares about the poor, feeds the hungry, delivers the oppressed, and brings peace to the world.

We do not spend the Sabbath trying to save the world. Rather, our very keeping of the Sabbath gives testimony to the efficacy of God's provision in our lives and to our trust for the future in his goodness. Out of the wholeness that Sabbath keeping creates, we will call the world to new wholeness.

FEASTING

Feasting on the Eternal

The primary components of our Sabbath traditions are study of the Torah and worship. In both of these elements we delight in the eternal but also recognize the ephemerality of our present time. Our *Havdalah* prayers bid the Sabbath Queen good-bye with great longing in our hearts, for we have tasted the delights of the day and long for their eternal fulfillment.

The wonderful folktale about a pious Jew who loses his way in the forest late one Friday afternoon and is given the privilege of spending the Sabbath in paradise[9] underscores this eschatological hope of the Sabbath and the importance of Sabbath activities of Bible study, worship, and prayer for experiencing in this time the presence of God. Such legends offer us models for observing our Sabbaths with practices that embrace and feast on the eternal.

Feasting with Music

No doubt Christians need this section more than Jews. What a thrill it was for me when first I heard the beloved Hebrew Scriptures sung at a Jewish Sabbath service. Our faith communities must carefully discern criteria for feasting with music appropriately in our Sabbath celebrations. Moreover, in a culture so much dominated by its music, it is imperative that our faith communities be deliberate about the training in music that we give our children, so that our Sabbath values in music carry over into the week. 2 Corinthians 5:17 literally says in the Greek, "if anyone is in Christ, there is a whole new creation." Similarly, Jews understand that to be Jewish places the individual in an entirely different milieu from the environment of the world. The strong emphasis on music in Hebrew and Christian Scriptures challenges us to be more deliberate about our use of it.

Feasting with Beauty

Similarly, in a culture that has become so violent and ugly, our faith communities have the opportunity to offer an alternative in our Sabbath emphasis on beauty. *Lechah dodi* [a Sabbath eve hymn], with its emphasis on the beauty of the Sabbath Queen and its charge to humankind to administer the creation in a godly manner, and other *Zemirot* [table hymns] challenge us to discover the secrets of creation and to refrain from even the smallest work which would deny that God is the Creator and Master of the world, to whom we are responsible for its preservation.

Observing the Sabbath gives us the opportunity to be as careful as we can to fill our lives with beauty and to share beauty with the world around us. Some of our faith traditions (especially mine in symbolic Lutheranism) create beautiful sanctuaries. Certainly all the instructions for the building of the tabernacle and the Temple in the Hebrew Scriptures point to the importance of the aesthetic dimension of our lives. Our *Kiddush* prayers underscore this emphasis as we ask that the Sabbath light might cause peace and happiness to shine in our homes and as we welcome the radiant and joyous Sabbath bride.

Feasting with Food

Contemporary Christians especially need to learn from Jews how best to feast with food. The willingness to live more frugally during the week in order to celebrate the Sabbath which characterizes Judaism teaches that true feasting is made richer and more genuine by fasting and simplicity on other days. Our Sabbath feasting with food reminds us that God provided for his people in the wilderness by giving them a double amount of manna on Friday.

Feasting with food also enables us to be more responsible in our lives for the many in our world who are hungry. This was the realization of the apostle Paul when he criticized the rich Corinthian Christians for their lack of concern for their poorer brothers and sisters when they celebrated their *agapē* meals. Similarly, Deuteronomy 14:22–29 lists three main ways in which the tithes of the Israelites' fields should be used. Besides the feasting of their celebrations and the care for the Levites, the other recipients of the tithes were the aliens, the fatherless, and the widows. The Jewish custom of welcoming into one's home any strangers at the synagogue points to the rhythm of fasting and feasting and to the hospitality of Sabbath celebration.

Feasting with Affection

One of the most terrifying aspects of the technological society in which we live is its loss of intimacy. Many people in our culture are desperate for affection and most do not know how to give or receive it. To keep the Sabbath offers us the possibility for learning to deepen our relationships and to embrace others with godly affection. Sabbath keeping offers us a deepening of relationships because of its emphasis on one's relationship with God, its rhythms of community and solitude, its gift of time, and its call to cease striving and productivity and work. Furthermore, the intentionality of the day lends itself to a conscious enjoyment of our relationships with and delight in each other as the outgrowth of our delight in Yahweh.

Throughout the Scriptures God is revealed as a caring and loving God. He walked in the Garden and promised to be with Moses and Joshua. According to the Gospel of Matthew, Jesus closed his earthly ministry by promising to be with his followers till the close of the age. In response to the character of God, Paul urges his readers in Rome to "love each other with brotherly [and sisterly] affection," which is kept pure by his next phrase, to "take delight in honoring each other" (Romans 12:10). Indeed, our faith communities have much to offer the world as alternative societies full of affection and intimacy.

Feasting with Festival

Feasting does not mean that our struggles are over. To observe the Sabbath teaches us the meaning of festival in the midst of difficulties. In his description of l'Arche communities, founded by Jean Vanier for the care of the handicapped, Michael Downey emphasizes that festival "intensifies as the suffering is recognized and appropriated." Celebration is not a compensation for affliction. Rather, "joy born of deep suffering is nourished by moments of celebration. . . . Celebration properly understood is the acceptance of life in an ever growing recognition that it is so precious."[10]

Festival involves the paradoxical combination of tradition and creativity, of the rituals and customs that become the framework into which we can pour all our creativity and in which all our senses are heightened. Each Sabbath becomes its own unique celebration while yet maintaining a thread of continuity with all of the world's celebrations through space and time and religious affiliations.

Festival also involves the paradoxical combination of memory and anticipation as we remember how Yahweh ordained our Sabbath keeping with his commands and his example at creation which we imitate. We also remember how Jews and later Christians have observed Sabbath throughout the centuries — so aptly summarized by other papers at this conference. Meanwhile, Sabbath points us intentionally to the future, when we will finally know the perfect ceasing of all work, the ultimate resting in the completion of God's purposes, the total embracing of all God's best gifts, and the eternal feasting in the very presence of God.

Because the Sabbath is holy time, it frees us to have festival fun, to play, to enjoy our guests and our activities, to relish the opportunity for worship, to celebrate the eternal presence of God himself. We feast in every aspect of our being—physical, intellectual, social, emotional, spiritual—and we feast with music, beauty, food, and affection. Our bodies, minds, souls, and spirits celebrate together with others that God is in our midst.

SABBATH CEASING, RESTING, EMBRACING, AND FEASTING

My concern about Sabbath keeping first arose in graduate study of its biblical basis and traditions. Then it issued in a desire to motivate lay-people to observe again more faithfully the Sabbath keeping of our Jewish and early Christian roots.[11] Now it returns again to the scholarly community in my attempt to outline the underlying theological principles and biblical notions of Sabbath keeping which unite rather than divide us. Jews and Christians need each other as both traditions seek to arouse our own communities to more faithful observance of the Sabbath. The world needs all of our traditions since our Sabbath ceasing, resting, embracing, and feasting lead to a holistic alternative life-style.

Each of the aspects of this presentation corresponds to major themes in both Jewish and Christian theology. Sabbath Ceasing deepens our repentance for the many ways that we fail to trust God and try to create our own future. Its Resting strengthens our faith in the totality of God's grace. Its Embracing invites us to take the truths of our faith and apply them practically in all our values and life-styles. Its Feasting heightens our sense of eschatological hope—the joy of our present experience of God's love and its foretaste of the joy to come.

NOTES

1. Martin Luther, "Treatise on Good Works," in *The Christian in Society I*, trans. W. A. Lambert; rev. James Atkinson; vol. 44 of *Luther's Works*, gen. ed. Helmut T. Lehmann (Philadelphia: Fortress, 1966) 72.

2. Abraham Joshua Heschel, *The Sabbath: Its Meaning for Modern Man* (New York: Farrar, Straus and Giroux, 1951) 23.

3. Jacques Ellul, *The Humiliation of the Word*, trans. Joyce Main Hanks (Grand Rapids: Eerdmans, 1985) 10–11.

4. J. Neusner, *Invitation to the Talmud: A Teaching Book* (rev. ed.; San Francisco: Harper & Row, 1984).

5. Mark Zborowski and Elizabeth Herzog, *Life Is with People: The Culture of the Shtetl* (New York: Schocken Books, 1952) 48.

6. David M. Feldman, *Health and Medicine in the Jewish Tradition: L'Hayyim—To Life,* ed. Martin Marty and Kenneth L. Vaux (Health and Medicine in the Faith Traditions; New York: Crossroad, 1986) 23.

7. Tom Sine, *The Mustard Seed Conspiracy* (Waco, TX: Word Books, 1981).

8. Samuele Bacchiocchi, *Divine Rest for Human Restlessness: A Theological Study of the Good News of the Sabbath for Today* (Rome: Gregorian University Press, 1980) 17–76.

9. Chaim Grade, *My Mother's Sabbath Days: A Memoir,* trans. Channa Kleinerman Goldstein and Inna Hecker Grade (New York: Alfred A. Knopf, 1986) 337–38.

10. Michael Downey, *A Blessed Weakness: The Spirit of Jean Vanier and l'Arche* (San Francisco: Harper & Row, 1986) 85 and 83.

11. Marva J. Dawn, *Keeping the Sabbath Wholly: Ceasing, Resting, Embracing, Feasting* (Grand Rapids: Eerdmans, 1989).

V

LITURGICAL PERSPECTIVES

15

SABBATH LITURGY: CELEBRATING SUNDAY AS A CHRISTIAN

John F. Baldovin, S.J.
Graduate Theological Union

> When the proconsul said to him [Saturninus]: "Against the decree of the emperors and caesars you have called an assembly of these people," the presbyter Saturninus, inspired by the Spirit of the Lord, responded, "Surely we have celebrated the supper of the Lord (*dominicum*)." The proconsul: "Why?" Saturninus: "Because it is impossible for us not to celebrate the supper of the Lord."[1]

I begin with these classic words from the tradition of the *Acts of the Christian Martyrs* because they provide a concise and at the same time powerful witness to the significance of the role of weekly worship in forming the identity of the Christian community. That weekly assembly will be the focus of this essay. My thesis is a simple one: The eucharistic assembly makes Sunday and Sunday makes the eucharistic assembly. In order to argue this thesis I will do three things.

First, I will argue that the Christian church was free to choose Sunday as its day of worship. Here I will place the idea of worship, specifically with regard to times and places, within a general theological context. Second, I will show how the Sunday liturgy as a whole (not just the Eucharist) shaped the contours of the Christian community in the patristic period. To do this I will rely mainly on the description of the Sunday liturgy in Jerusalem given by a late fourth century pilgrim Egeria. Finally, after some remarks on the significance and shape of Christian Sunday worship to the present, I will draw some conclusions with regard to the importance of weekly worship.

SUNDAY AS THE DAY OF WORSHIP

I have no intention of entering on a serious level into the debate that has
been carried on in the past twenty years between scholars like W. Rordorf,
S. Bacchiocchi, C. Mosna, R. Beckwith, W. Stott, D. A. Carson, and
others.[2] What follows will make clear that my sympathies lie with Rordorf
and with all who consider the Christian adoption of Sunday as a day of
worship (more than primarily as a day of rest) as a legitimate development
of early Christianity — even if the observance of the first day of the week
was not universal until the middle of the second century.

My approach to this question is at the same time simpler and more
radical. I see the issue not in terms of a historical debate regarding when,
why, and how Sunday became the day of worship and the ramifications of
the idea of a day of rest, but rather in terms of a hermeneutical question.
In other words, on what grounds does a religious community — in this case
specifically Christianity — form its practice? Too often, it seems to me, we
have fallen prey to what can be called the "genetic fallacy," that is, what
is earliest must be best.[3] This is a crucial issue for the method of theology,
since so much of classic theology has relied on an understanding of tradition as providing certain kinds of data for the formulation of doctrine.
This data can take the form of "types," as when Christianity is understood
in terms of the scheme Promise/Fulfillment, or it can be the search for
definitive divine prescriptions lodged in the Scriptures. The radical aspect
of my approach stems from a questioning of the value of this procedure
and an insistence that a religious tradition does not so much provide us
with normative answers to contemporary questions as with insight into
forms of life — in other words, patterns that arise from the living context
of a particular religious community.[4] Liberation from the procrustean bed
of this sort of normativity allows us to appreciate the variety and diversity
of Christianity in its period of formation[5] and provides us as well with a
means for adapting religious faith and tradition to contemporary culture.

I should be clear about a number of my philosophical presuppositions
here. Three of them are pertinent. First, it seems to me that to ground one's
doctrinal affirmations on the intentions of the historical Jesus of Nazareth
is a risky business. This has, of course, been a time-honored practice but one
that stems from a certain crypto-monophysitism (a complete swallowing-up
of the humanity of Jesus of Nazareth by the Logos), namely, that this
historical Jesus had not only a blueprint for the development of what came
to be called the Christian church, but that he also had foreknowledge. Such
an approach vitiates the humanness of Jesus and thus Jesus' significance
for salvation in the Christian scheme of things.

My second supposition has to do with the relation of Christianity to the
faith of Israel. It seems to me that this is a question that took some time

to sort out. On the one hand, Christians saw themselves as the New Israel in direct and profound continuity with their forebears. This is why Marcion and his denial of the God of Israel had to be rejected, a crucial turn for Christian doctrine and theology, and why Paul (on whom Marcion relied) seems to have remained somewhat suspect, even if canonized in the New Testament, up until the fourth century.[6] On the other hand, precisely as the *New* Israel, Christians felt themselves free to abandon any number of the religious practices of their ancestors as they confronted new religious and social situations. Early Christian liturgy, my own particular field of study, abounds with continuity and discontinuity of this sort, sometimes witnessing contemporaneous conflicting practices, for example, with regard to whether one fasted on Saturday (the Sabbath) or not.[7]

The third presupposition concerns the role of the Holy Spirit in the governance of the church. If, on the one hand, my first presupposition leads me on the basis of historical criticisms in what could be called a liberal Protestant direction, my third confirms that I am, after all, a Roman Catholic. I have no intention of denying the normative role of Scripture in matters both doctrinal and practical, but at the same time post-Enlightenment thought has demonstrated the impossibility of treating Scripture as though it were a norm that does not need interpretation and as if it were not read from the point of view of contemporary questioners. In other words, it seems to me that I must affirm God's continual guidance of the community (correctly understood this is what infallibility means), and this is what Christians call the role of the Holy Spirit. Confidence in this pneumatic guidance of the church should lead us to be wary of regarding Scripture (whether the Hebrew Scriptures and/or the New Testament) as containing extrinsic positive divine commands for human beings.[8] "What God wants," whether this be the Sabbath commandment or the command not to kill or not to commit adultery, is not something God imposes as it were from outside the human condition but expresses humankind's grasp of the implications of the ultimate mystery that is God and God's relation to us.

These then are my presuppositions. Now — what should one make of the imperative of a weekly day of worship and/or rest? It seems to me that the Scriptures do not provide clear answers when we ask them to produce a divinely mandated response to questions of this sort.[9] The New Testament does not seem terribly interested in the sacralization of time and space. On the contrary it appears to relativize both in terms of what it considers to be new — the revelation of God in a person, Jesus of Nazareth. (Hence the spiritualization of the cult in the Letter to the Hebrews.)

This is clear in the case of space — for example, in John 4:21, where Jesus tells the Samaritan woman that true worshipers of God will worship not in a particular place but in spirit and truth, and in Acts 2:46, where the community gathers for prayer, not necessarily in a sacred space but in their homes. In terms of time, we note the Pauline critique of days, months, years, times, seasons, festivals, new moons, and Sabbaths in Galatians 4:9-11 and Colossians 2:16. The person of Jesus of Nazareth becomes the sole criterion for worship and activity in the New Testament.[10] This leads me to the conclusion that, in principle, for the New Testament there are no such things as divinely mandated sacred time and space.[11] The second-century concept of Sunday as the "Eighth Day" may well serve as a symbol of this breaking the bounds of time. No doubt Christianity was not alone in the process of spiritualizing cultic activity, as Jean Laporte has well shown in terms of Philo of Alexandria.[12]

It would be unrealistic, however, to think that any religious community could do for long without some sacralization of space and time. Christianity accomplished this resacralization within a very short period and a parallel development can be seen in the adoption of sacral motifs for the ministers of the church. The religious terminology of the New Testament has an "oddity" about it that is missed completely when understood literally. Concepts like "kingdom," "priesthood," "sacrifice" are transformed in their meaning when measured against the criterion of Jesus of Nazareth, who is, when all is said and done, a rather odd candidate for divinity.[13]

But this transformation of religious categories is difficult to maintain, since religion is a world-constructing and world-maintaining activity. As Peter Berger has shown so well in terms of the sociology of knowledge, religious forms construct meaningful boundaries against a world that would otherwise be chaos.[14] In other words, it is impossible to conceive of a religious community that would not somehow shape its "world" in terms of defined boundaries. One of these boundaries is clearly the articulation of time as meaningful, which has been a universal human activity.[15]

Seen in these terms, the articulation of time has a highly political function.[16] It enables one group rather than another to define what is meaningful. A perfect example of this process can be found in the ill-fated attempt of the French Revolution to create a new calendar and destroy the weekly rhythm deeply engrained in Western culture, as Mona Ozouf shows in her recent book on the revolutionary calendar.[17] The ideology of the revolution was not powerful enough to carry this off. (It seems to me that secularizing economic developments may well succeed where political ideology fails.)

The articulation of time serves another function as well. It is a universalizing factor; that is, it takes what is germane to a particular place and makes it available to people wherever they are, as Jonathan Z. Smith has shown with regard to Jerusalem and the development of the Christian calendar.[18] In other words, the celebration of Easter is not limited to the

Holy Sepulchre in Jerusalem, nor are the feasts of the saints limited to their tombs. Similarly, one does not need to be in a specific place to celebrate the Sabbath or Sunday or a fast day; these can be celebrated anywhere that a community of faith assembles.

On the basis of these insights I argue that Christianity universalized not only a particular place but a particular event—its central event, the passion, death, and resurrection of Jesus of Nazareth—in the form of a weekly gathering taking the form of a ritual meal, the Eucharist. This weekly ritual assembly took place on a day that conveniently distanced the community from the Israelite Sabbath and at the same time corresponded to the climactic day of the paschal event, namely, the first day of the week. One need not resort to a positive divine command to ground this practice. In fact, they could have chosen any day of the week, but the first day of the week symbolized rather fittingly the correspondence: Lord's Supper/ Lord's Day. In other words the day and the event that shaped it belonged together.[19] To understand how this was carried out in terms of Christian worship we shall turn to the liturgy of Jerusalem in the fourth century.

THE LITURGICAL CHARACTER OF SUNDAY

Since no other early Christian church has provided us with as much information about its liturgical practices within a limited time frame, the Jerusalem liturgy has long been the object of detailed research.[20] No doubt there are special factors pertinent to the liturgy of Jerusalem that make it a less than ideal example for describing the Christian Sunday in general, namely, it contained the holy shrines associated with the passion, death, and resurrection of Christ and was therefore the object of pilgrimage, which probably influenced the development of its system of worship.[21] On the other hand, since Jerusalem was so important as a model for later churches in both East and West, it serves as a significant example of liturgical practice.

Our basic source of information for the shape of the Sunday liturgy in fourth-century Jerusalem comes from a pilgrimage diary by a woman named Egeria, most probably from Galicia in Spain. She visited the holy places in the latter part of the century, most likely ca. 381–384.[22] This eyewitness account is far more valuable than many liturgical manuscripts, for it gives us a sense not of the text of the liturgy but of how it was experienced by a participant. Part of her description of the liturgical services deals with the daily services, which need not concern us here, except to note that five services were held in the Anastasis, the rotunda enshrining the site of Christ's resurrection, each day from cockcrow until the onset of evening. The evening service—Vespers in modern terminology,

Lucernare or the lighting of lamps in hers—involved a long procession at the end of the liturgy to the cross at Golgotha and to the basilica that had been constructed behind it.

Egeria's description of the Sunday liturgy ("on the seventh day, the Lord's Day") is particularly rich (*Egeria* 24.8). The faithful gathered in the courtyard in front of the Anastasis rotunda well before cockcrow and sang psalms and hymns until the bishop arrived at cockcrow for the beginning of the liturgy. The liturgy itself involved three psalms, intercessory prayer, incensation of the cave of the resurrection and the whole building, the reading of a Gospel narrative of the passion and resurrection of Jesus, a procession to the cross at Golgotha, and a long dismissal involving individual blessings. This Sunday vigil was distinct from the weekday vigil in that (1) it involved the participation of the bishop (the symbolic leader of the community); (2) it included a reading from Scripture as well as the ceremonial act of incensation; and (3) it ended with a procession to Golgotha.

The Sunday Cathedral Vigil, as it has been called,[23] is significant, because it is the ancestor of a universal Sunday vigil in the Eastern Christian churches. This is still observed with splendor and devotion today, although the time has been pushed back and the vigil itself is combined with the first Vespers of Sunday, held on Saturday evening.[24]

Egeria does not mention the "morning hymns" that took place on other days of the week. Perhaps on Sunday morning alone this was left to the monks and nuns who usually observed the daily vigil that had been replaced by a Cathedral Vigil. Egeria turns instead to the assembly for the Eucharist, which begins at daybreak: "It is the Lord's Day and they do what is everywhere the custom of this day" (*Egeria* 25.1). She does not need to describe the service in detail, since the Sunday Eucharist is a well-practiced custom everywhere. At Jerusalem, however, the Sunday Eucharist seems to be considerably longer than elsewhere, since all the presbyters present have an opportunity to preach if they so wish. The bishop preaches last of all, and the dismissal from the liturgy does not take place until ten or eleven in the morning. Presuming dawn at around six, this would mean a good four or five hours of worship. Egeria explains why so many are allowed to preach: "The object of having this preaching every Sunday is to make sure that the people will continually be learning about the Bible and the love of God" (*Egeria* 25.1). After the dismissal from the main basilica at which the Eucharist has been celebrated, the people process with the bishop to the Anastasis rotunda for a service of thanksgiving and intercessory prayer that probably took the place of the daily prayer at the sixth hour.[25] Vespers followed in the Anastasis around four in the afternoon, as was the daily practice.

So the Sunday morning liturgy begins at cockcrow and does not end officially until around eleven or noon. Even if only the heartiest and most devoted of the faithful participated in the whole of these eight hours of services, clearly the intention was that the Sunday assembly, a corporate exercise, form the focus of the observance of the Lord's Day.

I would be remiss in not mentioning here that Egeria also provides some information on the liturgical observance of Saturday. It seems that in late fourth-century Jerusalem every Saturday (except for Holy Saturday, when fasting took place) was liturgical; that is, it included the celebration of the Eucharist. Indeed, this Eucharist took place at the Anastasis rotunda (a smaller place than the basilica — probably because of fewer numbers) after an all-night vigil held by the monks and nuns that followed Vespers (*Egeria* 27.8; 29.1, 3).

One can legitimately conclude that, in this special pilgrimage center at least, Sunday observance was characterized by an elaborate and ceremonial vigil of the resurrection as well as by an extended eucharistic assembly. The very length of these ceremonies bears witness to the fact that the relatively new public status of the Christian church in late antique society was symbolized not only by the conquest of space (the building of monumental structures at the heart of the city) but also by control of the time that society spent. The time and energy put into this corporate exercise of liturgy allowed for no other real focus to the day and may well have inspired the medieval Sabbatarianism that encouraged Sabbath rest on Sunday.[26]

Of course, one example from a specific place and time does not make a case for the importance of the Sunday liturgical assembly. Perhaps another example, this one from the practice of the fifth-century Roman church will help to build my case. In a famous letter on a number of liturgical practices to the Bishop Decentius of Gubbio (in Umbria) in 416, Pope Innocent I writes of Sunday eucharistic practice:

> Concerning the *fermentum* which we send to the titular churches on Sundays, it is needless for you to ask, for all of our churches are set up within the city. As to the presbyters who are not able to join with us (in the main eucharist) on Sundays because of the people they serve, they receive the *fermentum* made by us from the acolytes, so they may not consider themselves separated from us, especially on Sundays.[27]

The *fermentum* of which Innocent writes consists of pieces of the eucharistic bread, consecrated at the papal stational Eucharist and sent to the titular (or parish) churches within the city of Rome. The presbyters (or priests) would in turn drop a piece of the consecrated bread in the chalice at the parochial Eucharist at the time of the fraction rite. This practice provided a tangible and powerful symbol of the unity of the worshiping assembly, expressed horizontally by the *fermentum* as one celebration on each Sunday. In addition, eighth-century evidence indicates that the pope took a piece of eucharistic bread (called the *sancta*) from the previous Sunday Eucharist and dropped it into the chalice at the stational mass.[28] Thus, the Romans employed an elaborate symbolic system both vertically (in terms of time) and horizontally (in terms of space) to emphasize the unity of Christians expressed by the weekly assembly. This organic symbolic system fell apart in the translation of Roman eucharistic practice across the Alps, where practices such as the dropping of a particle of eucharistic bread into the chalice were retained but the larger context was lost.[29]

The Roman Sunday liturgy of the later patristic period in which the people would process to the church of the day (where the bishop of Rome was to preside) behind the banners and crosses of their own regions provides a striking example of the symbolic power of liturgical assembly in forming the religious and social identity of a people. It is on this basis that I want to claim that the Eucharist makes Sunday and Sunday makes the Eucharist.

THE SHAPE OF SUNDAY WORSHIP

Organic liturgical systems have a way of breaking down when they are translated to other cultures. As one contemporary liturgical scholar has put it, "Structure outlives meaning."[30] The classic Christian liturgical systems of the fourth and subsequent centuries, which I have described in the preceding section, were transformed because of social and political factors in the medieval West. One of the results of the significant mutations[31] that occurred in the West was a solidly hierarchical and sacerdotal understanding of Christian faith articulated by the theologians of the Carolingian period (the ninth century). Although Sabbatarianism, in the sense of a mandatory Sabbath rest, was already a legacy of the patristic period, it was often interpreted in Augustinian terms of a spiritual understanding of Sabbath rest as rest from sin.[32] The insistence on Sunday as a day of rest from labor, however, was to become commonplace in the Middle Ages and was certainly the case in medieval England.[33]

Along with this development, the expectation that Christians would primarily worship on Sunday remained steady. At the same time shifts in the character of worship from the participative assembly to a passive spectacle (at least for the great majority of the people) as well as the growth of the calendar of feasts tended to obscure what I have called the organic system of worship of the patristic period. Massive shifts occurred in the liturgical ethos in the course of the Middle Ages. It is not possible nor is it necessary to treat them in detail here. I will merely list some of them:

retention of Latin as the liturgical language, changes in church architecture including the eastward position of the priest at the altar, infrequency of communion, the withdrawal of the cup, an increased desire to see the host, elaborate ceremonialization by a trained elite including multiple incensations, and the like. All of these factors, while retaining the structure of the ancient liturgy, dramatically changed its meaning.[34] No longer do we have an assembly of active participants, but rather one of passive spectators. Despite these changes, however, the structure of medieval society made attendance at Sunday worship (Matins before Mass and Vespers in the afternoon as well as the morning Eucharist) a high value.[35] To be sure, the rest of Sunday (and feasts as well) was hallowed by the avoidance of labor, but Sunday worship was the constant factor and governed other uses of time.

Shifts in the Christian calendar also obscured the primacy of Sunday worship. As the Christian church conquered time and space—that is, the parameters of society—it was natural that it should shape the way people lived their daily existence. This calendrical development (which began already in the fourth century) had many specifically local elements (e.g., the celebration of a saint whose relics the town or monastery possessed) but was common to both medieval Christian East and West. Thus Sunday as *the* day of assembly tended to be obscured—as still occurs today when Sunday is used for special celebrations like Mission Sunday, or Worldwide Communion Sunday, or Mother's Day, or the placement of calendar feasts like Epiphany on Sunday by Roman Catholics.

The Reformation of the sixteenth century must be credited with the restoration of the primacy of Sunday both in the reduction of saints' feasts by the Lutherans and Anglicans and by the Sabbatarianism of the Reformed churches. What remained constant, however, even for Roman Catholics and especially after the Industrial Revolution, was the practice of Sunday worship as central to the observance of the day, even where Sabbatarianism prevailed.[36] But what of the contemporary situation? It seems to me that Sunday worship still holds pride of place in the observance of the day and, for those who are still active Christians, serves as the focal point of their weekly existence. No doubt there are any number of factors in contemporary postindustrial society that militate against the observance of Sunday as a true day of rest, and these may be lamentable. No doubt as well with the privatization of culture it would be worthwhile to stress domestic aspects of Sunday observance—a value that Jews and many evangelical Christians have maintained and one that many other Christians have lost. Liturgy, or the time spent in liturgical worship, is never enough to sustain a religiously committed life and (in my opinion) many Roman Catholics have forgotten this today by stressing liturgy over every other aspect of ecclesial life—that is, by expecting too much of it.

On the other hand, both in theory and in practice Roman Catholics have come to the same appreciation of the centrality of Sunday that the Reformers of the sixteenth century did. This is partly the result of a culture that will allow for Sunday worship at the most, but also partly a result of a renewed estimation of the place of Sunday in the early Christian church with its focus on the assembly. It is not insignificant that the current Roman Catholic *Norms for the Liturgical Year and Calendar* begin with Sunday "the first holyday of all"[37] and insists on its primacy in Christian celebration because it celebrates the paschal mystery—the passion, death, and resurrection of Christ. The same insistence is codified in the current Canon Law, where Sunday rest is prescribed: "They are also to abstain from work or business that would inhibit the worship to be given to God, the joy proper to the Lord's Day, or the due relaxation of mind and body."[38] Here the primary reason for Sunday rest is an orientation to worship, but the joy proper to this day of the week and the socially sensitive factor of the need for rest are mentioned as well.

There is one aspect of the contemporary Roman Catholic observance of Sunday that requires further comment. Canon #1248 considers the liturgical feast day to begin with the previous evening. Saturday evening liturgy has become a commonplace in Catholic practice and clearly represents more of an effort to accommodate contemporary culture than to restore an earlier notion of the liturgical day beginning with sunset. What is one to make of this? On the one hand, given the arguments of my first section, this development should not be considered negatively. In other words, the Christian community has the freedom to choose a mandated time for worship; what is important is that Christians assemble once a week to offer the sacrifice of praise and thanksgiving. On the other hand, however, one wonders whether such a development might not weaken the assembly of Christians in that a common time for worship undergirds the common religious identity of the people. Roman Catholics share a particular difficulty here in that the multiplication of worship services (in some large parishes even a dozen eucharistic assemblies over Saturday evening and Sunday) as well as daily celebrations of the Eucharist tend to undermine the notion of the gathering of God's people as a community and thus weaken the link between the content of worship and the community that is doing the worshiping.[39] One might get the impression from contemporary Roman Catholic Sunday practice that convenience rather than the symbolism of the Lord's Day is the governing factor.

On the brighter side one must note the increasing attention being given to the connection between observance of the Lord's Day and Christian initiation.[40] Baptism is no longer considered a private family affair but rather the business of the entire ecclesial community as it gathers weekly for prayer. Therefore in many churches Christian initiation takes place at the Sunday Eucharist.

In terms of what might be done to improve the connection between Sunday as a day of assembly and the observance of the day itself, it seems to me that mainline Christians have been too minimalistic in their expectations, supposing that people will only stand for an hour in church each week. The medieval ideal of Matins, Eucharist, and Vespers may not be replicable today, but at the same time might inspire mainline churches to be more aggressive as to the time they expect Christians to be together on Sunday. Here too the Eastern Christian practice of a Saturday evening Vespers combined with vigil of the resurrection might suggest a viable alternative to the convenience mentality I observe in current Roman Catholic worship.

Whatever the means taken to hallow the day both in communal and in domestic gathering, the assembly for worship remains the focal point of Christian weekly existence. Moreover, the connection between Christians assembling and the main activity that brings them together—the celebration of the Eucharist—cannot be overstressed, for it is in the Eucharist that we grow into being the Body of Christ by participating in the Body of Christ. That is why the martyrs of Abilitina, mentioned at the beginning of this study preferred to die rather than to live without the assembly for the Lord's Supper on the Lord's Day. That is why one of the current Roman Catholic eucharistic prayers prays as follows:

> "From age to age you gather a people to yourself
> so that from east to west a perfect offering may
> be made to the glory of your name."

NOTES

1. "Acts of Saints Saturninus, Dativus, and many others, martyrs in Africa," in W. Rordorf, *Sabbat et dimanche dans l'église ancienne* (Neuchâtel: Delachaux et Niéstle, 1972) 176. This trial took place in the Diocletianic persecution of 304.

2. The literature is, of course, ample: W. Rordorf, *Sunday: The History of the Day of Rest and Worship in the Earliest Centuries of the Christian Church* (Philadelphia: Westminster, 1968); S. Bacchiocchi, *From Sabbath to Sunday: A Historical Investigation of the Rise of Sunday Observance in Early Christianity* (Rome: Gregorian University Press, 1977); C. Mosna, *Storia della domenica dalle origini fino agli inizi del V secolo* (Rome: Gregorian University Press, 1969); R. Beckwith and W. Stott, *This is the Day: The Biblical Doctrine of the Christian Sunday in its Jewish and Early Christian Setting* (London: Marshall, Morgan, and Scott, 1978); D. A. Carson, ed., *From Sabbath to Lord's Day: A Biblical, Historical, and Theological Investigation* (Grand Rapids: Zondervan, 1982).

3. For a description of this fallacy, see S. K. Langer, *Philosophy in a New Key* (2nd ed.; Cambridge, MA: Harvard University Press, 1978) 54–75.

4. I am indebted here to Edward Farley's provocative book on theological criteriology: *Ecclesial Reflection* (Philadelphia: Fortress, 1982).

5. For example, see J. D. G. Dunn, *Unity and Diversity in the New Testament* (Philadelphia: Westminster, 1977); J. Robinson and H. Koester, *Trajectories through Early Christianity* (Philadelphia: Fortress, 1977) especially Koester's essay, "Gnomai Diaphorai."

6. On Marcion, see R. J. Hoffmann, *Marcion, On the Restitution of Christianity: An Essay on the Development of Radical Paulinist Theology in the Second Century* (Chico, CA: Scholars Press, 1984).

7. See, e.g., Augustine, *Letter (to Januarius)* 54.2.3, on the difference between North Africa and Milan on fasting practice on Saturdays.

8. Here I place myself firmly within the school of thought in modern Roman Catholic theology best represented by Karl Rahner.

9. This problem is even clearer when the questions at hand deal with ethics and Scriptural norms; see W. C. Spohn, *What Are They Saying About Scripture and Ethics?* (New York: Paulist, 1986).

10. For a development of this theme, see the treatment of R. F. Taft, *The Liturgy of the Hours in East and West* (Collegeville: Liturgical Press, 1986).

11. See J. Mateos, *Beyond Conventional Christianity* (Manila: East Asian Pastoral Inst., 1974) esp. 254–87; see also Y. Congar, *Le mystère du Temple* (Paris, 1958).

12. J. LaPorte, *Eucharistia in Philo* (New York: Mellen, 1983).

13. On this question, see the excellent essay of D. N. Power, "Words That Crack: The Uses of Sacrifice in Eucharistic Discourse," in *Living Bread, Saving Cup: Readings on the Eucharist,* ed. R. K. Seasoltz (2nd ed.; Collegeville: Liturgical Press, 1987) 157–75.

14. P. L. Berger, *The Sacred Canopy: Elements of a Sociology of Religion* (Garden City, NY: Doubleday, 1967) 3–51.

15. See J. T. Fraser, *Time: The Familiar Stranger* (Amherst: University of Massachusetts Press, 1987) 7–44.

16. For examples of how general calendar development brought the "polis" in line with Christian practice, see J. F. Baldovin, *The Urban Character of Christian Worship: The Origins, Development and Meaning of Stational Liturgy* (Orientalia Christiana Analecta 228; Rome: Pontifical Oriental Institute Press, 1987) 253–68.

17. See Mona Ozouf, *Festivals and the French Revolution* (Cambridge, MA: Harvard University Press, 1988).

18. J. Z. Smith, *To Take Place: Toward Theory in Ritual* (Chicago: University of Chicago Press, 1987) 74–95.

19. For the same argument, see Rordorf, *Sunday,* 294–307.

20. For further description and bibliography, see J. F. Baldovin, *The Liturgy in Ancient Jerusalem* (Alcuin/GROW Liturgical Study 9; Bramcote (Notts): Grove Books, 1989).

21. See T. J. Talley, *The Origins of the Liturgical Year* (New York: Pueblo, 1986) 37–47.

22. For an introduction to the text and the identification of the pilgrim, see John Wilkinson, *Egeria's Travels to the Holy Land* (2nd ed.; Jerusalem: Aris & Phillips, 1981). I use Wilkinson's translation here.

23. On the distinction between cathedral and monastic forms of daily liturgical prayer, see Taft, *Liturgy of the Hours.*

24. On the spread of the Sunday Cathedral Vigil, see Juan Mateos, "La vigile cathédrale chez Egérie," *Orientalia Christiana Periodica* 27 (1961) 308-12; on the contemporary Byzantine observance of this vigil, see Robert F. Taft, "Sunday in the Byzantine Tradition," in Taft, *Beyond East and West: Problems in Liturgical Understanding* (Washington, DC: Pastoral Press, 1984) 33-37.

25. This issue is controverted. On the various possibilities and my reasoning for this particular character to the service, see Baldovin, *Urban Character,* 58-59.

26. On medieval Sabbatarianism, see n. 32 below.

27. Robert Cabié, *La lettre du pape Innocent Ier à Decentius de Gubbio* (Louvain: Publications Universitaires de Louvain, 1973) 26-28.

28. See *Ordo Romanus I,* in *Les ordines romain du haut moyenâge II,* ed. Michel Andrieu (Louvain: Spicilegium sacrum lovaniense, 1935) 98. For further commentary, see Baldovin, *Urban Character,* 131-34.

29. See Angelus Häussling, *Mönchskonvent und Eucharistiefeier* (Liturgie-wissenschaftliche Quellen und Forschungen 58; Münster: Aschendorff, 1973) 181-82.

30. Robert Taft, "The Structural Analysis of Liturgical Units: An Essay in Methodology," in Taft, *Beyond East and West,* 152.

31. See Albert Mirgeler, *Mutations of Western Christianity* (New York: Herder & Herder, 1964).

32. On these developments, see R. J. Bauckham, "Sabbath and Sunday in the Medieval Church in the West," in *From Sabbath to Lord's Day,* ed. D. A. Carson, 300-304. See also W. Rordorf, "Die theologische Bedeutung des Sonntags bei Augustin: Tradition und Erneuerung," in *Der Sonntag: Anspruch - Wirklichkeit - Gestalt,* ed. A. M. Altermatt and T. Schnitker (Würzburg: Echter, 1986) 30-43. The entire volume is a valuable collection of historical, theological, and pastoral essays.

33. See Kenneth L. Parker, *The English Sabbath: A Study of Doctrine and Discipline from the Reformation to the Civil War* (Cambridge: Cambridge University Press, 1988) 8-23.

34. On these shifts, see Edmund Bishop, "The Genius of the Roman Rite," in Bishop, *Liturgica Historica* (Oxford: Oxford University Press, 1918) 1-23; Cyrille Vogel, "Echanges liturgiques entre Rome et les pays francs jusqu'à l'époque de Charlemagne," in *Settimane di studio del Centro italiano di studi sull'alto medioeve VII* (Spoleto: Presso la sede del Centro, 1960) 185-285; Theodor Klauser, *A Short History of the Western Liturgy* (London: Oxford University Press, 1969) 45-116.

35. See John R. H. Moorman, *Church Life in England in the Thirteenth Century* (Cambridge: Cambridge University Press, 1955) 68-77.

36. On the nature of the debates over Sunday as the Christian Sabbath in Puritan England, see Parker, *English Sabbath,* 92-216; Horton Davies, *Worship and Theology in England II* (Princeton: Princeton University Press, 1975) 215-52.

37. United States Catholic Conference, *Norms Governing Liturgical Calendars* (Liturgy Documentary Series 6; Washington, DC: USCC, 1984) 14.

38. *Code of Canon Law* #1247. Canons 1246–1248 all deal with the nature of Sunday as obligatory for public worship.

39. On this point, see John F. Baldovin, "Reflections on the Frequency of Eucharistic Celebration," *Worship* 60 (1987) 2–15.

40. On the tradition of this association, see H. B. Porter, *The Day of Light: The Biblical and Liturgical Meaning of Sunday* (Washington, DC: Pastoral Press, 1987) 63–73.

16

UPHOLDING THE SABBATH DAY: THE JEWISH SABBATH FACES MODERNITY

Lawrence A. Hoffman
Hebrew Union College—Jewish Institute of Religion, New York

> I raise my cup in love of You,
> Peace to you, O Seventh day!
> Six days of work are like your slaves,
> I work my way through them . . .
> Because of my love for you, O day of my delight!
> (Yehudah Halevi, *Al Ahavetekha*)

The assigned title, "The Jewish Sabbath Faces Modernity," sounds like the title bout for the heavyweight boxing championship in Madison Square Garden—between the people's favorite, who has enjoyed the championship for centuries now, and the young contender, who hasn't lost a match since the Enlightenment. Old, the champ seems hardly to have a chance, while the contender gets stronger every day. Come to think of it, Shabbat may not really even have nostalgia on its side anymore. As they say, nostalgia isn't what it used to be nowadays. Get behind the pious rhetoric of rabbis who, after all, are often paid to stand in the champ's corner; discount the recidivist old-timers who seem to yearn for nothing so much as yesterday; and what have you? No earth-shattering avalanche of cheers as the lonely old champion, the Sabbath, steps into the ring. Truth be told, it is not just the smart money but the popular support as well that has swung heavily toward Modernity. Nobody really wants to go back to premodernity again—not that they can anyway.

So, I have no intention of rolling back the gains of modernity, which (I confess) I rather like. Modernity's power is about as deniable as the presence of God was on Mount Sinai. A midrash holds that God gave the Torah while holding the mountain over the Israelites' heads, threatening to squash them like so many microscopic pests, should they refuse to accept it. So they took it, whereupon God put the mountain down, and went home, leaving the world to such worldly pursuits as household chores, taking in a movie, and shepherding the kids back and forth from Little League practice—all tasks inconveniently scheduled for Friday night or Saturday morning. All the cheering in the world won't negate modernity's nearly universal appeal; and, unlike God, rabbis cannot uproot mountains to make debating points. The days when you could yell at people to keep the Sabbath are over, victims themselves of modernity's knockout punch.

Before us then is the question precisely of how *modern* men and women go about the task of making sense of the Shabbat. I propose treating the subject in terms of accepting, not denying, their modernity. Let me summarize my argument in advance.

1. *To know how "the Sabbath faces modernity," we have first to define "modernity."* I assume here that "modernity" is not just some relative term, meaning "nowadays" as opposed to "yesteryear," but something specific— a set of circumstances that is by no means new. In order to see what it is, I will review with you two other instances of "modernity": first, seventeenth- and eighteenth-century Salonika, when we have evidence of Jews failing to keep the Sabbath; and second, classical Reform Jews of the nineteenth and early twentieth centuries. The goal will be to contrast the ways in which failing Sabbath observance is countered in these two instances, with the response that I advocate for today.

2. *We learn how different ages characterized the Sabbath by attending to the kind of hortatory language that the Sabbath's supporters used in urging its observance.* Extending Wittgenstein's notion of language games, we might say that the game being played here is the game of exhorting people to keep the Sabbath. The rules of exhorting vary from time to time and culture to culture. I will, therefore, contrast the Salonika game, the Reform game, and a third game for our time. I will call these three games Limits, Truth, and Meaning.

3. *The games of Limits, Truth, and Meaning provide alternative maps of reality.* From the rabbinic period until the Enlightenment, the Sabbath was discussed in terms of its *Limits,* a map of reality that categorizes everything as a case of "should" or "should not." With the Enlightenment, discussion switched to the game of *Truth,* whereby things are either true or false, not "shoulds" and "should nots." But Modernity has steadfastly remained as impermeable to arguments from limits as from truths. Thus we have invented a third vocabulary for keeping Shabbat: Shabbat as an issue of *Meaning,* whereby things are now either meaningful or empty.

4. *All three games may be played at one and the same time, so that exhortatory preachers may in fact use any one of them to make their point; but the preferred game in any culture always corresponds to that culture's cosmology.* The game of Limits corresponds to a prescientific world view. The game of Truth arises as a consequence of a scientific perspective, to some extent evident in the categories of Greek and, later, Moslem philosophy, but not really dominant in Jewish consciousness until the dawn of the Enlightenment. When relativity and quantum theory demolished the surety of the Newtonian cosmos, the game of Truth was replaced by a new game involving the interaction between observer and observed, namely, the game of Meaning.

Let me go step by step through each of the language games, demonstrating its genesis and cultural basis. Then I shall define modernity, showing why it is that recourse to the two games I call Limits and Truth failed in the cases of Salonika and Reform Judaism, respectively, and why the third game of Meaning must be the strategy we adopt.

THE GAME OF LIMITS

To read rabbinic literature is to get a sense of the undifferentiated cosmos the rabbis inhabited. One page of Talmud looks pretty much like any other. The only classification that matters is the things that are permitted to us and the things that are forbidden. For example, cows are edible, rabbits are not. The world is made not of what is but of what human beings may or may not do with what is.

The rabbis' map of the world is no series of essences. It is a map not of being but of doing. Rabbinic literature is not Greek philosophy, and the Talmud is not Aristotle. It was as if the world were one vast invisible maze, in which our task is to find our way from birth to death, without bumping into the walls. Rabbinic literature, literally, halakah, a way of "walking," is a map not of the world's objects but of its invisible walls. When they spoke of their world, therefore, the rabbis spoke in terms of its limits: what was permissible and what was forbidden. In Hebrew, we get the alternatives of *mutar/asur,* or, more colloquially, *kosher/tref.* A sort of caricature of the system is the picture of the eastern European householder who takes the chicken to the rabbi to see if it is *kosher.* Rabbinic literature is first and foremost legal literature, detailing what we may or may not do, just as rabbis, traditionally speaking, are neither pastors nor preachers, but *poskim,* that is, declarers of what is permitted and what is not.

This cosmology of a world fraught with invisible limits influences the rabbis' evaluation of human nature and even their view of God. Limit players see God as rewarder and punisher, the enforcer of the limits, in the context of which the case of the Shabbat is particularly instructive.

The liturgy describes the Shabbat as a gift—with, however, strings attached. Every Friday night saw the Sabbath inaugurated with the phrase *shabbat kodsho . . . hinchilanu,* "God gave us His [*sic*] holy Sabbath as an inheritance."[1] Similarly, we have: "You did not give it to the nations of the world, nor give it as an inheritance to idolaters; rather to Your people Israel You gave it, in love."[2]

But look now at a later line in the same prayer: this time, the verb *nchl* appears again, but not in the perfect—*hinchilanu, hinchaltanu*—but in the imperative—*vehanchilenu*—a petition that God should continue to give us this Sabbath as our heritage.[3] This grammatical change heralds a subtle theological point. The indicative mood reminds us that we received the Sabbath as a gift of God's grace. But the imperative implies that the continuation of the Sabbath as Israel's gift is contingent. What I want to emphasize here, however, is not the doctrine of grace, but the rabbinic concept of "gift" as that which God gives, but which can just as easily be removed, the moment we are unworthy of the thing given.

The fear of being unworthy is endemic to the Limit game, in which humans stand before God like children before a parent, who gives or takes, rewards or punishes. God gives. But once the gifts are given, it is the child's duty to live up to them by observing the regulations, or limits, relevant to them. The double entendre of the Hebrew phrase *shomer shabbat* is instructive here. It means one who "keeps the Sabbath," but a *shomer* is also someone on watch duty, or, legally, a bailee entrusted with a bailment. To keep the Sabbath is thus literally to keep it intact, to watch over it as if the Sabbath (as gift) were a bailment, its well-being entrusted to us temporarily until we can pass it on to the next generation.

I need at this point to prevent a misunderstanding. I do not want to be misinterpreted as holding in any way the pernicious nineteenth-century doctrine of rabbinism as dry legalism. Indeed, one of the obligations for the Sabbath is to rejoice in it (see Isaiah 58:14)![4] I am most assuredly not arguing that rabbinic Judaism, insofar as it is primarily limit setting, is pure legalism without spirituality, beauty, meaning, love, and so forth. Actually, people require all three maps of reality—Limits, Truth, and Meaning—so that any mature religious system incorporates them all in its recipe for human destiny. Indeed, to read rabbinic literature is to recognize how fully the rabbis struggled with the other two games as well.

My point here, however, is that Limits was the rabbis' primary game, and the result is the first of our three hortatory languages or rhetorical forms. The case in point is eighteenth-century Salonika, where a once-prosperous Jewish community had fallen into bad economic times, a situation that had thinned the ranks of the city. Nevertheless, the city still had at that time many wealthy Jewish merchants, who, however, no longer felt as tied to the ailing Jewish institutions and its way of life, including the synagogue and its keeping of the Sabbath. Their spiritual leader, Isaac Molcho, tried to correct this circumstance through his best-selling treatise *Orchot Yosher*.[5]

Molcho singles out an old habit that had been denounced by one of his rabbinic predecessors in Salonika, Chaim ben Israel Benvenista (1603–1673), in the year 1658.

> In our city [wrote Benvenista] there exists a bitter and evil custom, namely, people attend coffee houses and drink coffee that has been prepared on the Sabbath for the express needs of the Jews. . . .[6] You cannot find a soul—men, women, children, and even a majority of the students of Torah—who does not drink coffee made by non-Jews on Shabbat. The exceptions are so few that a child could write them down, and they would not amount to ten people.[7]

Benvenista attacked the problem the only way he knew: by a sermon on Shabbat, reminding people to return to God's ways. Needless to say, most of the people still remained confirmed in their old habit, and, after the sermon, went out to drink coffee.

All this had occurred in 1658. Almost a century later (1773), Salonikan Jewry suffered a drought, to which the rabbis reacted in their usual Limit mentality, by assuming it to be divine punishment for sin, and ordaining, therefore, as Molcho puts it, "a fast, prayers of atonement, and cessation from work. But our prayers were not answered. We therefore made inquiries regarding the affairs of the city, and discovered that people were attending coffee houses on the holy Sabbath day. We forbade them to go, and they listened to us."[8] But Molcho's success must have been limited, because when it rained and the drought lifted, he testifies: "This plague has spread, whereby many of the masses attend coffee houses on the holy Sabbath day, and there they drink these bitter accursed waters that have most certainly been heated expressly for them."[9]

The Limit game is still alive and well for some Jews, but most Jews remain undeterred by its traditional rhetoric. The coffeehouse patrons who remained unmoved by Molcho's protestations were just a sign of things to come. The nineteenth century is our next stop, therefore, as we unravel the second rhetorical system, the game of Truth.

THE GAME OF TRUTH

What was there about the pre-nineteenth-century world that supported the game of Limits, making it work so well? Imagine society depicted in a three-dimensional topographical map, its various institutionalized activities or role relationships marked by valleys, mountains, plains and plateaus. The more serious we take a relationship to be, the greater is the depth of its land mass. Such maps of modern societies would range dramatically from leisure-time activity (a mere strip of land running at sea level, having neither depth nor height) to things like family relationships and citizenship, which are presumed to be matters of serious religious and ethical consequence (and so would appear as deep valleys of tradition and enormous mountains of seriousness).

Maps of primitive society, on the other hand, would look very different. "In any primitive culture," writes Mary Douglas, "the urge to *unify* experience . . . has been at work,"[10] in the sense that *every* social state is *equally* undergirded by moral sanctions, *equally* thick with significant consequences. For primitive peoples, there is no such thing as leisure time, and family affairs are tribal issues, which in turn are divine concerns, as much as whom you go to war against or what you offer back to God of this year's harvest. These societies have no easy way even to differentiate one social institution or role from another.

The point is, these so-called primitive institutions do not divide human intercourse according to empirical categories. Their world is holistic, in, that everything is intertwined with everything else, a conception, I suggest, which sounds remarkably like rabbinic Judaism: not preliterate, certainly, but holistic in its assertion of a universe where, to quote Douglas again, "social reality [is sustained] by creating all-embracing universes of meaning."[11]

Each game presupposes its own unique supportive cosmology. Seeing rabbinic Judaism as a prescientific system helps us explain the rhetoric of limits. *Limits is the game favored by the holistic unempirical structuring of reality that characterized Judaism until the Enlightenment.*

With the Enlightenment, science demonstrated that the world of experience could better be cut up according to the empirical and, therefore, "provable," rules of the laboratory. It made little sense now to appeal to modern Jews by shouting about age-old limits that had depended on a crumbling premodern cosmology! So nineteenth-century Reform Jews developed a new rhetoric to justify Sabbath observance. It was the rhetoric of Truth.

Nineteenth-century science, the cosmology that was assumed, heralded its ability above all to provide truths. Reform Rabbis therefore concluded that religion also ought to be a truth-telling instrument. Insofar as Germany's enlightened nineteenth-century Jews flocked to temples at all, they did so to hear spiritual truths, from rabbis who had attended college and preferred to be called "Dr.," claiming that they were expert in *Wissenschaftliche Judentum*—note, "the *science* (!) of Judaism." Time spent in prayer shrank, as the sermon, which was the truth-telling spot in the program, expanded. Unwilling now to see God primarily as a keeper of limits, a rewarder and punisher, they revamped God until God emerged — to cite the 1885 Pittsburgh Platform of Reform Jews in America — as "the God-*idea*," that is, "the central religious *truth* of the human race."[12]

If we turn now to the Sabbath, we find that German Jews, like their Salonikan forebears, often broke the time-honored rules of Sabbath rest. Still living in a prescientific context, Isaac Molcho had contented himself with a reiteration of Judaism's limit rhetoric. Reform rabbis, however, adopted an entirely novel approach to the matter. Seeing religious issues as "truths," they endeavored to convince their recalcitrant laity to keep the Sabbath on the grounds that it, no less than God, was a scientific truth of which no rational being could fail to be convinced.

The key debate on the Sabbath occurred at the 1846 rabbinical conference in Breslau.[13] Assuming the truth rhetoric as their model, the rabbis divided over the question of the Sabbath's essence: Is it a day of rest or a day of sanctification? The majority report states the problem in *ontological* terms: the rabbis in Breslau barely discuss what a Jew should or should not *do* — that would be a question of Limits. Faced with nonobservance on a broad scale, they seek to return the Sabbath to the Jews by a discussion of what the Sabbath *is* — a question of truth, whence the issue of Limits, they think, will be solved automatically.

> The Sabbath is a day of consecration which is sanctified through our sanctifying ourselves; a day the distinctiveness of which is to be brought forcibly home to us by our ceasing from our daily toil and our daily tasks, and giving ourselves to contemplation of the divine purpose of our existence as indicated by Jewish teaching. Hence, no task should be forbidden which conduces toward recreation and spiritual elevation.[14]

How deftly they move from *is* to *ought,* from the truth of the Sabbath idea to the guidelines for Sabbath praxis. The Bible itself had discussed the Sabbath both in terms of work/rest regulations and in terms of its sanctified character. The former, of course, was more easily translated into Limit rules, so that earlier Limit-thinking rabbis of the Mishnah and the Talmud had said a great deal about what one does or does not do on that day but relatively little about the theological nature of Sabbath sanctity. Now Reform rabbis reverse the process. Ignoring the reams of rules regarding work, they concentrate on the idea of Shabbat as sanctified time and transform the rules against work into corollaries of the "idea" of Shabbat sanctity.

Samuel Holdheim, the radical rabbi of Berlin, took this argument to its logical conclusion. Recognizing that the Sabbath as idea, after all, is set free from the vagaries of any particular calendar, he argued in echoes of the moral versus ceremonial dichotomy that Shabbat may as easily be kept on any day of the week, even Sunday! His suggestion was strenuously opposed: as one objector insisted, getting rid of the Sabbath on Saturday would be equivalent to saying that "we will bury Judaism on Friday evening, to permit it to be resurrected as another religion on Sunday."[15] Our interest here, however, is not so much Holdheim's position as his rhetoric. Living in his scientific age, he believed in the power of truths. The Sabbath's essence can hardly be a specific day of rest, he argued, since God's resting on one day rather than another would imply an anthropomorphic deity. The Sabbath must therefore be a day of sanctification. Hitherto it has been marked in a symbolic way by adherence to a particular day of the week. But in this new age of scientific truths, Holdheim argues, "we take for granted that . . . religious truths . . . are no longer symbolized by man [sic] as before, namely by resting."[16] Modern men and women can thus bypass the merely symbolic and go directly to the essence of the thing in itself, the Sabbath as a day of sanctification.[17]

So there you have it: the Sabbath as a truth, a rhetoric of justification that continued here in America as well. Consider this retrospective analysis of the research done by Kaufman Kohler. Kohler, American Reform Judaism's theologian *par excellence* and the second president of the Hebrew Union College, turned to the issue of Sabbath observance in 1917, asking "whether the Hebrew Sabbath was from the beginning based upon the fixed institution of the week, which certainly rests on Babylonian astrology, or whether it originally corresponded with the four lunar phases, so that the 7th, 14th, 21st, and 28th of each month were the days of the moon's stand-still, that is, Sabbath days." Gunther Plaut, who cites Kohler for us, in an address of his own to a rabbinic convention gathered in 1965, correctly evaluates what Kohler was up to: "He was anxious to prove that Israel's Sabbath was not a derivative of the Babylonian *Shabbatu*. . . . Kohler spoke as a child of 19th-century idealism. . . . To him, as to the early reformers, the *original* ideas of the Sabbath, the *origins* of the day, were more important than what Israel had done with it over the centuries."[18]

Plaut is absolutely correct. Released from ghettos, both physical and mental, Holdheim, Kohler, and the other great rabbis of that era were discovering the world of European intellectuals, in which the scientific spirit had replaced religion as the formative influence. Imbued with a scientific claim to certainty, these Jews just naturally assumed that historical *truths* would in and of themselves clarify their inherited rabbinic *limits*. If, therefore, they could discover where the Shabbat came from, they would know how much of Shabbat to keep. If, that is, Shabbat were found to be historically derived from the Babylonian festival *Shabbatu*, then they could separate "foreign" Babylonian influence from "native" Jewish authenticity;

they would dispense with the former and keep the latter. Limits would thus be discoverable through Truth.

Let me stop and take stock, with the following chart.

SOCIAL BASE	COSMOLOGY	RHETORIC (GAME)	CONCEPTION OF SHABBAT	LITURGICAL METAPHOR
"primitive" undifferentiated states of social being	nonempirical boundaries	Limits	work/rest	gift to watch over
Newtonian science with differentiated states of social being	empirical boundaries	Truth	sanctity	day of sanctity

In the first instance, we have a typically prescientific cosmology based on nonempirical differentiations and invisible boundaries that are to be observed everywhere in life. This Limit mentality evokes discussion of reward and punishment, by a God who is the ultimate rule keeper of the universe—hence, in the patriarchal and hierarchical society which the rabbis inhabited, both father and king (*avinu malkenu,* in the liturgy's own words). Religious discourse is the rule rhetoric of Limit thinking, endlessly seeking to categorize this or that novel situation as permitted or forbidden, rather than the anomaly it first appears to be. It generates a dominant conception of Shabbat as a day of rest rather than work (which is "forbidden") and then spins out endless pages defining what constitutes work and what does not. In keeping with the image of God the beneficent father-monarch, and ourselves the children, the favored liturgical metaphor is Shabbat as gift, held by us in trust and deserving of our honor and respect.

But with Newtonian physics and its claim to know certain truths, an empirical division of social life took place, with most of life's provinces being excluded from the religious realm. Religion was left with ethical truths, so that the Sabbath was reinterpreted to be a truth in its own right or (using the language of nineteenth-century German idealism) an idea, namely, the idea of human sanctity.

The only thing left for our consideration, before rounding out the chart, is a survey of prayers in the Reform liturgies that came about as a reflection of the new system of thought. To be sure, old prayers were often translated as they stood, so that we do find the metaphor of gift. But in the *new* prayers, those composed *de novo* by Reform rabbis, we find a greater

emphasis on sanctified time as the essence of the Shabbat and the abstention from work as merely subsidiary.

Time and space prohibit a full citation of sources, but consider, as
typical, the way the first official edition of the Reform Movement's *Union
Prayer Book* (for Sabbaths) rendered the prayer known as the *kedushat
hayom*.[19] They inherited it with the following two adjacent Hebrew
phrases: (a) *vehanchilenu adonai elohenu be'ahavah uveratson shabbat
kodshekha* ("In love and grace, give us as our inheritance your holy
Sabbath") and (b) *veyanukhu vah yisra'el mekaddeshei shemekha* ("So
that Israel, sanctifiers of your name, may rest on it"). Turning to the original Hebrew first, we see that the second clause (b) is certainly related to the
first (a). Much of the prayer is composed of such couplets, in which God
is asked to do one thing (a), so that (as a consequence) Israel may do something else (b). The logic of each couplet is of the form God (a) → Israel (b).
Thus:

1. a. *sabenu mituvekha* ("Satisfy us with your goodness")
   b. *vesamchenu bishu'atekha* ("that we may rejoice in your
      salvation")
2. a. *vetaher libenu* ("Cleanse our hearts")
   b. *le'ovdekha be'emet* ("to serve you in truth")
3. a. *vehanchilenu be'ahavah uveratson shabbat kodshekha* ("In love
      and grace, give us as our inheritance your holy Sabbath")
   b. *veyanukhu vah yisra'el mekaddeshei shemekha* ("that Israel,
      sanctifiers of your name, may rest on it")

In keeping with their accent on the Sabbath as rest, the rabbis have thus
crafted a prayer wherein *rest is the end, not just the means.* The purpose
of God's giving us this Sabbath gift is that we may rest on it.

The *Union Prayer Book,* however, translates our phrase this way: "Help
us to preserve the Sabbath as Israel's heritage from generation to generation, that it may ever bring rest and joy, peace and comfort to the dwellings
of our brethren, and through it thy name be hallowed in all the earth."[20]
The translation is not exactly *wrong,* but it is not right either. Its logic is
reversed. Instead of the Sabbath existing so that Israel, who sanctifies
God's name, can rest; the Sabbath itself somehow provides rest (along with
peace, joy, and comfort), with the result that God's name is hallowed. The
Sabbath now is an ontic reality, an idea, which—in good German idealistic
fashion—is the most real entity one can imagine. It is the idea of human
sanctity. By observing the Sabbath, we raise ourselves to a higher degree
of sanctity.

I have often wondered why the generations of Jews my age and younger
complain that the *Union Prayer Book* prose is saccharin in its piety. The
answer, I think, is that we no longer relate to things in terms of their truths

alone. Unable to imagine the spiritual essences of which the nineteenth-century rabbis spoke, we find their rhetoric beautiful but empty. We are like positivist philosophers listening to metaphysicians and admiring their arguments, even though in the end we conclude that they are talking about nothing. Our denial of a metaphysical world of idealike things has involved us in a third rhetorical game, the search for meaning.

THE GAME OF MEANING

German idealism disagreed with the materialists on the *nature* of objective reality, but not on whether or not there was a realm of objective essences in the first place. Enlightened Jews who spoke about the Sabbath Idea and laboratory scientists who described molecules of gas were alike in that they both believed (1) in the theoretical possibility of total and absolute truth—what Richard Rorty has characterized as "the neurotic Cartesian quest for certainty"[21]—which (2) they, as objective observers of reality—Dewey's "spectator theory of knowledge"[22]—were in the process of discovering. The game of Truth has foundered because the cosmology has changed—which is to say, that both religion and science have been forced to scale back their earlier triumphalism.

To begin with, scientists themselves now deny the very possibility of such total knowledge. Meanwhile, philosophers question the very existence of a "realistic set of objects," be they tables, clocks, and ice cubes or just the network of subatomic particles that make up the atoms and then the molecules and eventually the objects themselves. Gödel's proof of 1931 did away with the old dream that mathematics would some day map a set of truths encompassing all that is, and the Heisenberg Indeterminacy Principle established the knower as part and parcel of that which is known, so that Hilary Putnam tells us: "The mind does not simply 'copy' a world that admits of One True Theory. But my view is not a view in which the mind makes up the world. . . . If one must use metaphorical language, then let the metaphor be this: the mind and the world jointly make up the mind and the world."[23]

In their usual prescience, the arts presaged this change in cosmology, almost a century ago, when impressionists rebelled against the realists' assumptions that such a thing as an independent nature could be captured in a single set of accurate brush strokes. Reality is transient, they insisted, dependent on the rapid play of light passing between the object (whatever it may be) and our own powers of observation. So Monet painted "the same thing"—Rouen Cathedral—over and over again, since it wasn't really the same thing at all but a different entity from moment to moment. Then cubists bravely disassembled human bodies, limb by limb, saying, in effect, that what we look like is partly what we wish to see. Developments in music and literature followed a similar sequence. By the turn of the century, Schoenberg was taking apart the octave, which, since Pythagoras, had been imagined to correspond to a mathematical ratio and, therefore, to a single world of reality to which both math and music correspond. Schoenberg knew better. He was taking apart the octave at the same time that physicist Max Planck was beginning to dismantle the old physics. Literary critics too now stress the slipperiness of meaning, some of them claiming (1) that even a simple declarative sentence has no objective meaning behind it,[24] and (2) that even the clearest author's intent can never be fathomed.[25] In such an environment, how can we continue to believe in an absolute realm of spiritual essences?

The notion of autonomous "ideas" with which nineteenth-century Jews had rescued both God and the Sabbath, in their conversion of Judaism as limits into Judaism as truths, has thus fallen on bad times, so that Jews today have responded with yet a third rhetorical strategy: seeing religion as the source of life's meaning.

MODERNITY

We can now be clear about what I mean by "modernity." Again, Mary Douglas's conceptualizations prove helpful. She plots human cultures on a two-dimensional graph, each axis of which corresponds to one of the two ways in which individuals experience solidarity with others. One is the measure of "group," and the other she calls "grid."

Grid-group diagram

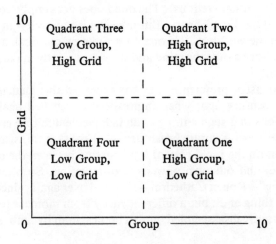

The variability of an individual's involvement in social life can be adequately captured by just two dimensions of sociality: *group* (the extent to which an individual is incorporated into bounded groupings with others); and *grid* (the extent to which the individual's life is circumscribed by externally imposed prescriptions).[26]

To simplify this slightly, we can say that "Group" is the extent to which we feel bound by commitment to other persons because of who they are; "grid" is the network of impersonal social structures that commit us to the system itself, whether or not we even know who the others in our system are. A California commune and a set of college roommates are examples of high-group entities, their members bound together by nothing but their allegiance to each other as persons. The bureaucracy of the army or a college administration is high grid. A platoon in battle, following all the army regulations but also committed to each other as persons, is both high group and high grid. But there is always the possibility that society will be formed with neither high-group nor high-grid capacity. That, says Douglas, is the case with an entrepreneurial society in which everyone is out for him- or herself, and where people cooperate only if cooperation promises a personal payoff in return.

We can identify the trends of modern industrial society which are progressively releasing the individual from the close control of strong grid, and the coercion of the bonded group. But instead of being released to freedom, the individual is then drawn into a very difficult social environment, the bottom left-hand corner of the diagram [I call it the fourth quadrant, in what follows] where he [*sic*] must either compete or be despised as a deviant; and if he [*sic*] competes, he [*sic*] must risk shame and seek honor, trust to luck and create ever more uncertainty for all in his [*sic*] entourage.[27]

This, then, is modernity: individualistic entrepreneurship; neither high grid nor high group. Let us see how grid-group analysis correlates with the games of Limits, Truths, and Meaning, and how the scheme we get sheds light on the Sabbath controversies at which we have already looked.

I suggest that the Limit game is particularly favored by high-group societies.[28] The idea of a personal God who gives the Sabbath as a gift out of love is, of course, an exact mirror of the personal ties on which high-group society depends. Rabbinic institutions in the first two centuries (the *chavurah,* the study academy) were clearly high group, the rabbis being teacher-mentors of study circles. Throughout most of Jewish history, the authority structure of Jewish society remained high group and professed the game of Limits.

But nineteenth-century Germany was quite different. Max Weber gives us an excellent picture of its rationalized social structure—the Prussian bureaucracy, for example, which substituted grid for group as the means of social cohesion. Instead of personal obligation to this or that person, one did one's duty to the state, to the army, to the Fatherland, or to whatever it was that the grid could conveniently be defined as. Again, for reasons beyond what I can adduce here, I argue that high-grid society depends on truth, not on limits as its favored mode of social control. Since a rationalized system sustains itself by the passing on of a group memory, it requires truths that go beyond any given person or personal relationship. By contrast, high-group sects have no use for impersonalized systematic theology; their theology is ad hoc, which people follow because the master says it, not because it is impervious to logical refutation. *Who* says it is more important than *what* is said. On the other hand, high-grid bureauc-racies distrust personal prophetic insight; they ban ad hoc pronouncements that might disrupt the stability of the grid, favoring instead objective systematic theology that retains a predictable status quo regardless of personalities who come and go only as part of the system itself.

Highly acculturated Reform rabbis of nineteenth-century Germany spoke German, dressed appropriately, and attended universities, learning to respect Max Weber's bureaucratic German culture with its high-grid loyalty and its basis in truths. They therefore replaced the personalist appeal of limit language with the impersonal rationale of objective truths, arguing that truths alone justify Sabbath observance and hoping that the people to whom they spoke, who were obviously impervious to limit talk, might be convinced by truth claims. However, neither the Salonikan nor the German rabbis successfully swayed the masses, who were increasingly moving into quadrant 4. Both rabbinic authorities missed the essence of "modernity," which is neither high group nor high grid, but an absence of both. Living relatively early, Molcho redirected a traditional limit rhetoric at his audience. German reformers, living later, made use of a new truth rhetoric with its claims to spiritual essences and ideas. But in either case, was anybody listening? Did people start keeping the Sabbath again? Did syna-gogue attendance rise? Is there any evidence that either strategy worked?

The truth is, their success was limited. The evidence on Salonika was given above, in the continuing appeal of the coffeehouses. Only briefly, when the drought threatened the town and people wondered if perhaps Molcho was right in claiming divine retribution, did some people listen — but not for long. Game theory discusses the possibility of a nonplayer, someone who refuses to role the dice, pick up the cards, or begin the race. In the simple game called "Greetings," I say "Hello, how are you," and count on the fact that you will at least smile back and say "fine." If you ignore me, you become a nonplayer, and the game is aborted. So too, the game called "Chastising," which is a subroutine in the game of Limits, calls for the rabbi to say, "You are sinning," and then for the sinners to do

penance. If they don't (if they go to coffeehouses instead), the game ends —
whether the rabbi knows it or not.

On the other hand, it is widely assumed that the efforts of Reform rabbis
enjoyed much greater success. The pertinent question, however, is, Compared to what? To be sure, compared to the enormous rate at which Jews
were leaving Judaism prior to the existence of a liberal Jewish alternative,
the success is striking. But in the very specific issue of Shabbat observance,
it is not so clear that the rabbis who redefined the issue in terms of truths
accomplished very much. Our records of synagogue attendance, home
ritual, or Sabbath observance are too sparse for us to know for sure. But
there is scattered evidence in America, at least, to suggest that despite the
successes Reform Judaism had overall, inspiring Sabbath observance was
not among them. The story of American Reform Judaism has been rather
bleak when it comes to Sabbath worship. At the turn of the century, huge
sanctuaries remained empty on Saturday mornings. Late Friday night
services rescued the Sabbath somewhat, but not very much and not for
long.[29] Most Reform Jews opened their shops, went shopping themselves,
and otherwise gave little indication in their own lives that the rabbinic
rhetoric of the *Union Prayer Book* had sunk very deeply into their personal
consciousness.

Using Douglas's model of grid and group, we can now see what went
wrong. In fact, all three examples of modernity — Salonika, Germany, and
our own case today — are the same, in that they all present the phenomenon
of people who have discovered that perilous fourth quadrant, where neither
grid nor group works efficiently to harness individualism. The rabbis —
whether Salonikan traditionalists or German Reformers — made use of
what they thought the best game to be, borrowing from the cosmology *of
their own class,* but in both cases, the merchants to whom they spoke were
way ahead of them. Fully modern, they had already gone beyond both high
grid and high group. Having entered the free-market system in which
neither grid nor group exercises much control over individual entrepreneurs, they were immune to the rabbis' message.

Take Salonika first. The merchants who ignored Molcho were modern,
even though Molcho himself was not. The truth is that they were becoming
lax about everything, not just Sabbath observance. We learn from Molcho
that they failed to say blessings, no longer kept the dietary laws, and
remained blissfully unconcerned in general about rabbinical ordinances.

The case of German Reform is only slightly more complex. Reform
ranks were filled with entrepreneurs. Hardly any of them were members of
the high-grid bureaucracies of the Prussian state, which were closed to
Jewish members. *The analytic problem we face is determining the relationship between a society's favored rhetorical method and the subcom-
munities within that society to whom the rhetoricians address their words.*

If truth systems are the rhetorical style of high-grid bureaucratic societies, it does not follow that everyone in those societies is equally amenable to the message of those truths. Thus, the Prussian bureaucracy and the Germanic social structure most certainly opened up the new rhetorical style of truth, and the Reform rabbis who were estranged from the old limit rhetoric made good use of it. Trained in German universities, they no doubt even believed it, but I am not sure their congregants did. In their search for acceptable social and civil status, the professional and merchant-class Jews of Germany may have been happy to hear their rabbinic leaders talk the appropriate Hegelian language of spiritual truths, like the God idea and the Sabbath idea, but whether they fully comprehended what all that rhetoric meant is questionable indeed. They supported the liberal rabbis as a means of retaining Jewish identity and still pursuing their own best business interests, but they had no intention of cancelling business plans on Saturday morning in order to attend synagogue.

In sum, merchants of Salonika, professionals and merchants in Berlin, and Yuppies in America are all modern in that they have opted for individualism over high-group and high-grid identity. The only appropriate strategy for communication with people in the fourth quadrant is the third style which I have yet to explain: the language pertinent to the game of Meaning.

THE GAME OF MEANING

What then is meaning? Simply put, Meaning is not a quality of any single entity so much as it is an attribute that an entity has by virtue of its connection to another entity. An uncatalogued book by an unknown author on an unknown subject is meaningless; but give me the author, topic, or call number, and I can relate it to other works — at which time, I file it away as "belonging" somewhere. It now has meaning. A single statistic is meaningless too, but give me the parallel statistic from last year, or the equivalent figure for the people next door, or for men as opposed to women, or for the south but not the north, and I nod with recognition of what the statistic means. Meaning is a relative thing, the importance a given piece of data has against the backdrop of other data. Things seen in isolation have no meaning at all.

The endemic threat to existence in quadrant four is precisely the characteristic of living in potential isolation. People on the frontier know neither grid nor group ties. Theirs is a life where only the ego is real, where self-centeredness and constant competition go hand in hand. There is always the realistic fear that some other equally self-made Nietzschean amoral "Superman" will come along and unseat whatever gain one has amassed.

At its extreme, quadrant four is life completely alone, for there are no necessary ties here, neither to persons nor to impersonal systems.

No wonder persons in quadrant four fear Durkheim's anomie. The ultimate threat of suicide is the ultimate threat of meaninglessness as I have defined it—the utter absence of connection to anything whatever. The issue of the Sabbath for modern men and women can finally be stated. For high-group society—Jewish communities for most of the medieval period—Shabbat is just one more example of a set of commandments to do or to abstain from doing; for high-grid society—the official world of Germany to which the liberal rabbis aspired—Shabbat was a truth, an idea. To moderns, however, Shabbat (if it is anything) is the opportunity for meaning, a moment in time to forge connections and to belong.

But meaning is not a "given" quality within the data of life; meaning must be supplied by the observer who posits a connection between isolated data and supplies a context. We understand now why the underlying epistemology of quantum theory and relativity is so attractive to moderns. Living as social isolates in quadrant four, we really do manufacture our own world after all. When modern scientists announce the good news that observer and observed are intertwined, we moderns in quadrant four know what they mean.

State the problem clearly: How do Jews retain a Sabbath in an era in which neither the rhetoric of "Thou shalt" nor the ontology of objective spiritual essences seems palatable? Whether we like it or not, the answer lies in a new rhetoric that captures the Achilles' heel of entrepreneurial men and women who suffer from only one thing: the threat of anomie, meaninglessness. If Jews will not keep Shabbat on the grounds that they are commanded to do so, or even because Shabbat is an eternal spiritual truth, perhaps they will do so because keeping Shabbat will provide their otherwise disconnected lives with meaning.

The key here is the concept of free choice. In three other quadrants people are constrained either by group or by grid or by both. But at its most extreme, where both grid and group measure zero, quadrant four knows complete freedom.

It is this enforced loneliness of the individual that Douglas describes as being "very harsh [with the result that] the will to escape from grid and group controls throws off small groups."[30] Unable to stand isolation, people choose their own favorite reference groups. As Putnam describes it, from his philosophical position, we may "celebrate the loss of essences" that marks the modern world of epistemology, but "private knowledge and incorrigible knowledge are empty and fallacious ideas."[31] To try on our own to formulate a world, to risk becoming "a cognitive minority of one" is to court disaster. So we complete the circle: having abandoned sect, become a church, and moved through all four quadrants on our way to leaving even the church behind, we find ourselves experimenting with sect once again. These are the small groups of which Douglas speaks, as modern men and women locate their favored high-group context in which their individualized judgments will be affirmed.

But we differ from our ancestors in the Russian ghettos or Iowan farming communities in that we may *choose* our own group. Some choose Jewish groups, and thus must choose also to find some sense of Shabbat that coheres with their chosen universe-in-the-making. Elsewhere, I have utilized the notion of "limited liability communities" and their opposite, "potentially total liability communities" to illustrate what I mean.[32] Most synagogues (and churches) function as purveyors of specific services that their members decide they want. But in joining them, parishioners do not simultaneously elect to accept the world of reality that synagogue and church assume. The sacred calendar, then, may mean nothing at all to them. They attend worship services only when their own list of needs coincides with attendance—perhaps they have a family Bar Mitzvah that day, for example. Rabbis have the right to bemoan that behavior, but it is by no means irrational. It fits harmoniously with the congregant's notion of the synagogue as supermarket.

To berate congregants for selective acceptance of Judaism or to speak of objective metaphysical truths is to reenter the lost worlds of Isaac Molcho or Samuel Holdheim. Neither one will do. We have no choice but to accept modernity, the challenger in the ring of modern life, and see Modernity's success as the affirmer of the good news of pluralism and personal choice. Synagogue and church must learn to become primary groups of total, not limited, liability, the kind of reference groups people look to for their own determination of the cosmos. Looking for meaning, they may well accept the Sabbath, if and only if they accept the Sabbath's supporters as a primary reference group that means more to them than a supermarket of limited liability.

I cannot now go into detail as to what I mean,[33] but I can specify the rhetorical style that will best accomplish the goal of Sabbath observance in the fourth quadrant of Modernity. It affirms people and their right to choose. It presents Judaism as an optional world of experience that successfully provides meaning in empty lives. It draws vertical ties to traditions of the past. It reaffirms sacred spaces and times, not as intact givens in the realm of nature but as worlds where "the mind and the world make up both the mind and the world." It repeatedly tells people not that they sin, but that they can be like God, a creator of a cosmos out of *tōhû wābōhû*, "the emptiness and void" of Genesis 1:2. It invites people who suffer the loneliness and insecurity of modernity to use the very freedom that modernity provides, to elect a reference point where chaos becomes cosmos and in which, therefore, they may *choose* to sanctify time and their own lives through a Sabbath.

Shabbat need not be Modernity's adversary after all. Shabbat and modernity may well take off their gloves, embrace, and forge a lasting alliance for the future.

NOTES

1. *Hasiddur Hashalem: Daily Prayer Book,* ed. Philip Birnbaum (New York: Hebrew Publishing Company, 1949; reprinted many times thereafter) 289. All liturgical references to the daily and Sabbath prayer book are to this book; my page references refer to the Hebrew, but a running English translation is given on facing pages.

2. *Hasiddur Hashalem,* ed. Birnbaum, 353–54.

3. Cf. ibid., 267, 353, 395, 453.

4. The concept of rejoicing is apparently unknown to the Mishnah, but receives attention in the amoraic period and beyond. See James Prosnit, "An Investigation of the Concept 'Oneg Shabbat' during the Tannaitic, Amoraic, and Geonic Period" (Master's thesis, Hebrew Union College – Jewish Institute of Religion, New York, 1981).

5. Isaac Molcho, *Orchot Yosher,* ed. Abraham Recanati (reprint, Tel Aviv: Va'ad Bet Haknesset R. Shlomo Ibn Gabirol, 1975). See, in general, the very fine treatment of this work by Deborah Ellen Zecher, "Case Study of Jewish Community in Decline, as Reflected by Isaac Molcho in Orchot Yosher" (Master's thesis, Hebrew Union College – Jewish Institute of Religion, New York, 1982).

6. The halakhic issue involved is the prohibition against getting around Sabbath work regulations – in this case, making a fire and heating coffee, by arranging for non-Jews to do it. If the coffee just happened to be available but had not been intended by its makers for Jewish consumption, drinking it on the Sabbath would have been acceptable. But this is a case of a coffeehouse owner's making coffee on the Sabbath expressly for Jewish patrons.

7. Molcho, *Orchot Yosher,* 117.

8. Ibid., 118.

9. Ibid., 119.

10. Mary Douglas, *Implicit Meanings: Essays in Anthropology* (London: Routledge & Kegan Paul, 1978) 57. See idem, *Purity and Danger* (London: Routledge & Kegan Paul, 1966) 92: primitive as opposed to modern society is characterized by "a personal anthropocentric *undifferentiated* worldview."

11. Douglas, *Implicit Meanings,* 76.

12. On the Pittsburgh Platform, see Michael A. Meyer, *Response to Modernity: A History of the Reform Movement in Judaism* (New York: Oxford University Press, 1988) 265–70; the Platform itself is cited on pp. 387–88. See also *The Pittsburgh Platform in Retrospect,* ed. Walter Jacob (Pittsburgh: Rodef Shalom Congregation, 1985), which includes a transcript of the conference proceedings and an introductory essay by Corinne Azen Krause on the Platform's historical setting.

13. Sources are cited in lengthy English translation in David Philipson, *Reform Movement in Judaism* (1907; reprint, New York: Ktav, 1967) 195–215; and W. Gunther Plaut, *The Rise of Reform Judaism* (New York: World Union for Progressive Judaism, 1967) 185–95. See also latest discussion by Meyer, *Response to Modernity,* 138–39.

14. Philipson, *Reform,* 197.

15. Leopold Stein, cited in Philipson, *Reform,* 210; and Meyer, *Response to Modernity,* 139.

16. Plaut, *Rise of Reform Judaism,* 193.

17. Ibid., 193–94.

18. W. Gunther Plaut, "The Sabbath in the Reform Movement: Fact, Fiction, Future," *Central Conference of American Rabbis Yearbook* 76 (1965) 2.

19. For a short discussion of the genesis of the *Union Prayer Book* (1894/1895), see Lawrence A. Hoffman, *Beyond the Text: A Holistic Approach to Liturgy* (Bloomington: Indiana University Press, 1987) chap. 4.

20. *Union Prayer Book,* 24.

21. Richard Rorty, *Consequences of Pragmatism* (Minneapolis: University of Minnesota Press, 1982) 161.

22. Which Dewey explicitly attaches to both realism and idealism, in that they both "hold that the operation of inquiry excludes any element of practical activity that enters into the construction of the object known. . . . The real object is the object so fixed in its regal aloofness. . . . A spectator theory of knowledge is the inevitable outcome" (John Dewey, *The Quest for Certainty* [Gifford Lectures, 1929; New York: Paragon Books, 1979) 23–24.

23. Hilary Putnam, *Reason, Truth, and History* (New York: Cambridge University Press, 1981) Introduction, p. xi.

24. "The claims of neither the text nor the reader can be upheld, because neither has the independent status that would make its claim possible. . . . The text as an entity independent of interpretation . . . is replaced by the texts that emerge as the consequence of our interpretive activities" (Stanley Fish, *Is there a Text in this Class? The Authority of Interpretive Communities* [Cambridge, MA: Harvard University Press, 1980] 12, 13).

25. See Gadamer vs. Hirsch, in E. D. Hirsch, Jr., *Validity in Interpretation* (New Haven and London: Yale University Press, 1967).

26. Michael Thompson, Richard Ellis, and Aaron Wildavsky, *Foundations of Cultural Theory* (forthcoming) manuscript of introduction.

27. Mary Douglas and Aaron Isherwood, *The World of Goods: Towards an Anthropology of Consumption* (New York and London: W. W. Norton, 1979) 43.

28. In general, my argument follows first and foremost from Douglas's view that sects (as she calls these high-group, low-grid social structures) must constantly worry about losing members. Hence they ring themselves round with pollution regulations, painting outsiders as evil, impure, the work of the devil, etc., and drawing strict limits to what members may or may not do. But limit thinking also dominates societies with undifferentiated cosmologies, as we saw above. Actually, we have the same phenomenon viewed in two ways. "Primitive" society (as Douglas uses the term) is undifferentiated in its cosmology; it erects arbitrary limits,

which it sanctions with the threat of impurity. It punishes its "evil" members with excommunication — being beyond the limit at which others may have any dealing with them — and promises rewards to those who follow its mandates.

29. See Hoffman, *Beyond the Text,* 164–66.

30. Douglas and Isherwood, *The World of Goods,* 43.

31. Hilary R. Putnam, *The Many Faces of Realism: The Paul Carus Lectures* (Lasalle, IL: Open Court Publishers, 1987) 52–53.

32. See Hoffman, *Beyond the Text,* 168; the nomenclature comes from Albert J. Hunter and Gerald D. Suttles, "The Expanding Community of Limited Liability," in Gerald D. Suttles, *The Social Construction of Communities* (Chicago: University of Chicago Press, 1972) 44–82.

33. For further elaboration on the context of liturgy as an artistic construct of reality, see Lawrence A. Hoffman, *The Art of Public Prayer: Not for Clergy Only* (Washington: Pastoral Press, 1988) chap. 7.

17

A RESPONSE TO
L. HOFFMAN AND J. BALDOVIN

William H. Shea
Biblical Research Institute

With clarity and picturesque speech Professor Hoffman has outlined for us the three main periods into which he sees Jewish attitudes about Shabbat developing through the Common Era. In the first of these, laws of limits were set up around the Sabbath to ensure its correct observance. This type of attitude has characterized most of the era down to the Enlightenment. Following the more reasoned approach of Western European civilization at that time, the Sabbath came to be viewed as a search for deeper meaning in the Sabbath.

Although it is easy to criticize any generalizing scheme as too simplistic and not meeting the complexity of human attitudes, Professor Hoffman has provided a useful framework for us to work with. He has illustrated that scheme well with the examples he has chosen. The century-long struggle of the rabbis of Salonika to stem the tide of coffeehouse visits on the Sabbath seems rather quaint in the light of our greater difficulties with the Sabbath and the problems with society in general. Nascent individualism of the modern age is already evident in the developing dispute over the Sabbath and sanctification in the nineteenth century. Finally, examples of the modern person's search for meaning in the Sabbath and elsewhere could be multiplied many times over.

The pattern proposed here could easily be applied to other religious groups and the development of their attitudes toward the Sabbath. My own religious tradition of Seventh-day Adventism has gone through similar phases of thought and experience. The search for the biblical Sabbath started out as a quest for truth in the nineteenth century, the same time as Hoffman's second phase in Jewry. Having arrived at their position on this subject, the early leaders of Adventism then went about developing the limits that Hoffman describes in his first phase. This has never reached the point of canon or halakic law, but informal personal discussions of this nature continue in local congregations to this day. What has developed in practice is a spectrum of limits. In some Third World countries and more conservative rural areas of the United States observance may be quite strict. In some parts of Western Europe and in Southern California practices may come close to more general attitudes about the use of Sunday. Practice in Adventist congregations in the great heartland of America probably falls in between these two poles. If one looks at the variations in these groups in the light of Hoffman's paper one might say that they reveal more about the attitude of members toward the God of the Sabbath than about their attitudes toward the Sabbath *per se.*

But neither the type thinking in the first phase nor that in the second is enough for the younger generation. The day when one could say to children, "We do it this way because that's the way we do it" has passed. Even to say "Well, because it's the Bible Sabbath" no longer carries much weight. Now it must be meaningful to me personally. It must be relevant to me now in my present situation. So the search for meaning in the Sabbath also takes place outside of Judaism. Adventists used to write books such as *Forty Reasons for the Bible Sabbath,* but now they write books about the Sabbath entitled *Divine Rest for Human Restlessness.*

This shift in emphasis has its advantages and disadvantages. It is better to be observant than not to be observant. It is better to search for truth than not to search for truth. But it is better still to understand the deeper meaning of what one does. Jesus said it well when he observed, "These ye ought to have done, and not to have left the other undone." Paradoxically, however, the Sabbath may become so relevant that its observance can be discarded or at least seriously minimized. This is the eternal tension of religion between external form and internal function. Happy is the person who can hold these two in creative personal tension.

I suppose that the one place where I might fault this general presentation of attitudes toward the Sabbath in Hoffman's paper is toward the end. In terms of volume of content, the third and final phase of the search for meaning seems to have gotten rather short shrift. Whereas the problem created by the modern search for meaning received a rather full treatment, Hoffman's answer to this problem is found only in the last two or three paragraphs of the paper. The suggestions found there are good and useful, but they could certainly have been unpacked and explained further. As a consequence, I came away from the paper feeling rather empty in terms of the final resolution to the problem. Perhaps a more Torah-oriented rather than sociological approach might have been helpful, even though we might view that Torah differently from the limit-setting teachers of times past.

As a final comment I might mention also that it seems to me that a number of papers presented at this conference have gone a long way toward providing the answer to that search for meaning in the Sabbath. I think in particular of the papers by Professors Wurzburger and Doukhan, John Primus's extensive quotation from Karl Barth in which Barth did indeed become almost rhapsodic over the Sabbath. Many of the comments made by these speakers fall into the category of "personal" theology and as such help to answer the question of meaning in the Sabbath for modern persons.

Like Professor Baldovin, I have no intention of entering on a serious level into the debate that has been carried on over the past twenty years, and up to this morning, between scholars like Rordorf, Bacchiocchi, Mosna, Beckwith and Stott, Carson, and others. I taught on the same faculty with Bacchiocchi for a number of years. He may not convince you in dialogue, but he certainly will overwhelm you!

Turning to the main content of the paper, we note that Professor Baldovin has given us an interesting liturgical history as it relates to the services of the church on Sunday. He has concentrated on fourth-century Jerusalem because of the wealth of information provided for us on that subject by the pilgrim Egeria. I have long been a fan of hers, but for other reasons. Because of the extensive detail she has provided us in recounting her travels, her work is especially valuable to persons interested in historical geography. Here now we can add another rich area of her work, that which provides us with information about the services of the church in that place and time.

Her description of the Sunday morning services, especially the lengthy series of sermons involved, reminds me of the experience of the Seventh-day Adventist congregation in Moscow. Because teaching the Sabbath school lesson was prohibited for quite some time (it is now permitted under Glasnost) it was the custom to have not one but a series of preachers hold forth from the pulpit. When they all finished, the congregation broke up for lunch. In the meantime, however, the members had either enjoyed or endured a series of several hours' worth of sermons. So the saints of both the fourth and the twentieth centuries have had their courage and patience tried by a prolonged series of preachers.

I have the feeling, however, that Professor Baldovin's paper begins quite abruptly with the section on liturgical history in the fourth century. Obviously the historian must go where sources lead, and it is undoubtedly true that our sources for the time prior to Egeria are more scanty. To fill in this gap Baldovin protests against the tyranny of the "earliest." He probably is right to lodge such a protest, but I fear that this kind of tyranny is going to be with us for a long time to come. Several years of my studies were in the field of Assyriology, and in that field the attitude is common that history effectively ends at the end of the Old Babylonian period, ca. 1800 B.C.E. Anyone strange enough to be interested in the Neo-Assyrian period was to be pitied, and anyone interested in the Neo-Babylonian period—as I was—was considered to be positively deranged. The same sort of thing is true in the field of biblical history, where the data for the reconstruction of the Israelite monarchy is seldom challenged but the discussions of origins concerning patriarchs, Exodus, conquest, and settlement still generate the most interest and heated controversies. The protest here in matters of Sabbath and Sunday is probably well taken, but it will also probably go unheeded.

To turn to that earlier period, which one might consider to be a gap in Baldovin's paper, I would cite but one text and one experience of the church. The text I refer to is the famous and much-discussed or debated letter of Pliny to Trajan, written about 112. Christians' guilt or error, he said, was this:

> They were in the habit of meeting on a certain fixed day before it was light, when they sang in alternate verses a hymn to Christ, as to a god, and bound themselves by a solemn oath, not to do any wicked deeds, never to commit any fraud, theft or adultery, never to falsify their word, nor deny a trust when they should be called upon to deliver it up; after which it was their custom to separate, and then reassemble to partake of food—but food of an ordinary and innocent kind. (trans. W. Melmoth [Loeb Classical Library; Cambridge, MA: Harvard University Press, 1915)

My purpose here is not to decide if such meetings on "a certain fixed day" took place on Sabbath, Sunday, or as an annual Easter vigil. My purpose is to point to a development of the liturgy from this point to the time of Egeria in the fourth century. Both services appear to have made use of hymns, and both services appear to have involved the use of the Lord's Supper. The major difference between them lies in the fact that, whereas the later service made considerable use of the preaching of sermons, in this case that central focus in the service was occupied by the swearing of an oath.

This oath looks very much like a covenant oath. In fact, it has certain resemblances to the covenant oath of the Hebrew Bible. In reading this quotation over carefully, it looks as if these early Christians had selected some of the Ten Commandments upon which to swear their oath. Thou shalt not steal, Thou shalt not commit adultery, and Thou shalt not bear false witness, come through quite clearly. Some of the other aspects of the oath may also be related to other commandments. Since the Ten Commandments are sometimes referred to as the Ten Words of the Covenant in the Hebrew Bible, the resemblance here is quite strong. My particular reason for citing this service and its oath here, however, is simply to point out that an evolution took place in the nature of the services of the church from Pliny's time in the second century until Egeria's time in the fourth. This is only to be expected on the basis of the materials that Baldovin has collected from the fourth century to the eighth, and on into the Middle Ages and modern times.

The experience in early church history that I would like to mention emphasizes a certain tension in Baldovin's thesis about the close interaction between sacred service and sacred time. I point here to the Quartodeciman controversy. Early Christians were confronted with a problem here as they moved toward their definition of sacred time. Should the crucifixion and resurrection be celebrated on the days of the week or the days of the month on which they occurred in the Jewish calendar. The eastern church preferred the latter (especially in Asia Minor, but in the Celtic church even down to the sixth century), whereas the western church preferred the former. Since the western church won out in this controversy, Easter is celebrated on Sunday, not on the 14th through the 16th of Nisan, on which they occurred in Jesus' time. This poses something of a problem for Baldovin's thesis because the Eucharist ultimately celebrates something that occurred on Friday, not Sunday. A fusion of these two events had to take place in their celebration in order to accomplish their principal commemoration on Sunday.

The occurrence of this controversy in the second century indicates that the church was then in the process of defining its sacred time, and this is not as late as Baldovin has suggested in his paper. Once it has been established, sacred time is not very easy to dislodge, modify, or abolish. Although the new year's or *akitu* festival varied in Mesopotamia as to the length of days and how the days were celebrated, it did not wander from the spring new year in a millennium and a half. More interesting is the Ptolemaic controversy over the calendar. The Egyptians had a calendar of 365 days or a quarter of a day short of the solar year. As a consequence, it moved forward through what we might call the Julian or Gregorian year. The Egyptians knew this as far back as the third millennium, but they simply chose not to change the calendar. One of the Ptolemies attempted to do this by royal decree in the third century B.C.E., and his efforts are preserved in a trilingual decree. The decree became a dead letter, however, because the priests refused to change the calendar. These two points illustrate the fact that it is not easy to change holy time. On the basis of analogy or comparative history of religions, therefore, it would not have been such an easy task for Paul simply to have swept the sacred calendar clean, as has been proposed here.

As a concluding comment I would note that the most controversial material in Baldovin's paper comes at the beginning, with the exposition of his presuppositions. In one case he himself refers to his own position as radical, and I would agree with his assessment there. That is the case when he states that it is of questionable value to search for definitive divine prescriptions in the Scriptures and that to ground one's doctrinal affirmations on the intention of the historical Jesus of Nazareth is a risky business. It seems to me that regardless of the religious tradition that one is examining, whether Buddhism, Confucianism, or Christianity—the place where one begins looking for the normative rule of belief is with the words of the founder of that religion and with the canonical writings that have been handed down by the recorders or writers nearest to that time. This still appears to me to be the most sound procedure to follow.

18

A RESPONSE TO
L. HOFFMAN AND J. BALDOVIN

Frederick E. Greenspahn
University of Denver

The papers by John Baldovin and Lawrence Hoffman share several intriguing features. Obviously central to both of them is weekly observance and the problems it has encountered in their respective traditions. That such should be the case can hardly be surprising, given the temptations of contemporary life; still, it may be worth remembering that, as the only holiday not rooted in a natural cycle, the Sabbath—in whatever form—is *literally* the most unnatural observance in both Judaism and Christianity. How important that dimension can be, even in our urban, technological culture, is demonstrated by Dr. Baldovin's reference to the tendency to turn individual Sabbaths into annual holidays, such as Mission Sunday and Epiphany, a process with parallels in Jewish life as well. However, this transformation of a weekly event into a series of annual commemorations is not an entirely modern development. Precedent can be found in the practice of the Qumran community of two thousand years ago!

Both Jewish and Christian practices also demonstrate the tendency to historicize their respective observances. An example of this is the book of Deuteronomy's description of the Jewish Sabbath as commemorating the Exodus. Christian ritual likewise reenacts events related to the crucifixion, although parts of Egeria's account may be problematic in this regard, since some of what she witnessed in fourth-century Jerusalem was characteristic of Lent and may not, therefore, have been practiced all year long.[2]

An underlying concern with the survival of the institutions they describe is also shared by these papers, even while their authors would allow for radical changes in detail. Here I must confess some skepticism as to whether intellectual musings can be readily translated into popular reality. In response to the shrinking role of religion, Dr. Hoffman proposes

236

presenting Judaism "as an optional world of experience that successfully provides meaning in empty lives." Although his description of the contemporary situation probably comes reasonably close to capturing the reality for many moderns, one must wonder whether religious partisans should be so willing to accept that stance. Judaism and Christianity have usually preferred to understand themselves as communities of shared memory and meaning, not as choices in some convenience mart of experiences, to be selected by the criteria of the marketplace. Nor should the problem be overstated, just because our own vantage point makes it look so threatening. Like all observers, we must guard against cultural myopia. After all, this is not only the age of Yuppies and VCRs, but also of Falwell and Chabad. However much members of some communities may find the Sabbath inconvenient, millions of others plainly find traditional weekend worship meaningful—if not in the "mainline centers," then certainly in Lynchburg and Boro Park.

The lack of Sabbath observance may be a symptom rather than the basic problem in communities facing much deeper issues for those in positions of religious leadership to address. Indeed, both papers may have skirted the real cause of the situation about which they are concerned—not, most likely, because their authors are unaware of it but as a by-product of this collection's focus, which lends itself so easily to detailed treatment of the Sabbath in isolation from the many other issues of contemporary religious observance. Separating one item from its larger context in this way can distort our perceptions and create a lack of perspective. We thus risk falling into the same trap as those who explain the Bible's dietary laws as a primitive effort to combat trichinosis, oblivious to the fact that neither the Bible nor, to the best of my knowledge, rabbinic literature ever singles pigs out as uniquely unacceptable, but simply includes them among dozens of animals that have split hooves but don't chew their cud. So too, for Jews the Sabbath isn't theologically different from the Torah's 612 other commandments, and a similar point could be made for Sunday observance in Roman Catholicism.

Jews and Christian Sabbatarians of various stripes regard the Sabbath as a commandment, an obligation imposed by God for reasons that are ultimately irrelevant. Is it any wonder that few choose to follow this practice in an age when obedience to divine imperatives has fallen into disfavor, whether the reasons have to do with theology or comfort? That may also account for widespread evidence that the proportion of Jews participating in weekend worship is about half that among Christians, since American Jews are notorious for rejecting the religious side of their tradition.[3] (One observer intriguingly notes that "without exception, *all* Supreme Court decisions involving the right to do business on Sunday involve Jews, and *all* the decisions involving the right *not* to work on Saturday involve

Seventh-Day Adventists or other sabbatarian Christians."[4]) Nor are any of the proposals offered here likely to resolve this lack of interest. In Dr. Hoffman's terms, the language of limits has little appeal these days, especially among Jews.

Having said that, however, we should also note that his Hegelian scheme of limits, truth, and meaning has problems of its own. However much classical Reform Jewish rhetoric may have gravitated toward "truth" or its more recent theoreticians been seduced by the language of "meaning," when the Reform movement issued a Sabbath guide some years ago, it included fourteen commandments, which were expanded to twenty-five when that section was incorporated into a volume on home observance in 1983.[5] Conversely, it is not entirely fair to characterize classical Jewish tradition as centered on limits. Although the depiction of rabbinic Judaism as comprising rules and punishments has a long history, Robert Goldenberg and Walter Wurzburger make it clear how little justice that does to the rabbinic view. In a famous essay, one modern student of rabbinic Judaism pointed out that although the Talmud devotes two tractates with over two hundred pages of practically pure halakhah to the Sabbath, their purpose is to create a day that is wholly aggadah.[6]

Further insight into the reasons why the Sabbath has fallen on hard times in some circles (and less so in others) can be derived from the observation that in biblical times Sabbath observance seems to have been of particular importance during the exilic period.[7] This is generally considered to demonstrate the high value accorded practices that set ancient Jews apart in a time when assimilation was a major threat. A similar explanation probably accounts for the emphasis on the Sabbath, along with dietary prohibitions and the laws of ritual purity, in modern Orthodox circles, where a high premium is placed on erecting barriers, whether social or psychological, between the Jewish and non-Jewish worlds. (The fact that Sabbath worship has become virtually the only form of regular liturgical practice in more liberal circles may have a similar cause.) Indeed, if the truth be told, this may be yet another reason so many American Jews have trouble with the Sabbath, since it is so visible a reminder of their differentness at a time when many would like to be just like everyone else.

But the basic reason for the lack of interest, among Jews and Christians alike, may be far more benign. Religion is ultimately a part of culture, an expression of fundamental values rather than an external force seeking to impose its views on a body of willing or unwilling adherents. This, I take it, is the point of Robert Bellah and his followers, who would remind us not to restrict our understanding of religion to what goes on in church or synagogue.[8] It may thus be misleading to equate contemporary religions with their historic forebears without taking into account the quite different roles they play in their respective societies. Contemporary Judaism may not be functionally equivalent to the Judaism of ages past, and today's Christianity may play a far different role in people's lives than it did in antiquity or the Middle Ages.

One of the hallmarks of modernity is the differentiation of elements that were previously intertwined—work and play, for example, or church and state.[9] In the past, religious practices were an organic part of culture—natural and accepted behavior, if not always convenient, given a whole system of assumptions and beliefs. The notion of secularization obviously rests on our having restricted religion to a certain time and place. As a result, our real beliefs may be very different from those proclaimed from our pulpits or recited in our creeds. The problems facing institutionalized religion must, therefore, be distinguished from the lack of religion.

Our tendency to use Yuppies as a paradigm for everything that has gone wrong is a case in point. Although often characterized as individualistic (or "low grid" and "low group," to use anthropological jargon), in some respects they seem highly social, as anyone who has witnessed their sacred convocations at 7:30 in the morning or 5:30 in the afternoon, when they gather in holy garb at exercise clubs around the country, can attest. Nor should their potential interest in religious traditions be too readily dismissed, given their urge toward conformity and conservatism, not to mention their willingness to invest in expensive status symbols, which may yet fuel a surge in membership at lavish churches and synagogues once their stylishly dressed children reach 5 or 7—the fifties revisited, alas.

The point is not to criticize Yuppie behavior but to suggest that we recognize that religion, in its truest sense, is not necessarily what priests and rabbis preach so much as what people believe, often unconsciously, in their heart of hearts, and what they do without even thinking about why. In this respect, those lobbying to keep Jerusalem's movie houses closed on Saturday or fighting to maintain blue laws, if that is still an option anywhere in this country, may have recognized an important fact—that rituals do not usually work very well when they are conscious or artificial.

The behavior vigorously urged on resistant audiences by today's clergy and implicitly by the papers under discussion is in many respects the unconscious habit of a bygone time. It is rather as if leaders of the twenty-fourth century were to try to force their parishioners to watch tapes of Super Bowl XXIII or pedal for hours on a stationary bike.

This, I take it, is what Dr. Baldovin meant when he quoted the statement that "structure outlives meaning." However, the facts may be more complex still. After all, our liturgies, both acted and said, are replete with evidence of structural conservatism, forms and words that have survived beyond their original context. But they are not necessarily fossils or dead skeletons enduring into a time beyond their own. Like species that survive the destruction of one habitat by finding a new ecological niche, religious structures can survive not only by gaining the support of institutionalized professionals but also by acquiring new meanings. That is not to say that these can be invented for the occasion, particularly in the absence of some kind of validating authority, but they may nonetheless find their own meaning in the life of the community that preserves them. Evidence for this is not difficult to find. After all, most of our major rituals, including Christmas, Passover, baptism, and circumcision, emerged in their present Jewish or Christian embodiments as the result of major transformations from their original meanings, and perhaps even without much assistance from liturgists or theologians. If we pay attention to what goes on in people's lives and not merely to what our traditions have taught us to expect, we may find religion adapting as it always has—albeit not necessarily in the ways we might choose.

Dr. Baldovin cites Canon 1248 and the growing practice of Saturday evening Mass in the Roman church. This is, of course, exactly the approach that has taken root in major segments of the Jewish community, where the Sabbath is celebrated on Friday night. That may disturb the purists, at least among Jews who would have wished for a twenty-four hour Sabbath, but it reflects accommodation rather than capitulation to the forces of modernity even among the ostensibly least committed segments of the community.[10]

Returning to our quest for those factors that are said to have undermined Sabbath observance in our culture, let me suggest that we include not only the weakness of institutionalized religion but also the power of Americans' real religion—and in this case the five-day workweek, which has created a double Sabbath (Saturday and Sunday), with football and Little League games, oversized newspapers, and family outings joining the Eucharist, candlelighting, and public worship of an earlier age. Collectively, these constitute both ritualized behavior and tacit expression of the values held by many in our land, whether we approve of them all or not. Nor are these entirely separate from what Judaism and Christianity had in mind by their weekly celebrations. Rest, family, God, community, joy—all have a place in our new and expanded "palace in time."[11]

Rather than lamenting the death (or maybe just the hibernation) of customs from another age, the authors of both these papers seem committed to finding a *modus vivendi* with the modern world. To the extent they are able to live up to that ideal, they will increase their chances for success while following long-standing custom in their respective communities.

NOTES

1. See Joseph M. Baumgarten, "The Counting of the Sabbath in Ancient Sources," *Vetus Testamentum* 16 (1966) 277–86.

2. *Egeria's Travels to the Holy Land,* trans. John Wilkinson, 27:1ff. (rev. ed.; Jerusalem: Ariel, 1981) 128ff.

3. According to the Gallup Organization, only 20 percent of the Jews surveyed in a 1986 poll had attended religious services during the preceding week, a number smaller than half the proportion of Protestants and Catholics (*The Gallup Report* #259 [April, 1987] 39). The same report notes that Jews are about one-third as likely as Protestants and Catholics to be among the "superchurched," but two to three times more likely to be "unchurched" (p. 41).

4. Marian Henriquez Neudel, "Secularism—Is it Good for the Jews?" *Sh'ma* 15/290 (March 22, 1985) 73.

5. Central Conference of American Rabbis, *A Sabbath Manual* (New York: Ktav, 1972) 9–13; and Peter S. Knobel, *Gates of the Season* (New York: Central Conference of American Rabbis, 1983) 21–33.

6. Chaim Nahman Bialik, *Halachah and Aggadah* (London: Zionist Federation of Great Britain and Ireland, 1944) 12–13.

7. See Ezekiel 20:13; Isaiah 58:13; Nehemiah 10:32; 13:15–22.

8. See Robert N. Bellah's classic essay, "Civil Religion in America," originally published in *Daedalus* (Winter, 1967) 1–21; reprinted with several additional essays discussing these issues in *American Civil Religion,* ed. Russell E. Richey and Donald G. Jones (New York: Harper & Row, 1974).

9. See Benton Johnson, "Modernity and Pluralism," in *Pushing the Faith: Proselytism and Civility in a Pluralistic World,* ed. Martin E. Marty and Frederick E. Greenspahn (New York: Crossroad, 1988) 12.

10. W. Gunther Plaut's description of these services suggests that they may not be altogether successful (see "Presidential Message," in *Yearbook of the Central Conference of American Rabbis,* ed. Elliot L. Stevens [New York: Central Conference of American Rabbis, 1985] 95:4–7).

11. The phrase is from Abraham Joshua Heschel, *The Sabbath: Its Meaning for Modern Man* (expanded edition; New York: Harper & Row, 1966); see pp. 12–24.

VI

LEGAL AND ECUMENICAL PERSPECTIVES

19

THE SABBATH AND THE STATE: LEGAL IMPLICATIONS OF SABBATARIANISM

Mitchell A. Tyner, Esq.
General Conference of Seventh-day Adventists

S abbatarians have been economically disadvantaged by America's more than three centuries of Sunday legislation. That disadvantage continues today, in spite of both the erosion of Sunday laws and the recent efforts of government to alleviate resultant religious discrimination. It is the purpose of this paper to show, first, that governmental efforts to assist religion are most proper and most productive not when aimed at aiding religious institutions but when intended to facilitate individual religious observance; and, second, that Sabbatarians should establish a coordinated effort legislatively and judicially to strengthen the protection society affords to one who finds his or her religious observance producing conflict in the ordinary affairs of life.

The earliest use of civil law to enforce the observance of a day as a Sabbath is now lost in the dim mists of antiquity, but it probably was an accepted idea by the time of Moses. The result of such laws, as seen in the experience of nineteenth- and twentieth-century America, illustrates the problem inherent in the majoritarian enforcement of religious convention: such an enactment both weakens the institution it was designed to support and penalizes those who conscientiously dissent from its presuppositions.

Although Christianity received from Judaism both the institution of the Sabbath and a general framework of ideas concerning its observance, the observance was transferred very early to the first day of the week. The change was occasioned in no small part by a desire to visibly separate Christianity from Judaism in the public mind.[1] As Christianity gained acceptance and political prominence, so did Sunday observance. Thus,

Constantine, usually regarded as the first Christian emperor of Rome, issued the following edict in 321:

> Constantine, Emperor Augustus, to Helpidius: On the venerable day of the sun let the magistrates and people residing in cities rest, and let all workshops be closed. In the country, however, persons engaged in agriculture may freely and lawfully continue their pursuits; because it often happens that another day is not as suitable for grain sowing or for vine planting; lest by neglecting the proper moment for such operations the bounty of heaven should be lost.[2]

The Sunday legislation of the Roman Empire subordinated the religious element to the civil. But during the Middle Ages, Sunday legislation took on a definite religious tone, as civil authorities, using an analogy to the Israelite theocracy, claimed the right to legislate in religious matters. Although the Protestant Reformation in Europe did not generally alter that pattern, a new theory did develop in England, where we meet for the first time the doctrine of the transfer of the fourth commandment imperative to Sunday. The laws of the Cromwellian period, although civil enactments, read like extended theological treatises.[3]

The Sunday law that had far greater influence in America than any other was chapter 7 of "An Act of the 29th Year of Charles II."[4] This 1676 statute, an act "for the better observation and keeping holy the Lord's day, commonly called Sunday," required "that all and every person or persons whatsoever, shall on every Lord's day apply themselves to the observation of the same, by exercising themselves thereon in the duties of piety and true religion, publicly and privately. . . ." Transgression by a tradesman or laborer was punishable by a fine of five shillings, but transgression by a "drover, horse-courser, wagoner, butcher, higgler, their or any of their servants" who might "travel or come into his or their inn or lodging upon the Lord's day" warranted a fine of twenty shillings. Presumably the tradesman worked in relative quiet, whereas a drover would offend the sensibilities of the pious by more visible activity. Offenders who were unable to pay their fines were to "be set publicly in the stocks by the space of two hours." The statute also prohibited the service or execution of "any writ, process, warrant, order, judgment or decree" on Sunday, and held any document so served to be void.

The statute of Charles II was, of course, applicable to the British colonies in America. After independence it was reenacted, often almost verbatim, into the law codes of the new states. North Carolina, for example, reenacted this statute, and when the western counties of North Carolina became the state of Tennessee, the same statute was adopted by that state's first legislature.[5]

Although colonial statutes were firm, their enforcement was not always so. Stephen Mumford, a member of the Bell Lane Seventh Day Baptist

Church in London, settled in Newport, Rhode Island, in 1684, and enjoyed sufficient freedom that gradually a small congregation of Sabbath-keeping Baptists grew. One of its members, Samuel Ward, was also governor of Rhode Island and delegate to the Continental Congress of 1774. Had he not died on 26 March 1776, he would most likely have been a signatory of the Declaration of Independence. Although the freedom of such dissenters was not legally protected, nonconforming groups were in fact granted considerable leeway.[6]

As revolutionary tempers cooled in the first decade of the nineteenth century, so apparently did zeal for religious equality, and powerful forces began to push for Sunday legislation at the federal level. The matter surfaced in 1810, when Congress acted to require postmasters to provide service seven days a week. A flood of petitions demanded that Congress rescind the law and made no secret of the petitioners' religious motivation.[7]

In 1815 the Thirteenth Congress reaffirmed its action, but the public outcry continued until 1830. Prominent in the effort to withstand the pressure for Sunday legislation was Senator Richard M. Johnson of Kentucky. When Senator Chambers of Maryland observed that the petitioners felt "the observance of the Sabbath was connected with the civil interests of the government," Johnson replied that, although he did not dispute the petitioners' motives, "some denominations considered one day the most sacred and some looked to another, and these petitions did, in fact, call upon Congress to settle what was the law of God."[8] Johnson further stated to his colleagues that "it is not the legitimate province of the legislature to determine what religion is true or what false" and that government's proper function is to protect all citizens "in the enjoyment of their religious as well as civil rights, and not to determine for any whether they shall esteem one day above another or esteem all days alike holy."[9]

Johnson's reasoning was compelling and carried the day so completely that not for another half century was any serious move again made for Sunday legislation at the national level. In 1888, Senator H. W. Blair of New Hampshire sponsored a Senate bill (N. 2983) to promote Sunday observance as a day of worship. Blair's bill (and a similar one in 1889) was defeated, but the effort to enforce Sunday observance was not. Rather, the scene of activity shifted to the states.

During 1895 and 1896, at least seventy-five Seventh-day Adventists were prosecuted in the United States and Canada under state or provincial Sunday laws. Some were fined, a few were acquitted or were lucky enough to have their cases dismissed. But twenty-eight served jail terms, aggregating 1,144 days: almost three and a half years in total.[10] Such prosecution was not happenstance, not just a small part of a broader picture of thousands of Americans arrested for a wide variety of Sunday activities.

To the contrary, it was a matter of selective enforcement. Those prosecuted were targeted not just for their conduct but for the reason behind it.

A case in point was that of Day Conklin of Big Creek, Forsyth County, Georgia, who in March 1889 was arrested, tried before a jury, and fined twenty-five dollars and costs, amounting in all to eighty-three dollars. His offense: cutting wood near his front door on Sunday, 18 November 1888. Attorney William F. Findley later gave the following recollection of the case:

> One of these Seventh-day Adventists was tried over here in Forsyth County, and I think there never was a more unrighteous conviction. There was a man named Day Conklin, who was moving on Friday. He got his goods wet on Friday, and it turned off cold. On Saturday he went out and cut enough wood to keep his family from freezing. On Sunday, he still hadn't his things dry, and it was still as cold as it had been on Saturday. He still cut enough wood to keep his family warm, and they convicted him for doing this. I say that is an outrage, an unrighteous conviction, for he was doing the best he could. One of the jurymen told me that they did not convict him for what he had done, but for what he said he had a right to do. He said he had a right to work on Sunday.[11]

Perhaps the most interesting of these cases was that of R. M. King of Obion County, Tennessee.[12] King had farmed in the community for twenty years and was held in high esteem by his neighbors except that, as a Seventh-day Adventist, he tilled his fields on Sunday. His neighbors labored with him, but he resisted. Finally "they insisted that he must keep Sunday and not teach their children by his example that the seventh day is the Sabbath and if he did not comply with their wishes he would be prosecuted."[13] King was subsequently arrested for working in his fields on Sunday, 23 June 1889. On 6 July, Obion County Justice J. A. Barker found King guilty as charged and fined him a total of $12.85. But since King refused to stop Sunday work his neighbors had him indicted by a grand jury for virtually the same offense.

Judge Swiggart and a jury heard the matter in Troy, Tennessee, on 6 March 1890, Attorney General Bond appearing for the state and Col. T. E. Richardson for King. The charge was that King's repeated Sunday breaking constituted a public nuisance—a charge that opened the way to a harsher penalty than did mere violation of the Sunday law. The jury heard five prosecution witnesses and one for the defense. They deliberated only half an hour before returning a guilty verdict and assessing a fine of seventy-five dollars. The judge denied a motion for a new trial and warned that Mr. King and his ilk would have to obey the law or leave the country.

Colonel Richardson appealed on King's behalf to the state supreme court, which in 1891 merely affirmed the trial court without opinion. Then

Richardson, joined by Don M. Dickinson, U.S. Postmaster General in 1888–89, appealed to the United States Circuit Court for the Western District of Tennessee. Their theory on appeal was a new one: since no previous case recognized habitual Sunday breaking as a public nuisance and no state statute described it as such, to convict King for such activity constituted denial of the due process and equal protection of law as guaranteed by the Fourteenth Amendment to the United States Constitution. Significantly, they also argued that he had been denied the religious freedom guaranteed him by the First Amendment religion clauses.

On 1 August 1891, Judge Hammond rendered his decision. He acknowledged:

> By a sort of factitious advantage, the observers of Sunday have secured the aid of the civil law, and adhere to that advantage with great tenacity, and in spite of the clamor for religious freedom and the progress that has been made in the absolute separation of church and state, and in spite of the strong and merciless attack that has always been ready, in the field of controversial theology, to be made, as it has been made here, upon the claim for divine authority for the change from the seventh to the first day of the week.

Nevertheless, the state court decision was sustained.

Was it proper to define such conduct as a public nuisance? It was, said Hammond, if a state court said so. A federal court would not second-guess a state court on the meaning of that state's law. Hence, no deprivation of due process existed. King also lost on his First Amendment claims, said Hammond, because that amendment did not apply to the states. According to the decision, "the Fourteenth Amendment of the Constitution of the United States has not abrogated the Sunday laws of the states, and established religious freedom therein. The states may establish a church or creed. . . ."

Upon that point King's lawyers appealed to the United States Supreme Court in the fall of 1891, asking the Court to clarify whether the Due Process Clause of the Fourteenth Amendment made the First Amendment guarantees binding upon the state. It was a strategy used successfully by Jehovah's Witnesses in 1940.[14] If the Supreme Court had adopted that theory in 1891, the course of Sunday legislation—indeed all religion clause jurisprudence—might have been different. But the Court did not have the opportunity to rule on the question: R. M. King died on 12 November 1891, before his case came before the Court.

The 1890s may have been the high-water mark in the prosecution of Sabbatarians, but the flood did not recede immediately. As the tide of fundamentalism rolled toward its crest about the time of the famous *Scopes* trial,[15] it carried with it a continuing volume of such prosecutions. And well into the twentieth century, as America experienced increasing industrialization and urbanization, with the concomitant rise of secularism and liberal thought, the pattern continued—and not just in the rural South. In 1923, three Seventh-day Adventists were arrested in Massachusetts and fined for painting the interior of a house on Sunday in order to get it ready for occupancy the next day. As late as 1938 a Massachusetts storekeeper was arrested selling fresh eggs on Sunday—at a time when it was legal to buy cooked eggs, beer, and liquor and to attend sports events and movies. In 1932, a deputy sheriff of Washington County, Virginia, arrested two Seventh-day Adventists for Sunday work: one, a crippled mother who walked on crutches, for washing clothes on her own premises, and the other a man who donated and hauled a load of wood to a church to heat it for religious services.[16]

Beginning in 1940, a line of Supreme Court cases established that the First Amendment, including the religion clauses, had indeed been made applicable to state and local governments via the Fourteenth Amendment, thus opening the door to Sunday-law challenges based on those clauses, and in 1961 those challenges found their way to the Supreme Court. The questions raised in R. M. King's case in 1891 would finally be answered by the High Court seventy years later. It's just as well that King didn't live to hear the answer.

There were four cases—one from Massachusetts, one from Maryland, and two from Pennsylvania.[17] All four challenged state Sunday laws as an establishment of religion.

The Crown Kosher Super Market of Massachusetts specialized in kosher products for a primarily Jewish clientele. It closed from sundown on Friday through sundown on Saturday and was open on Sundays from 8:00 A.M. until 6:00 P.M. One-third of its total sales were made on Sundays. When the market was cited for violation of the state's Sunday law, its owner went first to the state court (unsuccessfully) and then appealed to Federal District Court, alleging a violation of both religion clauses as well as denial of equal protection of law and an invalid exercise of police power because of capricious classification and arbitrary exceptions. The last mentioned charges noted that while tobacco could be sold on Sunday most food could not. Candy could be sold but not meat. A fish could be sold wholesale but the same fish could not be sold retail. A barber was forced to close completely, but a bootblack was allowed to work until 11:00 A.M., and professional football was allowed only after noon. Sabbatarians were exempted from the law and allowed to work if they "disturb no other person thereby." Apparently Crown Kosher disturbed someone.

In 1959 a panel of three federal judges rendered their decision. The court granted Crown Kosher the injunctive relief it sought and ruled the statute unconstitutional. It noted the law's religious purpose, rejected any suggestion that the religious character had been shed, and observed that subsequent amendments had created "an almost unbelievable hodgepodge." The court further ruled that Massachusetts had furnished special protection to the views of the Christian majority without furnishing comparable protection to others. The state appealed to the United States Supreme Court.

The High Court, in 1961, consolidated the four appeals which had arrived on its doorstep almost simultaneously and upheld the Massachusetts law in an eight-to-one decision. Writing for the majority in the *Crown Kosher* case, Chief Justice Earl Warren said, "We agree with the court below that, like the Sunday laws of other states, the Massachusetts statutes have an unmistakably religious origin." But he observed that a change "came about in 1792" when the statutory language declared that "the Observance of the Lord's Day" promotes the "Welfare of a Community" and provides "Seasons for Relaxation from Labor and the Cares of Business." Thus, said Warren, "the statute's announced purpose was no longer solely religious," therefore the statutes did not constitute an establishment of religion.

Warren admitted that "the statutes still contain references to the Lord's Day," but he found that "for the most part, they have been divorced from the religious orientation of their predecessors." He noted an expanded scheme of permitted activities, including dancing, concerts and sports, while "church attendance is no longer required." For Warren, "the objectionable language" had become "merely a relic."

For the majority in *Crown Kosher*, "the present scheme is one to provide an atmosphere of recreation rather than religion," and "the character of the day would appear more likely to be intended to be one of repose and recreation" rather than one of a religious nature.

The crimes of appellants in the second case, *McGowan v. Maryland*, consisted of Sunday sales of a toy submarine, a stapler and staples, a can of floor wax, and a three-ring loose-leaf binder. The sales occurred in a discount store in Anne Arundel County, Maryland, at a time when sales of food, auto and boat accessories, flowers, toilet goods, hospital supplies, and souvenirs were legal.

The *McGowan* appellants contended "that the purpose of the enforced stoppage of labor on that day is to facilitate and encourage church attendance, . . . to induce people with no religion or people with marginal religious beliefs to join the predominant Christian sects" and "to aid the conduct of church services and religious observance of the sacred day."

Chief Justice Warren acknowledged that "the original laws which dealt with Sunday labor were motivated by religious forces," but held that many years earlier "nonreligious arguments for Sunday closing began to be heard more distinctly and the statutes began to lose some of their totally religious flavor." As in *Crown Kosher*, the majority rejected the lower federal court ruling in favor of "the state supreme court's determination that the statute's present purpose is not to aid religion but to set aside a day of rest and recreation."

Similarly, the Pennsylvania law at issue was upheld in the third and fourth cases, the court stating "we hold that neither the statute's purpose nor its effect is religious."

Perhaps the Court came closest to the truth when it observed, in *McGowan,* that "Sunday is a day apart from all others. The cause is irrelevant, the fact exists." Or, more plainly stated, these laws exist because the majority of the populace wants them to exist.

In *McGowan* and *Two Guys,* the Court dealt only with the establishment clause. But *Crown Kosher* and the other Pennsylvania case, *Braunfeld v. Brown* also presented Free Exercise Clause arguments. Even if Sunday laws were not an establishment of religion, did their enforcement on Sabbatarians, who were forced thereby to rest two days instead of one, work an unconstitutional deprivation of the free exercise of religion?

Braunfeld argued that economic pressure required him either to give up his Sabbath observance as a tenet of his faith or to continue to operate at a competitive disadvantage. Chief Justice Warren, again writing for the majority of the Court, conceded that Braunfeld and "all other persons who wish to work on Sunday will be burdened economically by the state's day-of-rest mandate," but differentiated what he saw as an "indirect burden" from a law that would actually outlaw a religious practice.

The *Braunfeld* decision acknowledged that Sunday laws "operate so as to make the practice of their religious beliefs more expensive," and that Sabbatarians may well face "some financial sacrifice in order to observe their religious beliefs," but maintained that "the option is wholly different than when the legislation attempts to make a religious practice itself unlawful," implying that it would find infringement of free exercise only in evidence of *direct* prohibition, rather than *indirect* hardship.

Such reasoning is a bit curious in light of a decision just two years later in which the Court ruled that South Carolina could not deny unemployment benefits to a Seventh-day Adventist, Adele Sherbert, who lost her job for refusing to work on Saturday. Justice Brennan, who dissented in *Braunfeld* on the free exercise issue, wrote that the denial of benefits, even though an indirect burden on religion "puts the same kind of burden upon the free exercise of religion as would a fine imposed against appellant for her Saturday worship,"[18] and was thus unconstitutional.

In 1963, an indirect burden was enough to establish an abridgment of free exercise when a state denied unemployment benefits to a Sabbath-keeper. Two years earlier an indirect burden was not enough when a state forced a market to close on the day that produced 30 percent of its sales.

Potter Stewart, the youngest and newest member of the Court, also dissented in *Braunfeld.* He wrote:

Pennsylvania has passed the law which compels an Orthodox Jew to choose between his religious faith and his economic survival. That is a cruel choice. It is a choice which I think no State can constitutionally demand. For me this is not something that can be swept under the rug and forgotten in the interest of enforced Sunday togetherness. I think the impact of this law upon these appellants grossly violates their constitutional right to the free exercise of their religion.

The High Court was obviously aware of the scrutiny that would attach to its 1961 Sunday-law decisions, for it went to great length to elaborate its holding. The total number of pages required by the opinions, concurrences, and dissents in the four cases ranked second in quantity to any decision in the Court's history. Yet public opinion found the rationale less than compelling. Said *Time* magazine, "Seldom has an issue of liberty been argued on flabbier grounds."[19]

But walls that could not be breached by frontal attack eventually fell inward of their own weight and imbalance. In the years since 1961 a large portion of state and local Sunday laws have been repealed, declared unconstitutional for nonreligious reasons, or are being ignored. It was a development not unforeseen by at least a few. In his "Boston Monday Lectures" of 1887, Joseph Cook, lecturing on the subject of Sunday laws, said, "Unless Sabbath observance be founded upon religious reasons, you will not long maintain it at a high standard on the basis of economic and physiological and political considerations alone."[20] In 1961 the High Court removed the religious foundation for Sunday laws (or perhaps more accurately, the Court validated what had already been done by public opinion). As Cook had foreseen, the remaining reasons soon proved inadequate to sustain the institution.

A case in point is the Virginia Sunday law, invalidated by the Supreme Court of Virginia in September 1988.[21] Eight Virginia Beach corporations had moved for a declaratory judgment on the Sunday-closing law, alleging that their competitors, exempted by the statute, were able to sell identical products on Sunday. The plaintiffs contended that this placed them at a competitive disadvantage and that the statute, as amended and applied, constituted just the type of special legislation prohibited by the state constitution. The trial court upheld the statute and the retailers appealed.

The state supreme court reversed the trial court and struck the statute. In so doing it reviewed the history of Sunday legislation in Virginia. It conceded the clearly religious purpose of the statute of 1610, but found that the 1779 statute that replaced it had the secular purpose of providing a common day of rest. That statute survived until 1960, when a substantial revision, although continuing a prohibition of work "except in household or other work of necessity or charity," included a list of activities expressly deemed works of necessity.

In 1974 the General Assembly completely rewrote the Sunday-closing law. The resulting act granted blanket exemption to all activities of over sixty industries and businesses grouped in twenty-two categories. Since 1974 the legislature frequently had added additional exemptions and also allowed cities and counties, by referendum vote, to remove themselves from the ambit of the law. As a result, 50 percent of all employed persons in Virginia in 1988 were working in cities or counties not covered by the law, and 57 percent of Virginia workers worked in statutorily exempt businesses or industries. In total, 80 percent of Virginia workers were exempt from the operation of the law for one reason or another.

Although the state High Court reaffirmed its previous rejection of challenges to the statute based on equal protection grounds, it found that it had not previously been asked to consider the issue of special legislation. In approaching that issue, it observed that the special-laws prohibition was aimed at economic favoritism, and requires that laws "bear a reasonable and substantial relation to the object to be accomplished."

The court first asked whether the law affects all similarly situated persons and businesses and concluded that it did not, since only 20 percent of employees were subject to it. The court next inquired whether the statutory scheme, as applied, bore a reasonable relationship to the law's purpose. "Plainly," said the court, "the answer is no." The act, therefore, was adjudged to fail the tests distinguishing general from special legislation.

Wisely, the plaintiffs did not attack the law facially, but only as applied. In response, the court stated:

> We agree that none of these steps [creating exemptions] was in itself improper in any respect, but we further agree that their combined effects have reduced the application of general law to the kind of special legislation prohibited by Article IV, Sections 14 and 15 of the Virginia Constitution.

Over the course of 378 years, a statute that began as a rigid mandate of religious observance, through some amorphous evolutionary process, was transformed into a secularly based public welfare regulation, and in the end was simply amended to death.

In his 1891 opinion in the R. M. King case, Judge Hammond stated:

> This very principle of religious freedom is the product of our religion, as all of our good customs are, and if it be desirable to extend that principle to the ultimate condition that no man shall be in the least restrained, by law or public opinion, in hostility to religion itself, or in the exhibition of individual eccentricities or practices of sectarian peculiarities of religious observances of any kind, or be fretted with laws colored by any religion that is distasteful to anybody, those who desire that condition must, necessarily, await its growth into that enlarged application.[22]

Was Hammond anticipating a day when the attention of government would finally turn from *mandating* religious observance to *enabling* religious observance? Just such a turning occurred in the social turbulence of the 1960s. Only three years after the Supreme Court's pivotal Sunday-law decisions, Congress passed the monumental Civil Rights Act of 1964, which made religious discrimination in employment, among other things, an illegal practice.[23] Perhaps it was at least in part a response to the inherent unfairness of the Court's holdings in *Braunfeld* and *Crown Kosher*. Perhaps it was a realization of the changes wrought by the industrialization of society. In the nineteenth century most workers were farmers or craftsmen who set their own work schedules. By the mid-twentieth century, most workers were employees. It now mattered less whether a Sabbatarian was *required* not to work on Sunday as whether he was *enabled* not to work on the Sabbath. By 1964 Sabbath-keepers were being economically disadvantaged not for working on Sunday but for refusing to work on the Sabbath. For whatever reasons, Congress decided to "level the playing field" for ethnic and religious minorities.

But the Act of 1964 was less than effective. Although it forbade religious discrimination, it did not impose an affirmative obligation on employers to accommodate the religious practices of employees. In fact, in 1966 the Equal Employment Opportunity Commission, brought into being to enhance the effectiveness of Title VII of the Civil Rights Act, issued a guideline stating that an employer was not required to accommodate an employee who accepted the job knowing its requirements conflicted with his religious obligations.

In 1967, however, the Commission issued a very different guideline, requiring that an employer make a reasonable accommodation to the religious needs of its employees where such could be done without undue hardship on the conduct of the business. As a result, courts were faced with the question whether Title VII, which merely stated that it was illegal to discriminate on the basis of religion, could properly be interpreted to embrace this affirmative obligation. Several lower court decisions indicated a negative answer,[24] which led Congress to clarify the matter by amending the Act.

The 1972 amendment to the Act adopted the essence of the EEOC's 1967 guidelines. Largely at the behest of Senator Jennings Randolph (D-WVA), himself a Seventh Day Baptist, Congress added Section 701(j). That section defines religion as including "all aspects of religious observance and practice, as well as belief, unless an employer demonstrates that he is unable to reasonably accommodate to an employee's or prospective employee's religious observance or practice without undue hardship on the conduct of the employer's business." Randolph explained that this section was intended to protect workers whose religious beliefs "rigidly require them to abstain from work in the nature of hire on certain days" from being rejected for employment by employers that refuse to adjust their work schedules.[25]

Randolph's good intentions were largely undone by the Supreme Court. In 1977, the High Court interpreted both the 1967 guidelines and the 1972 Amendment in the seminal case of *Trans World Airlines v. Hardison,* still the standard against which all accommodation cases are measured.[26] The Court upheld the requirement of accommodation short of undue hardship, but seriously eroded the effectiveness of that requirement by defining undue hardship as (1) any action in conflict with a union contract or non-union seniority agreement, (2) any action that impairs efficiency or productivity, (3) any action that causes the employer to incur more than minimal cost, or (4) any action contrary to the rights or legitimate expectations of other employees. Those requirements—especially the first—have made it relatively easy for an employer to demonstrate undue hardship.

The Court in *Hardison* placed restraint on government enablement of the free exercise of religion in order to avoid an establishment of religion. It was telling us that too strict an interpretation of the accommodation requirement would be an impermissible establishment. In 1985 the Court made just that ruling, striking down a Connecticut statute that required accommodation regardless of the burden on the employer.[27] The Court has made it clear that too strict a requirement is unconstitutional, but it has not yet told us, except in generalities, what is too strict. As a result, employers have a relatively easy task in defending accommodation actions. Many such actions have been won since *Hardison,* but many more have been lost or have never gone to trial. Sabbath-keepers continue to be economically disadvantaged. In the United States, at least six hundred Seventh-day Adventists lose employment or are denied employment because of the Sabbath every year—a dozen a week. And that denomination is only a minority of the Sabbath-keeping community.

Improvement in the situation is possible. Sabbatarians could renew and coordinate their efforts to strengthen the accommodation requirement legislatively and judicially. Legislatures may be made aware of the seriousness of the problem and of the potential solution in strengthened federal and state statutes. Such measures might include diluting the near-total obeisance given union contracts and providing for recovery of punitive damages in accommodation cases. Sabbatarian groups should confer to develop a coherent legal strategy, identifying those cases worthy of support. Finally, non-Sabbatarian religious groups must be persuaded that it is also in their best interest to encourage government to facilitate the observance of individual religious conviction.

From the foregoing, five conclusions seem warranted:

1. Governmental efforts to assist religion (constitutional issues aside) are most proper and most productive when aimed not at aiding religious institutions but when intended to facilitate individual religious observance.

2. Governmental support of religious institutions is counterproductive. Efforts to legislate a general day of rest have failed and have at the same time had a negative impact on the free exercise of religion.

3. Governmental support of individual religious observance has come late and has been weakened by court decree, but it has made at least some progress in countering the economic disadvantage of Sabbatarians.

4. The interest of Sabbatarians would be well served by a renewed and coordinated effort to strengthen legislatively and judicially the requirement of religious accommodation.

5. As America enters the twenty-first century more religiously diverse than ever before, the interest of its citizenry would be well served by emphasis on tolerance of that diversity, mutual accommodation of religious convictions, and governmental enablement of religious observance.

NOTES

1. Samuele Bacchiocchi, *From Sabbath to Sunday: A Historical Investigation of the Rise of Sunday Observance in Early Christianity* (Rome: Gregorian University Press, 1977) 211.

2. Quoted in *American State Papers* (Washington: Review & Herald Publishing Association, 1949) 514.

3. For an early but still useful treatment of the subject, see A. H. Lewis, *Critical History of Sunday Legislation from 321 to 1888 A.D.* (New York: D. Appleton, 1888).

4. Quoted in *American State Papers*, 519–20.

5. *In Re King*, 46 F.905 at 916.

6. Warren L. Johns, *Dateline Sunday, USA* (Mountain View, CA: Pacific Press, 1967) 24.

7. *American State Papers*, 188.

8. *Register of Debates in Congress*, 5:42.

9. *Senate Report on Sunday Mail*, 19 January 1829.

10. *American State Papers*, 506.

11. Ibid., 498.

12. *In Re King*, 46 F.905 (U.S. Cir. Ct., West. Tenn.; 1 August 1891).

13. *American State Papers*, 488–91.

14. *Cantwell v. Connecticut*, 310 US 296 (U.S. Sup. Ct., 1940).

15. *Scopes v. Tennessee*, 289 SW 363 (TN Sup. Ct. 1927).

16. *American State Papers*, 508–11.

17. *Gallagher v. Crown Kosher Super Market* [Massachusetts], 336 US 617; *McGowan v. Maryland*, 366 US 420; *Braunfeld v. Brown* [Pennsylvania], 366 US 582; *Two Guys from Harrison—Allentown v. McGinley* [Pennsylvania], 366 US 420.

18. *Sherbert v. Verner*, 374 US 398.

19. *Time* (25 October 1963) 56.

20. Quoted in A. T. Jones, "The National Sunday Laws," *American Sentinel* (1892) 117.

21. *Benderson v. Sciortino*, 372 SE2d 751 (Sup. C. VA., 23 September 1988).

22. 42 USC Sec. 20000e et seq.

23. *The Equal Employment Opportunity Act of 1972* (Washington: Bureau of National Affairs, 1972) 324–25.

24. *Dewey v. Reynolds Metals Co.*, 429 F2d 324 (CA 6, 1970); *Kettell v. Johnson & Johnson*, 337 F. Supp. 892 (E.D. Ark. 1972); *Riley v. Bendix Corp.*, 464 F.2d 1113 (CA 5, 1972).

25. *The Equal Employment Opportunity Act of 1972* (Washington: Bureau of National Affairs, 1972) 324–25.

26. *Trans World Airlines v. Hardison*, 432 US 63.

27. *Estate of Thornton v. Caldor, Inc.*, 427 US 703.

20

A JEWISH PERSPECTIVE
ON SABBATARIANISM

Saul F. Rosenthal
Anti-Defamation League of B'nai B'rith and
the University of Denver

The legal issues surrounding Sabbath observances and the role of government in its enablement are both very clear and completely unclear. It is perfectly clear that for those Jews and Christians who choose to observe their Sabbath on the seventh day the role of government is to enable them to do so unimpeded. It is equally clear that American courts struggle with the notion that the seventh day is the Sabbath for Jews and some Christians. Courts, therefore, frequently muddy what is otherwise very clear by officially sanctioning Sunday as America's Sabbath, thus disenfranchising many Americans' religious liberty.

Since the legal issues are both complex and unclear, and since they are addressed quite well in Mitchell Tyner's paper, I will focus instead on the community-relations aspects of Sabbatarianism. I wish to say something also about the relationship between religious extremism and Sabbatarianism, as this is becoming an issue of some concern—at least within the Jewish community.

In my capacity with the Anti-Defamation League of B'nai B'rith I often serve as a point of first contact for Jews who believe they are experiencing some form of religious discrimination. Most frequent among the complaints are various difficulties in observing religious holy days. Some people report that employers will not permit leave for religious observance. Others find they are penalized financially for such observance. A few have even asserted that they were dismissed because of religious practice. What is uniformly true about these instances—where there is any merit to the claims—is that an honest disclosure of religious practice did not occur prior to the confrontations. Unfortunately, employers first learn of the need for religious leave as the date first approaches. This is rarely the case for Sabbath observance but is often true with regard to holy day leave.

What lies behind this failure to disclose? One theory would hold that employees fear the negative response of their employer and are willing to risk the minor confrontation rather than give an employer reason not to hire. Even though such discriminatory practice is clearly illegal, many people believe that covert anti-Semitism might be evoked by honest disclosure of need for leave for religious observance. Such a position suggests a disturbing attitude among American Jews—perhaps also among Sabbath-observing Christians.

Jews have ample history to demonstrate to themselves (if only by anecdote) that non-Jews look for reasons to discriminate against Jews. Why then, say some people, should we afford them the perfect reason by revealing our need for religious leave? Such an attitude reflects an insecurity that is certainly well understandable in this post-Holocaust period but may not be at all an accurate reflection of the behavior of employers.

More troubling still is the inconsistency of demand within the Jewish community for tolerance of religious observance. Too often I have heard of cases where employers are asked to provide religious accommodation simply because the person claims Jewish status—not because that person intends to use the released time for religious practice.

Without judging the behavior of American Jews, I would argue strongly that to assert our right to Sabbath observance without a concomitant commitment to put that time to Sabbath use hurts the case. Let me use the most extreme of examples. We know of cases where Jews imprisoned for heinous crimes against other persons "discover" their religious rights. Such inconsistency in value orientation does nothing to advance the notion that Sabbath (or religious) observers are genuine in their demands.

As Jews in America (and as Christian Sabbath observers) we should remind ourselves of our minority status. I hardly argue here capitulation to majority rule. The Supreme Court in recent years appears to be applying that standard in its action in this area. State courts, similarly, appear to conclude that that social policy is simply that policy which the majority of people evidence through their behavior—a point Tyner touches upon. Still, we are a minority and must live with the reality that our needs—as valid and defensible as they are—may be difficult to accommodate fully and always. Under these circumstances consistency in our behavior becomes an even more important tool.

Let me touch, finally, upon the issue of extremism and Sabbatarianism. The growth of religious extremist movements in the United States threatens all mainstream religious groups. Jews in particular have felt the sting of some of these movements, but others share our target status. I am thinking specifically of the Identity Church Movement, America's version of Anglo-

Israelism. Here is a theology of hate that masquerades as Christianity. It often cites Jewish religious behavior as evidence of the satanism of Jews. Likewise it smears Christians who profess Sabbath observance and other practices rooted in Judaism. A government endorsement of Christian religious practices (e.g., Sunday laws, creche installations) serves to embolden such extremism. Likewise, efforts to promote religious positions through the legislatures of our nation serve to validate a separatist and elitist view of Christianity among extremists.

Even within the mainstream religious movements, extremists (read fundamentalists) can be counterproductive to the acceptance of observances. Christians who trumpet the Jewish roots of their tradition, laud Israel for its fight to survive, and actively promote their love for Jews ultimately undermine the validity of a contemporary Judaism. By making the connection to Judaism so tightly they signal the insignificance of a separate and distinct Judaism.

Jewish fundamentalists who practice a "me too" ideology in the church–state arena are an obvious hindrance to accommodation. They encourage greater boldness by Christians and the courts to allow religious endorsement and entanglement. We need only cite the confused messages wafting down from the Supreme Court on religious displays. Context appears to be more important than content — a sad commentary on religion in America.

In short, I urge a realistic approach to what may be possible within this society and a recognition that we may shape that reality by our own communal behavior.

21

SABBATH OBSERVANCE AS A THEOLOGICAL ISSUE IN JEWISH–CHRISTIAN CONVERSATION

Michael E. Lodahl
Northwest Nazarene College

Three different conversations concerning the Sabbath that have engaged me in recent months will provide the centerpieces for the following reflections on Sabbath observance as a potential theological issue in Jewish-Christian dialogue.

I

The first conversation occurred in the home of an Orthodox, but rather broad-thinking, rabbi in Jerusalem. My wife and I were enjoying the Shabbat meal with him and his family, absorbing the rich beauty of the liturgy of Sabbath observance as we sat at the candle-lit table. As our rabbi friend explained some of the significant aspects of Jewish Sabbath observance, it occurred to me to volunteer that most of my father's side of the family is Seventh-day Adventist. The rabbi's elder son, of high school age, asked who these Seventh-day Adventists were. His father's response, brief yet enlightening, was, "They are Christians who observe Shabbat."

There is much that is attractive in such a definition. A most obvious implication is that, from the Jewish perspective, Christians who refer to Sunday as their "Sabbath" are, to state it kindly, misusing a Jewish term. Put more bluntly, they are simply wrong. To "observe Shabbat," at least in this particular rabbi's point of view, is to enter into public cultic and ritual practices on Saturday, the Jewish day set aside for observance, and not Sunday. Thus, for Christian ministers to welcome their congregations to worship on Sunday morning with some pious-sounding reference to "this beautiful Sabbath day" is an insidious religious imperialism on a most banal level. But of course this issue is hardly a matter simply of going to church on Saturday rather than a day later. The rather Jewish ring in this rabbi's designation, "Christians who observe Shabbat," additionally suggests that not only the day but also to a significant extent the meaning of Sabbath observance might be derived from Jewish practice and reflection. Given this possibility of theological resource, what might it mean for a Christian to "observe Shabbat"?

Certainly one of the most intriguing aspects of Sabbath in Jewish religiosity is its implications for a doctrine of creation. Sabbath reminds its observers of the utter gratuity of their allotted time in this life, calling them to an existence that flows within a universal rhythm of work and of rest and allowing them once a week to "catch their breath," as it were. In this day of rest, observers of Sabbath actually become imitators of God, who, according to Exodus 31:17, "made heaven and earth . . . in six days, but on the seventh day he ceased laboring and was refreshed."

Just as Sabbath allows and indeed invites its observers to rest, or simply to be, so do they in this day of simply being allow the rest of creation simply to be as well. Sabbath frees its observers from a purely functional, objectifying orientation toward nature, toward other people, and toward themselves, thereby encouraging a sense of enjoyment of "the world for what it is, not only for what it might become," and of relationship toward others and oneself "for what they are, not only for what they do."[1] David Hartman, in his book *Joy and Responsibility,* writes of this participatory, nonmanipulative orientation toward creation which begins to dawn on his consciousness with every setting of the Friday sun: "I stand silently before nature as before a fellow creature of God and not as a potential object of my control, and I must face the fact that I am a man and not God. The Sabbath aims at healing the human grandiosity of technological society."[2]

The value of this sabbatical orientation toward our world should be readily evident, given the almost compulsive expressions of manipulation with which modern technological humanity operates in relation to the environment. A Sabbath consciousness, in Hartman's way of thinking, can be a truly ecological consciousness. The environment is not an alien factor "out there" over against us, waiting simply to be tamed and controlled by human beings; it is, more fundamentally, God's handiwork, a creation in which and from which we live, and which has value in the Creator's estimation quite apart from its utilitarian value for human life. In the words of Christian theologian Franz Mussner, "The Sabbath makes the life of the human being festive and free and recalls to the human being that God himself desires a festive and free world."[3]

It is arguable that just such a consciousness of creation is sadly lacking in much of traditional Christian faith and practice. It is also arguable that the practical implications of a healthy doctrine of creation—for example, an affirmation and even celebration of this life, a recognition of our finitude, an acceptance of ecological responsibility, an awareness of our interrelatedness with every aspect of God's creation—do not receive rightful emphasis in most Christian teaching and preaching precisely because much of the church does not have a healthy doctrine of creation. If a more profoundly "Sabbath" consciousness can be arrived at through the practices of those whom my friend the rabbi called "Christians who observe Shabbat," then such practices carry their own persuasive argument. For the sad fact is that for the great majority of Christians of the "Sunday-go-to-meetin'" variety Sunday does not possess a Sabbath-like, re-creational significance.

In the midst of such reflections, though, it is crucial to recall that, although the biblical doctrine of creation is shared by Jews and Christians, it is not a generalized religious principle; it is, rather, specifically rooted in the ancient Jewish experience of Exodus from Egypt and covenant with God. That is, the doctrine of creation in Scripture actually is dependent on, and arises out of, reflection on God's creation of a responsible covenant people out of a motley bunch of rag-tag slaves—a bit of *creatio ex nihilo* on a small historical scale, if you will. Thus, when Mussner writes that "the Sabbath allows the glance of Israel to turn back to the event of the Creation of the world and in so doing reminds Israel of its liberation from Egypt," I want to argue that he has inverted the (theo)logical priority of these events in Israel's historical consciousness. It seems more correct to say that, as Sabbath observance encourages Israel to recall its liberation from Egypt, "thus again allow[ing] history to be experienced as the deed of God," in so doing it also reminds Israel of God's deed of creation.[4]

The point of such apparent hair-splitting is to assert that in the Jewish notion of Sabbath, even when its observance somehow recalls creation, that recollection itself is founded in God's covenant with the Jewish people. For although Sabbath observance is indeed an imitation of the God who labored in creation for six days and then rested on the seventh, it is also, and perhaps more specifically, "a sign between him [this God] and the children of Israel forever," calling that people "to observe the sabbath throughout their generations, for a perpetual covenant" (Exodus 31:17, 16).

II

The second conversion took place not long after I returned to the States, and the phrase "Christians who observe Shabbat" still rang in my ears and intrigued my thinking. I was at a family reunion of my father's side, and as often occurs at such affairs, I was engaged in friendly theological debate with a cousin who is a Seventh-day Adventist minister. As usual, he was attempting to restore me to the family faith of observing Sabbath, and I must admit he was doing a rather persuasive job of it. I then asked what became the critical question upon which the entire conversation turned: "Is it possible that observance of the Sabbath is a sign of the Jewish covenant with God, and not particularly intended for Christians?" He replied, "But isn't the church the new Israel? Haven't Christians taken the place of the Jews in covenant relationship to God?" It is this long-standing theological tradition of Christianity's displacement of Israel, lurking just behind my cousin the minister's question, that most quickly raises my suspicions concerning Christian observance of the Sabbath. Is Sabbath observance simply another expression of the Christian tendency to attempt to assimilate Jewish history and religion? As a Christian theologian who labors to overturn the traditional theology of displacement, I wonder about the extent to which most Sabbath-observing Christians believe Christianity to have displaced and negated Jewish faith and practice, relegating it to the preparatory role of an "Old Testament," now fulfilled—and so, to a certain dangerous extent, made obsolete—by the "New Testament."

It has been effectively argued by recent Christian theologians such as Franklin Littell, Clark Williamson, Roy Eckhardt, and Rosemary Radford Ruether, among others, that the anti-Judaism which is an inevitable upshot of a theology of displacement has contributed significantly to the disastrous history of Jewish suffering—not the least example of which, to be sure, is the Holocaust. Thus, even if only in view of the history of effects which the displacement or supersessionist theory has exercised—and in the light of the principle of love of neighbor—it is morally incumbent upon the church to reject this theory as the basis of its identity.

But the Holocaust is not, in fact, the sole basis for a reversal of the traditional Christian doctrine of displacement. Rather, the very heart of Christian faith, resting as it does in the faithfulness of God, receives a self-inflicted deathblow if Christians deny God's continuing faithfulness to Israel. Such a denial has functioned all too often as the basis for the Christian claim to legitimacy and priority, as in the claim in Hebrews 8:6–13 that Christianity represents a new and better covenant over "the first . . . [which] is becoming obsolete and growing old [and] is ready to disappear" (v. 13). Christians have assumed the convenience of reading Jeremiah's prophecy about a renewed covenant through the lens of Hebrews and its abbreviated quotation, leaving them with the smug impression that God has abandoned the Jews (v. 9). But a further reading of Jeremiah 31, beyond v. 34, would instruct Christians that the sun, moon, and stars, and the sea of its tides, will sooner vanish than will "the offspring of Israel . . . cease from being a nation before [God] forever" (Jeremiah 31:36). My argument is that God's covenant faithfulness to Israel ought to be axiomatic for Christian thought and practice, both out of regard for the witness of the Hebrew Scriptures and for a sure sense of divine reliability.

A close heeding of Jewish reflection on the meaning of Sabbath certainly shows this consciousness of and confidence in God's covenant faithfulness to his people Israel. It is written in the book of *Jubilees:*

> Behold, I will separate unto Myself a people from among all the peoples, and these shall keep the Sabbath day, and I will sanctify them unto Myself as My people, and will bless them; as I have sanctified the Sabbath day and do sanctify it unto Myself, even so will I bless them, and they shall be My people and I will be their God. And I have chosen the seed of Jacob from amongst all that I have seen, and have written him down as My first-born son, and have sanctified him unto Myself for ever and ever; and I will teach them the Sabbath day, that they may keep Sabbath thereon from all work (2:19-21).

It is clear that, in the Jewish religious consciousness, the observance of Sabbath is a sign and seal of God's election of Israel—an election which, in the words of the apostle Paul, is irrevocable (Romans 11:29). The Sabbath, it can be argued, is a temporal mark of Torah upon God's people Israel, a people established by the covenant initiated at Sinai. For what we call the Ten Commandments, including the Sabbath commandment, was, after all, addressed originally and primarily—if not exclusively—to Israel. And the historical ground and context of that Sinaitic covenant were Israel's Exodus from Egypt: "And remember that you were a slave in the land of Egypt, and the Lord your God brought you out of there by a mighty hand and by an outstretched arm; therefore the Lord your God commanded you to observe the sabbath day" (Deuteronomy 5:15).

It is evident, then, that the Sabbath theology in the second chapter of the book of *Jubilees* is profoundly biblical when it avers, "And the Creator of all things blessed [the Sabbath], but he did not sanctify all peoples and nations to keep Sabbath thereon, but Israel alone: them alone he permitted to eat and drink and to keep Sabbath thereon on the earth" (2:31). Thus in *Jubilees* the Sabbath is "the great sign" given to Israel by God; Mussner summarizes the *Jubilees* passage: "In the keeping of the Sabbath by Israel its specialness among all the nations is shown."[5]

If Christians choose to observe the Sabbath, they ought to be willing to do so as a sign of solidarity and celebration first of Israel's covenant election, still sustained by the faithful God of the Exodus. To do so with any other attitude would be presumptuously to steal another's divine birthright. How such Christians might then secondly reflect theologically upon their own Sabbath observance moves us toward the third and final conversation.

III

The third conversation occurred most recently, though the subject of conversation was a controversy that had raged several years earlier at Nes Ammim, a Christian *moshav* (cooperative community) located in the western Galilee, which operates within Israel as a Christian witness to solidarity with and support for the Jewish state. I spoke with a friend who is a member of the board of directors of Nes Ammim about the controversy surrounding Sabbath observance at the *moshav*.

Several years ago some of the community's participants began to raise protests concerning its Saturday worship services. These protesters felt that Sabbath worship reflected a forsaking of an aspect of the Christian heritage and in fact threatened Christian identity.

"Of course there was a pragmatic issue involved in Nes Ammim's Sabbath observance," my friend remarked. "It is the day of rest in the state of Israel, so if you're going to function economically within Israel, it makes sense to work on Sunday and observe Shabbat. Certainly that was a factor.

"But I think," he continued, "something else was going on too—a sense that to live and work in solidarity with the Jewish people somehow meant keeping their day of rest, and therefore some sense of identity or solidarity with Judaism. I think there was some sense in which they acknowledged the biblical basis of the early church worshiping in synagogues on Shabbat, while also gathering on the first day of the week to have Eucharist. This reflected a concern to return to the pristine community."

To be sure, such a desire for return has been expressed time and again in the church's history, though not predominantly in terms of Sabbath worship. The notion of returning to the pure, more spiritual church of the New Testament era has exercised a tantalizing effect upon countless serious followers of Jesus Christ. The difficulty in such a notion is that it does not take history seriously; it is an impossible dream to imagine that an individual or community can somehow leapfrog back over centuries of historical development and land in a pristine church. (Of course, such a church was never there to land in anyway.)

The point is, Sunday has been the primary day of worship for the vast majority of Christians for many centuries, and it will continue to be so. I would not try to dodge the arguments of Sabbatarian Christians who point out the probable pagan basis for Sunday worship any more than I would for similar arguments against Christmas and Easter. Sunday worship, in fact, serves as a witness to what Paul van Buren has called the "part Jewish, part pagan" heritage of the Christian church. He states further that "the tension between Gentileness and [walking] in the way of Israel's God will remain central to our identity and mark our conversation."[6] Christians exist, in Franz Rosenzweig's phrase, "between Israel and the world," and perhaps Sunday worship is a most potent, every-week sign of the same.

Sunday worship, too, can be a way by which Christians affirm their allegiance to the very God of Israel but at the same time recognize that their drawing near to God occurs on a surprisingly different basis. God established covenant with the Jewish people through the gift and task of Torah; but we who are Gentiles, says the epistle to the Ephesians, though once "separate from Messiah, excluded from the commonwealth of Israel, and strangers to the covenants of promise, having no hope and without God in the world" — we "who formerly were far off have been brought near by the blood of Christ" (2:12, 13). I am a Christian who can find no reason to believe that God's covenant with the people Israel at Sinai is no longer in effect; thus, I understand that the commandment to observe and to hallow the Sabbath is directed primarily, if not exclusively, to that people. Meanwhile, I find myself part of a religious tradition which, while claiming also to have heard and responded to the gracious voice of the God of Abraham, Isaac, and Jacob, celebrates its reconciliation to this God, through the crucified and resurrected Jesus of Nazareth, on Sunday.

It is not entirely surprising, then, that some of those Christians at Nes Ammim found themselves struggling with the implications of Sabbath observance. For Sunday has become, for the great majority of Christians, the day of the week on which Jesus' resurrection is especially celebrated; it is, for the church, not so much the first day of the week as a symbolic temporal witness to the eighth day, the eschatological day of the new age begun in Christ. Thus it points to the saving future of God spoken of in *The Life of Adam and Eve,* a pseudepigraphal work in which the archangel Michael tells Seth not to mourn the dead any longer than six days. "The rest on the seventh day is the sign of the resurrection in the coming age; on the seventh day the Lord also rested from all his works" (51:2). Mussner comments: "Christianity underlined this eschatological dimension of the Sabbath by making the resurrection of Jesus into its 'Sabbath.' In so doing it lived from the 'sign' which the Sabbath according to the Scriptures of Israel presented."[7]

Do such observations entail the rejection of Sabbatarian Christianity? By no means! Although Sabbatarians will always be an extreme minority, they nonetheless fulfill an important mission to the church at large: to serve as concrete witnesses to Christianity's roots in Jewish faith and practice. From the time of Marcion to the time of the German Christian movement under Hitler, and even yet today, the church has had to deal with the temptation to betray, if possible, its "part Jewish" heritage in favor of a fully pagan, wholly idolatrous orientation. Thus, those Christians who "observe Shabbat" are crucial witnesses pulling the church back to consider its Jewish foundations — as long as they avoid the supersessionist trap.

I have already mentioned that Sabbatarian Christianity's first step in tiptoeing around this dangerous ideological pitfall is to affirm its Sabbath observance as an indication of solidarity with and celebration of God's ongoing covenantal relationship to the Jewish people through Torah. Sabbatarian Christians might then proceed to interpret their own Sabbath observance as a testimony that the same God of Israel has called them to covenantal relationship through Jesus as the Christ. Their testimony, then, would not differ essentially from that of Christians who worship on Sunday; the latter's emphasis falls on the surprisingly gracious novelty of the work of salvation through Jesus of Nazareth, while the former's emphasis lies on the identity of the God active in this Jesus with the God who cut a covenant at Sinai. Thus, in their own distinctive ways, and certainly without having intended consciously to do so, "Christians who observe Shabbat" and Christians who worship on Sunday together bear witness to the creative interplay of continuity and discontinuity between Judaism and Christianity.

If in the midst of such a mutual witness, Christians of the "Sunday-go-to-meetin'" variety could begin to learn from all serious Sabbath observers—either Jew or Christian—a touch of the re-creative, restful, and even ecologically significant possibilities inherent in such observance, both they and their doctrine of creation would certainly be the richer for it.

NOTES

Quotations from *Jubilees* and *The Life of Adam and Eve* are taken from *The Apocrypha and Pseudepigrapha of the Old Testament,* ed. R. H. Charles (Oxford: Oxford University Press, 1913).

1. Shalom Hartman Institute, "Shabbat and the Human Experience of Labor," (Jerusalem: Joint Program for Jewish Education of the State of Israel, n.d.) 65.

2. David Hartman, *Joy and Responsibility* (Jerusalem: Ben Zvi Posner, 1978) 92.

3. Franz Mussner, *Tractate on the Jews* (Philadelphia: Fortress, 1984) 102.

4. Ibid.

5. Ibid., 101.

6. Paul van Buren, *Discerning the Way* (New York: Seabury, 1980) 26.

7. Mussner, *Tractate,* 102-3.

CONTRIBUTORS

SAMUELE BACCHIOCCHI, PH.D., is Professor of Theology and Church History at Andrews University. His books include *The Marriage Covenant* (1991), *Wine in the Bible* (1989), *Women in the Church* (1987), *The Time of the Crucifixion and the Resurrection* (1987), *The Advent Hope for Human Hopelessness* (1986), *Hal Lindsey's Prophetic Jigsaw Puzzle* (1986), *From Sabbath to Sunday* (1986), *Sabbath in the New Testament* (1985), and *Divine Rest for Human Restlessness* (1980).

JOHN F. BALDOVIN, S.J., PH.D., is Associate Professor of Historical and Liturgical Theology at the Jesuit School of Theology/Graduate Theological Union, Berkeley. His books include *Liturgy in Ancient Israel* (1989) and *The Urban Character of Christian Worship, the Origins, Development and Meaning of Stational Liturgy* (1987).

CRAIG L. BLOMBERG, PH.D., is Assistant Professor of New Testament at Denver Seminary. His books include *The Historical Reliability of the Gospels* (1987), *Interpreting the Parables* (1990), *Gospel Perspectives. Volume VI: The Miracles of Jesus* (ed. with D. Wenham), and *Matthew* (forthcoming, 1991).

MARVA J. DAWN, is a freelance theologian who heads Christians Equipped for Ministry. Her books include *To Walk and Not Faint* (1980), *To Walk in the Kingdom* (1982), *I'm Lonely, LORD—How Long?* (1983), and *Keeping the Sabbath Wholly* (1989).

JACQUES DOUKHAN, PH.D., is Professor of Old Testament Interpretation at Andrews University. His books include *At the Gate of Hope* (in French, 1983), *Drinking at the Sources: Essays on the Jewish-Christian Problem* (1981), *The Genesis Creation Story: Its Literary Structure* (1978), and *Hebrew for Theologians* (forthcoming).

TAMARA COHN ESKENAZI, PH.D., is Associate Professor of Bible at Hebrew Union College-Jewish Institute of Religion in Los Angeles. Her books include *In an Age of Prose: A Literary Approach to Ezra-Nehemiah* (1988), and *Telling Queen Michal's Story: An Experiment in Comparative Interpretation* (ed. with D. J. A. Clines) (forthcoming, 1991).

ROBERT GOLDENBERG, PH.D., is Associate Professor of Judaic Studies at the State University of New York, Stony Brook. His books include *The Sabbath Law of Rabbi Meir* (1978).

FREDERICK E. GREENSPAHN, PH.D., is Associate Professor of Judaic Studies at the University of Denver. His books include *Essential Papers on Israel and the Ancient Near East* (1991), *Pushing the Faith: Proselytism and Civility in a Pluralistic World* (ed. with M. Marty, 1988), *Uncivil Religion: Interreligious Hostility in America* (ed. with R. Bellah, 1987), *Contemporary Ethical Issues in the Jewish and Christian Traditions* (ed., 1986), *The Human Image in the Jewish and Christian Traditions* (ed., 1986), *Nourished with Peace: Studies in Hellenistic Judaism in Memory of Samuel Sandmel* (ed. with E. Hilgert and B. Mack, 1984), *Hapax Legomena in Biblical Hebrew* (1984), and *Scripture in the Jewish and Christian Traditions: Authority, Interpretation, Relevance* (1982).

DANIEL J. HARRINGTON, S.J., PH.D., is Professor at the Weston School of Theology, Cambridge, MA, and General Editor of *New Testament Abstracts*. His books include *John's Thought and Theology* (1990), *The Maccabean Revolt: Anatomy of a Biblical Revolution* (1988), *The Bible in the Churches* (1985), *The Light of All Nations: Essays on the Church in the New Testament* (1982), *Interpreting the Old Testament: A Practical Guide* (1981), *God's People in Christ: New Testament Perspectives on the Church and Judaism* (1980), *Interpreting the New Testament: A Practical Guide* (1980), and *A Manual of Palestinian Aramaic Texts (Second Century BC–Second Century AD)* (1978).

KENNETH HEIN, O.S.B., is a Benedictine priest from Holy Cross Abbey, Canon City, CO, and Chaplain at Fitzsimmons Medical Center, Catholic Archdiocese of Denver, CO.

LAWRENCE A. HOFFMAN, PH.D., is Professor of Liturgy at Hebrew Union College-Jewish Institute of Religion, New York. His books include *The Art of Public Prayer: Not for Clergy Only* (1988), *Beyond the Text: A Holistic Approach to Liturgy* (1981), *The Land of Israel: Jewish Perspectives* (ed., 1986), *The Canonization of the Synagogue Service* (1979), *Gates of Understanding* (vol. 1, 1984), and *The Making of Jewish and Christian Worship* (vol. 1, ed. with P. Bradshaw, 1991).

REV. DENNIS KENNEDY, C.M., is Assistant Professor of Liturgy at St. Thomas Theological Seminary, Denver, CO. His books include *The History of the Eucharist*.

MICHAEL E. LODAHL, PH.D., is Professor in the Division of Philosophy and Religion, Northwest Nazarene College, Nampa, ID. His books include *Shekhinah/ Spirit: Divine Presence in Jewish and Christian Traditions* (forthcoming).

DENNIS R. MACDONALD, PH.D., is Professor of New Testament and Christian Origins at the Iliff School of Theology, Denver, CO. His books include *The Acts of Andrew and the Acts of Andrew and Matthias in the City of Cannibals* (1990), *There Is No Male and Female* (1987), *The Apocryphal Acts of Apostles* (1986), and *The Legend and the Apostle* (1983).